THE LETTERS OF FRANZ LISZT
TO
MARIE zu SAYN-WITTGENSTEIN

THE LETTERS OF

Franz Liszt

TO

MARIE zu SAYN-WITTGENSTEIN

TRANSLATED AND EDITED BY

HOWARD E. HUGO

GREENWOOD PRESS, PUBLISHERS
WESTPORT, CONNECTICUT

To Marjorie Church Cherkassky

EDITOR'S FOREWORD

The letters of Franz Liszt to Marie zu Sayn-Wittgenstein were bought in 1931 by Mrs. Robert Woods Bliss and her mother from the Swiss musicologist and collector of Lisztiana, Robert Bory, and the late Ernest Schelling was the intermediary. Schelling had been connected with Weimar and the Liszt circle: he was a close friend and music teacher of Duchess Jean-Albert von Mecklemburg, born a Princess of Saxe-Weimar and daughter of Liszt's early patron, Grand Duke Carl Friedrich. Schelling, Mrs. Amalya Prendergast, and Dr. Edward Waters of the Library of Congress undertook tentative and valuable scholarly work on the manuscripts soon after, which was interrupted by Ernest Schelling's death; and the correspondence became part of the Dumbarton Oaks Collection — now the property of Harvard University. Except for eight letters published by Bory in the *Numéro spécial de la Revue musicale*, "Correspondance inédite de Liszt et de la Princesse Marie Sayn-Wittgenstein" (May 1, 1928), and six letters with their translations brought out by Carl Engel in the *Musical Quarterly* for July 1936, the correspondence has never before been made public.

Most of the letters are written on octavo sheets: those from 1848 until 1860 are on pale blue paper, and the remainder from 1869 to 1886 are on ivory stationery. The sole letter possessing any decorative charm is Number 6 — "Les Deux Roses," Liszt's fable composed for Marie's birthday — where the white sheets are bordered by gold and blue lines, and hand-painted pink roses ornament the four corners. Mrs. Bliss also obtained a copybook of 150 pages belonging to Liszt. This treasure still awaits the cold eye of some examining scholar, since in many instances the musician's original letter has been destroyed, and the rough draft in the copybook is the only extant version. Letters 108 through 118 of the correspondence to Marie, with Letter 112 omitted, may be found in the copybook with a few negligible changes.

Liszt's handwriting was fortunately legible, and the few occasions where the editor found a word undecipherable have been noted

vii

either in the preface to a letter or in a note. Liszt's mistakes are more important: there are, for instance, completely incomprehensible passages (cf. Letters 19 and 146), where any translation is dubious. Other peculiarities existing in the manuscript are the use of "d" for "de," "m̄" and "n̄" for "mm" and "nn," and the older "ſs" for "ss." The letters written in the 1848–1860 period reflect an interesting orthographical shift in the French language as a whole: words now ending in "ents" and "ants" were spelled in the eighteenth-century manner (for example, *flottans, évenemens, importans, divertissemens*). After 1869 Liszt's terminal endings assumed the modern form.

The chief difficulty posed in translating Liszt's letters arose from his own linguistic peculiarity. Almost all the letters are written in French, with much scattered German throughout; and French was a secondary language for the musician. Liszt himself stated in several letters (not in this correspondence) that despite his birth on Hungarian soil, German was the tongue spoken at home during his childhood. This situation is not unusual: Raiding, near Oedenburg, is a town in a predominantly German-speaking section of Hungary, and certainly German rather than Hungarian would have been ordinarily employed on the estates of the Austrophile Esterhazy family. After Liszt left Vienna for Paris, French entirely supplanted German for the youthful virtuoso; and for some twenty years he doubtlessly used German only sparingly. It is known that when he returned to Weimar in 1848 — when our correspondence opens — he was forced to relearn German in order to improve his failing accent.

Yet despite Liszt's Romantic pretensions, displayed during the 1820's, that he was the wild Magyar child bringing new dynamic vigor to effete, sophisticated Western society, Liszt never spoke fluent Hungarian; and we will have occasion later to speak of the belated appearance of his ardent Hungarian nationalism. Hence it is almost as if it were Liszt rather than Goethe who was the real "citoyen du monde" — at least in linguistic terms. Unfortunately Liszt's eclectic cosmopolitanism had to pay its price, not in the inarticulate regions of music, but when he chose to move in the more precise area of language. It is difficult to define the exact quality of Liszt's written French. Villon remarked several centuries earlier, "Il n'est bon bec que de Paris." Alas, Liszt's sojourn in that city during the 1820's and 1830's was perhaps too short to allow him to attain such Gallic perfection. His constructions and idioms are often on the edge of being incorrect; the movement of the prose is sometimes muddy and turgid, and prolixity replaces precision. While one might construe the poetic and rhetorical passages in the spirit of full-blown French Romanticism, actually they exhibit a sentiment more Teutonic than Latin; and whenever Liszt philosophizes, it is either a blend of Lamennais with German Pietism, or else the breath of Hegel or Schopenhauer blows over the page. Liszt's prose might best be compared with that of Henri-Frédéric Amiel, another product of the meeting of two distinct linguistic traditions. The musician suffers only slightly when contrasted with his literary contemporary.

The editor's translations have been made with cognizance that "even the best translation is, for mere necessitie, but an evill limped wing to fly withall, or a hevie stompe leg of wood to go withall" — as the Elizabethan critic Roger Ascham said long ago. The usual idiomatic problems presented themselves. There is the unhappy necessity of transforming mid-nineteenth century slang into its nearest English equivalent; tenses have been occasionally manipulated, since in many cases the historical present in French is poor in English and conversely the future tense in French is often better rendered by the English present. A graver alteration was performed when sentence order was radically changed, and Liszt's lengthy compound-complex sentences have sometimes been broken into simpler, shorter, and more coherent units. Whenever the choice between an excessively free and a stringently literal translation arose, the editor deliberately erred on the latter side in the interests of accuracy. At times the temptation was strong to weed out Liszt's discursiveness. At other moments, it must be granted, the editor's honest search for the right English word may have led him to employ several *mots injustes*. But his intention was expressed by another Elizabethan author, Philemon Holland, when he pleaded: "If the sentence be not so concise, couched and knit together as the originall, loth I was to be obscure and dark: have I not englished everie word aptly?"

The reader interested in consulting the original letters may consult the manuscripts and photostats at Dumbarton Oaks, Georgetown, Washington, D. C. The editor's typescripts are in the Archives, Harvard College Library, Cambridge, Massachusetts.

In order to give organic unity to this correspondence, thirty-one prefaces have been inserted as an aid to narrative and biographical continuity, and as a means of treating pertinent phases of Liszt's life and work which could not legitimately come within the province of the explicating endnotes. It will also be noticed that many of the letters have the date and place from which Liszt was writing enclosed in brackets, indicating that the musician himself did not contribute the information. The method employed was simple. Other correspondences were consulted, principally that of Liszt to Princess Carolyne, and the letter in question was dovetailed into its proper chronological position. In the case of several short notes to Marie where a lack of any real subject matter made such a procedure impossible, a similarity to other dated *billets* of purely social nature afforded a quick solution. As in the Introduction and in the short Preface, prose passages in foreign languages have been translated by the editor, but the text references are always to the *original* source. For the most part poetry has been left in its own tongue, and titles have not been translated. The reader should refer automatically to the Index for the location of notes containing additional information about persons, places, musical compositions. The occasional footnotes to a letter are Liszt's own, since the editor's notes all occur at the end of this volume. All the italicized words in the text of the letters represent Liszt's own underscoring. The dots too are his, and are not to be taken as ellipses for editorial omissions; for no deletions have been made.

The editor wishes to express his gratitude to Harry T. Levin and Jean-J. Seznec for their constant encouragement and valued advice, to André Michel for his criticisms of the translations from the French, to Miss Patricia Freda and Mrs. Jacqueline Cooke for their labor and solicitude which far exceeded any official obligations, and to Mrs. Robert Woods Bliss, Eugene H. Bland, and the staff of Dumbarton Oaks.

Finally, Frau Winifred Wagner is given grateful acknowledgment for her kind authorization to print these letters with permission of the heirs of Franz Liszt.

HOWARD E. HUGO

Eliot House
Cambridge, Massachusetts
October 1952

CONTENTS

THE LETTERS OF FRANZ LISZT
TO
MARIE *zu* SAYN-WITTGENSTEIN

INTRODUCTION

The letters of Franz Liszt to Marie zu Sayn-Wittgenstein, daughter of Princess Carolyne Wittgenstein, begin in 1848 and end in 1886 a few months before his death. Thus they span some thirty-eight years, although a hiatus of eight years — discussed in the Preface to Letter 61 — actually makes the correspondence incomplete for that brief period of the musician's life.

We offer them here for the first time to the public with a triple aim. First, the letters have intrinsic literary merit, despite Liszt's often cumbersome prose which he himself aptly described in a letter to Carolyne: "Alas, my epistolary style is rather restricted, and is a terrible parody of the Napoleonic manner." Second, the correspondence reveals certain little-known aspects of Liszt's manifold career and complicated personality. Last of all, the letters possess considerable cultural and historical value, and through them we arrive at a fuller understanding of an age at once so close in time and yet so remote for the modern comprehension.

We would venture to say that this correspondence belongs to a major artistic tradition, where charm and human warmth take precedence over profundity and greatness. Swift's *Journal to Stella*, Goethe's letters to Bettina von Arnim, Mme. de Sévigné's correspondence with her daughter Mme. de Grignan, Lord Chesterfield's letters to his son, the epistles of Lady Mary Wortley Montagu to her daughter, the Countess of Bute — all these are examples of age taking upon itself to instruct youth by means of the most genial of literary forms, the letter. News, gossip, and a certain amount of pedagogical instruction compose the subject matter. One moves neither in the arid areas of business relations and weighty intellectuality nor is one suffocated by the hot blasts of a passionate love affair. Here is the steady, inconsequential flow of everyday life undisturbed by high tragedy or low comedy, where the emotions are recollected in a state of such absolute tranquillity that we are far removed from the upsetting effect of artistic creativity. When Dr. Samuel Johnson said, "The qualities of the epistolary style most

1

frequently required are ease and simplicity, an even flow of un-laboured diction, and an artless arrangement of obvious sentiments," he was describing Liszt at his best. We might add that the noted critic, always quick to speak the whole truth, also pointed out that "there is, indeed, no transaction which offers stronger temptations to fallacy and sophistication than epistolary intercourse." Once more Liszt might be used as an example for Johnson's discerning statement, but here we defer to the reader's later judgment.

While the epistolary novel has long been out of favor as a literary genre, no one has ever questioned its claim as a rightful art-form. A correspondence — even a "one-way" affair such as this one — shares certain qualities with its fictional counterpart; and one of the pleasures of reading a collection of letters is to observe the gradual emergence of the writer's personality, the subtle shift in personal relations between him and the recipient of his letters, and the impact of historical events upon two persons not directly caught up in them. The late Virginia Woolf, in a sensitive essay called *The Humane Art*, mentioned that the letter-writer attempts to record no history of his times in a surreptitious fashion — that is, unless he has one eye cocked on posterity; and such was certainly not the case with Liszt writing to Marie. The letter-writer's world is a small one. What Mrs. Woolf called "the drag of the face on the other side of the page" is his motive force, and not the usual, more public demands of the *dulci et utile*. Consequently the aver-age reader is apt to feel excluded and indeed cheated when he tries to participate. At this point enters the lonely, unloved editor, offer-ing his services as a pander for the cynical, a marriage-broker for the more affable and idealistic. His office is triple. He mediates be-tween the letters and the outside public desirous of comprehension as well as affection; he tries to give substance to the shadow of the ever-present, yet mysteriously absent, correspondent; and finally the editor attempts to place a private, rather restricted correspond-ence within the context of the large — in Liszt's case, almost mythi-cal — life that time has chosen to leave as a heritage.

The notes and introductory prefaces scattered throughout this volume are intended to afford an adequate presentation of Liszt's life from 1848 — the year the letters began — until 1886, when the correspondence ended some three months before Liszt's death. There remains the task of sketching his earlier existence. The reader is advised to consult any of the standard Liszt biographies (for example those by Ramann, Corder, de Portales or Sitwell) for additional information. The purpose here is merely to offer the barest factual summary.

Franz Liszt was born October 11, 1811, on the estates of the Esterhazy family in Raiding, Hungary — the son of Adam Liszt, one of the Esterhazy stewards, and Anna Lager. His father, himself an amateur violinist and pianist, provided his son with rudimentary musical training. The boy's first public performances at the piano were in Oedenburg and Pressburg at the age of nine, when the Esterhazys — famous as the patrons of Haydn, Hummel and Cherubini — as well as a Baron von Braun, acted as Liszt's sponsors. His precocious talents were so apparent that a subscription was taken up by several Hungarian noblemen to enable the youthful prodigy to study in Vienna, and it was there that he became the piano pupil of Czerny and a composition student of Salieri. Liszt's Vienna debut was made late in 1822. The Liszt legend may be said to date from a concert six months later, when Beethoven is claimed to have embraced the boy publicly — and thus conferred the apostolic succession.

Vienna was succeeded by Paris in 1823. The *Lehrjahre* were over, brief as they had been. The full-fledged virtuoso, managed by his doting and ambitious father, entered his so-called *Glanzperiode*. Soon Liszt's fame was equaling, if not supplanting, that of the violinist Paganini, and the musical circles of London and Paris discussed nothing but his incredible technique. He even tried his hand at opera chiefly to display his versatility: on October 17, 1825, *Sancho* was performed at the Paris *Opéra*, where it enjoyed a brief, violent success. (The manuscript was lost by fire in 1873. Of all his youthful musical indiscretions Liszt apparently regarded *Sancho* as his worst: he never referred to it in later years.) The death of Adam Liszt in 1827 put a temporary end to Liszt's strenuous concert-tours. He settled in Paris with his mother for the next five or six years and devoted most of his time to teaching and practicing.

To attempt to describe the artistic life of Paris around 1830 is similar to stopping a turbine-wheel with a toothpick. The Romantic movement in the arts was at its greatest moment of ex-

3

travagant triumph. The first real *avant-garde* in history was publishing manifestos with the regularity of modern news-broadcasts; political and cultural revolutions were identified — with confusing, often disastrous effects; the cleavage between the artist and the "Philistine" public was at last felt to be complete, and both sides enjoyed this potentially tragic situation with mutual and articulate recriminations. This was the Paris of Hugo's *Hernani* and *Cromwell* — the latter with its aggressive preface. The salons of Nodier and Deschamps collected all the Romantic rebels, and Vigny, Musset, Lamennais, Sainte-Beuve, Saint-Simon, Ingres, Delacroix, Berlioz, and Chopin may serve as brief reminders, with all that these names connote. Liszt was a welcome addition to this community of exalted souls, since his flamboyant temperament was more than a match for any that he encountered. His aristocratic, gaunt, daemonic features enabled him to become a kind of physical embodiment of the Romantic artist (an advantage he had over some of his more prosaic-appearing contemporaries who would have been as anxious as he to accept the role). The *haut monde* lionized him, and wealthy hostesses with cultural pretensions vied with each other to do him homage. Because his role of piano virtuoso was almost unique and he was removed from a position of possible rivalry, even his fellow Romantics showered him with adulation.

It is by now a commonplace that the Romantics were also romantic in the everyday use of the word. This aspect of the Romantic myth found no better embodiment than Liszt: Ramann's *Liszt und die Frauen* records with feminine hyberbole some twenty-six affairs throughout the musician's lifetime. The first of these was with young Caroline de Saint-Cricq, but the great liaison was with the Countess Marie d'Agoult.

They met in 1833 when she was twenty-eight and the mother of two children. A middle-aged and indifferent husband provided no obstacle, and from 1835 to 1839 Liszt and Marie d'Agoult traveled together when he was on tour and she was occupied writing novels under the name of *Daniel Stern*. George Sand, another "emancipated" woman and herself at one time enamored of the pianist, acted as their companion on several excursions. These *Années de Pélérinage* found the pair settled at Geneva, which served as their most extended refuge from a critical and hostile society. It was inevitable and indeed desirous that such a combination of

4

two powerful egos break up after a relatively short period of bliss. Marie returned eventually to Paris; Liszt continued his concert engagements around the Continent. Their three children — Cosima, Daniel, and Blandine — were somewhat summarily legitimized and left chiefly under the care of private tutors. (The marriage of Cosima to Hans von Bülow and later Wagner, that of Blandine to Emile Ollivier, and the death of Daniel are discussed at length in the Notes.) The rupture took place in 1840, and all possibilities of reconciliation disappeared by 1844. Countess d'Agoult used their great affair as material for her novel, *Nélida* — another example of the truth of Keats' remark, that "what shocks the virtuous philosopher delights the chameleon poet"; and for a while the French reading-public of the 1840's delighted in reading the thinly-veiled biography of the lovers. There is no written evidence of Liszt's reaction to this *exposé*, although it is hard to believe that the later pious *Abbé* found the novel comforting.

In 1840 Liszt's famous competition with the pianist Thalberg took place in Paris. Thalberg had attempted to usurp the younger pianist's preëminent position during Liszt's absence with Marie d'Agoult. After simultaneous concerts, one at the *Conservatoire* and the other at the *Opéra*, the opponents battled it out before an excited *salon* audience — a scene reminiscent of the *Sängerkriege* of the medieval Minnesingers — and Liszt was declared the winner. His tours throughout Europe from that date until 1848 were received with a hero worship probably unequaled in musical history. It is safe to say that his triumphs surpassed those of Paganini — the artist from whom Liszt had learned so much about the technique of being the virtuoso.

Liszt the pianist had reached the peak of his maturity by 1848. The composer was yet to be revealed. During the 1830's and 1840's he did produce an amazing amount of piano music, when one considers the demands made upon him by an active concert career. There were, for example, the popular virtuoso pieces: *Grands Galops Chromatiques*, brilliant *Fantasies* consisting of unplayable technical fireworks; endless transcriptions of symphonies, whole operas, and songs by other composers. The empty, rhetorical taste of the early and mid-nineteenth century is one explanation, and certainly the modern tendency has been to rebel against such examples of grandiosity, sentimentality, and baroque pomposity. One should also remember that in that happy pre-radio, pre-phonograph age, the desire to hear orchestral and operatic compositions could not be satisfied except by piano transcriptions. Hence the piano enjoyed a disproportionate popularity and importance qua instrument. (Indeed, piano music itself suffered when the keyboard lost its tonal uniqueness: with much of Liszt's music, for instance, one is continually aware of hearing imitation string, horn, wood-wind, and vocal noises which are actually beyond the scope of the instrument.) Nevertheless, Liszt's contribution to piano literature up to 1848 must not be underestimated. The *Études* based on the Paganini *Caprices* for violin and the *Grandes Études Transcendentales* employed the piano to the fullest extent of its dynamic and tonal limits; while the several series of *Années de Pélérinage* foreshadowed Wagner's daring harmonic innovations, and with them Liszt displayed great formal ingenuity in his treatment of extramusical subjects. It is regrettable that modern taste has virtually driven off the concert platform such compositions from the *Années* as the *Tre Sonetti del Petrarca*, or *Après une Lecture de Dante*. Historically they are works of the utmost value since they embodied all of Liszt's radical theory concerning program music; and from a more absolute point of view, these pieces also possess great merit.

Our correspondence starts in 1848 — a convenient date not merely for its political connotations. It was the year that marked the commencement of Liszt's liaison with Princess Carolyne zu Sayn-Wittgenstein, the mother of the girl to whom these letters were written; and it was the end of Liszt's career as a piano virtuoso, a great refusal he made with considerable sacrifice. All his major orchestral works were written in the time covered by these letters to Marie — a significant shift, if one considers the paucity of his orchestral writing before 1848. In short, the serious musician and leader of the musical *avant-garde* emerged from the youthful showman and public performer; and his friendship with Wagner, with their resultant interchange of ideas, became one of the most important elements in the development of nineteenth-century musical theory. The notes and prefaces scattered throughout the letters take up both the biographical narrative and the various aspects of Liszt's intellectual growth after 1848.

There yet remains to discuss the Liszt of our particular correspondence, his times, and the mutual influences of these two inter-acting elements. "But who was able to understand Liszt? And could anyone, who had not seen this magician, describe him?" So cried one of Liszt's many female admirers, Adelheid von Schorn, and our feelings are sympathetic. Whether it really is personalities rather than principles that move an age, as Wilde said, is irrelevant: the Romantic period believed it was, and Liszt was one of the in-dividuals raised by Romanticism to almost mythic stature. It is no accident that painters such as Ingres, Delacroix, and Scheffer vied to use him as a model; for his features incarnated the physical qualities found in every literary hero of the age and coveted by all the sensitive young men who read about them. Even Liszt's severest critics were willing to grant his preëminence: Heine called him "the silly, hateful, riddling, fatal, and withall the very childish child of his age"; Nietzsche, describing Liszt and Wagner as "the advent of showmen in music," was still compelled to admit that it was chiefly Liszt (along with Paganini and Wagner) who taught the nineteenth-century *plebs* the meaning of the word "artist." Indeed one of the documents that stands as a summary of Romantic thought about the nature of the artist is Liszt's essay, *De la situation des artistes et de leur condition dans la société* (1835). Written while the musician was under the spell of Lamennais when both were con-vinced that they were "priests of art, fired by a sublime mission and desire to teach," Liszt's article is infused with the typical zeal of the Romantic manifesto. His purpose is clear if somewhat ambi-tious.

To determine today, with scope and precision, what is the situation of artists within our social order; to define their individual, political, and religious relations; to tell of their sadness and their misery, their weari-ness and their betrayals; to rip the bandage from their constantly bleeding wounds and to protest energetically against the oppressive iniquity or the insolent stupidity that blasts them, tortures them, and at best uses them as playthings; to find out about their past, prophesy their future, and to produce all their titles of glory . . .

When Liszt goes on to describe both the delights and the dep-rivations of "la vie de Bohème" which Henri Murger was to idealize some twenty years later, the phenomenon of the real "Bohemian" treating a less actual artistic world introduces another

7

element in his personality that raised him from individual to legend: his Hungarian-Gypsy background. Any real claim he had to such origins is rather shaky (cf. the Preface to Letter 168 and the discussion of *Die Zigeuner und ihre Musik in Ungarn*); but it is a truism that myths arise in order to satisfy a need and their validity is extraneous to the actual fact of their existence. The entrance of the Gypsy into polite literature dates from the late eighteenth century and the German *Sturm und Drang* period, where H. M. G. Grellmann's *Die Zigeuner* (1783) was indicative of the interest in the natural man and the rebel against society. Hugo's Esmeralda, Merimée's Carmen, a number of melodramas by Pixerécourt and Caignez all attest to the mysterious attraction the gypsies had for the Romantics — their primitivism, supposed prophetic talent and erotic and barbarous charm; the folk quality of their culture, and finally their nomadic and unbourgeois way of life which affronted both the middle-class respect for the law and its prized sense of property. That Liszt could arise from such an exotic milieu and also be the artist gave him a prominent place in the Pantheon of Romantic culture-heroes.

Similarly, his role as the virtuoso-musician provided him with yet another distinction. It is not within the scope of this Introduction to discuss the slow shift in the hierarchy of the arts that evolved during the eighteenth and nineteenth centuries. Generally speaking, the movement in aesthetic theory shows a gradual displacement of the plastic arts from their earlier preëminent position — Lessing's *Laocoön* might be taken as definitive of the Neo-Classic position — until music, once the stepchild, comes into its own with Schopenhauer's dictum (echoed throughout the century): "The goal of every art is to become like music." One of the best systematic studies in this area is Ferdnand Baldensperger's little book *Sensibilité musicale et Romantisme* (Paris: 1925), which approaches the subject less along the line of intellectual history or the history of ideas than it documents with precision the sociological changes — the increase in concerts in Paris after 1800, the rise of French musical criticism in newspapers, the new interest in popular balladry. Liszt's contribution to nineteenth-century music and culture will be assessed later: at this point, it is merely sufficient to emphasize the new elaborated role played by the musician as artist in the Romantic movement. For it was then that the notion of the virtuoso was first conceived; and here both Liszt and Paganini — to whom were attributed mysterious and Satanic powers — must be given chief credit for the creation and embodiment of the idea. The dynamic and passionate instrumentalist mediated in other than purely intellectual terms between the composer and his audience. The virtuoso literally brought his wares to the market place, more than could the unread, unseen poet or the creative musician; and certainly the concept of the artist possessed by *un homme moyen sensuel* in Paris during the 1830's must have rested partly upon his observation of Liszt's dramatic, overpowering performance at the keyboard.

Our correspondence begins in 1848, when the Romantic era was waning or was already finished. Hence the following letters, written when Liszt turned from his immense successes on the concert stage to the more cloistered activity of the composer and theorist, often have the quality of "emotion recollected in tranquillity" so far as they present either the Romantic artist or the age he symbolized. Intellectual movements do not terminate with the neatness historians wish them to have; in one sense, perhaps Liszt outlived his time. At the very zenith of Liszt's pianistic career, Chopin — the only other virtuoso of the time who rivaled Liszt technically — made an amusing but keen observation:

He [Liszt] will live to be a deputy or perhaps even a king, in Abyssinia or on the Congo: but as for the themes of his compositions, they will repose in the newspapers, together with those two volumes of German poetry.

Nevertheless, these "compositions" and their "themes" actually marked the next and major phase of Liszt's life; and the beginning of his role as a serious composer neatly coincides with the start of the letters to Marie Wittgenstein. The career of the virtuoso disappeared along with the character of the great Romantic — even the second love-affair, his middle-aged liaison with Carolyne, had little of the *brio* that distinguished his romance with Marie d'Agoult. While Liszt's own personal triumphs may have been fewer in this later stage, the problems he dealt with and his relation to contemporary ideas and personalities are no less important for the cultural historian.

Even as the later artist — the Liszt of our correspondence — was

9

no longer the fiery and impassioned character of the *Glanzperiode*, so was the new age itself a more reposeful, unpretentious time. When the old names of his former friends occasionally crop up and remind us of the intensely dramatic 1830's and 1840's, they tend to put the references to actual contemporaries in the shade. True, the mid-century was an *Epigonen-* und *Biedermeierzeit*, and the artists it produced tended to be all too aware that giants had walked the earth in the previous generation. Philosophical idealism gave way to a soberer materialistic attitude toward life; the high political, Utopian hopes of the Romantics reached their explosive climax in 1848 — but the expected bang was a whimper.

> *Reisst die Kreuze aus der Erden!*
> *Alle sollen Schwerter werden,*
> *Gott im Himmel wird's verzeihn.*
> *Gen Tyrannen und Philister!*
> *Auch das Schwert hat seine Priester,*
> *Und wir wollen Priester sein!*

So sang the poet Georg Herwegh in 1841; ten years later, however, the "Tyrannen und Philister" were secure in their quiet triumph, and before twenty-five years had gone by, Liszt — himself once a "Priest" in Lamennais' great army of humanity — embraced a more respectable, less revolutionary role within the peaceful sanctuary of the Franciscan Order.

If the persons mentioned by Liszt after 1848 lack the color and the fame enjoyed by his earlier acquaintances, they possess equal importance for the reader anxious to establish the cultural *ambiance* of the age. Ary Scheffer was no Delacroix, nor was Peter Cornelius the peer of Chopin, or Fanny Lewald another George Sand. Nevertheless Liszt's relation with them had added significance since he now saw himself and his fellow artists as part of a single, conscious, intellectual movement and no longer merely a collection of separate, unhappy — albeit titanic — egos. As far back as the 1830's, Sainte-Beuve had characterized Liszt as one of the "young people enthusiastic at all costs and forever marching in the van-guard" — a judgment the reader may find, along with more vitriolic remarks, in Sainte-Beuve's *Mes Poisons*. The critic was referring to Liszt's literary ventures with George Sand, Didier, and Lamennais (cf. Letter 22, Note 21) which ended in ludicrous fashion. Such *avant-gardisme* happily never disappeared for Liszt. It took a more serious form after 1848 when he turned to the task of composing and acting as the head of the *Neudeutsche Schule* of music. And since the principal theory of that group centered about the composition of programmatic rather than absolute music, the concern with contemporary writers and painters was a necessary correlative of Liszt's creative technique. One senses in these letters that Liszt's interest in artists engaged in other aesthetic media was more than merely personal: his conviction was strong that the *Kunstwerk der Zukunft* — to use the phrase Wagner made famous — would arise when music had come into happy alliance with its sister arts. The idea had appeared in a tentative form in Liszt's writings as early as 1835, when he declared of music that "no art, no science (with the exception of philosophy) is so sure to revindicate at once the glorious past, to effect an ancient and magnificent synthesis." Liszt's friendship with Berlioz and the increasing respect he had for that composer's works provided added substantiation for his embryonic theories; and by the midpoint of the century the burden of leadership was transferred from the French musician to Liszt, his younger disciple.

Liszt's conscious acceptance of his new role as leader is evident throughout the correspondence with Marie Wittgenstein. His own compositions occupied much of his time, and he naturally spent considerable effort to present them to the public. Liszt's was no "cloister'd and fugitive virtue," and he was the last composer who would have contented himself with the dubious reward of posterity. Yet his constant hobnobbing with the "great" — which one feels formerly to have been pure youthful snobbism — takes on the semblance of a higher and more legitimate purpose during the last forty years of his life. He realized all too well that "épater les bourgeois," the battle cry of the Romantics, meant the death of the arts in the world as it really was. That Marie d'Agoult had been a countess was a feather in the cap of young Lovelace, but the social prominence of Princess Carolyne Wittgenstein — an ardent believer in Liszt's mission — meant a greater likelihood of success for the older man's theories. For those who persist in regarding him as the prototype of the selfish, egotistical artist, his genuine altruism in furthering the cause of Wagner and a host of minor artists is an effective antidote.

11

The limits and purpose of this Introduction do not allow for an extensive analysis of Liszt's contribution to nineteenth-century music and general culture, nor are we able adequately to pursue the fascinating development of the notion of program music. The eighteenth-century rigid separation of the arts in Lessing's *Laocoön* had tended to dissolve during the hundred years intervening between that neoclassic German aesthetician and Liszt, and the potential or actual merger of the various categories became a favorite Romantic speculation. Baudelaire's often-cited *Correspondances* has been offered by critics as the definitive statement of the fundamental identity of the arts and the concomitant synesthesia:

Comme de longs échos qui de loin se confondent

. . . . .

Les parfums, les couleurs et les sons se répondent.

But actually the idea was already a commonplace well before Baudelaire's poem was written. German writers such as Novalis, the Schlegels, Tieck, and E. T. A. Hoffmann were fond of stressing the metaphysical unity that underlay all artistic creativity: music was regarded with special favor, since its lack of affinity with the sensuous world of experience gave it a uniquely indefinable and mystic quality. Even a less philosophically-minded French poet like Vigny reflected at once the quest for artistic interrelation and the role that music was to play in the new synthesis.

Descends donc, triple lyre, instrument inconnu,
O toi! qui parmi nous n'est pas encor venu
Et qu'en se consumant invoque le génie,
Sans toi point de beauté, sans toi point d'harmonie;
Musique poésie, art pur de Raphaël,
Vous deviendrez un Dieu . . . mais sur un seul autel!

If the influence of music on Romantic poetry was apparent in the increased "musicalization" of verse, and on the graphic arts by the attempted introduction of elements of "rhythm" into painting and sculpture, conversely the sudden prominence of program music was the result of a conscious transference of certain elements into music which hitherto were felt to be outside its domain. It is important to see this development as a matter of relative emphasis rather than actual novelty; and Niecks's book *Programme Music in the Last Four Centuries* abounds in hundreds of examples of pre-nineteenth century programmatic attempts — although Niecks's position as self-appointed defender of the genre makes him exaggerate in the interests of partisanship. For Liszt, as for Berlioz, the idea of an extramusical program must also be seen as a historical continuation of the rebellion against traditional musical forms. The breakdown of strict sonata form is already obvious in Beethoven, and the influx of *nocturnes*, *fantasies*, *impromptus*, and other experimental innovations shortly after the turn of the century demonstrate that the dialectical synthesis of eighteenth-century music was gradually being supplanted by a unity of mood. To the accusation that his works were inchoate and without structure, Liszt answered that the old forms were inadequate; and in order to achieve a new and more vital framework for expression, he felt that the composer must have recourse to the other arts. The historicism of Liszt's thinking, with its Hegelian overtones, emerges in his continual reassertion that the artist must speak for his own time; and the major accusation he leveled against his musical rivals — of whom Brahms may be considered the chief — was their "academic" adherence to the past. The critic Sir Henry Hadow, while he dismisses the issue of program music as actually extraneous to the main line of musical development, gives Liszt his due when he makes the pertinent observation that Wagner's music-drama, the asserted *Kunstwerk der Zukunft*, was much less radical in its theory than were Liszt's symphonic poems: the former involved no new redefinition of music *per se*, but was merely a modern attempt to reunite drama and music in a happier synthesis. Liszt's compositions, on the other hand, represented the logical culmination of an independent trend. Whether his works succeeded is irrelevant to the problem at hand, since such a consideration rightfully falls within the province of musical criticism and not aesthetics.

The battle between the absolute and the programmatic school continued throughout the century, and indeed the struggle is not over. One is reminded of the rebuke of Gines de Passamonte to Don Quixote when that valorous knight inquires whether the captive's autobiography has been completed — "How the Devil can it be finished and I yet living?" In Liszt's own day the opposite camp protested against his endeavor to break with the established tradition in the direction of excessively unique modernity. His opponents also resented what they deemed to be Liszt's destruction of the categories of the arts. The latter sin was interpreted as making music the handmaid to poetry and painting with a resultant loss of autonomy. "Sounds and the sensation of sounds are completely unique in themselves and their effect is entirely independent of their relations to any other objects," said the theoretician Helmholtz; and he and Hanslick (cf. Letter 30, Note 3) vigorously maintained that "the beauty of a piece of music is specifically musical; that is, it dwells in the sound-relations without any recourse to any foreign extramusical frame of reference." Hanslick foreshadowed many of the modern tendencies in aesthetics with his interest in the physiological aspect of the impact of a work of art, and in his book one finds long disquisitions about musical therapy and the effect of pleasant sounds on the nerve endings. After a heavy onslaught on both the mistaken emphasis of "Gefühl" in music and the fallacy inherent in program music — music can neither represent any specific feeling, nor can it imitate any aspect of nature — he concludes, "The content of music consists of sound-impelled shapes." In short, the beauties of music arise out of the delight of the mind contemplating pleasing forms; and the so-called "world of music" is nonexistent except for the poetically-minded metaphysician. Here Hanslick may well have been thinking of Liszt, since the intellectual disagreement of the two men extended to a personal level.

It is significant that the last period of Liszt's career was marked by his return to the composition of oratorios and masses — both conventional forms that exhibited neither the dramatic daring of his friend Wagner nor Liszt's own earlier orchestral heterodoxy. Does this mean that in his own mind Liszt felt his theories were defeated? Part of the shift toward the composition of church music was naturally occasioned by Liszt's active role in the Catholic Church and his assumption of lay orders with the Franciscans. Yet we cannot help feel his increasing sense of disappointment — partly with his own high aspirations and the course of his life, partly with the times that more and more appeared out of joint. Wagner had triumphed; but in many ways Wagner's task had been easier, since the age was friendlier to any art that lent itself to the grandiose and the spectacular. The coterie of musicians, painters, and poets, on which Liszt had pinned his hopes for the cultural renascence whose center would be Weimar, displayed little promise of great things to come. Liszt's musical disciples turned for the most part into piano virtuosi — a fine irony for the pianist who had virtually created the species only to forsake it; the painters of the *Biedermeier* generation and their successors were too content to cater to the conservative tastes of the complacent German public to desire membership in any doubtful *avant-garde*; Saar, Dingelstedt, Fallersleben, and the other poets accepted their lot as unassuming imitators of their Romantic predecessors — and in any case prose was to be the medium of the realistic-naturalistic 1870's and 1880's. Finally, Liszt presents us with the paradoxical phenomenon of the artist who made his fame too young and too quickly — and within a field he later abandoned for what he regarded as more serious activity. Perhaps a high-flown and hypothetical comparison is illuminating: Liszt's career was as if Keats had lived until 1860 and had then rejected the lyric for some unsuccessful and experimental form of the novel. It is the prerogative of the cultural historian to make the cruel judgment that a man can outlive his own times.

Philosophically, one might view Liszt's life as three successive stages in the quest for religious consciousness. First there was the ardent follower of Lamennais who embraced the vague and ultimately unsatisfying cult of "Humanity." The second was the attempt to raise music itself up to the status of a faith — and here Liszt joins the "solemn saints and sweet societies" of assorted nineteenth-century artists who pursued the same end. The ultimate phase was his identification with the Catholic Church. Is it too conjectural to interpret the supramusical demands Liszt made on music as the heritage of the Romantic search for the Absolute? For Schopenhauer, and to a lesser degree later for Nietzsche, music and a mystical insight into reality were synonymous. Perhaps *this* was the condition to which Liszt aspired; but temperament, intellectual limitations, and religious conditioning made such a conclusion unobtainable and essentially inimical.

It has already been noted that the letters to Marie Wittgenstein commence at a convenient year, 1848 — when Liszt abandoned his concert career for that of the composer-theorist and took up residence with Princess Carolyne Wittgenstein at Weimar. If the reader keeps in mind that Marie was eleven years old in 1848, the gradual shift in tone of Liszt's writings to her will be more easily comprehended. The first seventeen letters were written from 1848 to 1851, and among them is the charming fable composed for Marie's birthday, *Les Deux Roses*. Here we find the musician in a playful, quasi-parental mood. But as Marie approached adolescence, Liszt felt more and more the necessity to play the role of the spiritual adviser and pedagogue. Letter 18, for example, contains the interesting description of a visit to Wagner in Switzerland; and there is a group of letters, starting with the twenty-third, that deals with the new school of German painters. When Marie and her mother left Weimar on their trips to Berlin, Vienna, and health resorts — travels that increased in frequency during the 1850's, when Weimar society looked with disfavor upon the household arrangements at the Altenburg — Liszt was full of concern that Marie be the experienced observer; conversely, his own absences from Weimar as a visiting orchestra-conductor produced letters of an edifying and descriptive nature. Similarly, his own reading was reflected in the literary advice he sent to her. From 1850 to 1860 was the period during which he composed the majority of the symphonic tone-poems — his chief orchestral writings and the works that caused the most controversy in musical spheres: Letters 25 through 60 abound in statements about this phase of Liszt's creative activity, since Marie was now becoming his artistic confidante as she entered maturity.

Throughout this earlier portion of the correspondence one catches a glimpse of the problems besetting the musician at Weimar: the opposition Liszt encountered at the Theater when he attempted to make Weimar into the musical center of Europe; the rebuffs he suffered by insisting that unsympathetic audiences hear the "New Music"— mainly that of his friend Wagner; the thirteen-year fight with the Russian Court and Church to annul Carolyne Wittgenstein's marriage, which ended in the dramatic wedding *fiasco* on October 22, 1861. No letters exist from Liszt to Marie between that year and 1869, when the correspondence resumes in a casual fashion. The argument has been advanced — and indeed it has validity — that Carolyne prohibited Liszt's writing Marie. The young girl had married Prince Constantine von Hohenlohe-Schillingsfurst in 1859; her mother later was convinced that his brother, Cardinal Gustav, had been active in preventing the proposed match of Liszt and herself. There is no doubt that a certain coolness existed between Carolyne and her son-in-law; yet Liszt's letters to the mother between 1861 and 1869 refer continually to Marie in the friendliest of terms, and there is even the occasional mention of mutual visits between the Wittgenstein and Hohenlohe households. Furthermore, the same Liszt-Carolyne correspondence contains several statements concerning letters from Liszt to Marie — and these must presumably be lost. A neat scholarly problem is presented here. It is hoped that at some future date the answer may be found.

The period of the hiatus found both Liszt and Carolyne in Rome: he hard at work teaching and composing, she engaged at her monumental twenty-four volume labor, *Les causes extérieures de la faiblesse intérieure de l'Église.* Liszt's incipient religiosity, apparent in his relations with Lamennais during the 1830's, assumed a more positive shape in 1865 when he took the first four orders in the Franciscans and soon after Abbé Liszt became the Canon of Albano. Of the many histrionic acts performed by the great showman, none received more sarcastic comment by his contemporaries than did his assumption of clerical vows — and much was made of the fact that the fifth vow, that of chastity, was not taken by the middle-aged Don Juan. Only the saints themselves presumably act out of unmixed motives, and Liszt could scarcely have joined their glorious company. A witty critic has described Liszt at Mass in the morning, paying tribute to the demands of the spirit — and in the evening letting his corporeal nature have its due in less austere surroundings. Liszt was not a person to abandon the sure pleasures of this world in favor of the less certain rewards of the next. Nevertheless, in the interests of kindness and the whole truth the reader ought to admit what genuine elements of religious fervor were there. Liszt set about the task of reforming the music of the Church, and from now on his principal compositions were to be of a liturgical order. This fact alone should suffice as an artistic guarantee of the sincerity of his intentions.

Again our correspondence serves as a commentary upon the changes in Liszt's intellectual development. From the sixty-first letter to the last, written not quite four months before his death on August 1, 1886, the letters abound in references to his musical-religious concern: and the *vie trifurquée* that kept Liszt in a peripatetic existence between Rome, Weimar, and Budapest is all carefully recorded for the interested reader. Indeed, the three cities might be taken as symbols of his triple quest: the intellectual groping for spiritual faith, the artist seeking a cosmopolitan and universal vehicle of expression, and the lifelong *emigré* looking for his national roots. Even after the little "Magnolette" and "Magnette" of the 1850's turned into "Madame la Princesse," she still remained the recipient of his confidences — and perhaps it is this quality that gives the correspondence its uniqueness. In a sense, Marie became the daughter for Liszt that he never had in either Blandine or the willful Cosima. He was also able to lavish upon her an easy warmth and affection for which neither Marie d'Agoult nor Carolyne Wittgenstein could be the object.

It is regrettable that Marie's letters to Liszt do not exist — or if they do, that they are not published. It is hard to believe that they would possess any great literary or intellectual merit. Both from Liszt's correspondence and from contemporary accounts of her, one gathers that Marie had average charm and intelligence but no more than that. Nevertheless we would then see the other side of the coin, so to speak; and think of the wealth of information her letters might yield about the musician! It is not merely scholarly motives that lead to such a wish. Of all the vast number of persons within Liszt's wide acquaintance, it appears that Marie Wittgenstein remained his oldest and truest friend. His many pupils played too well their roles of zealous disciples to enjoy that coveted position. Wagner's affection for Liszt — while apparently as strong as his colossal ego ever displayed to anyone — was inconstant and full of disappointments for the pianist; and finally Carolyne Wittgenstein turned more and more to her writings and endless theological speculations, and her sole later dealings with Liszt were along the line of hypochondriacal complaints, ill-founded suspicions, and absurd recriminations. For human warmth and understanding the aged artist had only Marie, his confidante for almost thirty-nine years. Of her he might have said, as did Viscount Bolingbroke of Jonathan Swift, "I seek no epistolary fame, but am a good deal pleased to think that it will be known thereafter that you and I lived in the most friendly intimacy together."

PART ONE

1848-1860

LETTER 1: *Preface*

"The success of musicians, pianists, and singers with women is well known . . . women pull them to pieces: this has been the fate of singers ever since Orpheus." Sainte-Beuve made this penetrating remark about Liszt (cf. *Mes Poisons*, ed. Giraud; Paris: Plon, 1926, p. 70) before the musician had encountered the second of his two principal maenads, Princess Carolyne zu Sayn-Wittgenstein; our correspondence, written to her daughter, starts in the interim between Liszt's departure from Russia and Carolyne's arrival at Weimar.

Aside from marking the commencement of Liszt's new *amour*, the moment has added significance in the development of his career as artist. The concert at Elizabetgrad (now Stalingrad) in October 1847 virtually brought to an end the era of Liszt as leading virtuoso pianist of his age. The child prodigy of nine, who had made his *début* at Oedenburg, Hungary, in 1817, amazed the Viennese musical world four years later; Paris and London followed in 1823 and 1824, and the *Glanzperiode*, which saw him playing in all the major Continental cities, lasted from 1839 until 1847. Except for occasional benefit recitals and a few isolated instances when public opinion forced him into performing, Liszt abandoned his earlier profession to become a serious composer and the self-appointed leader of the "New Music." Perhaps, in this respect, Sainte-Beuve's comment is partially unjust: for even as the Countess d'Agoult (cf. Preface to Letter 26) had inspired him along virtuosic lines, so did Princess Wittgenstein encourage him in his new — and often criticized — role as composer-critic. The public was loath to lose one of its idols, and Liszt's detractors were all too quick to accuse him of having made the great refusal.

They met at Kiev, early in 1847. Carolyne had been born "Karolina Elzbieta Iwanowska," daughter of the wealthy Polish landowner Peter von Iwanowski and his wife Pauline Podowska; she married Nikolaus zu Sayn-Wittgenstein (1812–1864) when she was seventeen, on May 7, 1836, and one daughter, Marie — the recipient of these letters — was born on February 18, 1837.

Part of the complicated history of the Wittgenstein family will be treated later (cf. Letter 135, "Léonille W."). It had been a mediatized sovereign house of the Holy Roman Empire since the days of its founder, Eberhard von Sayn (1139–1176); the first Prince zu Sayn-Wittgenstein-Berleburg was created in 1792; and the Russian line came into being when Louis Adolphus, Graf zu Sayn-Wittgenstein-Ludwigsburg (1769–1843), was made a Russian field marshal. This Slavic branch of the original Westphalian family included Prince Nicolas, adjutant to the Czar. At the time that Liszt and Carolyne met, the Wittgensteins had been separated some six or seven years, and she was living in somewhat bizarre splendor on her Woronince estate in Podolia — with an estimated entourage of thirty-thousand serfs.

Her plan was to divorce Nicolas and marry Liszt, and Carolyne immediately set about obtaining an annulment. Her status as a Russian citizen and a Roman Catholic, plus the existence of a ten-year-old daughter, was to prove an insurmountable barrier to this projected second match (cf. Prefaces to Letters 25 and 57). Nevertheless, Liszt returned to Weimar in February 1848, and Carolyne, after settling some of her affairs, arrived in July. (Actually, she departed from Woronince with Marie in early April 1848, after eluding the Russian border police; and the rendezvous took place at Prince Lichnowsky's castle of Kryzyzanowitz in Austria. The sojourn there was succeeded by trips to Vienna and Hungary — a difficult period for the couple, since their own domestic disorder was placed within the larger historical framework of the 1848 Revolutions, and even peaceful Weimar had its own small share of political confusion.)

For Liszt to take up residence in Weimar was to realize a long-considered project. His first visit to that German city had been in November 1841. The actor Eduard Genast describes him sweeping into the *Russische Hof*, the epitome of the gaunt, daemonic, and aristocratic Romantic hero, in Leonhard Schrickel's *Geschichte des Weimarer Theaters* (Weimar: Pause, 1928; pp. 181–182). He played at Court on November 26 and in public on the 29th; the Grand Duchess Maria-Pavlovna was delighted with her new artistic discovery, and in 1842 Liszt was appointed *Hofkapellmeister*. The position was a nominal one until he returned to stay in 1848.

For information about the Wittgenstein family, cf. The Marquis of Rovigny, *The Titled Nobility of Europe*, London: Harrison, 1914. The biographical background concerning Liszt may be found in Sacheverel Sitwell, *Liszt*, London: Faber & Faber, 1934 — or in any other standard biography; also Adelheid von Schorn, *Das nachklassische Weimar*, Weimar: Kiepenheuer, 1911, and *Zwei Menschenalter*, Stuttgart: Greiner & Pfeiffer, 1920. The chief primary source, however, and the one most referred to throughout this correspondence, is *Liszts*

Briefe an die Fürstin Carolyne Sayn-Wittgenstein, ed. La Mara, Leipzig: Breitkopf & Härtel, 1899–1902. For convenience in citation this reference is shortened to *L. M.*, followed by the number of the document.

LETTER 1

I hope that these lines, my charming pupil, will arrive on your birthday,[1] and will remind you of someone who is quite humbly devoted to you from the best and deepest part of his heart.

The countries and the cities that I have crossed since leaving Woronince[2] have had no attraction for me, other than the idea of seeing you again soon. Despite my denials of a month ago, I confess that at this hour I no longer have the courage to give up the hope of your trip. Heaven grant that there isn't too much delay! Today I am sending the Princess, your mother, the design for the carriage that will have the honor and the good fortune to carry you; I like to think that it will be according to her taste and to all your requirements.

Your Cousin's Lamp,[3] with the triple crown of Prince, Painter, and Musician, ought to have reached you by now; at least it is through no fault of mine if M. Hausner hasn't used the utmost haste dispatching it to you. If only I could *dispatch* myself! How promptly you would see me arrive! That *Sorrel*[4] of glorious memory for Miss Anderson,[5] that three-gaited *Sorrel*, would step like a tortoise by comparison!

Remember me affectionately, my charming pupil, to Miss Anderson; tell her how happy I would be to resume our famous games again; and when Cyrus or Pantheus or even little Ernest[6] comes to your mind, remember me too, a remembrance of which I will try to show myself as worthy as I am happy and grateful.

Weimar, February 4, 1848.   F. Liszt

LETTER 2a

Missiou[1] kisses Magnette[2] most devoutly and tells her again to see him this evening —

LETTER 2b

Yet still your mouth, from so much boredom dumb,
Deigned not to open to complain of him — [3]
(Andromaque, Act IV, Scene 2)

LETTER 2c

Finish your lesson peacefully — and come to see me afterwards.

LETTER 3a

Dear Magne,[1]

I am bowed down with calls and with jobs to be done; would you be so kind, my dear sweet majesty, to excuse me if I don't come to pay my humble respects this morning? Around 4 o'clock I hope to be set at liberty, and shall immediately profit from it by undertaking my usual climb up to the Altenburg — [2]

I kiss at least fourteen times the kind hands of Farfadet XIV [3] and am prostrate at her feet.

Sunday morning —   FL.

LETTER 3b

UKASE for March 18th.

It is hereby commanded that Magnolets [4] and Floup [5] be so silly as to go to Mme. Sup's [6] reading this evening.

Fainéant I.[7]

LETTER 4a

It seems to me better that you go, dearest Magnolette,[1] even at the very likely risk that nobody will tell you anything that interests you, since in these types of dealing the intermediaries *of nothing* are indispensable in order to get at something, and if possible at something better. At least, this is the humble opinion of him who is your passion's slave.

LETTER 4b

Fainéant is still a big fool for not being able to get up and run and fly toward his dear Magnolette. But "blessed are the poor in spirit" — when they get such delightful little letters such as the one you have just written me.

Sleep well and long dearest child —

I hope to come to pay court to you tomorrow —

LETTER 5a

In this situation also the two blunderers of the house have settled themselves in the most blundering fashion by thus remaining separated at the two ends of the house.[1] But whether far or near, disabled or in good health, they are invariably and indissolubly good company for each other, aren't they?

May God's[2] good and beautiful angels watch over you, my dearest child —

LETTER 5b

All is well, dear Magnolette, very well, because you are feeling better. Scotland[3] has just given me some good news about you — bad little Ahriman who wrought havoc with your lip will soon be succeeded by good Mr. Ormuzd,[4] and the *criticism* which still has me by the legs, if not by the throat, will also end by going away —

Minette will soon come back, I hope, since I don't care to sup before her return, and hunger is getting the better of me. I very obediently drank Goulon's[5] medicine right down to the dregs — although homeopathic doses hardly sustain one more than certain prevention! —

Fortunately, as the Proverb says, "he who sleeps, eats." So let's sleep soundly — and trust in God —

LETTER 5c

No matter what science may counsel, I beg you to arrange to return here — wrap yourself up in three cloaks, if need be. Minette is waiting for you at home, and you can imagine her agitation.

LETTER 6: Preface

The charm of these early letters lies in their revealing the great affection felt by Liszt for Marie, and the constant interest he took in her education. That he considered himself to be her literary as well as her musical mentor is apparent in the number of books he suggests that she read. Letter 6 is unique, however: it offers us the sole example of Liszt the creative writer, and so far as I can ascertain, it was his only excursion into the literary field proper — if one excludes his critical writings.

The sentimental-religious tone of the little tale is slightly reminiscent of the *Paroles d'un Croyant* by Lamennais, whose influence on the musician sixteen years before certainly helped to determine Liszt's spiritual attitude (cf. Letter 22). From a visual point of view, the scene might be taken from any of a number of paintings by Schwind, Kaulbach, Schnorr von Carolsfeld, or Waldmüller — all admired by Liszt, and discussed later in the correspondence, and all part of the Nazarene-Biedermeier tradition that distinguished so much of mid-century German painting. It was the type of *tableau* that had much appeal for Liszt; note, for example, his admiration for Hébert's *La Sventurata* (Letter 63, Note 2), which depicts essentially the identical dramatic incident.

The allegory behind the story is unmistakable: "cette belle enfant de quatorze ans" is Marie, then in her fourteenth year, and the sorrowful widow can be none other than Carolyne. Since Liszt speaks often of the rose bushes around the Altenburg, it does not seem too far-fetched to regard the setting as that of the Wittgenstein house at Weimar. In an effort to redeem this narrative from absolute banality, one is tempted to speculate that in the character of the two distressed widows in the fable Liszt was representing both Carolyne Wittgenstein and Marie d'Agoult; and that he was identifying himself with the young maiden who brought them comfort.

Carl Engel, in the *Musical Quarterly* for July 1936 (vol. XXII, no. 3), translated and published this letter with an accompanying article, as well as numbers 4 ("a" and "b"), 8, 10, 21, and 24.

LETTER 6

The Two Roses

Once upon a time there was a castle; — and a garden; — A woman walked up to another who was sitting down. One could see that her face was lined with care; anguish was in her eyes. She murmured at length, and although her voice was low, the words loneliness, hunger, distress, kept coming back; and when she spoke the phrase, "my sick child," a sob choked the words on her lips! . . .

The woman who had been sitting answered in a low tone, the way one does to a mysterious tale. She obviously spoke from the depths of her soul, and she was rewarded with a heartrending look. Both of them talked yet for a while, and more than one secret sorrow was mutually confided, for both were as sympathetic as they were unhappy. Finally the woman who had entered the scene departed, much paler than she was when she had come.

Behind the perfumed honeysuckle and the fragrant jasmine, sat the little mistress of the castle. To her surprised ears came the sobs of her mother, and the sounds of helpless distress. She ran around the thicket, and awaited her who was courageous and unhappy, in the clearing. . . . And even as the latter came forward, the look in her eyes paved her way before her like a carpet beneath her bruised feet . . . and her poverty's solemn majesty was upset by this unexpected homage, as if it found this last refuge of its dignity invaded. She, however, gave a cordial blessing to the fourteen-year-old child, who was crowned with long blond hair, dressed in blue, and whose bright tender look seemed like that of an angel glimpsed across the Ether's azure heaven! —

And when these two faced each other, the juxtaposed picture of Sadness and the picture of Innocence, was like two of the earth's most sacred inhabitants standing before God, visible only to themselves, and concealing their finest glory from the eye of mortal man — The lilies in the bed of flowers seemed only to grow to bloom at the feet of this pensive and innocent creature, whose name was that of the Queen of the Heavens. . . . The shoulders of the widow were hung in a long mourning dress, like the robes of exiled royalty . . . and on the silent face of the latter could be read "*Death, suffering*" . . . which was answered by the former's ineffable smile, — "*Resurrection, — bliss.*" . . . And their eyelids were bedewed with tears! . . . These were colorless on the first, even as is the evening dew; for she had paused beneath the sharp shadow of a poplar tree, as if beneath a funeral obelisk. . . . But on the second they shone like a many-colored prism, even as the morning twilight is colored and caught up by the sun's rays, when the radiant day blends the waving folds of its azure curtain, in a golden background. . . .

And the angel of such radiant beauty knelt before the angel of the dying and the sick. Then, like a tribute from a novice to a hierophant, she held two Roses out to her . . . the loveliest of the garden. She had picked those whose hundredfold petals breathed the farthest air . . . and from them she had plucked their thorns. "Take these, dear Lady, to your sick child," said the timid little girl to the unhappy woman, and she blushed as she shook the hand which took the flowers. And she, who day and night had felt the iron fingers of misery pierce her side, found balm in the touch of this velvetlike hand. She wanted to grasp it again; but the trembling roses let fall, between their leaves, the generous gift that was to bring recovery to the child who was in pain, as well as bearing Nature's sweetest perfumes. Much moved, shaken, and blushing in turn, the disconsolate woman raised her eyes, where her sadness shone in a heavenly mirror. . . . The child was no longer there! —

She then considered that God must have angels, whose entire beauty He made apparent only to those who grieved. August fifteenth, Assumption Day, 1850 — Weimar.

LETTER 7

Fainéant doesn't want to go loaf with Walbrul,[1] Cornelius[2] and his Club,[3] without telling Minette and Magnolette that he is completely adoringly, *devoutly*, and devotedly

Their very happy slave
Fainéant I —

LETTER 8: Preface

The court at Weimar was a model of German nineteenth-century diminutive elegance. The Ducal Residence was originally at the Wilhelmsburg, an old castle on the outskirts of the city; and there the first Weimar Court-Theater was established in 1756. It was here, for example, that Koch's Leipzig Company settled, in 1768, to perform the new "Singspiel."

The Wittumspalais and Fürstenhaus were also occupied at various times by the ruling family; but its chief habitation, and the one to which Liszt most often refers in his letters, was the Belvedere, built by Ernst-August (1688–1748) between 1724 and 1732. This was a rococo palace famous for its *Menagerie* and *Orangerie*; and Bode (*Das Leben*, p. 22) says that Goethe wrote a sketch about the botanical curiosities of the *Orangerie* in 1823, although I have been unable to find any such essay in his scientific writings.

Vehle's little book, *Der Hof zu Weimar*, contains some interesting figures indicative of the growth in magnificence of the Weimar court. There was no "Kammerherr," for instance, in 1767. By 1791 there were eleven; thirteen in 1806; and forty-one by 1841. The year of Liszt's permanent attachment to the Court, 1849, saw the appointment of four "Hofmarschälle." The financial demands made upon the small state to maintain such splendor must have been huge: Liszt alone received 1200 Thalers a year, and the Court budget for 1848 was 250,000 Thalers — a figure that suffered serious reduction after the revolution of that year. An excellent description of an evening at Court is found in Schorn, *Das nachklassische Weimar*, I, chap. iii.

Vehle (*Der Hof zu Weimar*, p. 330) comments that "the court was the most magnificent of all the small German courts; this was made possible by the money that the Grand Duchess received from the Russian court"; and her dowry helped defray expenses. She was Maria Pavlovna (1786–1859), wife of Carl Friedrich von Sachsen-Weimar (1783–1853), whom she married on August 3, 1804. Bode describes the festivities occasioned by her entry into Weimar in the following September, when Schiller declaimed his ode, "Wir kommen von fernher, wir wandern und schreiten" at the Weimar Court-Theater. It was not until 1828, however, that her husband became ruler.

Her interest in music was partly responsible for Liszt's advent at Weimar; and the shift from the straight dramatic productions of the Goethe-Schiller period to the presentation of operas at the Court-Theater was also to some degree due to her influence. Liszt supervised the musical training of her daughters, Marie and Elizabeth. (Cf. Schorn,

29

Das nachklassische Weimar, vol. II, p. 18). Vehle says of her that she was "a woman of no great personal attraction, but who owned the most superb manners." (*Der Hof zu Weimar*, p. 321.) The Grand Duchess's role in the intrigue centering around Carolyne's attempts to marry Liszt and to get her marriage annulled was important, since Maria Pavlovna was sister to Czar Nicholas I of Russia.

LETTER 8

Thank you, dearest Magne, for your dear little lines which certainly gave me more happiness than they caused you trouble to write. You can scarcely imagine how lively an interest I take, *meal by meal*, in your progress of emancipation from the tyrannies of art and science, joined as it is to the friendly and affectionate solicitude the tyrannous Möller[1] bears for you, for whom it would be only fair to revive the old meaning of the word *tyrannos*,[2] quite opposed to the one we give it today, and to which honor and glory were formerly attributed, as Pericles will attest!

Well, here you are already permitted to taste the delights of herring and to savor ham! Such happenings! and what a party! . . . and what a sweet party it would be for me, were I allowed to witness these pleasures and to season your banquets with a few libations of Seltzer-Water.

Speaking of happenings, I shall have so many to tell you that I won't know where to begin; for you know that the capital and the residency of Weimar is a hotbed of all sorts of excitements and catastrophes. For today I'll restrict myself to the most important. First, then, Mux[3] has become a quasi-lordly animal, of rather handsome size, but with manners too noisily demonstrative and almost embarrassing in their mordant expansiveness. *Mr. Rabbit* * (pronounced in the Polish manner, for you must know that Hermann Becker[4] is of Polish origin, and consequently has full claim to the title of *Mr. Rabbit*, as a citizen of one of the districts of Posen[5] whose spelling I would mangle if I attempted to write it, where he was born, as he has just told me, perhaps he may even be that famous offspring of the carp and the hare, which the most learned naturalists have thus far vainly striven to obtain, despite all their

* Pronounce *Pan Lapine*.

care and vigil — and I am planning to send him to the next London exposition [6] in that capacity. If only John Bull doesn't make a Lion out of him! that would obviously be a scientific degeneration) but let's get back to Mux via Mr. Rabbit, who has taught him a most effective trick which I call the Dance of the Dervishes. Picture Mux turning and turning fifteen minutes at a time, trying to catch his tail, and filling up the intervals with his own brand of Music! — It's really the most cheerful kind of silliness, and one which denotes in this worthy animal the most incontestable aptitude for transcendental mathematics; for it is apparent that it is only because of his concept of the circle and of the superiority of this figure above all others, that he thus uses all his ardor in making a circle out of himself, by swallowing his tail and singing and dancing quite like a Dervish. "Die anderen Hunde. . . ."

For his part, Mr. Rabbit had the honor of displaying his artistic talent before the mighty ones [7] a few days before my arrival. He was *invited*, no less, to a children's party at the Hereditary Grand Duke's. [8] His juggler's cups (he has loads of them) bedazzled the little audience, and Their Highnesses very graciously displayed their satisfaction. Furthermore, they asked him about me (C.F. [9] in particular, by which I was really touched) and he was given two gold crowns as an honorarium.

Yesterday in the afternoon, coming back from Z's [10] — I met Lisi [11] in the Greek Chapel Square. [12] I was naturally very civil to him for your sake, as well as to Zeiss [13] whom I met with one of his little chaps a little further on, and whom I tried to convince that the interruption of your chronology lessons had had the most unpleasant consequences. He thinks, erudite professor that he is, that the lost time might easily be made up, and he is keeping in reserve several thousand numbers and dates, which will certainly strengthen your health.

I wrote Abbé Floup, that Her Grace the Grand Duchess, as well as Monseigneur C.F. and the heirs apparent, has urgently asked for news of you, and that Her Grace the Grand Duchess in particular *wishes* to obtain some through the intermediary of Countess Fritsch, [14] before your return —

Tuesday, tomorrow evening, there is to be a small Court Concert, whose Program I'll send you — As for operas, I have none to conduct until King Alfred [15] (on the 16th of the month), due to Höfer's [16] illness which makes the performance of major works impossible.

Concerning Höfer, I am definitely taking his *Mouxian* prerogative away from him, because he can no longer claim any analogy either with the black or the white —

Imagine a thousand, and a thousand times a thousand, good, lovely, and tender things; and tell yourself that I wish them for you and bespeak them to you from the bottom of my heart — and count on me as you would on one of Mux's "watchdog" † friends, with this difference, that the *chains* are my liberty and my happiness as long as they retain me near Floup and you (and I hope that it will be for ever).

Monday, January 27, 1851.   F L.

Please give my best regards to Miss Anderson — I am joining two notes to this, which you will give to Minette.

LETTER 9

Tuesday, February 3, 1851.

Dear Magnette,

I intended to give you some details about *Carl Friedrich's* [1] party, in my role as *historiographer* of the Weimar court; but now Abbé Floup has taken it into her head to write me such lamentable, gloomy letters that I haven't the heart to wander all around — Hence I rid myself of the Court yesterday morning, and quite naturally give up the honor of the dinner and the ball today —

The great event of the day for me yesterday, which really made me celebrate *Carl Friedrich's* party, was your cute *Moux Furet* [2] letter, for which I kiss your poor little skinny hands and the two ribbons on your braids. That Moux Furet signature immediately carried my mind back to some of the animals invented in that story, and particularly to the Hippogriff [3] — for *Moux* ought to have four paws, and Furet can scarcely be without wings — only these are

† The same family are scarcely watchdogs, says my Pan Lapine. They have no humor and no agility. Mux, however, is an outstanding example who stands *head and shoulders* above the rest of the family!

32

swallow's wings gotten up in most beautiful hummingbird colors —
and in so musing I've come to create a Symbol of Moux Furet for
my own exclusive use, which I wish I knew how to design that I
might send it to you.

A few days ago I went to call on our English friends, Miss Williams and Mme O'Brien.[4] I found them, as always, charming and
wonderful. Mme O'Brien asked me a great deal about you, and on
this subject kept the tone of the conversation most ladylike and full
of deep affection for you. As you may well believe, there was equally (that is to say quite otherwise) talk of S.,[5] whom she reproached
above all for his excessive leanings toward chattering and *cancans*.
Mme O'B. is enjoying herself at Weimar, where she sees almost no
one with the exception of M. Sach W.,[6] with whose teaching she is
most content, saying that she never could have imagined that a boy
of that age would be capable of so much seriousness and of such
application with his pupils. (Tell that to Abbé Floup.) Miss W.
works what she calls six hours a day at her piano, and in any case
owns an excellent instrument by Härtel of Leipzig, for which she
paid 500 Thalers.

Oh dear! I am vexed to announce to you officially: Ulysses
Stock[7] has committed his depredations on the chestnut trees, and
even on the hedge of roses that was in front of your windows. Soon
part of that little forest of pines will also disappear, they tell me, for
a *beer-hall* is to be built on this site, opposite the bridge. This Stock
really deserves a *caning*, doesn't he?

Abbé Floup is mistaken, or what is more likely, I explained myself badly concerning Pan Rabbit's opinion about Moux. Pan Rabbit
is too much a *Buffon* to class Moux among "watchdogs" — On the
contrary, he has the highest idea of Moux's superior origins, and he
certainly believes that Moux is in the same relation to other members
of his family, who are good only to serve as watchdogs, that Napoleon was in regard to the rest of the Bonapartes.

Tell Minette that in order to alleviate his amorous sorrows, I
have engaged Raff, to compose a great Andante for a symphony in
the *Doric mode*,[8] in imitation of Beethoven who wrote an andante
for a quartet in the Lydian mode.[9] *Little* Morning-Roamer[10] can
console herself that she doesn't yet know these scholarly tonalities;
for I scarcely understand them any better, and I'm reserving myself

some fine evening to have them explained to me by Raff, if he'd care to chat about them.

Speaking of *chatting*, has anyone told you that Messer Daniel [11] took it upon himself to let off some paper-pellet fireworks around his teachers' seat! What a nice example of fine scholarly respect! Zeiss can truly boast of getting off easily with the Fifth-Fourteen,[12] who would no doubt be quite as inventive, supposing that there were a professorial chair in your room! —

Please give my most convincing *"regards"* to Miss A's beautiful eyes, and add to them my respects and compliments without mincing matters. But what will be left for you? Oh, always quite enough, you need have no fear. . . . Furet is aware of what to believe on this score, and there's no need to teach her more than she already knows — and will always know.

If it is at all possible for you, fix it so that we may spend your birthday (18) [13] together either at Halle or Weimar. In the meantime I sign my name as Moux of Moux Furet.

FL.

LETTER 10: *Preface*

The issue of the *Revue des Deux Mondes* mentioned by Liszt contained his article on Chopin, who had died two years before; in 1852 Liszt expanded his essay into book form (Leipzig: Breitkopf & Härtel). Written by the musician who, by Chopin's own admission, could play his piano compositions better than Chopin, it is an extremely fascinating tribute. Upon reading it, one is aware of seeing one of the last critical documents of Romanticism: the rhetoric and ideas, while presented with passion and lyricism, both convey a sense of being out of joint with the more prosaic 1850's. It is almost as if Liszt had been schooled too well by Lamennais, Musset, Hugo, Lamartine, and their literary followers. Consequently his essay is as much a lament for an age gone by as it is for a late friend and fellow pianist, and it is declaimed in the very terms of the era now disappeared. When Liszt describes Chopin as the tragic, unhappy artist — physically ill, spiritually sick from the contumely of a hostile society, proud and aristocratic, driven by a daemonic urge to pursue his calling — we realize that perhaps the identification of Romanticism with youth is a proper one, and that Liszt was already an anachronism.

34

Of more immediate interest to this correspondence is the hand of
Carolyne that one detects throughout the book: the extolment of the
noble Polish spirit and the Slavic (particularly Polish) female — "for
are they not incomparable, these Slavic women?" — and the long three-
page footnote, pretentious with dubious scholarship, concerning the
peculiar beauties of the Polish language (cf. p. 59 and pp. 126–128).

LETTER 10

Weimar, February 8, 1851.
Saturday evening

Best and dearest Magnet,

How happy I am to see that you are already taking your place
among the most *fecund* of our letter-writers, and how much I thank
you for your last sweet and charming penciled letter! But, I beg
you if you are so kind as to write me again, please try to use ink,
because the wretched pencil blurs dreadfully, and that causes me
much sorrow. Well, here you are already up, but falling over back-
wards from an excess of strength and animation. Milord Sach[1] has
just told me (according to Minette's letter) that you are doing
marvelously well, and that in ten or twelve days we'll see you here
again. Unfortunately I don't dare delude myself with this hope, but
at any rate I will *concoct* something quite as subtle as Belloni[2]
would, and will soon consult you as to the odds you would give my
concoction.

Poor Floup! Now a round of abscesses has hit her! It's really too
much! . . . Tell her to mail me first class right away these boorish
abscesses. I won't treat them very ceremoniously and probably they
wouldn't be happy for long in my company, which is scarcely
charming at present. Black Moux soon had enough of it himself,
and no longer comes each morning when I arise to present his canine
compliments, as he deemed it proper to do the first 3 or 4 days. His
sensibilities were probably frozen by my indifference, and I think
he is quite ready to handle me with his "*best regards.*"

On the other hand, Ulysses Stock did me the honor to smoke a
cigar and drink a glass of Hungarian wine this morning (in the
dining room) here at home. The vandalism of the chestnut trees is
to be completely atoned for; and he has just planted, or rather trans-

planted to the same spot, three superb chestnut trees higher than our ceiling (he assured me) and which he hopes will bloom beautifully, beginning this summer. As for Laertes Stock,[3] he hasn't stood around doing nothing, and has stuck a superb — guess what? — a *superb cucumber plant* in front of the windows of the little twins' rooms![4]

We settled things in a very friendly way with Stock, who firmly agreed with the general maxim I spouted at him: "that it is better to improve things, than it is to worsen them," a maxim from which one might draw false conclusions, but which taken in its rather vague and philosophic general sense contains nothing contrary to good manners . . . even to Stock's own! —

As for events, there is one that has upset the Institute:[5] Milde[6] got hoarse, and they had to replace *Czar and Carpenter*[7] with Montagus and Capulets.[8] All the hopes and dreams of the Institute now bank on the success of Raff's opera,[9] and I have reached the conclusion that in such cases the above-mentioned Institute undergoes emotions rather similar to those of ardent roulette-players — with this difference, that its agitations and worries are in marked disproportion to the pleasures and gains. But that is the fate of human joys — to swim constantly in a sea of misery and suffering. Abbé Floup could make some nice homilies on this theme. Poor Abbé! My heart is completely broken by the thought of all that she has had to suffer. . . . Since I won't write her until tomorrow, would you please take upon yourself 1st — to embrace her, and more than once. 2nd — Tell her that Gerhard[10] hasn't sent me any sign of the *Revue des Deux Mondes*,[11] and that I recommend that Harpagon[12] demand, without further delay, the 1st of January number that is due him for the money he paid down. 3rd — Inform her that I am bored with my daily meals at the *Erbprinz*, and that on odd or even days (depending on rehearsals) I'll set up my little household at the Altenburg and give myself the pleasure of dining *Solo*. 4th — Both of you be so kind as to remember me to *Möller tyrannos*, and fix up as well as you can the blunder of my recommendation of the *Hofrath*, about which my conscience is all confused; although I did it with the simplest and best intentions in the world (*Behold and listen, my child*, how good intentions facilitate follies, and beware of them!)

Speaking of good intentions, have I talked to you about the Album of *intimate* portraits that Dosnay[13] left with me, upon departing? — To my mind these portraits aren't so bad; and I am convinced that the artist did his best, which doesn't prevent each of his models from holding a first-rate grudge against him — Joachim [14] claiming that his portrait looks like Pütsch,[15] — and Milde believing that his own would suit Winterberger better, etc. etc. — The poor devil thus finds himself displeasing and disaffecting everybody, and each emulates the other — in all truth this situation disposes me quite favorably toward him, because I have the bad habit of being contrary . . . a method I recommend immediately using against your own feet, while you exercise with walks *"run"* the way Scotch does. For that, I urge you to proceed as in 66 [16] — begin at first with 20 steps — then the next day count forty (the forty will help a great deal) and finally one fine day not too distant, make it your business to do *66* steps up and down in your room.

If, unhappily, Minette suffers too much to write me, ask her merely to dictate four lines to you, so that I don't continue not hearing from her. V.[17] told me effusively the other day that if Eilsen [18] were as far from Weimar as is Erfurt,[19] he would have been able to keep posted about the dear health of this dear Princess, despite his numerous jobs. Figure that out: if V. would go as far as Erfurt, I'd have to go at least to China!

Goodnight, dearest Magnet, and I'll see you soon!

In the meantime I remain not only at the feet, but beneath the sweet paws, of white Moux, with all my heart and soul.

FL.

LETTER 11: *Preface*

Letters 11 through 17 contain little of importance, except as they indicate the amount of activity Liszt was undertaking at the Weimar Theater during 1851. The production of new operatic works, including Wagner's *Lohengrin* and *Tannhäuser*, occupied much of his time. He conducted Berlioz' difficult and extraordinary composition, *Harold in Italy*, and made plans for a *Goethe-Stiftung* — the organization, unfortunately short-lived, that was to perpetuate the literary glories of the past at Weimar and guarantee the musical triumphs of the present.

Liszt was also engaged in his own musical creation: the endless transcriptions for the piano of songs and orchestral pieces and the *Symphonic Poems* — for which he was busily studying orchestration (cf.

L.M. I, No. 101). His correspondence alone must have absorbed several hours each day. Added to all these assorted tasks was the elaborate and demanding social life into which Liszt entered at Weimar. The lure of the fashionable world had always been strong for him, ever since the early days at Paris; and Weimar, with its pretension to being at once the elegant nineteenth-century Versailles and a provincial Paris, would scarcely have suited an aesthetic recluse.

His personal life, if letters to Carolyne are any index to it, was complicated by her lengthy complaints: there was always the problem of settling her first marriage, since both Prince Nicolas and the Russian government were proving obdurate. Evidently a corollary of this difficulty involved certain financial losses on her part: Liszt commiserated with her, in April 1851, for some 8,000 rubles confiscated by the Czar (*L.M.* I, No. 85).

In these letters to Marie, passing references to Kossuth and ex-Queen Marie-Amélie of France remind us that even quiet Weimar was feeling the repercussions of 1848.

LETTER 11

Saturday evening, February 15, 1851.

Knowing all the hot and *feverish* interest you feel toward the good fortune of the *Institute*, I'm sending you today, dearest Magnet, the Program for tomorrow evening. Please tell Abbé Floup about it, although she ordinarily is not up to the important level of such major questions; and you may profit by this occasion to hasten her recovery, no matter how slightly, as well as her entire cure, and it will be quite in proportion to the imperious incapacities of the dramatic situation.

It is fated that Your Ladyships will escape in no way the melodious charms of *Alfred*; [1] and you will probably hear it at your first theatrical sallying-forth on Saturday, March 1st, unless by a special favor the illness of Mlle. Agthe [2] and the hoarseness of Milde (for you will notice on the program the sentence, calamitous and disastrous for the Institute, "on account of the sickness of Miss Agthe and the *hoarseness of several of the members*"!) does not indefinitely postpone Messire Raff until Doomsday! But in this case, there would truly be something to fear from Abbé Floup's *emotional outpouring* (she, who seems to have cast an *evil-eye* — have this Neapolitan word explained to you — upon the dramatic fate of the pagan Raff from her Eilsen solitude) for how could Floup ever accustom herself to these two awful things — 1st, a prolonged interruption in operatic performances. 2nd — a mischance for Raff! —

Your dear little leaves, cut as the result of a pupil's accident, are more than a compensation to me for my boredom at home and in the city. This boredom has literally reached such an insupportable point, that I can't stand it any longer. Despite all the wise and eloquent arguments of Floup, I will not stay here one hour longer than it is strictly necessary, and will start on my way to join you beginning Tuesday morning, come what may. Please make Floup understand, what up to now she could not get into her head, so limited is her intelligence! that is, that I am not going to Eilsen to please her at all, or to surprise you, but quite simply out of *egoism*, because I absolutely have to see both of you.

This month I haven't been able to work, or to read, or to live at all as I care to — somehow your quarters at Eilsen weighed continually on my thoughts, and poor Floup's distress and illness *magnetized* me from afar; so that I was left with neither breath nor motion for my spirit.

This morning Her Highness the G.D.[3] called me in at 1 o'clock, to thank me in advance for my acceptance for tomorrow — She received me in the cedar room, with which you are familiar, and asked me for news of *Eilsen*. "Princess Marie is so-so," I answered her — "Her complete recovery is again delayed another two weeks" — As she was very much rushed, I didn't think it relevant to talk specially of your mother. That would have been a longer chapter, to which I'll have occasion to come back another time.

Zieg.[4] having accompanied me, I hinted casually that I had asked him for a week's leave of absence — which will allow us three, I hope, to return as peacefully as we left. I imagine that Weimar, that is to say the Altenburg, won't make a bad impression on you this time; and I implore God to bless your stay there, from the bottom of my heart —

I have just been told that the Jena Court of Appeals has completely absolved me, and I will neither have to pay a fine nor submit to prison for my supposed insults against the magistrates of the Grand Duchy. I confess to you that the result almost surprised me; for no matter how absurd Uzlar's[5] accusations were, I couldn't deny that the official position of my antagonist, with his colleagues and superiors on the bench, gave him a big advantage and a marked superiority over me —

I hope you haven't misconstrued my epithet about the most "*fecund* of our letter-writing authors" — God forbid, dearest Magnet, that I deprecate the exceptional charm of this exceptional fecundity of yours. To me your letters are a little treasure, of which I am as proud as I am happy. Unfortunately I hardly ever know how to say nice things; and even if I were less clumsy in this line, I wouldn't cultivate it with you, for I love you too seriously for that. If you could reserve a tiny little bit of your heart for me, which I know will be a large piece, you would be sweet and kind. Perhaps later on I will be allowed to give you a more real proof of my profound attachment, and I warn you ahead of time, you will never succeed in ridding yourself of it.

For today, dear Magnet, Moux Furet, Fifth Fourteen, etc. etc. etc., I wish you the best of all possible birthdays. May Abbé Floup neither suffer more, nor moan nor cry on this 18th of February, when these lines will no doubt reach you — The next day on the 19th I will come to crave an audience with you, and invite myself to Rinne's[6] pot-luck. Tell Abbé Floup not to write any more, since the letters can no longer get to me — I will write her a couple of words after tomorrow's concert, which will be the last from here for a long time — forever, I hope —

As for Moux, would you believe that he has taken a liking for Bloss,[7] and that he goes to visit the Institute from time to time? This morning he even walked into the orchestra, to the great amusement of the *Kapelle.* If he had a less expansive disposition, he might possibly be used for Faust. —[8] M. de Bury[9] hasn't yet arrived, nor anyone else I know. The Leipzig people are waiting for Raff's first performance before moving — Princess Charles and the Prince of Prussia[10] are expected tomorrow. If I am not mistaken, Princess Charles has already been here since yesterday. I've kept myself at a respectful distance from the Court during the past two weeks, — but tomorrow I plan to put on my new green uniform and a borrowed hat, since mine is crammed in some box or other. If only I could stay wrapped up all the time, I'd be a lot better off myself.

Goodbye then, until three days from now!

FL.

LETTER 12

Wednesday (sad octave of my name day) [1]
9 April 51

Dearest Magnet,

How can I tell you how sulky, crotchety and almost corpselike I have become, since the day I left Eilsen? For several days I haven't left the Altenburg, except at the hours of the frequent rehearsals and the operas (postponed), and the Concerts — but unfortunately I am scarcely left in peace, and there's a perpetual procession of blind singers, fleeced and fleecing tenors, disconcerting boors and bunglers, etc., etc., etc.

However I forgot all this gang, at the sight of an excellent Zrazy [2] with which Thérèse regaled me today for dinner, accompanied by *Kacha*,[3] which I devoured to the health of the Podolians [4] of Eilsen; but shortly afterwards I had to hear "Dies Bildniss ist bezaubernd schön," [5] and I was immediately carried back to our memories of Vienna, and to that portrait of ill omen which Dosnay did of Abbé Floup, a masterpiece which only the same master could equal when he undertook to paint yours. . . . May his conscience be as light, as his brush proved heavy! . . . Poor fellow, — he told me here that he had been Ole Bull's [6] protégé at Hamburg, and that he had been commissioned by him to do some kind of a statue of Kossuth.[7] I'm going to write him right away asking him to engage Ole Bull in my name to come here after Easter; and perhaps in consideration of the sounds of this Norwegian Amphion,[8] you will excuse poor Dosnay his monumental blunders.

Whatever you may say, you still will not be excused from Raff's opera, which will be given shortly after your arrival. Since I do not intend to take it upon myself to direct it, we shall hear it together from the depths of our little ground floor hen roost, decorated with the name of *Parterre Loge*. During Easter week *Laroche* [9] of Vienna is coming here and will give several *Casserolles* (Gastrollen) among others Faust,[10] and Cromwell.[11] This evening I am going to the *Institute* for the first time, to listen to *Nathan* der Weise,[12] a loathsome play according to Abbé Floup, and mephitically oozing the pantheistic stink through its bourgeois and philosophic triteness! — This type of drama mixes passably with rhubarb and senna, but falls

41

far short of castor-oil . . . an admirable Drug which was forever rehabilitated by an incomparable Dithyramb.

Did you laugh a little at Ulysses,[13] who has made himself my champion in the little daily tabloid called "das Tage Blatt"? I'm going to call on him presently, in order to keep in the same key as much as possible. — Moux is prospering; and I imagine you'll get some pleasure out of seeing such a jovial creature. Mr. Rabbit had a very pretty silver-plated collar made for him, with a little chain and name-plate, on which will be engraved the name of his master. Pan Rabbit did not care to continue playing the part of Pyrrhus[14] opposite one of the tribe of Astyanax, due to lack of classically romantic culture, or romantically classical, and he claimed that Astyanax was too *ugly* and, moreover, of too sickly a nature; consequently the most urgent thing for him was to get rid of Mux, thus exposing him to all the whims of harsh fate!

Since Zeuss[15] wanted the Ginguené[16] back badly, I thought it better to wait until your return to have it requested again at the Library. Besides, I hope Sismondi[17] will suffice you. Beg Minette to take care of herself and to let herself be cured! — and may God bring you back soon to this now-so-painful desert of an Altenburg, where I don't know what to do or where to turn without the Podolians; and where, however, I feel as if nailed until your return. Where should I go, if not toward you? And what should I seek in Heaven and earth if not . . . that which is all my heart, and all my life? Goethe says somewhere "Among all the possessions on earth, a real heart is the rarest, and scarcely two exist among thousands."[18] If I knew His Excellency,[19] I would tell him that I have a *double*, and even a *triple* one; so that great as he is, he would not even question it — for he had never been in Podolia! And this miraculous happiness was hardly for his eagle beak.

Kiss Moux — Jan — Gha—,[20] tenderly, and come back —

LETTER 13

Friday, April 11, 1851.

Your nice, sweet little letter with its rose perfume revived my true life for me, for a moment; and I thank you from the bottom of my heart, dear, dearest Magnet.

The analysis of Josika's[1] *Batory* was done by the hand of a master; and there is no doubt that if ever the fecund epistolary writer who penned this analysis should ever tackle the novel, or history, nay even dates, she would become a model for the class. In the meantime, my sole wish is that she set herself about writing a few travel *impressions*: as for example from Bückeburg[2] to Weimar, with a great deal of thought on the inconvenience of the small baths to be found in the little German principalities, — which are more than compensated for, it is true, by the benefits that a prudent population receives from the paternal, patriarchal governing system of its rulers, etc., etc. —

These paternal governments take me right back to the superb dried *codfish* that Abbé Floup sent me as a gift. What a magnificent and delicate creature it was! . . . but I'll give you a hundred to one if you can guess whom I invited as partner to this gastronomic treat . . . M. von Beidenfeld,[3] if you please; for I indirectly had a little service to ask of him, and the codfish furnished me with an excellent pretext. As for the remainder, Zerdahely also had his portion — indeed, so well that there is nothing left for *backstairs* —

This great feast took place today, Friday at 2 o'clock, after my rehearsal. Elkan[4] came at 4 o'clock, and tomorrow I'll write Abbé Floup the result of our talk and send her the letter that the abovementioned Elkan is firing off at her.

I feel all worn out and dull this evening, and I don't know what to say to amuse you a little. It is true that I feel very miserable in my isolation, and that I would willingly give the Institute for the king of Clubs! Here, indeed, is something which could have dramatic interest: a game of sixty-six between Za-hatte[5] and Scotch (please don't forget to give her my very worshipful compliments); but silly plays such as Nathan der Weise, or rather "Der Naseweise," how can I stand them in my present frame of mind? Tell Abbé Floup that I heartily subscribe to her opinion of this philosophically boring and insupportable drama. Next week, thank God, there is to be neither Court nor Institute, due to Holy Week, which this year coincides, through some strange chance, with the Holy Week of the Greek Church; for I have been told that tomorrow Her Grace the Grand-Duchess commences her devotional retreat.

In the way of news, I can tell you that according to the newspapers, Queen Amelia[6] (the widow of Louis Philippe) will soon

43

live in Eisenach [7] with the Duchess of Orleans; [8] Milde is definitely going to marry Mlle. Agthe at the end of the theater season — Genast, [9] however, requests that this be not before next October, so that the performances of the 2nd and 16th of February 1852 may not be disturbed! (Abbé Floup will be edified by this demand!) C.F. [10] frequently attends an olympic circus held at the riding-school, whose daily performances do a fair amount of damage to the gate receipts of the Institute — so Z. [11] has tried to find a way to avert this competition, by having these equestrian artists forbidden to perform on theater days — but he went about it too late, as they very nicely had the official permit in their pockets for which there was no recourse. — Raff has become sensible once more and is postponing his Sans Souci [12] *madness* for a few weeks. You surely will see his Alfred, [13] which Z. is reserving to celebrate Floup's return!

Moux is getting along fine, but completely avoids my society, which probably seems too monotonous for him. — It is true that I often feel in a currish mood which doesn't at all compete with Moux's joviality.

Goodnight, dearest Magnet — I shall write Abbé Floup tomorrow evening, after having seen Elkan. Kiss her tenderly for me, and don't delay much longer in dispelling my interior and exterior shadows with your presence —

This morning I forwarded an issue of the Britannic Review, where you may read a rather good article on the end of the Roman Republic, and some excerpts from the English novel, "Poet and Tailor" — [14]

Bonzoir again — and let us pray to the good Lord that He be good to us —

L.

LETTER 14

Weimar, the end of April, 1851

Dear Magnet,

This morning, when Mr. Lapinousz came into my room, he woke me with a rosebush from the garden you committed to his care when you left. "To kings and princes one should only offer flowers gathered from their gardens," [1] so said the diplomat I have often quoted to you. And so I send you this rose, informing you that according to Mr. Lapinousz, the same rosebush bore *twelve* others. I maintained that it must have been thirteen, so as to make the number *fourteen* [2] — and he raised no objection and immediately discovered the possibility that a fourteenth may soon bloom — Then there will be, my dear Magne XIV, fourteen roses on your little rosebush now in my room until your return, as a discreet symbol of your most serene charm.

Yesterday morning I paid a brief visit to Miss Williams, who sighs for your return. They are charming people of distinguished good sense; it is useless for me to add that they particularly entrusted me with compliments, etc. for you, your mother, — and Scotch too, (with the whys and wherefores sketched in).

Please tell Abbé Floup that her letter to my uncle [3] was immediately forwarded. I particularly enjoyed the paragraph where she instructed him to raise the sum of money she intends for M.Z. [4] — by reason of his poverty and honesty — and accordingly to decrease it for inverse reasons —

I felt obliged to go see two bad plays last evening, "Die Vorleserin" (translated from the French of Bayard) [5] and "der höfliche Mann." [6] Faroche played the chief role in both — and to my taste, as an accomplished comedian. Tomorrow he plays for the last time, in a drama by Raupach, "Cromwell's Ende." [7] C.F. [8] has recently signed a decree that will cause a certain upheaval in the Institute's orchestra, when it is published. Chelard [9] is politely *unattached* and invited to make his request soon for a pension. Your very humble servant becomes *Kapellmeister* (oh! oh!) and has the whole crowd under his command . . . with the exception, however, of der Frau Kapellmeisterin, [10] of whom C.F. inadvertently neglected to mention. Wednesday Fidelio, [11] will be given, and *Alfred* on the 3rd of May. Raff now insists that I direct his opera; but I am holding off, unless C.F. personally asks me.

In the way of interesting news, you might tell Abbé Floup that *Panine*, [12] the Petersburg Minister of Justice, has been here for several days. The *Sepia* of Helgoland (Fanny Lewald) [13] also arrived this afternoon. I've seen neither one nor the other up to now.

You wrote me delightful things about your Easters and Christmases at Podolia: such as no Sepia in the world could ever imagine. Please don't let your *writer's* talents lie fallow; and continue your

stories and descriptions, which will certainly never meet a public
so moved and touched as

Your incompetent servant
FL.

LETTER 15

April, 1851

Dear Magnet —

Since I can separate you from your mother neither in my heart
nor in my mind, I am writing you these few lines after my letter to
her, to tell you *Bon zoir* . . . be patient . . . and the good Lord
will grant us His help. You must find me a very *sterile* correspondent; for in exchange for your charming, interesting, and gracious
little letters, I can scarcely find time now and then to scribble you
a few dry and dull words, in my Institute style. But the fault is
somewhat Abbé Floup's, and this is why I hope you'll forgive me,
— for Abbé has given me much to think about, and quite a bit to
read, and even to do, these last days. Furthermore, I have an obses-
sion (unhappily all too well founded) that I was guilty of some
business blunder in the simple negotiation with Elkan, with which
Abbé entrusted me; and the thought that I deserve to be scolded
drives me wild. It's a bit like the *sensation* and the *emotion* you
experienced at the completion of your great piece of embroidery,
which earned you the nickname of Mlle des Gobelins! [1]

I hope this week to be partially freed from my *forced labor* at
the Institute — but I will have to take care of my two copyists, and
send the Eilsen manuscripts — before you get back — alas! — to
Härtel, Kistner, and Senff — [2]

Thank you for your *Zabatique* [3] analysis of Josika's Novel. If
ever we meet J., who is now in exile in Brussels, I shall tell him what
a delightful little Serial Writer he has discovered in V–XIV [4] — and
this tale itself may furnish a charming subject for a novel, where
little Minnie and her sister's introduction would also play a small
part. As for me, I haven't read anything but newspapers since I left
you — and you can even tell Floup that I didn't open the package
of Charivaris [5] that she sent me . . . . — Don't weary of writing

46

to me, even when I answer so stupidly; your letters are for me not something to read, but rather stars that rise in my heart.

FL.

LETTER 16

May, 1851

You are a pet and a thousand joys to me, dear Magnet. Thank you, thank you for your pillow. Tonight I shall place it under my head (which is very heavy and aching, since I no longer see you!) and may all the dreams I have for your happiness and your soul's joy come true.

Did you say the 2nd of June? . . . This date frightens me; and in any case I will see you before then, since I literally could no longer stand leading such a life of fits and starts.

Your rose bush is now bearing five delicately full-blown roses that resemble the five fingers of your hand — I'm sending you a tiny little bud which I don't want to let wilt here.

Bonzoir — and a happy return!

LETTER 17

Ballenstedt, Wednesday, June 23, '52.

What must you think of me, for not having yet thanked you for your very nice letters? . . . But then why have you become such an important person — Little Miss *Big*, if you please — and are taking to writing not only in your crystalline style of those things which touch your heart, but also to having personal envelopes (what must Minette say of these extravagances?) your own sealing-wax; and to top it all, a handwriting designed to excite at once the curiosity and the envy of the post-office employees!

Dear, dear Furet, you certainly are becoming a rare wonder of charm and perfection. "I wouldn't have believed it" think you — and here am I nicely caught.

My Ballenstedt [1] exile is coming to an end; and shortly after these lines arrive, you shall see me arrive in person. I thank you again for telling me that I am not an intruder at the Altenburg. This is a feeling that comes from my *"bruises"*; but from which I'll not be able to rid myself, any sooner than from the one which most of the time makes me feel superfluous to myself, and as though disagreeably useless to others wherever I have to stay longer. I assure you that this is neither vanity nor affectation on my part; and the idea to *fish for compliments* never entered my head, since this kind of fishing is no more to my liking than that with line and net.

Would you be sure to tell Minette that I'll be able to give her a good account of my good conduct at Ballenstedt, and that evidence will not be lacking in its support? Mme. O'Brien and Mme. Fabrice (Mlle. von Asseburg) [2] will testify on my behalf, that the honor of Weimar is safe with me. Mr. *Lapinousz* has made about a hundred of my medals with sealing wax; and I have been invested with a kind of provisional government over this county town, from which I'll rid myself as soon as the last chord is played at today's after-dinner Concert. —

I have to close now, so that these lines may yet reach you before I do — Until tomorrow, then, dearest Furet, and forever and always

Your very humbly devoted
FL.

LETTER 18: Preface

The forty-year friendship of Liszt and Wagner is a separate chapter in nineteenth-century musical and cultural history. There can be no doubt that despite momentary irritations felt by Liszt at some of Wagner's more flagrant examples of ingratitude and arrogance, the pianist always considered Wagner as the chief embodiment of the "New Music" — even at the expense of Liszt's own claim to eminence. The idea for establishing Weimar as a cultural center, with the two musicians reënacting in musical terms the roles of Goethe and Schiller, was Liszt's. It was he who saw most clearly the dichotomy between the Leipzig school of "absolute" musicians — Brahms, Schumann, Joachim, etc. — and the Weimar tendency toward programmatic and dramatic genres. Liszt's modesty with regard to Wagner is striking; indeed, this is the quality that so infuriated Carolyne Wittgenstein, who resented Liszt's easy acceptance of his friend's artistic superiority.

Liszt's unceasing efforts on Wagner's behalf would indicate that the burden of their friendship rested with him; although it might be argued with cogency that he, as musical director, was in a better position to have Wagner's works performed than was Wagner with reference to Liszt's orchestral and piano compositions. An examination of that huge collection of letters, however, the *Briefwechsel zwischen Wagner und Liszt* (Leipzig: Breitkopf & Härtel, 1910), does serve to reveal the open and generous nature of the pianist, which contrasts markedly with Wagner's reserve and general ingratitude. But again, when one reviews the personal side of Wagner's life, the conviction emerges that he was probably incapable of any stronger demonstration of affection, and that Liszt was indeed one of his best friends.

One of Wagner's many essays deals directly with Liszt: "Über Franz Liszts Symphonische Dichtungen — Brief an M.W." (*Gesammelte Schriften und Dichtungen*, Leipzig: Fritzsch, 1872, vol. V). It would be interesting to know who "M.W." was. It is highly unlikely that it was Mathilda Wesendonck or Minna Wagner, *née* Planer. Several references to Liszt as their mutual friend make it possible that the initials belong to Marie Wittgenstein. This open letter, written admittedly for publication, is curiously ambivalent in tone, and gratitude and affection are mixed with rather censorious criticism. After a long panegyric to Liszt's powers as a virtuoso pianist, Wagner then casts off on this entire branch of reproductive musicianship and hails Liszt's shift to more fruitful composition and operatic direction. There is a fascinating discussion of the development of the symphonic tone-poem out of the "dance" elements of strict symphony form; and Wagner sees first Berlioz, and then Liszt, introducing a new formal ingredient into orchestral music: "a poetic motif" (p. 246). The essay turns into a spirited defense of program music versus absolute music, eloquent if perhaps not logically convincing; and Wagner concludes, "Nothing is . . . less absolute, than is Music" (p. 249). His highest praise of Liszt is the statement that of all contemporary artists, Liszt is the most musical — high praise from Wagner.

LETTER 18

[Zürich] Sunday, July 3, '53.

All hail, and worship, limitless homage and fealty to Magnolet! —

Fainéant I is delightfully established in a very clean little room on the 2nd floor, decked by a pretty white stove, very useful at this season, by a sofa and three chairs upholstered in velvet (not of

Utrecht).[1] This room has a single, but high and wide window; and the view looks right out on the lake, whose waves almost wash up against the ground floor of the house which is separated from the lake only by a little garden parterre that acts as a promontory bedecked with roses. — To left and right are charming borders of pretty houses, pleasantly rising above one another on hills undulating in sweet laziness and capriciously intermingling their ranges. When you come to Zürich, I strongly urge you to live in that house, called the "*Annex*" of the big *Bauer* hotel, the town's finest.[2] One can certainly be more comfortable there than at most annexes; all the more so, since they serve an excellent honey there for breakfast, according to the custom of the land, of which I'd like to send you a few combs to compensate for all the honey ordinarily lacking in my words.

I am writing to *Pasabée*[3] how happy Wagner and I were to see each other again, and shall continue keeping you in touch with our every move during the week I spend here. At this moment there are few foreigners of distinction at Zürich — Countess L. Bathyany[4] no longer lives here, and Herwegh[5] is the sole literary celebrity who has been pointed out to me. I shall see him at Wagner's, with whom he is intimate —

On the whole, I'll have no difficulty spending my time; and I rather fear that little of it will remain for me to devote to my day-dreams and memories. Wagner has a truly incredible fiery energy and rebound, and *Pas Floup* is the only one I know who is capable of sustaining in this manner six to eight hours of solid conversation which very often turns into monologues —

Independent of the delight that any and all must have in chatting with you, dearest Magnolet, these lines also have quite a serious purpose: to invest you with the dignity of *Mentor* for *Pas Abée*, and to entrust you with the supreme management of her cure, which it is extremely desirable, nay even necessary, that she undertake, continue, and complete during the 4 or 5 weeks that you'll stay at Carlsbad. Be good enough, then, to point out to her that it would be completely unreasonable not to set to work *immediately*, swallowing *with conviction*, as is her way, the waters and the medicine that will be prescribed for her, not to mention the baths and other amusements which are more to her taste. Have our dearly beloved Pas Abée get up every morning at 5; take him for a walk, rock him, and in the absence of M. von Maltitz,[6] even *calm* him; and in your next letter give me detailed and edifying reports on his conduct and way of life.

Toward the end of July or the beginning of August, I shall probably join you; and before leaving Weimar I'll ask M. von Watzdorff[7] for some great big decoration that I will award you, as a recompense for the zeal you will have shown in your new functions.

If you write me immediately (General Delivery) your letter may still catch me at Zürich, from whence I shall leave Saturday evening, July 9th — but if by chance you delay, write to *Frankfurt-am-Main*, where I shall arrive Monday the 11th, and stay probably until the 12th —

I kiss your sweet hands, and remain forever your own irreplaceable and most unalienable, by the Grace of God and your own

Fainéant I

LETTER 19

[Zürich, Saturday, July 9, 1853]

Dear Sister in St. Francis,[1]

What, a new little pink letter for me!! . . . why, it is scarcely believable — and thus all the more real. Thank you for your details about the church, the bishop, etc. — Behold how great minds are in agreement! at the same moment that I was besieging you to *tutor* Pasabée, Mercure[2] suggests Fulda[3] to you as an example. May the buzzing of his words leave some honey behind him! — in the meantime I have asked Mme. Wagner[4] to send you some of this excellent honey I found here, so that Magnolette and Floup might have a treat. If one could add to it the view of the lake and the glaciers, it would no doubt be infinitely better — but I mustn't claim too much. Still, I hope that we'll be able to give ourselves a bit of Switzerland next summer, and undertake a few Alpine excursions. It's really very beautiful; and we're so nicely at the level of the highest mountains, without having to take the least trouble to climb them and get out of breath! The lake of the four cantons will make you dream sweetly, profoundly; — this winter we are limiting ourselves to looking at it, just as M. Händl will

paint it in William Tell![5] — it will be a little like the difference
there is between Minette at the Belvedere,[6] or Pas Abbée in our
little room, or "God makes a fine cup of coffee."

How are you set up at Carlsbad? Is the countryside pretty?
May I come to join you? — In any case I'll come to meet you at
Dresden; and I hope that due to your influence as teacher, Pasabbée
will come back fat and lusty, fresh and pink. Please calm her if I
write less often this week — I have all sorts of small errands and
long conferences ahead of me at Badenweiler[7] (at Edouard
Devrient's),[8] at Carlsruhe with His Highness the Threefold Marshal,[9] with Schott[10] at Mayence, at Wiesbaden with all kinds of
fancy people, and at Frankfort with the same — and with this heat
I'm really not good for much. I delayed my departure from here
24 hours; and I'm only getting under way tomorrow evening
(Sunday) at 7 o'clock for Bâle and Badenweiler, where I will stop
for just a few hours. Tuesday evening I am going to a performance
of Lohengrin[11] at Wiesbaden, and Wednesday to one of Tannhäuser[12] (with Johanna Wagner)[13] at Frankfort; unless M. Wagner senior[14] is afraid to compromise his daughter's success by
letting her play a part where she takes a strong chance of not being
called back on the stage. There is neither a final rondo nor any
great whip-snapping at the end of Tannhäuser — a most peremptory reason for the Prima Donnas not to accept the part of
Elizabeth, and a reason which was proved victorious by the
Wagners, father and son, in the several cities where Johanna was
asked to sing Elizabeth. Well, they say small causes have large
results; but as for important things, the man in the street is never
used to them, unless you make him accustom himself, willy-nilly.

I shan't speak to you about Wagner — it would take a book.
My dealings with Herwegh[15] will lead, I hope, to a fine work we
will do in collaboration. I have also discovered one of my former
friends, M. Wille,[16] whom you caught a glimpse of in Hamburg.
He's a very witty fellow and one who has profited greatly from a
very unusual life. Heine,[17] whom he saw lately in Paris, compares
Wille's sword-furrowed face to an Album "where an academic
youth has inscribed himself with sword-cuts." He formerly edited
a Journal at Hamburg, and Pasabbée had a bit of a philosophic
discussion with him, at the Hotel d'Europe in Hamburg.

Tell Floup about a whim of the Mail-service. Her Halle letter arrived 24 hours ahead of the one sent from Weimar. Naturally I didn't understand much about it, not knowing that researches had been made about the Prometheus; [18] but everything came out so well, that the effect of a sermon getting to me the day after, about my disastrous tendency to lend manuscripts, got weakened; and consequently I still feel capable of continuing my system of negligence, without paying too much attention to it. — Hug our dear Minette, and kiss her hands for me — and in the moments of respite from the cure, both of you tell each other how much I love you, through God and for all eternity.

F. L.

I'll be at Frankfort on the 12th and 13th — and the 14th and 15th at Weimar — I'll immediately go to see Talleyrand [19] who took care to inform me by telegraph of the death of the Grand Duke.[20] It goes without saying that I approve of, and in a pinch I command, your correspondence with Talleyrand to which, more-over, I hope to have several emendations to make, because he will certainly want to tell them to me.

LETTER 20

Tuesday, July 19, 1853.
Weimar.

I have neither stories, nor meetings, nor events to tell you about, dear and dearest Magnolet. My poor days are going to slip away dull, monotonous, and languid — "The root of patience is bitter, but the fruits thereof are sweet," as they say. How I would love to come to you, roam around your *white lion*,[1] feel your presence there, and know that you are close, providing moral tonic for Minette, and bring you the loveliest strawberries and the most beautiful crystals from Carlsbad! But instead of that, I have to chew and chew my *root* of Patience.

Zieg.[2] is at the Belvedere, bowed down under reports and procedures — it is he who is now taking over the functions of Marshal to His Imperial Highness, since Beaulieu [3] is headed for the honor of *Grand Master* to the reigning Court. For the time being, Beaulieu has been sent on a mission to The Hague; General

Beulwitz [4] to Berlin, Hopfgarten [5] to Vienna, Werthern [6] to London, Beust [7] to Petersburg, Lieutenant-Colonel Watzdorf to Stuttgart — all to announce the accession of Carl Alexander.

Rt. [8] goes around staring vacantly up and down the corridors of the Belvedere and of Ettersburg. [9] He will leave for Paris a day after tomorrow, Thursday; and in order to give himself some relaxation, I suppose he has released M. Dominique [10] from the job of packing for him. The discovery of the passage from Dumas [11] that Remenyi [12] made, and which I cited yesterday to Minette, was only mildly pleasing to Rt.; and he then told me that d'Israeli, [13] in one of his novels, had mentioned Dumas in a way that suited Rt. better. I'll ask him the title of the novel tomorrow. — If Minette now has enough leisure time for reading, recommend Thackeray's [14] new book to her; the title I forget, but she may easily find it for herself. These are the *Sketches* that he did in London. — I am very proud of Scotland's remembering me, and please give her my sincerest and most cordial regards — The details you give me about Mme. de T. [15] interest me keenly; you know how distinct and separate she has always remained in my mind; although I had very little chance to see and know her, that little bit, however, was enough. I keep an admiring respect for her, and have one of those far-away feelings for her which is perfectly useless, but which is understood by someone with a delicate and susceptible sensibility — I told you that there was something providential for me in this Weimar business, and in your reconciliation with Mme. de T.; and I can't keep from guarding some hope for a happy solution to the difficulties so painfully encumbering your fate, when I juxtapose certain dates and facts, among which shine with an inextinguishable light *Fulda* [16] and *Krzyzanowitz* — [17] Minette did not yet like music at Fulda, and at Krzyzanowitz Magnolet was the little Dominican.

Speaking of Dominicans, at Mayence I bought two charming little volumes which are a part of the Railroad Library (published in Paris) — "Joan of Arc," by Michelet, [18] and "Saint Francis and the Franciscans" by F. Morin. [19] The latter volume delights me. The dreams, the parables, the prayers, the teachings of the Saint all strike me as tender and impressive. Although you already know his famous Canticle, I wish to write it to you just as I found it in my little book: [20]

"Highest, most powerful, and gracious Lord God, to You all praise, all glory and honor! To You all thanks! Everything comes from You alone, to You alone all returns — and no man is worthy to call upon You.

Be praised, O Lord, with all creatures, and above all for His Grace our brother the Sun; through him the day shines that illuminates You; he is beautiful and beams in his splendor; he is Your emblem O Lord! —

Be praised, O Lord, for our sister the moon and for the stars; You made them in the heavens, clear and beautiful!

Be praised, O Lord, for our sister the water; she is useful and lowly, precious and pure!

Be praised, O Lord, for our father the fire; he lightens the shadows; he is beautiful, pleasing, vigorous, and ever-ready!

Be praised, O Lord, for our mother the earth, who sustains us; she begets the fruits and the herbs and the multiform flowers!"

The Franciscan's Chronicle says that St. Francis "rejoiced heartily when he saw this Canticle sung with grace and fervor; after hearing it, his spirit ascended wondrously up to God" — At the moment when the fight was the liveliest, he added the following strophe:

"Be blessed, O God, for those who pardon in the name of Your love, and who bear misery and tribulation! Happy are those who live in peace! Heaven will crown them!"

At the moment of leaving for France, he made an admirable short speech to his brethren, of which I will only quote these lines to you: "No matter where we may be, we always have our cell with us. This cell is our brother the body; and the soul is the hermit, who dwells therein to think upon God and to pray to Him; thus if the soul of him who is religious rests not at peace within the cell of the body, the outward cell serves him little" — and further: "Our mission is to cure the injured, and to console the afflicted; to lead back those who have strayed; and, mark you, many are those who appear to be in the ranks of the Demon, who one day will be among the followers of Jesus Christ! [21]

There is also, in this catalogue of the Railroad Library, a book about St. Dominic and the Dominicans,[22] and I am going to get and read it in honor of our ex-Dominican, our dear Sister of St. Francis, whom I pray God will shower with His grace and blessing —

FL.

Don't forget to present all my compliments to Alexandra and Henri [23] — and tell them that I am quite jealous of their being near you. Now, for once, you have become a "little morning-wanderer!" — When you write me, tell me how you are planning your day — at what time Minette Pas takes her waters and baths, when and how the meals are, and if there is an "*Institute*" —

Recommend that Minette go to the Wollmers [24] Concert, and listen to the Wieniawskys,[25] and tell me about them —

P.S.

By the same mail I'm writing a *registered letter* to your mother, owing to an enclosed letter; tell her immediately so that she mayn't worry, because there is nothing the matter.

LETTER 21a

[Gotha, March 23, 1854]

I reveled in your little *Bulletin*, and thanks a thousand times for having so well fulfilled your promise to write — Abbé is a little lazy; and I will not neglect to reproach her, which she deserves, on Sunday morning — The Duke [1] will only return from Berlin tonight — Thus it's better that I stay here tomorrow and the day after — Besides, I have a three-to-four-hour rehearsal every day — and next week the dress rehearsals start at the theater. There needn't be more than three, and the first performance can very nicely start a week from Sunday —

The course of my days is very monotonous — I get up at seven — work alone in my room until ten — Then my rehearsals begin and last until two — I come back to take up my scribbling again and we eat at five — Yesterday a brother of the Duchess sat down with us, Prince William of Baden [2] — and today I ate at the Hotel, because the Duchess went as far as Naumburg [3] to meet her husband, and accompanied her brother who is going to Berlin.

I spoke to Abbé about my black servant — [4] He makes a

56

fetching contrast with the grand piano with its white tail (what wood it is I don't know), the main ornament in my room — Yesterday evening I took my siesta at the Barber of Seville,[5] since it's had neither charm nor interest for me for a long time; for I've heard it too often before, and too well done for me to get used to the mediocre performances such as Weimar, Leipzig, or Gotha offer — and besides you know that I have no liking for Italian works, except in Italian, and given by an Italian cast. The German language gives me a lemonish feeling and it in no way takes the place of the orange.

As for news, I can tell you that I long for my sweet home! — May God bless your every hour.

Goodbye until Sunday morning — Kiss poor Abbé tenderly for me — Beg her for me not to cry too much — and don't forget

Fainéant the Last

Thursday, 10 o'clock in the evening —

Ira Aldrige[6] is here for the second time, and will play Othello next Monday — I hope to profit from this performance, by staying all day Monday at the Altenburg.

LETTER 21b (fragment)

(Gotha, March 31, 1854)

. . . frightful chords — which I will ask sweet Cornelius to explain in a friendly way. Anyway, we are still happier than the Duke of Parma![1] Poor fellow! He excelled in the *narrow* style that the Rhetoric books have forgotten to record. Milord of Gotha told me that he amused himself at Windsor by cutting capers in the Queen's salon, without anyone asking him to devote himself to this type of recreation. I knew him slightly at Lucca,[2] when he was exceedingly young; and he then already displayed strong tendencies toward the cretinism which he has since cultivated and developed — It was a rather sad marriage for Mademoiselle, whose fate is marked by two sinister events — the murder of her father[3] and of her husband! —

My days go by very lonesomely here. I don't budge from my room, except at meal and rehearsal times. Hermann[4] had a complete

57

success last evening; and if I thought to take up my career of a
traveling virtuoso again, I'd associate myself with him in order to
lure the public —

Good night, good Magnolet — We'll wait for you Sunday
morning at ten o'clock sharp — unfortunately I can't come tomorrow evening — Pray to God for all three of us — who are of one
heart and soul — I kiss Abbé again, and beg her not to cry —

LETTER 22

[Rotterdam]

We promised a narrative account of the *Venetian Festival* for
Magnolet — we'll keep our word as well as we can.

Rotterdam and Amsterdam have often been compared to Venice
— but yesterday a Dutchman made the wise observation to me,
that the comparison could only be understood in a very advan-
tageous way for Rotterdam and Amsterdam: since in these two
cities the canals are big enough to hold large merchant ships and
steamboats, while at Venice there is only room for insignificant
and tiny gondolas. What a difference between these ships full of
all kinds of cargo, and the little shells skimming over the Adriatic
pond, good at the most for having barcarolles [1] sung in them! —
There we have all the difference between solidity, positive reality,
the useful: all that which makes for a country's greatness and
power — and futility, the useless, and the imaginative! —

For all these good reasons, the Dutch can very well dispense
with the whim of planning Venetian festivals; while the Venetians
would be decidedly embarrassed to treat themselves with this kind
of Dutch festival — The Lion of the Netherlands can be hospitable
to the lion of Saint Mark; but the latter has become too poor a
fellow to do likewise — The *Venetian Festival* of the day before
yesterday (July 12th) consisted simply in the *daylight* illumination
of several small-craft and ships — A *four-master* (which is an
innovation) particularly attracted attention by its sleekness and
good proportions, and the whole roadstead presented a far from
shabby appearance. If you remember the Alster basin at Hamburg,
you will quickly get a rather approximate idea of this part of the
Meuse (a half-oval shape) which is commanded by the Yacht Club

building — only add to it quite a number of merchant ships and steamships, and cut off a whole wing of houses —

Wednesday morning there was a yacht race — I followed a half-dozen of them for a quarter of an hour. They're long rather narrow vessels, with no complications. Young *gentlemen* acted as rowers (6 or 8 on each yacht) in costumes appropriate to the occasion. This time it was the Amsterdam crowd which won over the Dilettantes of Rotterdam — Prince Henry [2] presided at the Festival, on the Yacht Club balcony; and distributed the prizes consisting of several bronze objects, a silver coffee-pot etc. — Fainéant kept to the second story Rooms, which they had thoughtfully decorated with the title of "Artists' Salon" for this week, by putting this inscription on white pasteboard over the door. The great Hall intended for the Concerts, which holds about 4000 spectators and from 7 to 800 performers, was made of wood, on the bank of the Meuse, within gunshot of the Yacht Club — Thus it is possible, during the rehearsals, to come and take refuge in the Artists' Salon, and settle the excessively-lively emotions that one would experience.—

After the ceremony of distributing the prizes, at which I was not present, a very nicely served dinner took place at 5 o'clock. I bowed to Prince Henry from five steps away; and later I was told that he intended to toast me — but since I had to leave the roast (around seven o'clock) before the toasts had begun, in order not to miss the rehearsal for the Four Seasons,[3] I missed the honor of participating in H.R.H.'s graciousness, for which I am no less obliged — This evening (Saturday) after the end of the 3rd and last Concert — which parenthetically, will last from 4 to 5 hours, for they will play a large Psalm composed by Verhülst,[4] and the 5th Symphony, followed one after another by 9 pieces sung by the soloists: Roger,[5] Formes,[6] Pischeck,[7] Miss Ney,[8] etc. (there will also be the Beethoven Sonata dedicated to Kreutzer,[9] played by two young Dutch artists) the whole thing capped by a quartet from *Lucia*,[10] which will no doubt be the same piece as the inevitable Andante finale — the Festival Committee will give a big dinner on the Yacht Club premises, of such a size that I likewise will have the honor of belonging. They promise us a lovely fireworks display after dessert, in order to terminate the Festival celebration; and then we can go to bed content.

Up to now, none of the members of the royal family have appeared at the Concerts. For this morning (with the exception of today's Concert, which begins at Noon — yesterday and the day before they took place at 7 o'clock and lasted until 11) they are announcing Prince Henry and his wife . . . at least if the King of Portugal's [11] arrival doesn't disrupt their R.H.'s plans by making them stay at The Hague — but we don't know whether we will have the honor of having him at the Concert Hall.

It was explained to me how Rotterdam was not only a rival of Amsterdam, but was still tiffing with The Hague. At this moment it is a question of a ministerial upset in this country; and at the last election, Rotterdam appointed the opposition candidate.[12] They say that the King is pestered by contrary sentiments: French sympathies on one side and the influence of the North on the other. Lately, there was the gift of a Carpet made by the King to the French Emperor, which threw much oil on the burning rage of the Court. H.M. the Queen-Mother [13] was furious about it, and speaks of the French in words written only at St. Petersburg, and even then not "from the lips." But above all, it's perfidious Albion who is the scapegoat. How, indeed, can one understand a *Christian nation* (since the French are Voltairian dogs) that allies itself with Mohammedans in order to fight the *Godcpoiedoff* of *Bevelleriowich!* — [14] Speaking for those who are on the side of the Grand Duchess Sophia, some persons who seem well informed told me that she was on wavering terms with her brother, depending on how the latter followed his own instincts as a Prince of the House of Orange, or yielded to foreign influences. These are personified by his mother, to whose party the Grand Duchess completely allied herself, according to the popular opinion — Prince Henry likewise passes for a strong conservative, and his wife does not seem to have yet taken the opportunity to declare herself — Whatever it is, Rotterdam is in bad standing at The Hague; although there were several Ministers and Important People at the music festival, it is doubtful whether there will be a distribution of crosses (as is usually the custom) at this occasion — and the King declined the Committee's invitation, since Rotterdam wasn't sufficiently *right-thinking* for him at the moment.

Tomorrow morning we're going to Scheveningen with Hiller [15] and several other persons, to call on Ary Scheffer.[16] It's only a short ride from here to The Hague (by railroad), and three-quarters of an hour from The Hague to Scheveningen. We will return here by evening — Monday there is to be a large picnic at Mr. Nottobom's,[17] who owns a superb collection of paintings, among others Scheffer's Faust and Marguerite — and that night I will take off for Antwerp, where I will arrive after an 8-hour crossing in the afternoon of Tuesday, the 18th, so that I may be at Brussels a few hours ahead of Mme. Patersi — [18]

Beg Minette to excuse me for not having written more often — but you can gather how badly upset I am here, and how little I am master of my own time — This letter was started yesterday morning — Some callers stopped me from continuing; and in the evening I was so harrassed, that I could only pray the Good Lord to watch over kind Floup and kind Magnolet.

Yesterday morning I saw at the Exposition a painting by Tassaert [19] of Paris, which touched me profoundly — It is two figures — a mother and daughter — based on an episode from *Les Paroles d'un Croyant*, by M. de Lammenais:[20]

"From time to time the old woman warmed her pale hands at a little brasier. A clay lamp lit up this humble dwelling, and a ray of light came from the lamp to expire on a painting of the Virgin hung on the wall. . . . My child, happiness consists not in owning much, but in hoping and in loving much. Our hope is not here below, nor our love either; or, if it is, it is but transitory.

Except for God, you are all to me in this world — but this world fades like a dream, and that is why my love ascends with you toward another world —" [21]

Saturday, July 15, '54 — 8 o'clock in the morning.

LETTER 23: *Preface*

In Letter 22, Liszt mentioned the painters Tassaert and Scheffer. In this letter, we find the first of many references to contemporary German painters. Ordinarily any treatment of the relation of musicians to painters would have general cultural interest and would possess merely incidental merit, but in the case of Liszt such a connection must be viewed with more serious attention. His whole theory of music and his own compositions were based on a necessary interrelation of the arts, and one need but scan the list of titles in the catalogue of his works to see the dependence that musical inspiration had on literature and particularly painting. Hence a study of German fine arts of the mid-nineteenth century reveals not only a similar climate of opinion and taste, but — in the case of Liszt — we also comprehend more fully the feelings that moved him, the rhetoric of the age, and even certain formal parallels.

While Weimar was no center of painting in the 1850's and 1860's as was Munich, Berlin, and Vienna, the Court invited many of the prominent artists of the day to vacation there and exhibit their canvases. A more positive step in the direction of establishing the little city in the world of fine arts was taken by the Grand Duke in 1859, when the portraitist Kalckreuth was invited, along with four other leading painters, to found an Academy of Fine Arts (cf. Letter 57, Note 6). While this step was taken to guarantee Weimar's preëminence in *all* cultural activity — the Golden Age of Goethe and Schiller had represented the glorious literary past, and Liszt and his followers exemplified the musical present — actually the move meant an awareness that these two arts were now better pursued elsewhere; and Carl Alexander, that noble dilettante and self-appointed imitator of Renaissance princes, was turning to the last remaining asethetic field in order to restore Weimar's fading splendor.

Specific details about the painters to whom Liszt refers may be found in the various scattered notes. Focillon (*La peinture au XIXe siècle*) points out that the school of German historical painting came about twenty years after its French and Belgian predecessors, and the peculiar shape and emphasis it assumed was due in part to the intensity of German frustrated nationalism — and to the aftermath of Hegelianism. It is all too easy to caricature this pretentious, flamboyant, and excessively serious genre; Rebecca West brilliantly describes the German historical scenes executed during the mid-century: "enormous flushed nudes which would have set a cannibal's mouth watering; immense and static pictures showing what historical events would have looked like if all the personages had been stuffed first." A more serious estimate is given by the critic Richard Hamann in *Die deutsche Malerei vom Rokoko bis zum Expressionismus* (Leipzig and Berlin: Teubner, 1925; p. 123), where he discusses the German painters' penchant for feeling rather than seeing, and the lofty demands they made upon the fundamental simplicity of nature: "They were nearer to the world-spirit and to what one guesses exists behind nature, than they were to the physical body of the world. They sought 'nature' at every turn and yet did not dare to look her in the face."

Perhaps the most familiar example to American readers would be the *tableau* hung in thousands of high-school auditoriums, Emanuel Leutze's *Washington Crossing the Delaware* (1850).

German art in this period also produced vast numbers of religious paintings belonging to the so-called "Nazarene" school. Here all the elements of German pietism and mysticism were blended with a technical interest in Italian Renaissance art, and the fusion was augmented by the perpetual stream of German painters who went to study at Rome, and often stayed there, usually to the detriment of any indigenous qualities in their art. Johann Friedrich Overbeck (1789–1869) was the chief representative of the Nazarenes, and Julius Schnorr von Carolsfeld (cf. Letter 23, Note 6) may be taken as one of the exponents of the school. His *Verkündigung, St. Rochus teilt Almosen aus,* and *Die Flucht nach Aegypten* exhibit the characteristic marks of Nazarene painting — flat colors with sharp contrasts and clear lines; light, rhythmic, and easily-grasped figures, and a primitivism that tended to move into symbolic portrayal.

But the bulk of German painting contemporaneous with Liszt must be classed as simple *Biedermeierzeit* art. The Romantic revolt gave way to a quiet acceptance of bourgeois and sentimental values; the "Philister," once the foes of culture, now triumphed with fine historical irony. In a sense, Biedermeier painting stood halfway between Romanticism and Naturalism, and it is not false to interpret it as a part of the general spirit of *Epigonenthum* that pervaded German culture. Any collection of paintings of the period yields endless scenes of domestic bliss, where "the family, completely self-satisfied, sits on the sofa — in order to be suitable for the moment when their existence was to become historical by means of a painting" (Hamann, *Die deutsche Malerei vom Rokoko bis zum Expressionismus,* p. 172). Babies, the institution of the *Kaffeeklatsch*, elderly men drinking toasts, Sunday promenades where nature herself has put on her best go-to-meeting clothes, card and chess games, complacent and prosperous portraits — these were the popular subjects. Again, Hamann (*ibid.,* p. 169) sums it up: "The portrayed characters presented themselves with bourgeois simplicity, the women generally staring wide-eyed at the world: healthy, solidly built, and gladly turning to their household and daily tasks."

An excellent series of reproductions of Biedermeier art is found in Paul Ferdinand Schmidt, *Biedermeier-Malerei* (Munich: Delphin, 1922), and one is able to see examples of the mild humor free from any harsher satiric note — Hasenclever, *Weinprobe*; Haemann, *Die Vagabunden*; Becker, *Heimkehr der Schnitter* — as well as the qualities already noted.

63

(For the best brief survey of this early and mid-century cultural phenomenon, cf. Richard Hamann, *Die deutsche Malerei im 19. Jahrhundert*, Leipzig and Berlin: Teubner, 1914.)

LETTER 23

[Weimar] Wednesday July 15, '55.

Dearest Magnolette,

This comes to tell you very sweetly that I love you very tenderly. This isn't any newer than getting up every morning, or the spring of each year — but if there is nothing new under the sun, the sun still shines none the less for it, and our spirits preserve his gleams without any other need for renewal. Floup being at odds with those persons who project their statues, like shadows, ahead for Posterity, we are going to keep our own *little company* for today, and babble as we please —. Before bothering with other persons and things, I'd like to inform you that I was delighted to know that you spend your time well at Berlin, and that, as you tell me, you are enjoying yourself there; despite the shutting of the *institutes* specially planned for public amusement, and the almost proverbial disagreeableness of summer days in Berlin.

The *country air* of Weimar has laid so heavy upon us this past year, that the sands of Berlin may seem a restorative! — and the heaps of celebrities you meet there, should cause you a certain intellectual amazement, which I take to be one of the sweetest and most salutary of emotions.

You will now see M. von Humboldt,[1] and I am delighted for you. His conversation is like some miraculous beehive, where all the rhythms and perfumes of space and Ether come and go, and harmonize together in their continual movements. It's like a Symphony with Chorus, for which Pythagorous[2] [*sic*] would have done the vocal parts and Cuvier[3] the orchestration. Occasionally, also, His Excellency deigns to play the jew's-harp a little bit, and tells anecdotes and infinitely diverting pieces of gossip with most ingenious cleverness — In all truth, I'd like to be the King of Prussia, for the sole pleasure of giving *Floup* such a chamberlain — with the reservation that I would not delay my hour of retiring; and I'd never link myself with their nightly discussions, which would run the great risk of lasting forever.

64

And if I were King of Prussia, I think I'd also appoint Kaulbach [4] as painter to Sire Floup — for inasmuch as I can remember and allow myself to discover, he is all-in-all a genius, and not merely a *showman* as our friend Rietschl [5] says, who is only repeating what his friend Schnorr [6] says —

Try to convince Kaulbach to come spend a few days with us at Weimar; it will be very pleasant to see him again; he has a healthy and sufficiently *lively* disposition to cheer me up.

Speaking of Painting, tell Floup that Schirmer [7] (of Carlsruhe) is at Berlin now. You might be interested in getting to know him, and it would be very easy with Olfers [8] as intermediary. One of his chief scenes is the way of Good and Evil. Schirmer was connected with Mendelssohn, who dedicated the 114th Psalm to him, "When Israel out of Egypt Land," — [9]

Egypt takes me back to Jews and Jewesses — I ate at the Belvedere last night, where there was only the usual crowd, Mme. Fritsch,[10] Mlle. Mandl,[11] Their Excellencies, Werthern, and M. Soret — [12] Her Highness the Grand Duchess questioned me about my Dante; and I turned the talk to a lighter vein, confessing that I had undertaken this work in order to have a yoke of two, not wishing to limit myself to the Faust Symphony,[13] which represents to me what in Paris they call a *one-horse carriage*; that is, a carriage for four horses pulled by one. Later on I will drag in Schiller and Petrarch,[14] in imitation of the Petersburg style, where 4-horse teams are customary — To the query as to whether I would treat the Ugolino [15] episode, I answered her "No, Madame; Ugolino has become too rococo — despite his heroic devotion for his children, whom he didn't hesitate to eat in order to preserve their happiness at having a father." She didn't seem to get this pleasantry, and had me explain and repeat it. Then she cited a charade to me, about a M. von Seebach,[16] who had acquired a most merited reputation for dryness —

> "My first is a little body of water
> My second a still smaller body of water;
> and my whole, something very dry."

Her Royal Highness dismissed us around 5 o'clock, telling me that she would have me sent for, one of these days before I go to Wilhelmsthal.[17]

From the little enclosed note, you will see that Fainéant is most properly invited there; and he will not show himself in the role of an intruder, no matter how much of an intellectual intrusion he may make.

Upon returning to the Belvedere I called on Vitz.,[18] who had left for Elksleben [19] yesterday noon; and from there I went to see Pohl [20] and Mme. Marr,[21] who are both of them "Grass widows."

I had spent about an hour in the morning with the Princess and Prince Latour,[22] in order to apologize for not being able to accept their friendly dinner invitation. It was decided that I would make amends for my involuntary absence, today, Wednesday at 6 o'clock —

We had our Club meeting [23] last night (Fischer's [24] musical-racket made us change the day from Monday to Tuesday), where there was nothing of interest except a rather long explanation and discussion about the "Schiller Club" at Dresden, about which I will have the opportunity to tell you in detail, when we return.

Mention Kugler [25] again to Floup (he did a history of art which is found in your Library, and publishes articles in the "German Art News," edited by F. Eggers [26] at Berlin) — Kugler is, I think, quite forewarned about me by Hoffman's [27] friends, the Weimar "Privy-Councillers," with whom he is connected. I know nothing of Eggers, but I suppose he acts as a screen for Olfers. — Since you have seen Rellstab,[28] perhaps through his intervention you might correspond with Varnhagen von Ense,[29] whom I value as a distinguished person and intellect, (although not *well-coördinated*.) Rellstab's visit will be most pleasant for me, for I do not alter my feelings toward those who have shown me kindness and affection. As for Hans,[30] I'll receive him with drums and trumpets: first, because he will bear news of you, and after that because I love him extravagantly.[31]

There is still a philosopher at Berlin who has done two or three dramas — "Colombus" and . . . his name is Werder or Werdern — [32] He is the same person whom Teleky [33] took as guide through the labyrinths of Hegel's philosophy, and who refused to give his *word of honor*, as proof of the truth of the axioms of this *science of confused components*. If the occasion presents itself, I would press Minette to make his acquaintance —

Well, this is long enough, don't you think, dearest Magnolette?

The carriage awaits you, wherein are Kaul.,[34] Olfers, Marx,[35] and Cosmos — [36] So I break off my poor empty prose — and kiss both your hands and bow reverently before Your Most Serene Highnesses, so gracious and kind to

your
Fainéant

P.S.

By order of Fainéant the First, it is commanded that Sire Floup and Little Sire Magnolet do not return too soon to Weimar, and that they conscientiously "*do*" the town of Berlin.

I shall go to Erfurt a week from Thursday at 4 o'clock to hear Taubert's [37] Symphony. I'll probably take Hans,[38] as well as the Club-members who are still present at Weimar —

I will write to M. Sach that I am going to W.[39] toward the end of the month.

LETTER 24

[Weimar] Saturday, July 21, '55.

Dearest Magnolet,

Fainéant comes to beg you to plead his cause with Minette, and to obtain his pardon for the sin of omission he committed yesterday by not writing you. As you can well imagine, there was a driving rain *of Music* all day long; and from 8 in the morning until 11 in the evening I never left M. Hans, to whom I showed and played a pile of things (the Faust, the proofs of the 2 Scores, etc., etc.) At 1 o'clock Hoffmann came to lunch with us, and did some nice verses from Hans which will be transcribed in Sire Magnolet's Album — at 3 o'clock we went to Preller's,[1] who completed an excellent portrait of Hans in an hour and a half, for the Gallery of Today's famous members of the *New-Weimar Club*!

Mme. O'Brien, whom we saw while leaving Preller's, is rather suffering from your absence; and Miss Williams deplores it greatly. I've tried to console her in my own way, by telling her that you were fine in Berlin, and that I wouldn't stop urging you to prolong your stay there —

About 6 o'clock a little piano-playing *prodigy*, age 13, from Warsaw, and named Tausig,[2] came to see me. He bears very special letters of recommendation (completely justified by his talent) from Casimir Lubomirsky [3] and Halpert.[4] He'll probably spend a year or two at Weimar. He's an amazingly gifted boy whom you will enjoy hearing. He plays everything by heart, composes (fairly well) and seems to me destined to make a brilliant reputation for himself very quickly —

After we had him perform a half-dozen pieces, Hans played his Fantastic Revery for us, his Mazurka and his Invitation to the Polka (three charming pieces, and even rather *exquisite*); I ended the session with my Scherzo and my Sonata [5] — and after that at the sound of nine o'clock, the whole crowd ate at the Erbprinz, from whence we did not return until Midnight.

Here is yesterday's story — to which I add our trip to Erfurt the day before yesterday, as complement — where we had the pleasure of swallowing huge portions of musical *Bread-soup*, under the guise of a Symphony, Overture and "Free Fantasy" in M. Taubert's style — although for my type of mustard-lover and Grog-drinker, the *Bread-soup*, as you know, has lost all its savor. Upon returning from our trip, Cornelius made up the following anagram: "Who is the composer who remains even bigger than he is, if you take away the first and last letters of his name?" — *T*auber*t* (Auber —!) [6]

Hans will be back tomorrow, and shall give you the very freshest news concerning your most humbly attached and unalterably enslaved,

Fainéant.

LETTER 25: Preface

From 1847 until 1861, Carolyne was actively attempting to obtain an annulment of her marriage to Prince Nicolas Wittgenstein. It will be remembered that one of the initial reasons for Liszt and Carolyne settling in Weimar was the hope that Grand Duchess Maria-Pavlovna, sister to the Czar, would mediate in their projected marital affairs. Unfortunately things turned out otherwise. Prince Wittgenstein was a close friend of the Czar; the Consistory of Zytomir, headed by the Metropolitan Holowinsky, found her claims invalid, and a Petersburg Decree was issued by the Czar. Carolyne was ordered to return to Russia under pain of banishment. She refused to comply. Her property was confiscated, half of it, including the Woronince estate, going to Nicolas and a part of the remainder being held in trust for Marie. Furthermore, social opprobrium was added to this financial blow: Maria-Pavlovna was asked by her brother *not* to receive Carolyne at Court, and this also served to reduce the constant crowd of callers at the Altenburg.

Wallace (*Liszt, Wagner, and the Princess*, pp. 100 ff.) introduces a speculative element into this elaborate intrigue, and his remarks are at least factually corroborated by simple research into the *Almanach de Gotha* for 1855 through 1861. In the *Almanach* for 1860, there is a note that Nicolas was himself divorced from Carolyne in 1855 — although there is no entry concerning the event in the 1855 volume — and that he married a Princess Marie Michaeloff in 1860. This is not tolerable under the laws of the Church. A further complication enters when one discovers no reference in their correspondence to indicate that either Liszt or Carolyne was cognizant of Nicolas's act.

For a discussion of the attempted marriage of Liszt and Carolyne Wittgenstein, see the Preface to Letter 57. The facts concerning the Czar's stand may be found in any standard biography of Liszt, although the best secondhand account is found in Schorn, *Zwei Menschenalter*, pp. 48–87.

LETTER 25

[Weimar]

Thank you, dear Infanta, for your wise lines. I am answering them with a copy of my letter which will be sent this evening to RD.,[1] and I merely say to you as did Dante to Beatrice:

"Your command is so agreeable to me, that to have obeyed it were to have been dilatory: there is no need further to disclose your will to me." [2]

Tuesday, July 31, '55.   FL.

LETTER 26: *Preface*

"My draft for an answer" refers to a letter just written by Liszt to his two daughters, Cosima and Blandine, in Berlin. Their mother, Countess d'Agoult, had filled them with accusations against their father and Princess Wittgenstein; Liszt's letter was an attempt to refute, or at least to temper, the libels of his former mistress.

No love affair conformed more perfectly to the pattern established by the Romantic myth — or perhaps no romance did more to produce this pattern of behavior — than did that of Liszt and Marie d'Agoult. It was a variation on the story of Julie d'Etanges and Saint-Preux, and thus had literature behind it: yet once again life and art were intertwined in their usual problematic relation, and Marie d'Agoult produced *Nélida* (cf. Letter 28, Note 14) — that extravagant mixture of *Dichtung* and *Wahrheit* — out of her experiences with Liszt.

Only a few details and a short outline of Liszt's relations with her will be sketched; since the affair, which antedates this correspondence, is only of secondary importance in clarifying any remarks made by Liszt to Marie Wittgenstein. Marie d'Agoult, born Vicomtesse de Flavigny in 1805, had married the Comte d'Agoult in 1827. He was twenty years her senior. Despite the two children resulting from the match, it was apparently not a happy marriage. She met the pianist at the Marquise Vayer's in 1833, and he soon became a leading member of her salon, which included such figures as Ingres, Heine, Berlioz, Vigny, and Chopin. The Romantic legend has it that they sat and read Lamartine and Byron together, and "quel giorno più non vi leggemmo avante." It was even hinted that the Countess "avait été enlevée dans un piano à queue" (Bory, *Une Retraite*, p. 25). When her response to Liszt's advances became more serious than he had intended, he fled to Lamennais for spiritual comfort. One has the feeling that he relinquished his role of Hungarian Don Juan with regret; and Marie d'Agoult forced Liszt into dubious domestic bliss when she publicly gave all for love — and abandoned her husband, who seems to have accepted the loss with surprising good grace, and her two children. Trips to Italy and Switzerland followed, and the couple settled in Geneva in 1835, where Liszt practiced, wrote, and taught at the Conservatory and Marie continued her prolific literary career. Blandine, Daniel, and Cosima were born within the next five years; Bory (*ibid.*, p. 34) shows a facsimile of Blandine's birth certificate — "fille naturelle de François Liszt . . . et de Catherine-Adélaïde Méran" — and he makes the amusing observation that Marie put her age at twenty-four instead of thirty in order to agree with Liszt's. (Both Blandine and Daniel are mentioned in Letter 57, Note 6, and Letter 28, Note 4. Cosima's history is easy to find in any biography of Wagner, since she married Hans von Bülow and Wagner in succession.)

A combination formed of two such unstable elements was bound to dissolve, and indeed the best tradition of Romantic liaisons would have had it thus. The two artists clashed temperamentally. Marital inconstancies, either actual or fancied, brought about a decline in mutual affection; the musical career of Liszt and the literary pretensions of Marie made a continuance of their "Maison du Berger" existence impossible. After a series of dramatic separations and reconciliations, the final break took place in 1844. In 1857 Blandine Liszt married Émile Ollivier and Cosima married von Bülow. Liszt and Marie d'Agoult saw each other only once more in 1864, on the occasion of Liszt's visit to Paris in order to receive the Officer's Cross of the Legion of Honor, which their son-in-law Émile Ollivier had procured for him.

The Appendix to Bory's *Une Retraite* includes several interesting and previously unpublished letters by Liszt, Marie d'Agoult, George Sand, and Adolphe Pictet, dating from the Geneva days. His book is also one of the best sources for information about the famous lovers, and it contains many facts not included in Liszt biographies. Paul Henry Lang, "Liebestraum" (*Saturday Review of Literature*, January 25, 1947) is a recent attempt to revaluate their relationship, but it is an article that adds no new material to that already known.

LETTER 26

[Weimar]
Behold, dear Infanta, my draft for an answer, in exchange for your nice copy, and it may amuse you. Show it to your mother; and if she thinks it suitable to pass on to Mme. Patersi and to Scheffer, be good enough to make or have made a legible copy — for I wrote this draft in great haste, and it would be difficult for anyone to understand it who wasn't used to my hand. There are also two references and several addenda, that were obtained from the copy sent to Berlin by the same messenger.

I spent all day at this nice job — and in fifteen minutes I have to go to the Belvedere, where I have been ordered by Grand Duchess Maria.

I hope that you are having a better time in Paris, and that you please won't curtail your stay there on my account. I promise you to *loaf around* patiently another ten days — after which I'll come to meet you at Kösen[1] with much joy —

In the meantime, I kiss your lovely, sweet hands while reminding you of

September, '55   One of the Altenburg watchdogs.

71

Please try, if it's possible, to bring back a sketch or painting of Minette. With your diplomacy, I'd guess that you could obtain one from her and from Scheffer.

Preface: LETTERS 27 through 39

These letters, from 1855 through 1857, reflect Liszt's activity at that time: in general, a period of rather unimportant artistic development if his life is considered as a whole. Carolyne and Marie were away from Weimar a great deal of the time — a reflection, no doubt, of Carolyne's status as *persona non grata* at the Court; hence in Liszt's letters to both of them we find much advice concerning places of interest in various cities. He, too, was frequently on tour — no longer the virtuoso pianist, but now the hard-working conductor attempting to spread his own compositions and those of the "New School." The tone of these letters is tired and fairly despondent. The following passage may well be taken as typical: "My days are gray and obscure, as is the weather. I continue merely to 'stand guard' by dint of my fame — that function, which as 'advance sentinel' of art, I must perform willy-nilly." (*L.M.* I, No. 202.)

The situation at Weimar, once so full of promise, was also gradually changing. The Intendant Beaulieu, who succeeded the friendlier Ziegesar, was mildly hostile to Liszt's emphasis on the opera as opposed to straight drama — his gesture of forbidding Liszt to take a group of his Weimar musicians to Aachen for a concert may be viewed as typical of the increasing tension that existed between music and the theater.

Liszt's snobbishness, perhaps a heritage of his earlier days as the social lion, cannot be discounted. We are aware of it in a few of the letters to Marie, where he points with almost childish pride to the honors paid him by the aristocracy and the Great.

It was approximately during the first five years of the 1850's that Liszt's real interest in Hungarian culture began. One looks in vain, for example, for evidence of any particular concern with Hungarian politics during the 1848 revolutionary period and the fight for national freedom. The *Rhapsodies* for piano, the compositions most associated in the popular mind with the musician, appeared from 1851 to 1854; and the *Graner Mass*, for the Church of Gran, near Budapest, was first performed in 1855. But his chief efforts in musical creativity were devoted to writing the twelve symphonic poems which form the major portion of his orchestral contribution. On the subject of these he was curiously silent. The letters to Marie and Carolyne barely mention the *Poems* when they were in their formative stage, and those to Wagner are scarcely more revealing.

LETTER 27

[Weimar] Saturday, 15 September 1855

My lines yesterday were rather brief, dear Infanta; but I really had a sore hand from the 6 or 7 pages of writing, done from 9 in the morning until 6 in the evening, (with all the inevitable interruptions due to my way of life) to be sent to the address of the "proud children." [1] Even while I was still writing you, the court "carriage" was at the gate. I then had to dress as fast as possible, in order not to be late at the Belvedere. Her Grace the Grand Duchess is in fine health and this Franzenbad [2] cure seems to have guaranteed her health for many long years. In the way of outsiders, there were only the 2 Gross's and Mlle. von Pogwisch. [3] Berlioz's [4] letter, which I had M. von Minkwitz [5] give Her Grace upon entering, enjoyed a great success. It has both original conciseness and perfect ironic humor. "My Benvenuto Cellini, assassinated in France several years ago, has somewhat regained a spark of life due to the care of a famous Doctor, your Weimar Choirmaster. [6] A German editor has been located who really wants to take him out into the wide-open public eye; and I am taking the liberty of begging Your Highness to continue your patronage of the convalescent, by allowing the dedication of this work etc. — " The Grand Duchess was greatly amused by this style, not customary under such circumstances; and tomorrow Vitzthum will reply to Berlioz that she accepts with pleasure the homage rendered her by this score.

M. von Minkwitz, with whom I made the ride up to the Belvedere, told me that Vitzthum had planned to come to see me; I thought it would be decent to forestall him, and went to see him this morning to pay my respects. He, too, is as perfectly recovered from his illness as he can be, and welcomed me with complete cordiality. I told him some of your artistic information about Paris, which greatly interested him. His Excellency has fully approved of your trip to Paris; consequently I urge you to have no *Weimarian* scruples about lengthening or shortening your stay there. Vitzthum leaves for Elksleben in three days, and he will stay there about two weeks before again taking up his winter quarters here. He, too, was unaware of the death of the Princess-Marshal and is as surprised as is Mal.[7] — to be still without any news relative to your affairs. I took advantage of the chance, to hint to him that your lovely head of hair would not tend to turn grey, if RD let himself be overcome with impatience — and unless I'm wrong, he understood the apologue — When the snow and skating returns, we'll see how to go about it without getting too swallowed up.

I have nothing to tell you about the Altenburg, my dear Infanta. My sole events are Minette's letters, which happily arrive nearly exactly after each dinner at about four-thirty. The finest days are those when they arrive morning and evening — Daniel[8] keeps to my room very quietly most of the time, and reads V. Hugo's *Rhine*,[9] Pascal's *Pensées*,[10] and *Paradise Lost*.[11] Naturally I told him of the sketch I sent you yesterday, and at that time I tried to clarify his ideas a bit concerning the conduct he and his sisters ought to follow. He was already familiar with the 3rd letter (which I annotated), but up to now he has not envisaged the problem of the *foreigner*[12] from the same point of view as mine. One may believe that if good reasons and the most palpable facts have any power of conviction, his mind, which isn't lacking in fairness, will not resist them. I imagine that you won't be displeased with him; even though you have been in the company of so many important persons and aesthetic-and-intellectual heralds, I fear that you may find his society a little dull.

The inauguration of the Merseburg[13] organ will take place on Wednesday, September 26. Perhaps things will arrange themselves so that you can get to Merseburg on that date; as for me, I'll have to be there from the evening of the 25th on, in order still to try out some of the new registers. Sacha Winterberger will play the Prophet Fantasia,[14] which is now taking on quite a different character under his fingers after the work I had him do.

Goodbye, dearest Infanta — Kiss Minette for me, and tell her that I fully approve of all that she says, does, and writes in Paris.

If there is any way of seeing David and Niton [?] Keck,[15] I urge you to do so.

LETTER 28

Weimar September 22, '55.

For the Infanta

Well, another little letter from the Infanta, who really doesn't want to forget poor old Fainéant! Now here is something very nice and very charming — and I thank you warmly, while still hoping that our correspondence doesn't go on indefinitely, which is a little selfish wish I trust you don't hold against me. In my letter yesterday to Minette, I urged her not to neglect St. *Ouen* of Rouen,[1] and to add this architectural wonder to her list — It won't take you more than a day; and if you are fortunate with the weather, you will enjoy the trip.

Nothing is happening or going on at Weimar. Last evening I took Kamiensky [2] to the Eckeburg [3] ball, where I introduced him to the Frohrieps [4] and to Mlle. Schmidt — [5] He was a courageous dancer and didn't return with Daniel until after 1 o'clock. Fainéant naturally went to bed at 10 — As for Daniel, he was content to *watch the dancing* while waiting until the time when his lessons with M. *Voss* [6] allow him to do it with skill, something he seems to want to acquire quite badly.

In the way of foreigners, we now have Rosaļie Spohr (now the Countess Sauerma) [7] and her husband, who look as if they're going to extend their visit here — and Roquette,[8] with whom I am entering into rather advanced negotiations for a musical *legend* about St. Elizabeth.[9] Perhaps Minette will scold me; but I imagine Roquette will do this sort of thing very well, and furthermore I am afraid Cornelius may be taken up with his outline of an opera for a long time. Tonight after dinner, Roquette is reading a manuscript of his own tragedy at Genast's, to which I shall listen . . . and he's promised to send me our St. Elizabeth for Christmas, since I want to start it as soon as the *Dante* [10] is finished — that is to say, during the course of next summer.

You have admirably made up for Scheffer's blunder — and in this case it is likely that the Altenburg Museum will be enriched by two masterpieces instead of one —

Try to see to it, that Her Gracious and Whimsical Majesty doesn't put us off until Doomsday; and if you succeed in getting her to leave Paris for a few weeks, you'll have something to boast about. In the meantime I hope that you soon send me Magnolette's picture, for I have no idea how it looks, no matter how I try to imagine it, sometimes in a white dress sometimes in a coat of elusive colors — with varying skirts — sometimes a profile of the face, or a three-quarter likeness of several aspects, etc., etc. — No matter how it turns out, I hope Scheffer *"will be worthy"* of his subject, as much as possible.

The little girls [11] seem to be changing their minds a bit (as you will have seen by their letters), or at least concealing their feelings behind the obedience to what they perhaps term my tyrannical requirements. I can't ask more of them for the time being, and there will be plenty of time to reflect on what to do later. I wrote some-think like the following to B.[12] last night, in answer to her letter to Mme. P.[13]:

"I approve of you and thank you — my child. You did what there was to do, and as it should have been done. May this con-scientiousness always be your guide; it will gain for you the greatest measure of satisfaction and happiness that it is possible to get in this world, etc. —"

Daniel is continuing to behave, and he doesn't at all share these *foreign* feelings for the *foreign lady* shown by his sisters — The letter whose sketch I sent you helped greatly to coördinate his still rather vague ideas, since it provided me with the opportunity of reciting a litany of arguments to him to which there is scarcely any reply. As for the *poetic* feeling my children have for their mother, far from trying to destroy it, I've even sought to feed the flame by reading half of *Nélida* [14] to them, as well as several other things written in Daniel Stern's [15] honor. There has just come out, along with several others, a German book, "Mitteilungen aus Paris" by a M. Seiffarth,[16] where there is a long discussion about the author of *Nélida* (lasting at least 40 pages) which I will arrange to have you read when you return.

Scotland is very sad not to hear from you and if you still have fifteen minutes, you will make her very happy if you will chat a little with her. To console her, I told her that I was expecting you a week from tomorrow (Sunday, September 30th); but if you still find something pleasant to do in Paris, I urge you not to hurry, and give you leave of absence up to the end of the first week in October.

Vitz.¹⁷ is in Elksleben; thus nothing is urgent in Wey.,¹⁸ except the great desire to see you again, felt by

Your very proudly
humble slave
FL.

LETTER 29

[Berlin] Friday, December 7, '55.

Fainéant comes to kiss your sweet little hands, my dear Magnolet; and he wants to tell you right away that he will be very happy to see you again, to take once again his place beside you, and to fulfill his role in "dragging you along" — because it is the only way for him to avoid *dragging* himself (which often seems very arduous) through all sorts of discouragements, tiresome affairs, and vexing boredoms.

In my capacity as Magnolet's confidant, I also want to inform you about my minor success this winter. It was only a bit of a one — but we are not completely through with it — and Rubinstein,¹ who came yesterday morning, told me after the Concert that it seemed like a good entering wedge. As for me, I confess that for the time being I have no exact opinion about it — They clapped after each number on the Program — and there was one encore each after the Préludes and the Concerto ² which Bülow played superbly, so well that he was honored by being eagerly called out again — The Tasso ³ seems to have made a fairly good impression (even at the rehearsals); but it was less warmly applauded — and after the Psalm,⁴ which went perfectly, there were several *St's* or *Szt's* (the last letters of my name), and these occasioned a roar of Bravo's, amid whose noise I climbed down once more the steps of this hall which formerly I knew so well, in much the same way you've seen me more than once on the proscenium of our Institute after a performance of Tannhäuser or Lohengrin.

The hall was filled; and their Majesties the King and Queen,⁵ and if I'm not mistaken Prince and Princess Carl as well as several other Princes, were also present. Among the visiting artists I noticed Rubinstein, Joachim (who had come from Leipzig, but whom I didn't see, since he left this morning and did not have supper with us, for lack of the *tail-coat* appropriate to the occasion), Damrosch,[6] Goltermann (from Schwerin),[7] Jaell,[8] etc. — Even M. Taubert didn't stay away. Needless to say, the most tense silence filled the hall during the performance; and I conducted it with apparently the necessary calmness. All are unanimous about its success.

I went back to the Arnim Hotel at 10 o'clock, where about 300 had gathered, including 250 musicians, in a *magnificently* illuminated hall, extremely spacious and brightly decorated. We drank to the King — and then Marx spoke eloquently and with restraint about Fainéant. Wendt[9] had written a Grand March in my honor, and Wüerst[10] a men's chorus, equally in my praise. Following that, I answered Marx's toast fairly briefly by drinking my own to the "Society for the Arts"; and Rubinstein commented on the sentence, "If you want to understand me, you'll have to grasp me." — [11] Bronsart[12] will write you the other details. Be good enough to tell Minette that I didn't touch a *single* drop of Cognac, and I merely drank a few glasses of Champagne — I took Hans home around 2 in the morning; and I think he's quite smitten with Cosima and the idea of marrying my daughter, so we are to have a talk tomorrow morning, in the presence of her mother and my daughters.

At the dinner at M. von Humboldt's, — where there was everyone mentioned in his letter to you except Rauch,[13] who was forced to stay home where he was indisposed — Humboldt did me the particular honor of drinking to the health of someone whose identity I could guess, and I was most grateful. The conversation was of course extremely animated, and there was a marked tone of goodwill on the part of the Greatest of the Great toward your poor little Fainéant — who hasn't the time to write you further, and sadly enough, not time to adore, bless, and kiss you, you and Minette. He does this in his heart, however, every minute — and he entreats dear God to preserve your tenderness, sympathy, and sweet affection, for all time and for eternity.—

FL.

I shall go on with my Bulletins to Minette tomorrow morning — Don't expect me before Tuesday evening —

LETTER 30

Thursday, January 31st,
Vienna (1856)

Well, soon I'll be through with my dull days, and after tomorrow evening I shall turn back to my lair. Monday I'll be at Dresden, and Tuesday evening at Altenburg. In the meantime I *kiss the walls* of our little blue room!

Fainéant has been very neglectful this time in the matter of letter-writing — and this comes from the small number of persons and interesting things he had to tell you about — and also from the expectant position he had to keep — and as a result, he will leave Vienna just about the way he came there. Opinion, public and press, are quite unanimously favorable toward him — notwithstanding the feeling against him for his refusal to play the piano (something no one cares to understand, and about which "admirable" and unadmirable friends, *with the exception of Eduard,*[1] bore him from morn to eve) notwithstanding also the skeptical attitude, at the very least, concerning his capacity as an orchestral conductor, which he met upon his arrival here. This attitude displayed rather disagreeable nuances right up to the last minute in several of the personnel with whom it was a question of conducting; and it caused scarcely restrainable agitation to our friend Löwy.[2] Everyone concurred generally in praising my appeal and my personality; and Hanslick,[3] who in this respect is an excellent thermometer and the best critic around, did a *very fitting* article in yesterday's *Press* on the Mozart Festival, where he in no way begrudged me the good portion that was my due. I'll tell you a few details verbally — in brief, I think that they are pleased with me, for which I have occasion to be satisfied for the moment. In every way these two weeks served me perfectly as *preliminaries* for Gran[4] — and I'm about to start another *mass* after the one for Gran, in the church at Fôt[5] (three-quarters of an hour away from Pesth), built by Count Étienne Caroly.[6] It is virtually the center of Catholic propaganda in Hungary. As for Vienna, I should stick to my reserve, and let other people talk and act. My natural appearance is that of a *very serious* man, and one sincerely *modest.** In short, the soil is favor-

* sure enough of himself, so that other people have no doubt about *him*!

79

able for me, outwardly much more favorable than that of Berlin —
although it's likely to be the latter I will cultivate beginning next
winter.—

What remains is only very secondary — and if I plan a concert
in Dresden on the way, it will be principally to conform to Minette's
instructions.

Prince M.[7] had invited me to dinner the day before yesterday
(Tuesday); but I was obliged to excuse myself, since the Burgomaster was giving a big dinner at the same time to end the *Mozart
Festival*, where he did me implied honors by proposing a toast to
me *in first place*. I saw His Highness again yesterday afternoon —
and this visit yielded an exquisite story about the Semiramide[8]
overture, written during the Congress of Verona.[9] Brendel[10] could
profit from it. Strictly speaking, the Prince might reinvite me; but
I doubt it, although I flatter myself at having lost none of his good-
will, which always remains several thousand feet above sea level!

In the way of *society*, I've only seen Princess Kevenhuller
[*sic*],[11] Princess Esterhazy,[12] and Countess Banffy.[13] The latter
gave a large party for my benefit, where Madame Schumann[14] and
the Marchesis[15] did the musical honors on the program. Before
leaving Saturday, I will dine (at 4 o'clock) at Mme. Banffy's, who
is most friendly toward me, and who plans to see us at Weimar.

Princess Kevenhuller's daughter (the sister of Felix Lichnowsky),[16] is the *Magnolette* of Vienna at this moment. She is sixteen,
and made her entry into society this winter through the Court
balls and the *elegant* Schwarzenbergs, Lichtensteins, etc., etc., with
the most complete success. She is the first on everyone's lips —

An elegant young woman, a Social Lioness, and an Artist, whom
I see rather often and who will also pass through Weimar this
summer, is the Hungarian Princess Nako.[17] She plays Bohemian
songs in a ravishing way, sketches and paints with a kind of genius,
and maintains at her expense a troupe of Bohemian musicians whom
she has shown to Meyerbeer.[18] Villiers[19] introduced me at her
home. Her husband is quite a young fellow, perfectly well-bred
and His Majesty and Emperor's[20] *Chamberlain*. I am dining with
them today — tomorrow at Mme. Eskeles'[21] (probably with Count
Schlick,[22] whom I have seen only in public, since it is impossible to
meet him at his home) and Prince Gortchakoff,[23] who lives in
Mme. Eskeles' house) and the day after tomorrow at Mme. Banffy's

— then I'll try to sleep until Prague (where I'll stay until Sunday evening); for here I don't get my *thirty winks* either in the daytime or at night, and it tires me greatly. Henry [24] claims that I look badly — and I can well believe it. One of my compatriots (Duneiski) [25] has made a colossal bust of my sad face for the Pesth Museum — and Kriebhuber [26] has made a watercolor, which he'll send you when he has finished the lithograph he plans to design for the watercolor.

Edouard,[27] whom I see every day, has just told me that Minette had a bad dream on my account. Tell her that it was a deceiving dream, and that there is not the *least reason* in the world for her to worry about me. I'll only be very bored for four or five more days, because *without you* I can't be anything else — but you are loved entirely and exclusively, since one can't do otherwise without ceasing to exist —

Add for Minette's sake, besides, that we are not drinking small Cognacs,[28] and that we are in no way about to do any sort of foolishness.

I kiss your sweet hands, dearest Magnolette, and I remain your slave and your chattel with all my soul.

FL.

This three-day extension has become quite indispensable, and I hope that you don't disapprove of me. Neither Prague nor Dresden shall stop me — and Tuesday evening I will see you again!

I am sending you a few autographs by the same mail —

LETTER 31

Sweetest and dearest Magnolette —

I hope that these lines get to you right on your birthday, and remind you of all the perfume and incense which my heart lavishes on your picture. If only our good *little brother* the sun, and our pretty little sisters the stars were at my command, I'd send them to you; and I'd ask you to keep them in the *Portfolio* that Minette will not fail to decorate and embellish this August 15th, as she did in former years. Alas, I'm not even there to be the bearer of your charming treasures, and to come to wake you at 7 in the morning, and to arouse your incredulity by insisting "that this time there won't be anything," to take you to Church and then remain with you the whole blessed day! Keep my place in your heart, dearest angelic Magnolet; and pray God to leave us always together, invincibly united by our thoughts, our prayers, and our hope! —

August 12, '56 — Pest.   FL.

I am practicing from afar our little deaf-and-dumb language, and am amazed at the nice pantomimes with which you favor me!

LETTER 32

. [Pesth]

Dearest Magnolette,

This for you today: a tender kiss for your two dear hands, and a big Thanks for your delightful letter with the trilogy of stars and all of God's Heavenly Music, which you are so worthy to hear and whose sweet echo you transmit to me!

How I long to see you — and how empty my heart is, by your being away! . . . Be sure to tell Minette this, and repeat it every morning. I'm still going to Prague in order to notify them of my acceptance, and will arrange it so I arrive on the 20th. Since St. Wenceslas [1] is on the 28th, I hope to be free by the 30th — and will run immediately to you and spend at least a few days at the Altenburg, before going to get our friend Wagner. You will no doubt tell me that I look badly, since I am very tired and don't succeed in getting the sleep I need; but 3 or 4 days of rest in the blue room will completely fix me.

Happily I've come to the end of my job here — and will probably resist the invitations I've received to give a second and a third Concert. Yesterday evening's made too great an impression on me to begin again right away — The "Preludes" ought to have been played right through again; and as for the Hungaria, [2] which was the last piece on the Program, there was better than applause — all wept, both men and women! Make a note of this 8th of September, which will be one of your anniversaries, dearest Magnolette (the Birth of Our Lady — the Hungarians call it the Little Lady's Day, and the 15th of August, Great Lady's Day!) make a note of this date on our little calendar, because on that day I was very happy.

"Sirva vizad à Magyar," "Tears are the joy of the Hungarians," is a Proverb of this country . . . and yesterday evening proved to me that I made no mistake in style when I wrote the Hungaria, which I now do not wish to hear again.

Zellner [3] left again for Vienna during the night, his eyes also filled with tears. . . .

In the morning, my first Mass, which you heard at Jena, was very well sung in a little chapel which the Cardinal Primate consecrated yesterday. It bears the name of *Herminie Chapel*, in honor of the late Archduchess, sister to the Archduke Stephen. This chapel is only able to hold about a hundred persons — but outside there were several thousand, and the sermon was delivered from the steps outside — After the Mass, Curé Santoffi [4] gave a large dinner at his home — His Eminence [5] honored me by a few words in a toast, stressed still more distinctly . . . by the master of the house in a toast that followed, when he called me "the regenerator of Church music" — The idea is starting to take hold among the intelligent portion of this country's clergy —

Before returning to Vienna, I will stop again for a few hours at Gran, at the special invitation of His Eminence. I shall probably arrive Sunday, Sept. 14th — at Vienna — Would you be so kind to ask Minette to write me at the "Empress of Austria" until I give her new directions from Vienna?

Goodbye, dearest Magnolette, until we meet again during the first days of October. — I will leave abruptly from Munich and go right to Weimar, Stuttgart, Winterthür [6] and Zürich. We will chat about that at length — Make allowances for my letters, for I don't know how to express myself. Give my best to Minilaws [7] — and don't forget my regards to Scotch, of whom I think constantly and with keen affection. Kiss Kossenessa [8] for me, too — you know how much I love her! Moreover, tell sweet Harpagon that I am being quite economical and avoiding all unnecessary drinking —

May God be with you and may we love each other through Him, in this life and for Eternity!

Tuesday, Sept. 9, '56   FL.

I am going to write to Beaulieu, to ask him to let me keep Gross [9] until the first of October; and I'd be very grateful to you if you'd ask Minette to speak with Beaulieu about this —

83

Dearest Magnolette,

This will not be the sort of surprise for you, that Beaulieu contrived for me last evening — but our invalid's [1] last words and looks are so much with me, that I chose to stop at Cassel [2] in order to write to you a little sooner — Read these lines to Minette, and tell her that she shouldn't worry about me. Wahlbrül and Gross are extremely attentive in taking care of me. Up to here, we have been alone together in the train all the time — and tomorrow we shall continue our trip to Aix tranquilly in the same manner. We will be at our destination about 4 or 5 o'clock. Hemsen, [3] of whom I caught a glimpse at the Eisenach station, will write you soon after his return to Munich; and he told me to convey his most devoted regards to you and Minette.

I suppose Spohr [4] will come to see me in the course of the evening, because they were notified here of my trip by the father of Concertmaster Schöler [5] (who gets himself regularly applauded in Weimar in the Flute-prelude preceding the 2nd act of the Huguenots) — [6] His son, the Cassel Concertmaster, waited for me at the train; and I asked him to apologize for me to Spohr. Due to my foot trouble, I neglected to come see him this time and I invited him to call on me without further ado. Schöler just told me that Spohr, in the course of the winter, regularly plays quartets at the homes of several of the city's *finest*; but ordinarily his repertory was limited to quartets of Spohr and to a few of Mozart — and the latter in the proportion of a double dose of Spohr to a single one of Mozart. As for Beethoven, they claim that he can't play a single one of his quartets without committing some obvious mistake; and he takes his revenge by stating that no matter how lovely one wishes to find these works, they absolutely lacked *form*. How right was the good, dull Loke, [7] with his cheap simplicity (as de Maistre [8] said of his pupil Condillac) [9] when he repeated incessantly, ". . . define your terms! — " For that is what M. Hanslick, for example, never does, whose brochure on beauty in Music I reread on the way. It has a kind of cunning and rather persuasive skillfulness — But as for me, I wouldn't care to follow in his footsteps, and I define myself precisely and definitely: Someone

who loves you kisses your sweet hands, and blesses and honors
Minette with his whole soul.

Cassel, Tuesday, May 19th [1857]   F.L.
6 o'clock in the evening
(The King of Prussia Hotel)

LETTER 34

[Aix-la-Chapelle]
Thursday, May 21 — [1857]
(Ascension Day!)

Leaving Cassel yesterday morning at five-thirty, I arrived here
nicely and quite quietly at six-thirty in the evening — Suermondt [1]
had joined me at Cassel, and we made the trip together — After
Paderborn [2] I began to see, in the charming forests magnificently
illumined by the sun, the slim shape, the sweet and proud air, and
even the *green* dress of my dear Magnolette, whose picture at this
moment looked like both Diana of the Hunt and Saint Geneviève.[3]
Then, while slowly passing through the streets of Düsseldorf by
bus in order to reach the other train, my heart tenderly filled with
the memories of our stay in '51. "The lady seems to love you!"
I saw again in my mind all the Italian drawings in the Gallery, but
much more beautiful than they ever could be. — I chatted with
Suermondt the rest of the time (whose wife is one of the Coqueril [4]
daughters — a very well-known name in big business — they've
been married for about fifteen years, and there are *six children*);
and in order to fulfill my role of traveler with honesty, I finished
reading Hanslick's brochure, and appended a fair number of notes
to it, which are summarized by the formula borrowed from
Minette:

I understand only too well, hence I protest against it.

At the Aix station, Burgomaster Dahmen and M. Van Houtern,
the Committee Chairman, were waiting to welcome me; and they
accompanied me by carriage up to Suermondt's house, where I am
now comfortably established. Suermondt gave me the choice between a rather spacious apartment on the second floor and a very
nice room on the third. "I swung myself up there," and can climb

the stairs now like a young fawn. All the furniture is in good fine mahogany — and the red bedspread is exactly like the one on my bed at Weimar. Moreover, there is a charming green carpet and chintz curtains that are quite cheerful. The whole house has a grand and handsome look such as we are not familiar with at Weimar with well-spaced windows; and it bears the stamp of the new order of patricians, that of solid comfort and elegance without gingerbread, like W.'s [5] Grecian villa —

At Aix, the big industries are clothing, pins, zinc and several other accessory metals — and mirrors too, if I am not mistaken. In the second-story sitting-room, there are some Velasquez [6] portraits (originals), several pretty landscapes, and Érard [7] piano (which figured in the Paris exposition), a double-action harp, etc. — the stairway is well-carpeted and decorated by vases with lilacs and other flowers, and there are several bronze figures in the style of Kiss — [8] In Su.'s [9] work-room I first noticed a portrait of *Beuth* [10] (for whom they have erected a monument in Berlin), and a big Bust, which I gather to be that of his father-in-law, Coqueril — Madame S. has kept rather nice features, and speaks French almost more fluently than German. No more than he, has she any of these nouveau riche and parvenu traits. Her oldest son (so I gather) is in the Prussian army; and we had supper with him yesterday, and Turany [11] with his better half — The bill-of-fare consisted simply of beefsteak, potatoes, asparagus, crayfish, and a dessert of oranges, apples, etc., without any pretension to *high-fashion* in cooking.

I shall go to the Rathaus at eleven-thirty, to introduce myself to the Committee; and in the evening I'll no doubt attend a quartet session which I saw announced in the Aix paper. I've been told they are friendly. As soon as the situation concerning the Music Festival is a little clearer in my head, I'll talk to you about it — In the meantime, I have rather good hopes for its success. Berlioz, who was especially invited, excused himself — but perhaps Fétis [12] will come. Furthermore, I was assured that since the Festival in which Jenny Lind [13] figured, about ten years ago, there had not been a similar stimulation of curiosity, now evident by the large number of subscriptions for the one taking place. In any case, the receipts ought to be excellent. The Music Festival Committee of Cologne has specially asked for a loge — and Hiller answered the Committee's request, saying that they were already assured of tickets, and that he thanked them for their attention. Her Grace Countess d'Outremont,[14] widow of Mme. Sacha's grandfather, put herself down for a loge, and it has already been difficult to get for her. I suggested that the Committee immediately write a few lines of thanks to Beaulieu — and also to Mme. Milde — and for my part, I will write to M. Sach. Please send my letter to the castle after you seal it.

I hope to hear from Minette this evening, and I kiss her with all my soul while asking God to shower both of you with all his blessings.

F.L.

Find the letter from Brandt[15] in Pesth, in the letter-drawer of my Desk (on the left), and send it to me. I want to give it to Turanny whose pupil Brandt was.

By the way, rumor has it here that the *Wanderer's* Article, copies of which were spread around here in profusion, is the editing of Bischoff[16] and Hiller! — As for me, I don't believe it.

LETTER 35

[Aix-la-Chapelle]
Saturday, May 30, '57.

Alas! my dearest, sweetest and adorable child; this time things have turned out as I feared, rather than as I had hoped. Nevertheless one shouldn't give in, and should trust in God while persevering right up *to the last*. There are, even as there were martyrs for the Faith, martyrs for love! Minette is one of the latter. Let us pray God to test us in accordance with our strength, and don't give up hope.

Considering things from the *human* point of view, one could foresee that the priest would not immediately bring back a favorable answer, and that we would have to resign ourselves to several more stages of waiting. For the moment there is nothing to say, nothing to do, except to maintain ourselves strictly in the *passivity* we have kept for the past two years. — I shall be back in a week and hope to find Minette sufficiently recovered, so that I may gently exhort her to be patient. Ask her to pardon me if for the

87

next three or four days I only write her very brief letters. I have two daily rehearsals, each of 4 to 5 hours — and since the performers add up to almost 600 persons, I have to shout a great deal, which makes me middling tired — Besides, it is necessary that I see a certain number of persons in the intervals between rehearsals, at dinner and at supper, and no other free time is left me save when I write to you upon awakening (6 o'clock in the morning) —

Make my excuses for me to *Daniel*, whom I will not be able to answer until later in the week —

In short, things look promising and are going well here — and Suermondt assures me that my adversaries of a week ago admit themselves to be completely beaten and in the process of conversion. Yesterday we repeated the Infancy of Christ[1] in its entirety, of which several parts produced a good effect. Dalle Aste [2] is excellent and Schneider[3] very good — as for Mme. Milde, I am most certain of her success — Bülow arrived yesterday morning — and Hiller ditto; but up to now my Cologne colleague has not yet called, and we scarcely said hello to each other at the rehearsal —

I kiss dearest Magnolette's fingertips, and remain with you in spirit from morning to night —
P.S. My feet and legs are feeling *fine*.
There is no trace of an inflammation any more.

LETTER 36

[Aix-la-Chapelle]
Saturday, June 6, '57.
7 o'clock in the morning.
Dearest Magnolette,

Please tell sweet Minette that I will try to arrive tomorrow evening (Sunday) a little late — but if that isn't feasible for me, she shouldn't worry; and I shall certainly arrive during the course of Monday —

We are leaving immediately for Wesel[1] with the two Hans's (Bülow and Bronsart) and Sascha Winterberger, where I will spend the night; and according to the train timetables, I shall get under way tomorrow to be with you as soon as possible. All things considered, I will give up stopping over at Wolfenbüttel,[2] and shall come right back to where my soul ever dwells. —

Goodbye, then, until tomorrow evening, and I imagine, the end of your supper.

Kiss Minette tenderly and pray God that we may remain *one*, through Him!

L.

LETTER 37

[Aix-la-Chapelle]
July 26, '57.
Sunday evening, 10 o'clock.

I can never stop saying to you, dearest Magnolette, that you are grace, kindness, *wisdom*, and even *perfection* itself. My happiness is to accompany you with heart and soul and ever to delight in you unreservedly —

The condition of my *scaffolding* is improving, as I wrote to Minette yesterday. I have scarcely gone out except to attend Father Roh's [1] sermon; and following that I heard Mass, during which I prayed for you both the whole time. Since Mme. Suermondt was ill, the picnic we planned was dropped; and we ate quite simply in the only room at the Suermondt's town house not littered up with masons, furniture, and paintings. Afterwards I went back to my pigeon-roost, where I have been working since 4 o'clock at my *Marches*,[2] without even letting myself be tempted by Mlle. Krall,[3] who is singing Agatha in the Freischütz [4] with Gross's trombone accompaniment — At the Suermondt dinner, there was Kehren,[5] who is completing Rethel's [6] frescoes; Dare,[7] the architect for the Town Hall, Turanny, a painter from around here named Thomas,[8] and two or three other persons. We talked about a lot of things, and of our *worthy friend* [9] among others; nothing was said worth the trouble of remembering, which is usually the case in society.

But let's get back to Father Roh's preaching. In the series of sermons he is conducting here this year, he chose for his principal theme the Church: its authenticity, its unity, its apostleship, the holiness of its teachings, the absolute obligation we are under to practice its commandments and to follow its decisions, etc. — He is a concise dialectician, expert, who derives excellent profit from the contradictions of others, and who is not afraid to use a simple conversational tone, and even willingly to risk a few witticisms. For example, concerning fasting on Friday, today he complimented unbelievers on their faith in the stomach: (Congratulations for belief in the stomach)!

His sermon for today developed this idea of St. Cyprian's: [10] "He who calls not the Church *his mother*, may not call God his father," which he quoted in conclusion. As a necessary concomitant, he put the 5 commandments of the Church [11] in the same category, since they are quite as obligatory for Christians as the command-ments of God — "Has there been a society, an enterprise, a corpora-tion, a meeting of stockholders" — he asked — "whose statutes could be reduced to a few lines, and to such manifest simplicity, as these five commandments of the Church?" — The latter reminded me of the "Laws of the Theater" which Ziegesar and Beaulieu made for themselves, a pair of Sysiphus' more than they are Solon's! — [12]

Here is a letter of Cosette's [13] I am sending to you which I shall answer in two or three days, as soon as I have gotten along with the absorbing business of my marches —

Kiss Minette, and God Bless you —

LETTER 38

[Aachen]
Tuesday, July 28, '57.
How sweet and good you are, my dearest Magnolette, thus to take care of my intellectual nourishment by sending me Chateau-briand's Memoirs! [1] You've catered to my tastes perfectly; for I don't know why, but through some chance or hidden coincidence, it is one of those books that forces me to read: a virtue not possessed by many volumes! —

And since you like quotations, I'll continue to give you some: beginning with the first pages of Book 7, describing the hustle and bustle that took place at Ghent the day after the battle of Waterloo, M. de Chateaubriand confesses his awkwardness; and he sagely remarks that he *continually handicapped himself, and was always* in his own way.[2] That's even better than the speaker who contradicts himself! and there is no lack of persons we know well, to whom these words would apply wonderfully.

I would give a lot to rout out another Father Thornpillier;[3] but up to now I haven't found anything analogous, although I haven't neglected rummaging around in several libraries. In lieu of, and in order to ease Minette's medical concerns, I am enclosing part of Rodenburg's[4] letter concerning my health (which is improving) and Müller's[5] little book, where you'll discover, commencing with the first pages, a comparative table of the non-volatile substances and of the gases dissolved in cubic centimeters in the various springs around Aachen, according to Dr.'s *Liebig*,[6] Monheim,[7] Bunsen,[8] etc. — If, as I imagine, my cure continues its progress, I'll pick up my bags in about a week and see you at Weimar on Thursday, August 6th — By the end of this week, I shall have finished my Marches, which, if I am not wrong, are most successful. In the *Goethe March* there is a *"cultural-historical"* second Trio that has a serene quality, and is calm and majestically sweet. For M. Sach's March, I discovered a motif from a *non-Protestant* Chorale, yea-saying and as if overflowing with love; and it blends in marked contrast with the militant and warrior spirit of the first motif — I should like a courageous, daring, almost reckless Prince, who announces his reign with this ray of love and faith that should shine on royal heads like the sun glowing on mountain peaks! —

When is Hoffmann[9] going to send me his poem? It may be that I can adapt it to this same motif, which seems to me so well chosen.

At daybreak we are to make a little trip to Rodenburg's country house with Father Roh, and I'll tell you all about it. Mme. Suermondt has been continually sick, and I haven't yet seen her. Bronsart will come toward the end of the week — and Hahn[10] and Winterberger also plan to make me a bit of a visit. —

It's my mother's birthday today, and I'm going to write her. Give me her address in tomorrow's letter. Cosette's marriage will probably be set for Sunday, August 9th. The Catholic Calendar shows it to be St. *Amor's*[11] Day: this is a patron beset by all my wishes!

Ask Minette to prepare a *legal document* to help me atone for the blunder I made at Berlin, which caused me so many unhappy hours. I hope this experience will serve me for the rest of my life. I've taken a firm resolution never to rush into business dealings, and never to give up something without bringing it to the best conclusion I can. If it's a good thing to mull over your words seven times before talking, one oughtn't to hesitate pondering even more when it's a matter of signing something with the pen. Without relying on anyone at all (for *you* don't bank on me any more than I do on you!) I have occasionally made the error of becoming involved in untimely dealings: out of boredom, weakness, ineptitude and inexperience in business; and these have more than once played me the trick of forcing me to confess myself a first-class fool, as in this particular instance — My motives being usually honest, I don't indulge sufficiently in that drop of suspicion that is so rigorously necessary for peace of mind, as well as for the dignity of existence: that ingredient from which I theoretically at least, am not exempt. The fact is, that on the one hand I esteem myself too highly, and on the other I give myself too cheaply to others. There is something there that has to do with pride, inadvertence, and a premature laziness; and I ought to be on triple guard against them.

I feel obliged to confess this to you, my dearest child, because willy-nilly you will be called upon to make decisions, sign papers, undertake plans — and all on a much different level than does a poor fellow in my station. Don't ever rush into these things; and always look for the most *precise*, the most *detailed* and the most noble elements. I don't say you have either to escape from or compromise with your own conscience, for you couldn't be in that quandary; but rather you must deal with the customs, decorums, forms and formulae which are the tools you must learn to use well. In this respect, as in all others, you have the consummate model of your mother before you, whose lofty character, prodigious perspicacity of intellect, firm yet flexible, zealous courage, in her daily and hourly defense of her carefully weighed and reflected convictions, will triumph even in failure; and this is the rarest crown reserved only for the greatest souls! — Thus no matter what rancor, what cheapness, mediocrity, envy, lies, and sordid counterfeits of the concern and kindliness of others may pursue

92

her, nothing can harm and trouble her in that region where God Himself guides and protects her as an adviser, friend, and father.

May she be forever blessed! or rather, like old king Lear to his daughter, I say to her: "When thou dost ask me blessing I'll kneel down and ask of thee forgiveness: so we'll live, and pray, and sing!" [12]

F.L.

LETTER 39

[Aachen] Monday August 3 [1857]
3 o'clock in the afternoon.

Dearest Magnolette,

I want you to intercede with Minette for me, that she take into account how sorry I am not to have written you; although every minute that went by, my heart kept telling me to do so. The arrival of Sascha Winterberger, Hahn, a Dutch pianist who later will come to Weimar, and of Bronsart, has upset my daily routine and has stopped me from doing anything except look through rather bulky manuscripts brought me by fledglings, take my baths, and sleep. — Yesterday I spent the day hearing Beethoven's Mass [1] (a mediocre work by a first-rate genius) at the Cathedral — looking at a painting which depicted the Cologne Dome as it will be when entirely finished, with its five-hundred-foot spires displayed for the benefit of those burned out in the Moselle fire, — dining at the Suermondts', — reading through half of Bronsart's *Spring Fantasia* [2] at the piano, a piece I feel to be remarkable, save for several gaps and unskillful spots in the transition passages, — posing for two hours for a new medallion by Mohr, [3] who came especially from Cologne to use me as a model for a second time: I posed without the aid of a laurel wreath and of Mme. Milde; since the protests of Bülow and Bronsart were echoed by several members of the Committee, who decided that the only present to give me ought to be my own, personal likeness, and they intend to have it done in silver at Berlin — and finally I dined on a chicken-wing and an apricot compote at the Suermondts' country house. I was barely able to take a half-hour out in the morning to write Minette; and even then I was obliged to curtail my letter, as M. Schorn [4] and Steger [5] came to call before the Mass. This morning Sart. [6] surprised me during my morning walk at the Elisa Spring — and I asked him back for coffee at my place. We chatted and made some music from 8 to 11: then Bronsart came, and we finished the *Spring Symphony*. Afterwards I just had time to bathe; for I now dine at one o'clock, and I had asked these gentlemen to eat at the general table at Nuellens's.[7] We met Formes there, who regaled us with opinions and stories about England. This evening we are to go hear Steger in The Jewess;[8] and in the meantime Hahn will read me a few chapters from his Chopin and sing me some of his songs. All this would be wonderful, at Weimar and with Minette and Magnolette; but I confess that away from there, the amount of things amid which I must remain a passive spectator is hardly to my taste. However, since a lot of fine young men have put themselves out for me, I consider it my duty to do the same for them; and I am obliging myself to render their stay here as profitable as possible. So I must resign myself to giving them all day tomorrow — but the day after we shall chalk up for ourselves; and I am going to spend a few hours at Mohr's in Cologne, in order for him to finish my medallion. I owe him this politeness; for he has an enormous amount to do at Cologne, and at this time he could absent himself only with great difficulty. I shall go see our friend Weyden [9] and will return here the same evening, around 11 o'clock. So excuse me, dearest Magnolette, for my short and breathless letters; and also crave indulgence from Minette for me. Here's a second letter from Cosima, in answer to my own. — In order to reconcile everything, both the medical advice and Minette's prayers and injunctions, I shall remain here until Sunday; but very *much against my wishes*. I hope soon to be able to tell you, — at a quieter time than this, when I am besieged with manuscripts, and with visits of the Aachen citizenry, — that I am forever

your slave out of free choice
F.L.

LETTER 40

[Prague] Sunday, March 14 [1858]
(2 in the afternoon — right after the Concert)

Very humble and tender greetings to Magnolette in Berlin, and my homage to Floup at the Brandenburg Hotel: May you find a little harmony and amusement there to make up for the monotonous Weimar boredom! —

The last chords of *Tasso* have just resounded — and I treated myself to the small pleasure of having the final march (the Triumph) played again, which pleased the public exceedingly. This piece, which was *acquitted* and accepted in advance by the *big-wigs* here, was a great success afterwards. At yesterday's rehearsal, during a pause between the two Adagio's, a dog started to howl — "another critic," I said to myself *under my breath*! — This critic was met (figuratively) in the person of a little man about whom Meissner [1] had spoken to me in Weimar; and I suppose our darling "Germany" will have nothing better to do, than to put the article in the Prague "*Daily Messenger.*" Everyone takes his pleasure where he finds it, and they all find so much fault with me, that I wouldn't dream of picking on everyone else in the same way! —

This evening I shall start off for Vienna. The Pflughaupts [2] are staying here, and are going to launch out into one or two Concerts. — I told Mme. Pflughaupt to write Minette a detailed account of the evening party we had yesterday at the Baroness Kotz's. — [3] If she fulfills my commission successfully, perhaps Minette will find a few words to send her in reply — Tausig is awaiting me in Vienna, and is keeping up his lofty role of the Hidalgo! — But haven't you noticed that *Brendel* is also attaining this high pitch? From that little note he inserted in his last issue (in the Augsburg Gazette), you will see that my talk with him wasn't in vain. I am curious to see how the Augsburg Gazette will take it —

I've seen Mme. von Prokosch [4] here two or three times. Contrary to her customary invalid habits (she has bad eye-trouble, and never budges from her house) she came to Thursday's Concert and the one we just had — and she is sending the *Dante* Program to her husband, who will find time to read about "the gates of Hell" during the hours he sits around at the "Sublime Gateway"! — [5] I am sorry not to have found her at Vienna, where she might have been of great help to me.

Consider all this as a telegram announcing my *relative triumph* at Prague, which may also act as Prelude for a *Lament* [6] at Vienna

— but come what may, we will imitate Boccage [7] and *remain respectable!*

F.L.

May the Good Lord shower you with His dearest, tenderest mercies —

LETTER 41

[Pesth] April 2, (58 —)
3 o'clock —

Without Magnolette, no party — Thus I am coming to demand my little bouquet and the sight of your pretty little face, even more blooming; since both are due me on this day — [1] I know that you prayed to God for me, and that later you drank to my health, didn't you? How I would have liked to have been near you! — but, oh dear, I still have to endure another twenty days away! My Mass [2] will probably be performed a week from Sunday, here at the City Church; [3] and although I really want to get away from here before, I can do nothing else but stay until that day — When I return to Vienna, I'll also have to spend three days there (in order to discuss the subject of *Jankó*, whose libretto I will bring back for you, with Beck [4] and Mosenthal [5]) — then almost immediately I'll go to Prague before going to Löwenberg.[6] From there I'll take off for the Altenburg, but in any case not before the end of the month! —

My stay at the Karacsony's [7] is very quiet this time. He is convalescing and his wife is still ill. Today, for instance, we didn't even see each other the whole time. On the other hand, Leo Festetics [8] paid me a visit and offered me as hommage some Hungarian compositions of his making that he has had published by Härtel. These are *12 Songs and Tunes without Words*: very good for him, although really not of any great value. Accustomed as I am to appreciating and sometimes admiring the pieces by my friends who don't admire mine at all which are not to my taste (like Joachim, Raff, Brahms,[9] etc.), I shall continue this same treatment with Festetics, by praising his Songs without caring at all what he thinks or says about my Mass and my symphonic poems.

I have just this moment received the telegram from Abbé and Abette,[10] which was delayed for at least an hour, because it was addressed to K.'s[11] *Ofen*[12] house, and I am staying at the one in Pest. Thank you, thank you, my dear sweethearts, for having evoked good St. Francis to intercede so much for me this day. When I arose, I went to the nearby Franciscan Church, and joined in spirit with you both, at the foot of the Cross! —

Up to the 8th of April, then, write me at Pest; and beg Minette to excuse me if I don't write her for two or three days — I have to correct proofs for Holle[13] and write a pile of local correspondence —

Give my most friendly and affectionate regards to Scotland, and *bedeck* the floors and the walls of the Altenburg for

your

Fainéant.

I am *very happy* about your fine friendship with Cosette, and charmed by the good success of your Berlin campaign — If you write Cosette, tell her of my leaving for Löwenberg around the 18th or 20th of April —

LETTER 42

Prague, April 20, '58.

Hello again from Prague, dearest Magnolette! — It's a great temptation, I assure you, for me to come back *right away*; because I can't explain to myself at all how it is that I can have anything else to do but to serve you, look at you, and be forever near you. Thus, when I awoke this morning, my heart felt lighter at the thought that I was already twelve hours closer to you! Our excellent friend Meissner was waiting for me at the station last night, and I felt better to see the face of one of *our* friends from the Altenburg — The rest of the world reminds me of Bedlam broken loose; and God help me to know as little about it as possible. —

When I get back with you again, I think I'll have a great many little things to tell you; but now I can only think of seeing you again as fast as I can — in ten days, I hope —

Tell Minette to write me at *Löwenberg* (at Prince H.'s[1] in Silesia), where I shall arrive after tomorrow evening (Friday).

If she could send me about a hundred crowns they'd be very welcome, as I don't think I have enough in my wallet to get back from there; — for Mr. Daniel took his holidays in Dresden and Berlin with part of the funds (in crowns) I had kept for my return. Excuse these details and my poverty, which your magic wand shall change into richness. — Speaking of Mr. Daniel, he got back to Vienna two days after me, and is once again settled in Tausig's room at the Empress Elizabeth Hotel. His Catholic leanings, it seems, are becoming more and more pronounced; and Tausig informs me that his thoughts revolve incessantly about the circle of truths, by which our Holy Mother the Church gives us our true liberty in making us God's prisoners and the coheritors of Jesus Christ. Daniel always maintains much reserve and a fair amount of embarrassment towards me. On the whole it's better that way, and I shall do nothing to change it. At Dresden, where I shall stop for just a few hours (to see Drähseke[2]), I shall make a brief visit to Mme. Krokow's,[3] once more to encharge her with D.[4] on whom she evidently has a strong influence —

Please, dearest Magnolette, give my very sincere regards to M. *Philotechnus*:[5] who has, among other merits, that of being more royalist than the king. His article is exquisite and excellent; the picturesque erudition that bloomed there, with the names of Bunzino,[6] Pordonone,[7] Cignani,[8] Crayer,[9] Polimenes,[10] Castiglione,[11] etc., etc. was very well handled; and the extension of Schwind's [12] witticism, "These fine folk ask for a giant, but he only has to be bigger than a dwarf," struck home. In the same issue, Dräseke's article on Orpheus [13] also pleased me greatly — above all by the complete understanding he demonstrated of the structure of the piece, and his praise of the final measures for which I have a weakness.

In the way of little details, I can tell you that after the supper we gave for Laub [14] the day before yesterday, Monday, (at the Archduke Charles Hotel) where about forty persons got together, I played the two first portions of the Schubert [15] Hungarian Divertissement with *Dachs* [16] (not our Dachshund!); [17] and afterward Hanslick asked me if I wouldn't do him the honor of playing the 3rd with him. I acceded very gracefully, and he played his part wonderfully. If only this little incident could later become a *symbol* and *omen* for the happy alliance [18] of Art and Criticism — We could ask nothing better than to have these gentlemen play the *bass* — as long as it weren't faulty and we kept good time. Beyond that, I was not willing to play a *Solo*. I left this *extra* exclusively to Mme. Banffy; and the musical evening (or rather night, since we sat down to eat at 10:15 and didn't begin to have any music until after midnight) ended with a 4-handed march by Winterberger and myself. Tausig and Daniel, who had been invited, stayed home —

Edouard,[19] Haslinger,[20] Doppler,[21] Winterberger, and Daniel went as far as the coach with me yesterday morning. Zellner wasn't there; and I'll have to take into account several stops with him, so we don't have a falling out, I suppose. Measure and proportion is necessary in everything; there really is none, between his demands and the services he renders me. His wife, sister-in-law, father-in-law, and brother-in-law, form a burden impossible to shoulder; and what is worse, they discredit him! — I am sorry for him, but I fear there is no longer any cure; and if there is, he will have to find it with his own strength, and not with my purse. I already have to reproach myself for being too easy in this respect. Tell Minette not to write him until I get back. Z.[22] has kept the Dante Score, and he will probably do the musical analysis she has requested — After we have chatted, we'll see what there is and isn't for him to do —

I am most impatient to know what opinion you have of *Janko*, whose script and the whole first act I sent you; and I'm asking Minette to write me *without any reservations*. It seems to me that I might do something with it; Mosenthal is accommodating with all the changes that are asked of him; and I hope that there will be some way of getting Janko really started, on the one definite condition that Minette doesn't consider the thing impossible and would give me advice, help, and support. I think I've written her that the inauguration of the Monument of the Palatine Joseph[23] (father of Archduke Stephen)[24] will take place in *May of '60* — This would be the favorable moment for the first performance in Pest — I shall have all this time to write my Score, and to translate the text during the course of next year; because this year I *have* to keep my promise and *finish* Elizabeth,[25] of greater concern to me than anything else since this work was specially planned for *Minette*: Johanna-Karo-lyne Elizabeth. Kiss her with all my heart's tenderness, and keep your love for him who lives only for and through you

F.L.

I shall write a few words from Dresden the day after tomorrow in the morning — Meissner has invited me for tonight, after the theater —

LETTER 43

Good news, dearest Magne! I shall leave from Berlin on *Saturday* morning, and will get to you shortly after luncheon time. Tell Minette that I would have gladly telegraphed her this time, had it not been that the telegraph office was 3 hours from here (at Bunslau);[1] and I hesitated to use the Prince's[2] carriages. Minette's letter, with the announcement of the Court Concert, arrived for me last night after the Postman left. Please let M. von Vitzthum know that I shall be at His Highness's command after Sunday. Only let us keep Saturday afternoon and evening for ourselves. I am happy to the point of idiocy at the thought of seeing you again, and I'm jealous of Tausig for beating me to it by two or three days!

At long last *Saturday*! — If by chance there is any delay, I will telegraph you from Berlin — You probably shan't have any more letters from me; tomorrow morning I am leaving from here with choirmaster Seifriz,[3] in order to attend a Concert at *Görlitz*[4] where several artists from the Prince's Chapel are taking part. Görlitz is 4 hours from here and virtually on my way to Berlin, where I shall arrive Friday morning at 5 o'clock.

If Minette writes me, tell her to send it to Berlin, Anhaltstrasse,[5] where her letter will reach me until after tomorrow evening, (Friday).

Excuse me, my dearest Magnolette, if I have no other idea for today but to be near you, as

Your *own* and your *darky*

F.L.

Löwenberg,
Wednesday, April 28, '58 —

Bülow played at the Princess von Preussen's last night, and she was kind enough to have me also invited via Hans. He received a note here from Countess Hake.[6] I asked him to apologize for me with my thanks and excuses as well as he could. Please thank Minette, too, for apologizing to Vitzthum about my small inclination to endure the forced labor of Piano Solos, since these seem to me to be truly unseasonable. Nevertheless, because I remember the Grand Duke of Baden with great kindness, I will perform with good grace if *it is necessary* or *fitting*.

LETTER 44

[Gotha, December 6, 1858]

Here I come to chat with you, my dearest Magnette, and to tell you how I am counting the hours I find so long, away from home. From the lines I wrote to Minette yesterday, you must already know that I have to wait until Wednesday now before getting back. In the meantime, here's a little sketch of my two days here —

Arriving here the day before yesterday (at 11 o'clock), I first took lodgings at the *Lion*, where I stayed only about an hour, for as soon as Wangenheim[1] knew of my arrival, the Hof-Courier[2] called to tell me that Milord[3] had reserved rooms for me at the castle. I immediately came here and took possession of a small living-room with a Piano, and a bedroom furnished with elegant comfort. The foyer both *joins* and *separates* my apartment and Dingelstedt's[4] — who didn't arrive until the 8 o'clock evening train, along with Pütlitz,[5] Platen,[6] (from Hanover) and Tempeltey[7] — all similarly housed at the castle, as well as the author of the libretto for *Diana of Solange*, Otto Prechtler.[8] He naturally has had his quarters here for the past few days, and had a double celebration yesterday: the performance of his opera, preceded in the morning with his Decoration by Grand Duke Ernest. Küken,[9] who also came with Dingelstedt, took the room I'd occupied at the Lion.

The dress rehearsal was set for 4 o'clock. The Duke came to see me an hour before, and talked most amiably and wittily, as he always does, about one thing and another. He didn't neglect to tell me that his new work couldn't fail to meet with a success as immediate as it would be complete — and this was in the same tone that he used with Platen yesterday (who repeated it to me still more clearly), when he said that no matter how slightly people might give it countenance, this success would attain at least the level of the *Huguenots*.[10] In Diana of Solanges there is not merely a profusion of Tunes and of striking scenes rushing in a *crescendo* from start to finish —

sure-fire effects which good singers can turn to an extraordinary advantage; but even more, the composer has courageously made use of the best of Wagner's ideas pertaining to the structure of the work. This includes the logical distribution of *Scenes*, instead of the old style with Airs, Duets, etc. In short, the new Score joins the virtues of Meyerbeer and Wagner — and I should add, for myself, even those of Verdi.[11] Thus it provides a triple alliance [12] between France, Germany, and Italy.

I was completely convinced by the dress rehearsal that the composer followed his own bent, and I could only applaud the happy success of his ideas. There was a large supper at 8:30 on Saturday, at which Her Grace the Duchess appeared — and after the supper we got together at Dingelstedt's — for cigars — and quite interesting talk.

Yesterday (Sunday) like today, lunch at 10 o'clock (in frock-coats, without the Duchess) for the guests of the *house* alone — the Chamberlains and Marshals of the Court shine by their *absence* — and a Gala Dinner at 4:30 — M. von Lüttichau [13] had come yesterday morning, and along with Dingelstedt and Platen composed a most impressive *Intendantish* Triumvirate —

I am being interrupted by a visit from Milord — and have time only to kiss your hands and hug Minette.

Tomorrow Meiningen,[14] and Wednesday Dinner at home.

Monday morning —

LETTER 45: Preface

The reference in this letter to Fallmerayer and Zeissing is interesting in that it reveals Liszt's constant preoccupation with aesthetic theory. The influence of Zeissing's master, Hegel, on Liszt's general thought about the arts is evident in the essay *Berlioz und seine "Harold-Symphonie"* (1855), Liszt's most ambitious literary attempt to justify the school of program music. After a lengthy preface, where Liszt demonstrates the historical precedents for his creative technique by alluding to "non-absolute" compositions by Bach, Kuhnau, Beethoven, Mendelssohn, and Spohr, he points to Berlioz as the first musician consciously to employ the programmatic form — and certainly the first composer to assert the necessary, rather than the accidental, formal elements in such a structural scheme. Hegel's *Ästhetik* is cited frequently; and the reader of the *Berlioz* essay is continually aware of the long line of German philosophic speculation behind Liszt's intellectual endeavor. There is much talk of genius being the mediator between Art and Nature — an example of a typically Hegelian triadic mode of thought; and Liszt asserts that the musician aims at following "the Law of Assimilation" in order adequately to incorporate spirit in its embodiment.

That Liszt saw the dangers of program music leading to mere natural imitation — Strauss's *Domestic Symphony* may be taken as a supreme example of this musical aberration — is a tribute to his intelligence. Again, his way out of a possible intellectual impasse is via the elaborate and meandering route of German Idealism. The new music, particularly in its orchestral manifestations, is the highest and most unified expression of the world of idea. Because music, of all the arts, is farthest from the region of simple phenomenal experience — a concept treated with brilliant insight by Schopenhauer — it is therefore placed at the summit of the aesthetic hierarchy. The imitations of natural sounds is but a naïve stage in the eventual realization of the true meaning of music and the proper awareness of its function. In any case, the old forms are outmoded, and progress — that god of the nineteenth century — demands that one abandon the sonata, the rondo, and all the other heritage of musical classicism.

The last portion of the essay contains some fascinating discussions about the relation of the epic to music. One is tempted to wonder, with perhaps excessive cynicism, from whom Liszt borrowed the ideas — although German Romanticism from the Schlegels to Wagner abounds in endless speculations about the place of the epic in modern times; and Liszt's arguments are best considered as part of the baggage of his contemporary aesthetics. The eighteenth-century oratorio and cantata were suitable musical representations of the simple and primitive epic (and here Liszt is negligent in providing us with illustrations). But the *modern* "philosophic epic" — Byron's *Cain* and Goethe's *Faust* — requires a more inward and subjective vehicle. This is to be the mission of the program music of the future.

Up to this section one feels Wagner and Liszt to be in agreement, and the essay might well have been written by the former as by the latter; but Liszt's subsequent and final denunciation of the inadequacy of the opera marks his own unique point of departure. The spoken word, he says, forces music to concern itself with mere externality and makes music the handmaid of the drama. The word is also the tool of the world of physical phenomena with which music has no concern.

Furthermore, the stage is too limited, and its demands and those of music can only inevitably lead to an irreconcilable clash of forms.

The *Berlioz* essay, despite its cumbersome terminology and elephantine reasoning, is worth reading. As an apology for Liszt's own technical method in composition it is revealing. More important in terms of the whole development of nineteenth-century music, it stands as one of the major attempts to explain the theoretical basis for program music. For those who cast off on Liszt as a serious thinker and who regard him as an extravagant musical charlatan and exhibitionist, the essay is an effective antidote: the work of no light-weight intellectual dilettante, but rather of a serious — albeit limited — artist who tried to grapple with one of the principal musical problems of his day. (Cf. Liszt, *Gesammelte Schriften*, ed. Ramann, Leipzig: Breitkopf & Härtel, 1880–1883, vol. IV, pp. 1–94 *passim*.)

LETTER 45

Löwenberg, May 6, '59.

Before leaving this room, I want to tell you that I thought of you constantly while I was there, my dearest Magne —

These six days went by very quietly for me, and the sole events were your letters from Munich. Except for a walk over Hohlstein [1] Castle, built rather recently without any style on top of an old cavernous rock — I have scarcely moved from the house, and thus imitate the way of life of the Prince: [2] he is convinced that his feet no longer support him, and has been spending seven-eighths of his time in bed for the past five months. He ate with us last night, however, for the first time, and was in extremely good humor and full of anecdotes. Among others, he told very amusingly how King Ludwig [3] put a whole crowd of *august* visitors into commotion at Tegernsee. [4] He arrived suddenly and commanded, via the Court Marshal, the King of Prussia, the Duke of Brunswick, [5] the Duke of Darmstadt, [6] and himself the Prince von Hohenzollern — to change their black ties into white ties in a hurry, since His Bavarian Majesty had a horror of the informality of black ties. — On another occasion, the English Minister presented one of his countrymen at Court in a black tie. King Ludwig turned purple with rage; and he had no peace until this subject of His Britannic Majesty was thrown out. This just missed causing a brawl between England and Bavaria, as

Milord scarcely found these severities in etiquette to his taste. — Prince H. imitates King Ludwig's *speech* to perfection (to whom, of course, he does justice for the great things he has done); and he amused himself hugely, by repeating with the accent and gestures of the royal spouse, the sacramental phrase he used for his wife[7] at every turn: "Theresa, you are a Tcherman woman!" —

While I'm on the subject of anecdotes, I'll tell you another one at the risk of being a little lengthy, and without guaranteeing its authenticity. A few weeks ago, M. Lenormand[8] (from the Institute) went to Rome to have his son blessed by the Holy Father. Pius IX[9] questioned him at length about France and the Emperor:

"What do you think about Louis-Napoleon's faith? — "

"Holy Father, it's hard for a Catholic to judge the faith of another Catholic. — "

"Nonetheless, I want to know your opinion — "

M. Lenormand, quite embarrassed by His Holiness's persistence, finally cleared himself; and he said that the Pope himself might well judge the religious sentiments of any King who wears in *one medallion* around his neck, a relic of the Holy Virgin, and a charm belonging to Mohammed, given him by the Sultan before the Crimean War.[10]

"What superstition!" cried the Pope —

They then spoke about something else, and M. Lenormand was excused. The Holy Father went with him to the door, which he closed — and then suddenly reopened it, and said to M. Lenormand "I really think that this man must be the evil beast of the Apocalypse."[11] (This last point is less apparent than the attribute of "Tcherman Woman" for Queen Theresa!) No matter what it is, the Emperor L.N. has shown that he doesn't lack the *cunning of a snake*, since the pigeon-like sweetness of M. Walewski's[12] last proclamation failed to convince everyone!

———————

I shall leave this room tonight, as well as the beautiful paintings by Bassano[13] (a large forge, a Holy Family) Pordenone, Franceschini,[14] and *Finkenboom*[15] (a landscape!) that decorate it.

In the room above, there is the famous fish-market painted by the *two* Teniers;[16] some Hobbema[17] landscapes; Salvator Rosa,[18] Bakhuysen,[19] Ruysdael;[20] a lovely head (three-quarter view) by Andrea del Sarto;[21] a charming Cupid by Guido Reni;[22] a small

Madonna by Francia,[23] etc. Several of these paintings probably come from the Sagan Gallery, since the Duchess was forced to make a distribution that in no way pleased her! —

I shall get to Breslau (the Zedlitz Hotel) tomorrow morning for the rehearsal of the Damrosch Concert, which seems to have been settled for Monday. I will tell you all about it later. Tuesday evening I shall start back for Weimar, where I plan to call on Scotland by Thursday morning. Please ask our most beloved to take note exactly of what I wrote in my yesterday's letter, concerning the address of her letters. If she writes me later than Sunday *morning's* mail, it will have to go to Weimar or better to *Brendel* at Leipzig; since I will see him in any case at the train, and even arrange it in such a way as to spend 3 or 4 hours in Leipzig. I have taken the necessary arrangements here for my letters to be forwarded to me at Breslau.

I am delighted that Abbé enjoyed Fallmerayer's [24] nasty remarks, and that you have also been seeing Zeissing [25] again. If there were any way at all to incorporate the latter with the "German Music",[26] it would be a very nice gain. He formerly knew Brendel, and perhaps he might decide occasionally to honor the columns of the "Neue Zeitschrift" with his fine style. — I am very much counting on you to indoctrinate him, as I also am counting on you to explain the secrets of the "Golden Model" to Fainéant: a method I would really like to apply to my own compositions. Mme. Zeissing gave me the impression of being a very well-bred-woman — have you seen her again? —

Thank Abbé for me for her invitation and conversation with Lachner.[27] I sincerely wish for peace — but for it to last, there must be mutually acceptable conditions.

Don't you think that Heyse [28] rather than Roquette would be more suitable, to arrange the 7 crows [29] as an opera? — The animal kingdom is certainly all the rage now in the opera — following Lohengrin's swan and Ploermel's [30] goat, the 7 crows ought certainly to have their fling! — As for me, I have no objection against it, providing that you always are good enough to keep me as

Your "domestic and travelling lap-dog" —

to be this is my glory and my joy.

F. Liszt

Please turn the page and read with Abbé —

"I pledge Abbé and Magnette less and less to deserve my title of Fainéant; and at the risk of cutting my six minutes down by a half, to be ready with the scores of Elizabeth and Kuma [31] at the indicated time, about a year from now."

May 6, '59 —   (ex-) Fainéant —

Please tell Abbé one more thing. My Iron Crown [32] decoration arrived a few hours before I left Weimar, and I put it under Miss Anderson's care.

(Don't be worried if I am a little late writing you from Breslau). It is likely that I'll see a great many people there. Bronsart is coming with me. Brendel has been back in Leip. [33] since the day before yesterday.)

LETTER 46

What wonders you do accomplish with me dearest Magnette! And now if it isn't my poor old symphonic poems, marching out triumphantly just like Esther, and followed by the most illustrious cortege of contemporary names that one could imagine! We will have to add also, to all our dearest Abbé's titles and nicknames, that of Ahasuerus! [1] Fainéant cannot recover from the shock of seeing all his unhappiness thus transformed into fame by you! — Only remain my guardian angels and my sweetest patronesses, my dears, and God will grant me the favor someday of singing you all my love.

Thank Kolb [2] and Baermann [3] for me, for the fine idea they had (or which was given them) about this morning's performance.* I felt a child-like joy at reading the letter of invitation, and to see my poor works attain their *true* goal for the first time: that of "being performed in your honor". Before publishing them, I sent a little casket to Minette with a few words written on it, telling her my plan to this effect. When Elizabeth is finished, Magnette, too, will have her little casket . . . with all kinds of explanations! —

* Don't you think it would be fitting to *pin* them up (as does Pohl with the dedications to his poems): now, however, while maintaining a slight difference between Pohl and Baermann, and not to the disparagement of the latter? I leave this little matter up to you —

Speaking of explanations, but of a completely different variety, I thought I had told you that M. Sach formally announced to me that he would not thank Heyse for the dedication to his *Thecla*.[4] M. S.[5] found it good to impose a kind of *regimen* upon a poet who, according to him, had not provided an adequate return for the advances made to him. Heyse would therefore be mistaken in attributing this temporary coolness to me; since Sach's silence is deliberate on his part, to use the phrase. It was only desired to let him know that more than mere literary relations were expected of him; and this wouldn't have been demanding excessive devotion to the person and whims of M. Sach, as a compensation for the prodigous kindness evidently wasted on Heyse. As usual, M. Sach attained his goal perfectly. If there is a way to do it, try to indicate sweetly the *softened* lineaments of these mighty dealings to Heyse. In any case, our poet-friend may be quite certain of a favorable reception for his June visit; and M. Sach won't have any rest until he has softened those stubborn persons who oppose the fulfillment of his desire . . . to take H. away to Munich!

I shan't fail to follow the instructions that Abbé has given me regarding Geibel[6] — at the same time without too much hope of success, since Dudin[7] is more stubborn than it seems.

Judas Maccabeus[8] is announced for tomorrow — and I have written to Brendel that I shall go to Leipzig on Saturday. Allow me to drop a small hint about this. I'd prefer you not to come to Leipzig until toward the end of next week. Fifty bad little reasons would prevent my being with and for you during these first days of preparation. Please be sweet enough to agree with me — and tell Abbé, that in case you leave Munich Saturday (as she has written me) it would be better to return to Weimar — where *I shall come to see you* in the interim, and where we can chat day and night in our *blue room* before going back to Leipzig. 4 or 5 days of the *Music Festival* is all you can stand, unless you're absolutely made to take more! After Munich, Leipzig will seem more unbearable to you than ever. Thus, let me *get your lodgings* ready for you and only arrive there on Sunday, the 30th of this month.

I exhibited your portrait[9] in the salon, already gloomy with your absence — This photograph gives a little *joy* to the house — and no matter what Scotland may say, I find K.'s portrait excellent and very much to my liking. There is, I find, an indefinable relation between the pose of this portrait and my memory of the "*Ideal*" crown you had, when I returned to the Altenburg last year.

I've just come back from Their Highnesses' — Judas Maccabeus has been postponed until *Friday*, due to the anniversary of the death of the Duchess of Orleans. (May 18th) — Is it possible that our friend Dudin might feel such delicate solicitude! but one should not lend to the rich, but only to the good Lord, while giving to the poor! I shall dine at Her Highness's on Saturday, as she has just deigned to inform me. She refuses to let me beg off a second time. I had to do this yesterday, owing to the rehearsal which kept me at the theater from 4 to 9 o'clock — I have to go back there today at 4 for a general rehearsal.

Here are a few words from my mother.[10] After more than 30 years in Paris, she still hasn't learned the simple idiomatic expression of *spendthrift!* — I am appending Dudin's [11] lines as an autograph.

I'll see you soon, my dearest Magnette — and I kiss both your dear hands with reverence, while remaining your very faithful

May 17, '59 — Weimar.   Haus Pudel.

I shall write to Abbé at length tomorrow morning. My Brendel correspondence and the proofs (of my *Lieder*) I have to correct, will take me all day, without including the rehearsal.

LETTER 47

[Berlin]

Praises and Blessings upon you, dearest Magnette!

Since 9 yesterday morning I've been settled at Hans's and Cosette's, who are strongly opposed to my taking back my room at the Hotel Brand;[1] and they have put a very nice bed in the Piano room. All of yesterday was spent chatting and making music. Hans's pieces (a Mazurka and an Impromptu) delighted me, and Minette now has one more reason, out of a thousand, for singing their praises to me. — In the evening friend Kroll [2] appeared, and we spent the time most cordially —

Poor Daniel looks badly, even though he is getting better. He still coughs a great deal — but Büking [3] (whom I shall see tomorrow morning) promises to pull him through.

This morning I saw Eggers (whom I shall tell you about) for a long time, and also Hildebrand,[4] who is staying in the same house with Schmitser.[5] I missed him — but he will probably come to Cosette's this evening — The latter with Hans and Daniel, insist emphatically that I don't leave before Sunday morning; and if you have nothing in particular for me to do tomorrow evening, I shall doubtlessly conform to their wishes. Don't expect me, then, until Sunday *lunch* * and take care of my apologies to the usual crowd at the so-called Sunday *matinée*. — If you don't have anything better to do, we three can go to the Church Concert to hear the "Beatitudes" [7] at 4 o'clock —

Kiss Minette sweetly for me — and may both of you be tenderly extolled and blessed a thousand and one times, by your most humble

[*September 30, '59.*]   Fainéant.

LETTER 48: *Preface*

The two chief events for Liszt during 1859 were his award of the Order of the Iron Crown by the Austro-Hungarian government and the marriage of Marie.

The first of these revives the unsettled problem of Liszt's social snobbery. That he drew most of his friends — and certainly his two leading mistresses — from the aristocracy is indisputable, and certainly the younger musician enjoyed the countless descriptions of himself as the "natural aristocrat." The myth of the Romantic hero as haughty, proud, disdainful, and usually nobly-born was one that he shared and even helped to formulate. The Austrian monarchy and the various German states created a horde of minor nobility throughout the century, and particules were showered upon the wealthy bourgeoisie and the intellectuals in what one feels was an attempt to shore up a tottering aristocracy. For the most part Liszt regarded this largesse of "von's" with mild amusement (cf. his remarks about Fallersleben and Dingelstedt); yet in April 1859 he accepted the Iron Crown and its accompanying patent of nobility with high seriousness. In a letter to Carolyne, for

---

* or lunsch, as Baron von Buttstend [6] used to say!

example (*L.M.* I, No. 339), he quotes the statutes appertaining to the award: "Paragraph 20 of the statutes concerning the Iron Crown: "All knights of the order also receive, differences of rank notwithstanding, the right of entry to all Court Banquets and appertaining ceremonies . . . 2nd Class Knights, if they desire, may attain the status of baronets, and 3rd Class Knights may be raised to the tax-exempt status of Knight-hood.'" In the same letter we find him considering adding his birthplace to his name; i.e., Franz Liszt von Raiding! Apparently Carolyne, whose advice he asked, disapproved, and there is no further mention of the matter.

The marriage of Marie on October 15, 1859, to Prince Constantine (Konstantin) von Hohenlohe-Schillingsfürst (1828–1896), while of some concern for Carolyne, was met with great joy by Liszt. The young man had promise — he had served as aide-de-camp to Franz-Josef during the Italian campaign — and the family was illustrious: the oldest brother, Chlodwig, Herzog von Ratibor, was already a prominent statesman and later became German Chancellor, while another brother, Gustav, was to be a Cardinal high in the affairs of the German Catholic Church. The family must have displayed some displeasure about Carolyne's relations with Liszt, and their feeling was known to Carolyne; for when her own marriage was blocked at the last dramatic moment by the Church, she put the major responsibility on the Hohenlohes — particularly on Cardinal Gustav — and for some eight years refused to see her daughter or to allow Liszt to correspond with Marie. (This was the probable reason for the hiatus in this correspondence from 1860 until 1869. The abrupt manner in which Letter 61 commences, however, leads one to think that intervening letters may have existed and are now lost.)

LETTER 48

The charming watch Your very sweet, kind, and Serene High-ness sent to me on October 22nd,[1] delighted me. The hand will not go by an hour without my heart overflowing with the tender, deeply grateful memories of the hours and hours that God granted me to spend near you. May He also grant me to be forever useful to you, in no matter what offices! or no matter how slight a degree! — You know how completely I remain Your slave — and this is neither an *empty word* nor a *metaphor!*

Minette won't get back yet for another two or three days, and she seemed happy with her stay in Paris. While she spent her days shopping, she also found time to see several well-known persons. Pauline Viardot [2] arranged a small evening party in her honor, with five or six excerpts from Berlioz's new opera, "The Trojans," [3] which she thought superb and the newspapers spoke wonders about. She'll tell you about it when she gets back.

Without mixing in things that are no business of mine, I suppose, however, that the changes effected in the Vienna [4] *powers-that-be* will not delay your establishing yourselves at Teinfalts Street.[5] The ministerial rule of my old quasi-friend M. von Hübner [6] was rather transitory — and that of Count Grunne [7] may well last longer, under the more *limited* guise of his actual position as Master of the Horse. Time will show. As for M. de Crenneville,[8] he'll have — as they say — to make his own bed, nay even turn it up with skill, if he wants to take a new line of action with any kind of facility.

Several letters have arrived for me from Vienna on the occasion of the performance of my 1st Mass (for men's voices). It took place last Sunday at the Church of the Augustinians, under Herbeck's [9] direction, as celebration for the anniversary (I don't know which one) of the *Founding of the Men's Choral Society*. According to what I am told, both the work and its performance made an equally good impression; and the church was crowded to overflowing.

How good you are, a thousand times over, thus to bother yourself with our fine old Hoffmann! The position of Librarian at Corvey [10] would suit him, in effect, as well as he suits it. Furthermore, I've heard said recently by persons well-up in library matters, that formerly he was of great service to the Breslau library; and his outline, *"Divisions and Cataloguing"* etc., which he had adopted, is still in use. The Duke of Ratibor [11] can verify this when he goes through Breslau —

I spoke in deepest confidence to Hoffmann (advising him in particular not to whisper a word to his wife) of your well-meaning plans on his behalf. He would accept this job with the greatest pleasure, and promises to leave nothing undone in order to make himself of value. If such would be the case, he has told me already in advance that he would undertake the studies and research about Corvey. The folios and manuscripts which are still necessary are to be found there in part. From 6 to eight-hundred crowns would be sufficient as salary — particularly if, as he hopes, he might retain his *Prussian Attendant's Wages* of roughly 450 crowns. It wouldn't be impossible, since the Corvey Library is a special establishment; and the Duke of Ratibor has more say in this regard than has anyone else. You must recall that Hoffmann kept his 450 Thalers of *Prussian Attendant's Wages* during the three years the Grand Duke extended his munificence to the *Weimar Year-Book*, edited by Hoffmann — Then, too, the fact that Corvey is in Prussia would be another item in his favor; and once Hoffmann is assured that he would not lose his *Wages*, in this case a salary of 600 Thalers with quarters, and perhaps as much firewood as he could use, would be sufficient.

If the Duke of Ratibor decided to give this position to Hoffmann, he will have in his employ a professor who knows all there is to know about classifying the Library facilities, editing the catalogs thereof, and who would gain for it all the possible fame and renown, through his conscientious rummaging-around. — In brief, Hoffmann would be a capable faithful servant for him * — and one who would also sing the Duke's praises in excellent dedicatory verses and toasts, if ever Milord would allow him. This would be no trouble — Thus you can recommend the affair to him, as a nice, good, deed to be done — and which would be perfectly sensible in the bargain (*really sensible* as the English say), and one offering the very best chances of bringing in a good *income* (if you don't want to limit this word to immediate and palpable pecuniary benefits). Such opportunities don't always present themselves with every nice, good deed — quite to the contrary — but that shouldn't deter us in this occasion; since we are on this earth to sow rather than to reap.

Excuse me for having been so long-drawn-out on this subject; my conscientiousness in these concerns is my only claim to pedantry, I feel, and you're well-accustomed to bear with it.

Please remember me, my dear Princess, to Constantine, and do maintain your good, sweet charm (as a good deed).

for your most constantly
grateful slave

October 27, '59.
Weimar.

F. Liszt.

* All his merits or faults notwithstanding —

Scotchy is still very saddened by your departure — but your letter of the day before yesterday did much to revive her spirits and comfort her.

In my next letter, I'll talk to you about our Schiller-Festival and other Weimarian diversions and entertainments.

LETTER 49

Although I am not able to pack myself in person into the trunks that have given Minette so much anxiety, I shall profit, however, from their dispatch, to send to you all my best wishes for a very good trip and a still happier return! May you always feel yourself warmly sheltered from Pet's [1] cold blasts by the nice wraps that are sent you, and which, in this case, you may regard as a symbol of our love! —

Our own winter here will be wan and grey — for consolation, I shall let the ink fairly snow on my Music-paper! I hope St. Elizabeth comes to my aid, and I shall try to remember you, in order to give my Saint's countenance the compelling grace with which I would like to endow her.

In the course of the winter, you'll hear the Prometheus again in Vienna (under Herbeck's direction) at one of the Concerts of the Philharmonic Society. Tausig, who returned to the Altenburg yesterday (from Warsaw) is also planning a surprise visit to you in Vienna. He leaves for Pest in a few days, and will doubtless spend the winter between Hungary and Vienna.

As for news, only what you give interests us — consequently, I have nothing to impart to you for the moment. Despite M. and Mme. Sach's strong entreaties, I shall fulfill, bit by bit, my absolutely *negative* [2] Program just as you know it, and when spring comes, we'll see what ought to be done.

May the Good Lord accompany you, and may His good angels make it their duty to see that all your wishes come true!

November 25, '59 —   F.L.

LETTER 50: Preface

The death of Liszt's son Daniel is treated so brusquely in this letter to Marie — and indeed another written at the same time to Carolyne (*L.M.* I, No. 360) reveals scarcely any more genuine feeling — that one is tempted to wonder about the depth of Liszt's affection for his three children. Perhaps it is unfair to expect an outburst such as Hugo's *À Villequier* —

> *Je verrai cet instant jusqu'à ce que je meure,*
> *L'instant, pleurs superflus!*
> *Où je criai: L'enfant que j'avais tout à l'heure,*
> *Quoi donc! Je ne l'ai plus!*

— yet Liszt's attitude is too close for comfort to that of Rousseau, who blithely sent his progeny to the *Enfants-Trouvés*. Liszt's role as the family man back in the early and mid eighteen-forties must have been already dim in his memory, and he had seen his three children only intermittently since the liaison with Marie d'Agoult.

LETTER 50

[Weimar]

I don't want to talk to you at all about my grief. You know what sad days I had to spend in Berlin. A few hours before his death, Daniel [1] said in his sleep "I am going ahead to prepare your places for you"! — So be it, and may God be blessed! —

The story you told Minette of your evening at Czarkoe-Selo [2] interested me keenly. The flowers given through the kindness of His Majesty seem to me a happy augury for the ripening of the fruits that are to follow — [3] Your two pertinent remarks *about* the paintings of the battle of Kotzebue [4] and the *compotes* were first-rate. Indeed, if one were to prepare things well ahead, one would not succeed as well!

What an admirable description you made of Raphael's Holy Family! — [5] This painting belongs all the more to us, thanks to what you've said about it.

As for Z.O., [6] *keep him in check* — I am angry at these banterers who do nothing but continue the old worn-out technique prescribed at W. [7] If this were to continue, he has nothing to do but to clear out and leave things as they were — Let's hope the powers-that-be will be so good little-by-little to see the whole simple question in its proper perspective — from a point of view at once more just and more human.

Since I suppose that Rubinstein will present his compliments to you, please tell him that I sent him, via M. von Maltitz, the Score of the "Spinning-Song" (in the 2nd Act) from the "Flying Dutchman."[8] I had it copied, as he wished. I presume that it will get to him on time; although M. von Maltitz, with the circumspection he acquired at W., made the observation that the courier may be late, that due to the shift in the regime it could even happen that there might not be any courier between W. and St. P., etc. — To increase the security, I asked M. von M. to turn the notebook over to the Berlin Legation. They will *no doubt* be sending out several Couriers in honor of the Congress of Paris.[9]

A million thanks for the news you have given us (because each time I take a goodly portion for my own)

completely at your feet

December 24, '59   F.L.

LETTER 51

[Weimar]

You never spoke more angelically, than in that letter of mourning[1] dated the day of the Feast of the Virgin. May your Holy Patroness guard you in all the paths of life, and shower you with the delights so much deserved by the holy purity of your soul! —

As for me, I shall pray *as you* asked me — and thank you from the bottom of my heart.

Cornelius, who arrived here last evening without our expecting him, will probably do a short obituary of Daniel. Hoffmann, Mosenthal, Wurzbach,[2] and several others, sent me poems on this sad event. The funeral ceremony in Vienna took place last Thursday at the *Schottenkirche.*[3] Edouard,[4] who is always the good-hearted and upright man, "reliably" took care to provide all the proper solemnities. They sang for the first time a Requiem by an Italian composer (Terziani),[5] which the Nuncio brought back from his trip to Italy. His Eminence was interested in it — he was also present at the performance.

But I don't care to go on any further with these mortuary details — It is not for death to absorb life — but rather for us to *conquer* death! So let me tell you that I have again taken up my work of writing fly-specks, in all truth a little haltingly. — I've begun by orchestrating the Schubert Marches [6] I promised Herbeck. They were already placed on the program of a philharmonic Concert at the beginning of the month — but I wasn't able to send them in time. You'll hear them during the course of the winter after you return to Vienna.

This morning Schlesinger [7] sent me your copy of the Chopin Songs,[8] humbly dedicated to you — Lassen's Songs,[9] which enjoy the same honor, are joined with them (in the proofs) — we will have to change the first sheet, since they put *Oehringen* [10] instead of *Schillingsfürst*; and your cousin might be surprised by this unexpected and accidental attention. I'll send you the two copies of the Dedication to Vienna in a few days —

Minette is very much occupied on your behalf with cataloguing your *masterpieces;* and by comparison, the most *elegant* Scores are merely the disorderly exercices of school-boys. Mother-love is like an endless ladder of fantasy and feeling, — moving to the point of being irritating — and one might put at both ends of the scale, in order to make the allegory more complete, the oldest magician and the most youthful fairy. Excuse me for making this rather far-fetched analogy, and believe me truly to be

forever your most humble slave

December 26, '59 —   F.L.

LETTER 52

[Weimar]

You speak of your *uselessness*. In all truth, there are, I believe, those physicists who claim that we can see quite well enough without the sun, and that after a fashion this lovely star is merely *useless*. Your own state is similar. —

But let's talk about some other *useless* things.

The day before yesterday (for the first time since the death of Her Highness) [1] there was a great Reception and Court Concert. Out of motives of "discretion" and "delicacy" — those are the terms that were used — Lassen was put in charge of the orchestra. Fainéant was relegated to wearing his green uniform among the spectators and to chatting with everyone. Their Highnesses were splendidly and royally bored — and the music suited their mood perfectly. I said to Mulinen [2] upon leaving: "Well, now you're even with Music" which annoyed him to the point of rage. Since Frohriep was there as a stranger, I turned to him to have him notice that *German squabbles* had become a *French speciality* at Weimar.[3] This put Mulinen back in good humor.

Tomorrow evening I'll probably go to Berlin for a few days. Count Redern [4] is having his opera "Christina of Sweden" performed (Tempeltey's text) on Monday — He invited me, in a most friendly way, to be present; and since I have maintained amicable relations with His Excellency the composer for a number of years, I feel I should give him this proof of my eagerness and past good wishes — I shan't see Hans any more, alas, as he is already on his way to Paris. On the way, or nearly so, he is to play at Basel and Cologne, at the *Male Vocal Society*, and I imagine that *he* wouldn't allow Hiller to invite him to the Gürzenich [5] Concerts, which the latter conducts. Hans's 3 evening-concerts at Berlin for the benefit of the Schiller Foundation were a great success. He has just sent me the profits (350 crowns), and these will enable the *Schiller Foundation* of Weimar to make a nice gesture to the Petersburg Committee, who made us the splendid gift of *6000* crowns! They may accept the sum without hesitating. I will explain sketchily this rather confused affair, which goes like this: The Petersburg Committee sent 6000 crowns to the Weimar one, expressing the wish that the Schiller Foundation immediately grant 300 crowns to a most deserving poet, M. Leopold Schefer [6] of Moscow, age 75. He had just been struck with an attack of apoplexy, and found himself completely penniless. At the time, the Schiller Foundation could scarcely scrape up 20 crowns; for it was not permitted to touch its capital, and hence it would have had to wait until June to get enough interest — From this point on, the various *legal advisers* fought about how to use the interest, and each tried to have his candidate put forth. It seemed almost inevitable that if Weimar proposed Schefer, the other Committees, who hold the majority, would have voted against him. So much for "German Unity"! — After a lot of tentatives, I was happily able to breach the difficulty by having Hans put his Berlin vote at my disposal with certain convenient restrictions. This now enables us to provide a means of satisfying the very legitimate desire of the Petersburg donors, and thus to come in the nick of time to the help of a very deserving person.

Excuse me for having related all these useless things to you; perhaps they'll distract you for a moment —

We ask God, morning and evening, to shower you with His blessings.

January 14, '60   F.L.

LETTER 53

[Weimar, January, 1860].

If you notice a janitor or a Swiss guard when you go into your house on Teinfaltstrasse, tell yourself that there is someone who sincerely envies him, and who would prefer his social position to that of the General Director of Music at Berlin and Munich, which the newspapers are playing up at the moment — all this, if said happy janitor has the honor of bowing to you as you go by. This is not at all a statement of gallantry but rather one *of principle*, if you please; and behind it I have the strength of a hundred thousand Turks! Minette treated me like a brigand, by speaking to you about my friend *Richard* [1] (how absurd, when the name is pronounced in French!) I wanted to tell you myself about our rehearsal the day before yesterday, which took place despite the previous resolution agreed upon by Mmes. Milde and Caspari,[2] and sent to Dudin, not to sing the parts they had been given. Tristan [3] shall still be given, notwithstanding, although some place else; and I gather even in the course of this year. Prague, Stettin, or Wolfenbüttel, if necessary (as long as it isn't Olmütz [4] or Brünn! [5]) would do. In the meantime, we are going to have ("Gustave") [6] Auber's Masked Ball here, with a broken-down section of the Brunswick Ballet Company and several other novelties of the *same brand*.

When you are a bit more settled at Vienna, I shall tell you the story of Ing.[7] and Bronsart's novel. It involves a most gripping *intrigue!* —

As for today, I send you my best wishes as a *Cretin* [8] (for they claim that this race brings good luck) for a happy arrival at Vienna!

F.L.

LETTER 54

It's a simple offering that I give you for this 18th of February [1] — merely my impoverished heart, bereft of all that makes for glory and fame in this world. I had arranged a little gift, however, to act as my interpreter on this date: Chopin's Songs, with your name inscribed. The binding, alas, wasn't ready in time, and it's so far from here to Vienna! Still let me be with you on this day and all others, with all my heart and soul, — to pray for you, and to remain in the years to come even as in the years past,

your very deeply
grateful servant
F. Liszt.

February 11, '60 —

Turn, please.

P.S. Since a painting ought never to be lacking on the 18th of February, there will be a Tony Johannot [2] to place itself at your feet —

LETTER 55

Well, now that Ash Wednesday is here, you've again become a little stay-at-home; cotillions will be supplanted by conversations of a more-or-less intimate variety; but with the help of a few parties and Concerts, we'll soon get to the fashionable season. Spring is really delightful in Vienna, and I presume that Constantine will be inclined to have you fully enjoy a great many walks about the neighborhood. I know no better setting for the *Pastoral Symphony* [1] than Mödling, [2] the Brühl, [3] and twenty other charming spots that are near by. Without casting off on the advantages of the Bois de Boulogne, the spectacular forests of Fontainebleau and St. Germain, and the superiority and charm of English Parks; still, the country around Vienna has a kind of more *natural* quality to it, and it would seem as if one might be happier there than almost any place else. Unfortunately, and even without being as mischievous as is Mathieu Lansberg,[4] one can foresee that this spring won't be so congenial for idylls; and the Prince Regent [5] doesn't risk a mistake, saying that "The Fellow in France will give other people some trouble" (The Man in France will give us plenty to do!) — And the biggest part of the *trouble* accrues rightly to Austria! — [6]

May your fair, good star be your guide! — and, speaking of stars, how may I thank you enough for that splendid *pair* [7] of gems shining on a blue background, which you picked out as messengers for your thoughts on the 18th of February? — I had to leave a couple of days earlier for Löwenberg; Prince Hohenzollern's party was brilliantly celebrated there by a grand ball on the 16th and a superb Concert on the 17th (where they performed the Pastoral Symphony, the Prelude to Lohengrin, *our* Tasso, and the Finale to Mendelssohn's Lorelei).[8] An hour after the Concert, I came back in a carriage; and at 1 in the morning on Saturday I was again at the Altenburg, to toast you there with Minette, Scotchi, and Cornelius (our sole guest), where for eleven years your presence alone has been a continual celebration! — The *stars* were immediately affixed on my humble self — They are much too brilliant to be worn often — but even when they aren't adorning my hands, they shall glow in my thoughts! —

Since yesterday I've taken up again my old abode in the right wing of the Duke of Gotha's [9] palace. To use a little whimsy and a mediocre pun, I might attribute myself with a little of the dignity of an "aide-de-camp" [10] [i.e., literally, "Wing-Adjutant"] in this dwelling! His Highness made me the very handsome gift of the piano-and-voice score of Diana of Solanges, published in German and French by Brandus,[11] in Paris. The double dedication to the *author of the Huguenots* [12] and *Tannhäuser*, with which the eminent composer had originally planned to adorn his work, was finally omitted. When I commented to him about it, he told me that *Giacomo* [13] had appeared only mildly flattered by the compliment of yoking together two names in such clashing harmony! As for our good friend Richard,[14] he would have doubtlessly had at least a touch of fever from it. Beethoven, Schumann, Berlioz, all would have shown themselves the same — since, alas! in our artistic world, every star plays at being Jehovah, and tells himself very seriously: I am that I am! —

As for myself, I've chosen a better role; and *am* and *remain* forever your most humble beneficiary, with all my heart and soul

Gotha — February 26, '60.   F. Liszt.

LETTER 56

Easter Sunday, '60.

Your wreath [1] will not get mixed up with any others — and no matter what Pythagoras may say, the shade of this *laurel* [2] neither inebriates nor puts one to sleep — When you get back to this room, you shall see what a fine place I have found for it — It's above my desk, near St. Francis, bordering Minette's picture (for which I've kept great affection these twelve years); and the Daguerreotype [3] reflects the branch and leaves like a mirror. The ribbon is draped over the little enameled box that holds the watch you gave me last October 22nd; [4] on the other side there is an eagle with outstretched wings, who turns his head around only to see the sun more determinedly. Okrazewski's rosary is entwined about this bronze piece — You may well imagine that for the past three weeks, all we've done is to wait for Okra's [5] arrival — Minette can neither eat nor drink nor sleep — As for me, I continue to hope and hope and hope; the way the pine and the yew retain their leaves despite the ravages of the weather.

Due to Easter Day, Mme. Sach's birthday will not be celebrated until tomorrow and the day after. Lassen's *Praise of Women* will appear tomorrow — and afterward the *New Weimar* Club is giving a big farewell supper to Hoffmann, who goes to Corvey toward the end of this month. Tuesday we shall have a large Concert at the Castle, with David [6] (from Leipzig), Mme. Ney, and perhaps Niemann.[7] I am going to have the Prelude to Tristan performed, the Grand March written by Meyerbeer for the Schiller-Festival at Paris, and my Mephisto Waltz for Orchestra (based on the episode in Lenau's Faust,[8] "The Dance in the Village Inn") — It's the only piece I have written this winter; when I've barely had time to orchestrate 3 or 4 Schubert Marches, to correct a few proofs, and to prepare various manuscripts for the printer — This last job is always a long and painful one for me. As soon as things get steadier again, I shall go back to work on *your* Elizabeth, which should be finished in three months — I want so much to do something for you — and though I am only good at doing useless things, the thought of you gives them a price beyond compare, for him who remains absolutely attached and devoted to you.

F. Liszt.

LETTER 57: Preface

Liszt's comments about the Weimar Theater and the formation of the new Academy of Fine Arts, remind us that the great days of that city's musical preëminence were drawing to a close. The succession of Intendants, each one more hostile to Liszt and his aims, has been discussed earlier as has the affair of Cornelius's *Barbier von Bagdad* on October 30, 1858 (Cf. Letter 44, Note 4). We find the musician writing to the Grand Duke in terms of bitter reproach and hurt dissatisfaction, on February 14, 1859, that "the excessively stringent and restraining limits by which I have been hemmed in, have not allowed me to continue in a manner worthy of myself or of Your Highness the functions I have fulfilled in a slip-shod way up to the present." (*Briefwechsel zwischen Franz Liszt und Carl Alexander*, ed. La Mara; Leipzig: Breitkopf & Härtel, 1909, No. 51, p. 70.)

In one sense the letter is a plea for artistic integrity and freedom from external compulsion. While Liszt is ostensibly attacking the specific interference of Dingelstedt and the general lack of coöperation on the part of the Theater staff, behind his statements is an implicit criticism of the archaic system of patronage represented by Carl Alexander — although it is equally evident that the musician had the highest personal regard for his ducal benefactor. In the same letter Liszt writes: "No matter what may be the decision Your Highness will be kind enough to take, I have no doubt that it will be for the best. I am quite aware how much the artist, or even art itself, may seem a useless luxury, and that in many ways I am no longer wanted at Weimar — that I find nothing but disdain on all sides and that everyone would like to make me shiver in a banal and bourgeois existence." (*Ibid.*)

Finally a letter from Liszt to the Grand Duke on December 4, 1859, offers his resignation: "My position at Weimar is no longer tenable . . .

in the immediate future, I shall have to find some place far from Weimar a way of life that at least will be less onerous than that here — less systematically badgered from both within and without." (*Ibid.*, No. 66, p. 84.)

Part of Liszt's motives for leaving Weimar had to do with his impending — and ill-fated — marriage with Carolyne. The complicated situation, involving her husband Prince Nicolas and the devious intrigues of the Russian Court and clergy, has been discussed in the Preface to Letter 25. The problem was somewhat simplified by the divorce granted to Carolyne by the Russian Church in March 1860. She departed for Rome soon after to obtain the necessary Papal documents and approval. Liszt stayed behind in Weimar and solicited Carl Alexander's intercession for both the Russian Czar and the Vatican Secretary of State, Cardinal Antonelli. When the musician left the Weimar Court for Rome in early August, 1861, he and his patron parted on the best of terms and with the understanding that Liszt would return whenever he desired.

LETTER 57

[Weimar — May 27, 1860]
Whitsuntide

I am deeply sorry that I haven't written you for several days! — Minette left on Ascension Day, Thursday the 17th of May. I spent more than half of last week without hearing from her — but yesterday two letters came simultaneously from Nîmes and Marseilles, and these made me feel better about the first portion of her trip. According to the plan of her itinerary, she ought to be getting to Rome today, at the very hour I am writing this to you (noontime —) — Several papers are saying, that good report has it, my marriage blessing will be performed by His Eminence the Bishop of Fulda. The "Frankfurt Journal" is careful to dress me up for the occasion with the title of *celebrated pianist*. I would almost be tempted to complain to Beurmann[1] about it, since he did my biography about 15 years ago in the collection of "Famous Contemporaries"; and it really seems to me that my name is sufficiently clear and distinct by itself, so that it might be spared the irksome encumbrance of a superannuated title. And the Augsburg Gazette, for its part, writes the surprising news that I am being put in charge of the *Euterpe* Concerts . . . in Leipzig. I'll probably ask

M. von Bronsart to direct them. At the same time, this paper, which had at least the nice taste to praise my "character" (and not as in German passports, where the word *Character* shows the individual's profession) also expresses the timid hope that Berlioz might be named to direct the Concerts at the *Drapers' Hall, to act as a balance for me.*

Here's a charming letter from Wagner, to whom I haven't written for the last six months. I telegraphed him a "Happy returns" on his birthday (May 22nd), and he answered this way, which seems to me delightful. When you've read his lines, send them to Minette in Rome — and ask her to keep them for me. The double-talk version of his letter to Berlioz is curious.

Guess how I foolishly spent my time last week? By setting, unsetting, and resetting in twenty different ways a "gibberishish" tune for these verses by Hoffmann: [2]

> *The fragrant bushes by the Au,*
> *The stalks (not Münch Bellinghausen!) with sparkling*
> *morning-dew*
> *The trees all clad in green*
> *And each one cries: I leave.*
> *Farewell; I leave!*

> etc., etc. (always with the same refrain
> "I leave — farewell — I leave")

These may be the last lines that Hoffmann wrote here. He read them with a voice full of feeling, at a farewell supper we gave him at the *New-Weimar Club.* I told him then that I would set them to music: — but he won't hold me to such a capricious wish, because I definitely have no bent for the sentimental. My faithful Achates, Cornelius, showed enough generosity, however, to find my piece a perfect success — and when and if you agree with him, I'll willingly come over to his camp.

To get back to Hoffmann, I've had good news about his position and frame of mind at Corvey, of a sort that makes me hope what *you* have so well accomplished, will be of good favor for him. In any case, one might say to him, like Frederick: [3] "They've put the ass in the stall" — and as a variant, may I add "why didn't he eat, instead of going for a walk?" —

Contrary to M. de Talleyrand's phrase "Everything is happening": here, nothing is going on. Milord is at the Wartburg [4] — from whence he will go to rejoin Mme. Sophia [5] at Geneva around the 10th of June. Their Highnesses will be back at Ettersburg or Wilhelmsthal a few weeks later.

Count von Kalkreuth [6] *netted* a few painters in Munich — Ramberg [7] (Baron von), Lenbach [8] (a student of Piloty's) [9] — and also a landscape-painter [10] whose name is, I think, Corräder. * Thus the Academy [11] is getting fatter, although at the same time there is the strong change of *wasting-away* here. — The Theater is closing earlier than usual this season (on the 17th of June), owing to the anniversary of the death of the late Grand-Duchess — since on that date the Grand-Duke and Grand-Duchess do not wish to be seen in public. Dingelstedt comes but seldom to his theater, on the pretext that the repertory is too poor. Lassen's *Praise of Women* was given again a second time. The *lack* of taste and of any kind of ideas at all, on the part of the Public, struck me even more at this performance than the half-empty house with which Dingelstedt had to reckon. Tomorrow Tannhäuser — the day after, The *Nixie of the Saale* [12] — and Wednesday, *The Last Witch* — a Bavarian "farce" arranged in Thuringian style by our popular-puppet-poet — Rost! [13] "The things of importance in this world, ought and must be treated *farcically!*"

Hebbel [14] (who is no "joker") has just written to Minette. She will tell you just how little deference he shows to the comments that have been made to him. — Cornelius *is expanding* his *Cid*. He is full of good ideas, and who knows? perhaps he'll do a masterpiece, and I hope he may with all my heart. He is returning to Vienna in about a week. Bronsart has settled down in Löwenberg; and starting with the month of October, he will act as *Concert-Master* and *Music-Director* for His Highness the Prince von Hohenzollern.† Furthermore, I imagine he will be appointed Director of the Euterpe Concerts at Leipzig. He is vacationing at Schwalbach [15] until the beginning of July, where Inga is taking a *cure*. This may profit Bronsart in another sense — but it's scarcely likely.

---

* They were more or less trying to seduce Piloty here, where he spent a few days — and it got him an increase in his salary at Munich. He is soon to marry one of the *prettiest* members of the Munich middle-class.

† With a salary of approximately 600 Thalers.

Have you read Prütz's [16] two volumes, which appeared this winter by Voigt and Günthe (Leipzig and Weimar) *"German Literature of the Present* — 1848 to '58" —? Would you let me send them to you? — You will find many of our friends there. Dingelstedt, Hoffmann, Gutzkow,[17] Meissner, Freytag [18] (the latter rather badly dealt with) — etc. — Hebbel shines by his absence — with the exception of a half-page which I think is in the second volume (page 276, Vol. II), where he is scarcely mentioned, and then only in an opprobrious way, — the kind of thing that Hemsen, who has recently become somebody through the correspondence of Humboldt and Varnhagen, had the wit if not to invent, at least to state, about his own feelings toward a performance of Grillparzer's Sapho [*sic*] [19] in Munich: "The Public has been disappointed as concerns the play"! — If by chance you don't have this work of Prütz's in Vienna, it would give me great pleasure to send it to you immediately.

I don't know whether you'll be able to decipher this scrawl. In proportion as my ideas become clearer, it seems to me (?) that my handwriting becomes more atrociously illegible. Nevertheless, even if you don't read me, at least you will get my intention. — Only please never forget, that I am with heart, head, and all my soul, forever your faithful slave and

servant
F.L.

Scotchi never stops crying over you. In order to give a little variety to her grief for having lost you, she now raves violently against Napoleon III — and as if that isn't enough, she has just become ardent for . . . Garibaldi! — [20]

LETTER 58

[Weimar, May 28, 1860]
From your letter to Minette, which has just reached me and which I am immediately sending on to Rome, I notice that a postscript was lacking in the one I sent you yesterday. Allow me to correct this omission, and to tell you in all truth, that I *approve* of you completely and even *admire* you for the perfectly simple and

at the same time dignified way of life you are following, in the milieu where you are called upon to live and take root. For my opinion, it would be impossible to give further proof than you have shown of tact, charm, nobility of sentiment, and calm superiority of spirit.

I suppose one might have expected it of you; still, it is with the charm of certain qualities, to which is added the perfume of noble virtue, as with the flowering of spring. One knows that it will come — yet at its approach, we feel a sort of thrill that is akin to surprise.

May God keep you and lavish His blessings upon you. I will yet add what is said in the Gospel for Whitsunday: "Let not your heart be troubled, neither let it be afraid." Jesus gave you *His peace* — not as the world gives it. Continue then to remain the joy and pride of your mother, the grace and honor of your Family; and if I may say it, a *delection* for him who has had the happiness not to leave you, for these last eleven years! and who stays deeply attached to you.

Monday of Whitsuntide.   F.L.

LETTER 59

[June 2, 1860]

Tender thanks for this morning's letter — which will now make its way toward Rome. I have been without word from Minette for a week — and will wait only until tomorrow or the day after. The 2 books by Prütz will immediately be sent you. You'll find there several nicely said things, neatly done, about some of our friends. The little chapter about Hoffmann particularly pleased me — Perhaps when things go better for our good friend Hoffmann, people will esteem him less. But one mustn't go off on this way of thinking, and one must take the good where one finds it. Hebb's[1] visit is a small poetic license in good taste for Vienna — and one would have to be bitten by I don't know what kind of a tarantula to disapprove of it.

Mme Kalergi[2] telegraphed me yesterday from Dresden, to inform me that she would spend several hours in Weimar today. I had heard nothing from her for the past few months, and I even neglected to thank her for a very cordial letter she wrote me after Daniel's death.

Blandine and Caroline d'Artigaux[3] wrote Minette with much feeling about her article, which they found *admirable* concerning Daniel's death. I don't need to say that I feel the same — but Cosette and others not knowing that these pages could only come from Minette's heart, merely displayed a reserved praise — and it was a pleasure for me to send her this as a *reparation*. You know that she is excessively inclined to think that she has an unhappy way of writing, that she fares badly in the eyes of others, etc. — These are old sores and wounds, and I should like to pour a little balm on them.

I am sending you Cosette's last letter — not because it contains items of some interest for you, but simply to keep you aware of Cosette's humorous tone. Send it back to me.

In the notices of Brendel's next-to-last Number you will find the Program of the Zwickau[4] *Schumann Festival* — 6th, 7th and 8th of June. I have decided to go to it. Brendel, David, Martha Schumann,[5] E. Genast, and other acquaintances of ours are coming too, — and all the more because Mme. Schumann[6] and her friends want nothing of *our* company, and their dislike of us makes one more reason for joining this commemoration in Schumann's honor. *Rietschel's* medallion will be mounted on the door of the house where he was born, and the rest of the time neither Music nor Champagne will be lacking. Mme. Schumann and Joachim have made their excuses to the Committee for their absence, motivated for the wife's part by the excessive emotion she would undergo, and for the friend by the absence of the wife. — From Zwickau I shall probably (Saturday morning) go to Magdeburg for Hans's[7] Concert.

Rosa Küstner's[8] marriage to Escudier[9] was announced to me by 2 letters inviting me to be present — from Escudier and from Mme. Küstner — Consequently the news is extremely genuine.

Forever, your entirely devoted,

F.L.

LETTER 60: *Preface*

The sixtieth letter is the last Liszt wrote to Marie before the trip to Rome and his famous, dramatic, and ill-fated marital attempt with her mother. It is fitting here that he should sum up the labor expended upon the twelve symphonic poems. They represented the main body of his artistic creation during the Weimar period from 1849 to 1861, and they are perhaps Liszt's principal contribution to music in general.

LETTER 60

Here is Minette's telegram. It took more than three days to get from Rome to Weimar.

I've already told you that I shall go to Zwickau (the Schumann Festival), and to Magdeburg. A few little things to take care of at Leipzig make me leave tomorrow morning. If by chance Hans's Magdeburg Concert gets postponed, I will return here Saturday — otherwise Sunday evening.

Mme. Kalergis, who notified us by telegram, hasn't come at all — in 3 or 4 days, Cornelius will be at Vienna. Perhaps you will do him the honor of letting him see you, and I shall tell him to present himself at your door, in any case.

It's been impossible for me to start a new job these last few days — but I am bringing to Härtel *Hamlet*,[1] the *Battle of the Huns*,[2] and the *Artist — Festival Variations*[3] (with the whole "*middle portion*" in polonaise rhythm), which I have revised, corrected, and expanded with care. With their publication, the cycle of *12* symphonic tone-poems will be complete. After that will come *Faust*, the choruses from *Prometheus*, and the Psalms — now entirely finished — and finally the Elizabeth which ought to be done before the beginning of winter. Excuse me if I speak to you so often of this musical crowd; but they have me by the heart — and *by the throat*, as Pascal says.[4] Apart from the feeling that dominates my whole life and for whose honor I would gladly give all ten of my fingers — one after the other — and all my worldly possessions, I have no other passion save that for my task. The contradictions, nay even the injustice occasioned by my work, far from thwarting me, arouse me still further; and they confirm me completely in the attitude I have had since my youth: that is, in the field of Music I have something to say; and no one else can say it for me. — Certainly this is a small enough thing. I take no great pride in it; but come what may, I shall fulfill my task by God's good grace, to Whom I pray with genuinely resigned humility for what good or bad fortune I may encounter. I was informed by the Augsburg Gazette that Prince Chlodwig [5] was present at the Passion Play at Oberammergau.[6] Did you hear about it?

I hope that Minette will enjoy her stay in Rome, and that God will grant her a few years of peace and quiet after so many trials and tribulations. Let us pray that it may be so!

Monday, June 4, '60.   F.L.

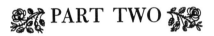 PART TWO

1869-1876

LETTER 61: Preface

Liszt stayed at Weimar for a year and a half after Carolyne's departure, and for fifteen months after his letter of June 4, 1860, to Marie. It was a period in which he composed and performed much sacred music; evidently he considered that he had finished with the symphonic poem genre, and his letters to Carolyne indicate an increased devout, theological concern. He even wrote, on September 14, what may be his first will, which he sent to Carolyne. Almost all his possessions were to go to her. "I cannot write her name without feeling an ineffable thrill. All my joys have come from her, and my sorrows always seek her for comfort . . . My last sigh will be to ask a blessing for Carolyne." (*L.M.* II, No. 27.)

Liszt finally took his leave of Weimar to go to Löwenberg, to Berlin, and thence to Rome — a departure not without emotional overtones, since it is obvious that neither he nor Carolyne ever expected to return. "It is impossible for me to bring to a single focus the emotions of my last few hours at the Altenburg. Each room, each piece of furniture, right down to every step on the staircase and the lawn itself — everything was transfixed by your love, without which I am as nothing!" (*L.M.* II, No. 79.) His last letter to Carolyne from Weimar is dated August 16, 1860, and Liszt arrived in Rome on October 20, 1861.

The melodramatic episode of the last-minute cancellation of the wedding has been treated by every biographer of the musician: the sudden entrance of the Papal emissary bearing the Pope's fateful message after the lovers had attended Mass together on the night of October 21, 1861, the collapse of the Princess, the empty flower-bedecked church of San Carlo al Corso which greeted the crowd of onlookers the next morning — all this has the character of third-rate Italian opera. The curious coolness with which Liszt accepted the decree from the Vatican has never been satisfactorily explained. Adelheid von Schorn simply says: "Liszt had become indifferent, during the period in which he was separated from her; and the thought of a legal union with her was no longer of necessity for him." (*Zwei Menschenalter*, p. 82.) Certainly he was no longer the amorous, youthful, and passionate lover, the role he played with Marie d'Agoult that so delighted the Romantic world of 1840; but one is forced to wonder how anxious he really was

135

finally to enter into a respectable marriage in his fiftieth year. A letter written just one month later to the Duke at Weimar does not even allude to his marital disappointment. Indeed, Liszt displays a quiet contentment. "The temperature of Rome suits me perfectly; up to now, we've felt no cold weather, and each day goes by for me without effort or boredom: I compose, read, and for recreation, I have made several visits to churches, monuments, art-galleries, and studios." (*Briefwechsel*, No. 84.)

Carolyne turned to the labors of her colossal *Causes extérieures* and the cultivation of an equally complicated hypochondria. Visitors had to undergo a period of "quarantine" in an anteroom before entering her salon, and she found all her doctors unsympathetic and incapable of diagnosing her peculiar and unique malady. Even the humble thermometer was held to be inadequate and suspect in her case. Liszt, settled in a state of what he termed "santa indifferenza," while he worked hard at a number of Masses and Oratorios and aspired unsuccessfully to be appointed as director of the Lateran and Sistine Choirs. The death of Prince Nicolas Wittgenstein, in March 1864, would have made possible the long-desired marriage, but it seemed to make no impact on either Liszt or Carolyne. "Both had already become so accustomed to the idea of separation, that there was no longer much idea of marriage." (Schorn, *Zwei Menschenalter*, p. 83.)

On April 25, 1865, Liszt took the first four of the seven degrees in the Franciscan Order: doorkeeper, reader, acolyte, and exorcist. The cassock and the clerical collar were now his, and no picture made after this date shows him without the latter; but evidently there was no need for the tonsure to replace the famous flowing locks. He could neither celebrate the Mass nor hear confessions, and he might have left the priesthood had he so wished. Sitwell (*Liszt*, p. 244), quotes a contemporary observer who saw the musician the day after his ordination: "Mephistopheles disguised as an Abbé. Such is the end of Lovelace."

He lived in an apartment in the Vatican until Cardinal Hohenlohe invited him to stay at the Villa d'Este in Tivoli. From 1863 until 1867 the interchange of letters between Liszt and Carl Alexander reflects the desire of the Duke for Liszt to return to Weimar. He returned for a visit in July 1867, and in 1869 — the year that marks the resumption of Liszt's correspondence with Marie Wittgenstein — occupied the *Hofgärtneri* in the park at Weimar, and began his "vie trifurquée" between Weimar, Rome, and Budapest.

The following letters present an interesting and somewhat disappointing change in tone from the earlier ones. "Votre Altesse" has replaced all the little pet names; Liszt's air of submissiveness with Marie, now Princess von Hohenlohe, seems excessively deferential, and at times it is hard to remember that the letters written after 1869 are addressed to the same person as those previous. The oblique references to "affairs at Rome" and similar statements may have to do with a possible estrangement between Marie and her mother, since Carolyne for many years was convinced that the Hohenlohe family had a hand in blocking her marriage with Liszt. Their disagreement has been offered as a reason for the hiatus in this correspondence between 1860 and 1869. Actually, I am not entirely convinced of the validity of such a thesis. Letters to Carolyne between 1861 and 1866 refer sparingly to Marie, but never with any sense of a conflict between her and Carolyne. On August 5, 1867, we even find Liszt writing from Weimar that he has spoken to the Grand Duke of a potential visit to be made there by the mother and daughter, and Marie came to Rome to see her parent during late August, 1868. (Cf. *L.M.* III, No. 168.) As late as 1873, Liszt alludes to some discord but fails to define it. This, however, may be a clue: "She [Marie] remains your devoted daughter — but her obligatory marks of respect do not always coincide with those she would be only too happy to demonstrate to you." (*L.M.* IV, No. 11.)

Again in a letter to Carolyne from Vienna dated April 17, 1874, Liszt says: "Lately my relations with Marie have taken on the character of a new, serious intimacy on account of you. In a few words, she has privately expressed to me, and has made me understand her filial affection — true, deep, and tender. On his side, Prince Constantin has taken me into his confidence by speaking of you without any false verbosity. He has assured me that he would be quite ready to display his devoted gratitude to you by coming to Rome, if it were necessary." (*L.M.* IV, No. 55.) This would seem to indicate that any differences between the Wittgensteins had their origins with the Hohenlohe relationship.

The abrupt manner with which the 61st letter begins makes it seem unlikely that this was the first letter written to Marie after a break of eight years. It is to be hoped that at some future date perhaps other letters will be found to close the gap in the correspondence.

LETTER 61

[Vienna, 1869]

If your very gracious Highness does not order her very humble servant to the contrary, he will have the honor of coming to the

Augarten[1] (after leaving *England*)[2] about nine o'clock this evening.
Regards and unlimited gratitude.
Wednesday, March 31st.   F. Liszt.

LETTER 62

[Vienna, Spring of 1869]
I shall be so bold to ask you for a little advice, Your Highness.
It was extremely vexing for me to miss (as if for a third time)
Fürstenberg's[1] very kind invitation on Saturday, and I am all set to
write my very humble apologies to His Excellency, Count Beust.[2]
Only please be so kind as to tell me if I may mention Fürstenberg
in my note to Beust, or whether it would be better to excuse myself
vaguely, on the grounds of a previous invitation. —

Baron Reischach[3] will give you a brilliant account of our dinner
at Hitzing,[4] with its musical *liqueur*. I hope that I didn't put the
recommendation you gave me to shame.

For tomorrow — I've accepted a "Sexardian" dinner with Augusz[5] at the Metternich's; and around seven o'clock I shall go from
Rennweg[6] to Palleske's[7] *Introduction*. Saturday evening, Leitert[8]
is giving a small concert at Bösendorfer's,[9] where my presence is
indispensable. The program announces *Orpheus* and the *Concerto
Pathétique*,[10] performed at 2 pianos by Leitert and Mlle. Menter;[11]
in addition, Schumann's *Carnaval*,[12] my *famous* Sonata and the
Spinning-Song.[13] Perhaps Count Willczek[14] might be so kind to
listen to these strange pieces, by your
most obedient servant
Wednesday.   F L.

I am still counting on the *meatless-meal* for Friday you were so
kind to mention to me.

LETTER 63

I am hatching a plot in your honor, Your Highness; but in order
for it to succeed I need your approbation.

Up to now we haven't met with a suitable painter to do a portrait of your mother.

"Finally Malherbe came,"[1] and our Malherbe's name is Hébert,[2] who lives in Rome as Director of the French Academy. I have told him that Your Highness wants this portrait, that She will put it in her salon — more glorious than all the Salons, past, present, and future, of the Louvre — and that finally you have instructed me to commission the illustrious M. Hébert to paint a masterpiece as quickly as possible (— at the most reasonable price possible, — 4000 francs) which will immediately belong to you.

I beg you, would you please do me the honor of writing two words to the Princess, your Mother? Convince her that you are yielding to the scheme of

Your old and most
grateful servant

June 15, '69, Rome.   F. Liszt.

LETTER 64

I am most happy for your much-coveted approval, Your Highness. There remains now for M. Hébert to fulfill the scope of his commitments, by completely satisfying you with a masterpiece. If you pass through Munich at the exposition there, you will see Hébert's last picture. They say it is very lovely. He calls it "The Unfortunate One"; its composition is extremely simple: A sorrowful, miserable widow, with a small urchin of a son whose appearance is scarcely calculated to console her.[1]

During the last ten days, the "Dance Pieces" of Herbeck have been keeping me busy from morning till evening. I have allowed my transcription to be singularly coquettish musically, more than usual; and I please myself in hoping that the composer will be pleased with it. Will Your Highness accept once more the humble dedication of these "Dance Pieces" — less dancing than dreamy — first cousins to both Schubert's "Evenings in Vienna,"[2] and the "Scenes from Childhood" of Schumann?[3]

Coming back to Herbeck, I am not at all surprised that he didn't show himself more of a Ulysses toward the "Sirens" of the theater. In this vicinity the Ulysses' are as rare as are independent souls at court!); and how could a musician of his strength possibly plug up his ears, while the treacherous voices sing "Come ye to the shore"?

He would only have to yield to the wrathful schemes of Neptune-Dudin, who is capable of sinking the whole grotto of Herbeck's desk; or better yet, of contriving some sort of trap there, to break the arms and legs of the unfortunate choirmaster!

And Meissner too, lured thus to the "Danube Shores!" But it isn't the Sirens' voices that are ensnaring him; he is listening to Beatrice, and he himself will sing well.[4] I don't know whether the poet-novelist will succeed in finding a place in the newspapers; butterfly or bird-wings can't be used to pull carriage-steeds. Nevertheless, he will cut a fine figure, even as a decoration, in Viennese society; and will find more there to his advantage than any place else.

I haven't seen your most illustrious brother-in-law[5] again since the departure of your august cousin Feo, whose grace and charm I esteem highly. She and her husband let me accompany them to the Villa d'Este,[6] where the rain did not hesitate to make itself a member of the party despite the illumination of the Sibyll's Cascades. The Duchess wittily omitted admiring them.

Be so gracious as to remember me kindly to Prince Constantine, — and I am taking the liberty to beg you to tell Scotchy "high Church," a thousand old sweet nothings, from

Your very humble and most
grateful servant

July 12, '69 Rome. F. Liszt.

Monseigneur Bauer[7] has just published in one volume, under the title of "The Goal of Life," his sermons preached at the Tuileries Chapel during Lent in '67. He has arrived at his finest eloquence in developing "the supreme formula for the Science of Life: to do one's duty in order to bring about salvation." —

LETTER 65

What a delicious feast your most charming letter was, Your Highness! I enjoyed it unselfishly, immediately conveying the pleasure it brought me to the one — alone — who knew how to understand it. The following day we learned of *your* happy event, which this time went well for all concerned. Would the youthful matron, surrounded by her brave *Quintet* of little heroes, be so kind to accept my heartiest congratulations?

I have been ensconced in the small tower of the Villa d'Este since the evening before last. Your most illustrious brother-in-law most graciously offered me this retreat. It is more than comfortable: above all during the winter, when the invasion of *civilized-barbarians* makes my staying in Rome insufferable. Here I find myself again at my best; my apartment is very nicely arranged: two fireplaces, a new lamp hung from the ceiling of a little parlor which acts as a boudoir, — books and music in abundance, — in addition, the magnificent terrace with the dome of St. Peter's at the edge of the horizon, and the venerable cypress-patriarchs you know so well.

I have been greatly touched by a delicate consideration on the part of His Eminence: in order to show that he feels me neither an intruder nor a visiting tourist, he had my initials (two very well marked L's) painted on the entry door of the tower. Thus, henceforth I consider myself as a faithful beneficiary of the Villa d'Este; and although I am keeping my apartment at Santa Francesca,[1] I shall only go rarely to Rome during the winter season. — To fulfill my duties as a Christian, and to spend my time suitably by continuing to write my notes, is my whole life: nothing else concerns me in the slightest.

Toward mid-April I shall return to Weimar. They are going to perform the Beethoven Cantata[2] (which I shall write here) there at the occasion of the "Musicians' Convention" at the end of May, — and at Saint Michael's,[3] I've promised a Mass to Augusz for the solemn dedication of the new church at Sexard.[4] Augusz is inviting several of our acquaintances for the anniversary of the bell-tower of his patron-saint; — notably Herbeck. This brings me back to another *Dedication*, not really having to do with a church, but at least it has no touch of worldly banality: that of the "Dance Pieces," twice decorated with the name of Your Gracious Highness. Before they start dancing again in Vienna, my Transcription (of small dancing value) will arrive for you. Mlle. Menter played it for me in a delightful way recently in Munich: allow me to add that if you are so kind to ask her to perform it this winter at the *Augarten*, it will be a "glowing moment" for the Virtuoso and for the entire little composition.

Yours ever,
Your very grateful debtor
F. Liszt.

October 26, '69.

Villa d'Este.

The Cardinal [5] sends you a thousand good wishes, and will soon write to you.

LETTER 66

Formerly I was very happy to bring you pictures on the morning of the 18th of February. Today, I bow before the memory of *your* picture, and write to tell you once again of my lasting good wishes. Praise God, and thanks to you, my principal wishes have been granted: You are a sincere Christian and a most worthy, infinitely charming woman. All else will come to you in good time, and in abundance. So let's not worry; and look instead, as it has been taught us to do, at the birds of the air and the lilies of the field, keeping complete faith in Our Father's goodness.

You knew that I have been virtually all winter at the Villa d'Este, enjoying the most peaceful contentment in the company of my notes and a few books. The Cantata for the Beethoven Jubilee is almost finished; my author talks a great deal about the stars in it. This affords me the chance to take a long stroll across ethereal fields, as well as to indulge in a little *"Tone-painting"* with these verses:

> *"As when from Heaven to earth*
> *The bridge of Faith falls in colors,*
> *And binds us to the other world. . . ."*

and again:

> *"Even as here the roar of the Rhine*
> *Resounds down as far as the Cathedral,*
> *So will his soul someday rise up*
> *Like stream of pure melody. . . ."*

You will hear about it all from Herbeck, since I hope that he will come to hear this Cantata at the *Musicians' Convention* at the end of May in Weimar. They've already asked Hellmesberger, at my request, to be the first violin for the Beethoven quartets.

I came back here for the 8th of February, when my chief occupation was that of posing. A young French painter, M. Layrand,[1] took into his head to do a masterpiece using my face: he has a most

142

stubborn temperament, and forced me into sitting after sitting. Furthermore, Her Grace the Duchess Colonna Castiglione [2] is being kind enough to make a little statuette of me; and Miss Ream,[3] an American sculptress who has been commissioned to do the Lincoln monument for Washington, is undertaking to do a bust of me. Thus my likeness is fast becoming a kind of international symbol, and I am forced to act, — at least in one way, — as a model.

Many humble thanks for the kind reception you gave the "Dance Moments," and for the one you have promised me for Mlle. Menter. The newspapers tell of the glowing success she had recently at Pest, where she played two Concerti in E-flat during the same evening: the first by Beethoven,[4] and the other by his all-unworthy follower,[5]

your very faithful and truly
grateful servant
F. Liszt.

February 18, '70 — Rome.

LETTER 67: *Preface*

The "troubled days" of 1870 included the start of the Franco-Prussian War (which must have upset Liszt, since despite his Weimar and German affiliations, he was a great admirer of Napoleon III), the confusing political situation at Rome, and his own usual domestic problems, now augmented by collapse of Cosima's marriage with Hans von Bülow.

Certainly Wagner, even more than Liszt, did much to establish the myth of the amorous artist. The stormy marriage with Minna Planer included a lengthy affair with Mathilde Wesendonck and a liaison with the actress Frederika Meyer, and by mid-1864 Wagner was openly in love with Liszt's daughter, Cosima von Bülow. Hans, Cosima, and Wagner all settled at Ludwig II's court in Munich in May 1864; and when out of this *ménage à trois* Cosima bore Wagner a daughter, Isolde, in April 1865, Bülow's unsuspecting innocence was so great that he thought the child his own. It seems incredible that the birth of a second child, Eva, in February 1867, should still find Bülow devoted to his wife, and it is hard to say when one's admiration for his charity turns into amazed humor at his being one of the prize cuckolds of all time. Finally, in 1868, Wagner and Cosima left Munich for *Villa Triebschen* at Lucerne. In June 1869 she bore him Siegfried. A divorce took place in July 1870, and the wedding of Wagner and Cosima took place on August 25, 1870, ten days after this letter to Marie. (Cf. Ernest Newman, *Richard Wagner*, New York, Knopf, 1933, *passim*.)

Throughout all these tangled matrimonial complications Liszt retained a surprising equanimity. It is safe to say that he was never very fond of Cosima anyway, and hence her troubles scarcely moved him as they might have the orthodox parent. Liszt was extremely attached to Von Bülow as a person; but his admiration for Wagner the musician evidently swayed any private emotions Liszt may have felt for Cosima's first unhappy husband. One does not find even the slightest note of censure of Wagner's conduct.

LETTER 67

Even on the most troubled days, there is certain peace for those who have the signal felicity to be Christians. It is this continuous, ineffable, indestructible peace, the summation of all the goods here below, which is besought for you from the Celestial Father by

your old servant

Sexard, August 15, '70.   F. L.

LETTER 68

How can I thank Your Highness enough for those exquisite lines of October 22nd? There is no memory that glows in my heart with such a pure and sweet intensity as does yours; this is one of the most precious gifts that God has granted me, and I never stop thanking Him and begging Him to continue His blessings for You and Yours.

The huge events that startle the world also bear on my little existence.[1] I had planned to return to Rome during the first days of October; but considering the actual state of things, I would be a great deal of trouble to myself, and superlatively useless to everyone else. Thus it wasn't much of a task for them to persuade me to prolong my stay in Hungary; and as you know, it's a question of keeping me there even longer. On this score, please excuse my lack of modesty in sending you the appended article. Its meaning conforms perfectly with the numerous articles published by the Hungarian newspapers on the same theme, during the last few weeks.

No matter what happens — and I still hope that nothing does happen, since I am so terrified by the prospect of being thrown back into an active career! — I have promised to go to Pest in mid-November and conduct the *Beethoven-Festival* Concert in December. I may also participate in the one in Vienna, for MM. Mosenthal, Dumba,[2] and Unger[3] had the kindness insistently to ask me to conduct Beethoven's *Missa Solemnis* and my Cantata. It seemed to me excessive to decline once more; and I simply begged these gentlemen on the Committee to deal with the new Pest Intendant, Baron Felix Orczy,[4] (who looks as if he may attain the heights of a Magyar *Ziegäsar*) so that the Pest Concert might not take place on the same date as that in Vienna.

If the affair straightens itself out, my dearest reward will be to come to the Augarten, and to place at Your Highness's feet the sincere testimony of my most respectful and my keenest gratitude.
Sexard October 27, '70.   F. Liszt

LETTER 69

Your Highness,

I am very proud of your "regret" concerning the Beethoven-Festival, and still more delighted by that which you were so kind to add to it. Whenever you talk or write, all things take on a charm: even the most common things, and often those which are in reality startling. For example, there was Dudin's momentary discomfiture, stemming from the business of the title of Excellency, and Herbeck's wailing over his "forced marriage" with his long-legged boss, and her still lengthier tricks. I imagine that W.[1] will succeed in calming the wailings of the latter, while he grants the former the ashes of his desire — the title of Excellency.

Speaking of Excellencies, we see some larger caliber ones here. The other evening, at the performance of Lala Rook (by Felicien David),[2] Beust, Kuhn,[3] and Longay[4] displayed themselves in the same box; and right next to them was Andrassy[5] with his wife, upon whom Beust made a ceremonial call, during the intermission: very much appreciated by the public.

My modest little exclusively musical way of life goes on. I am counting on a brilliant *Beethoven Concert* on December 16th, —

the kind that could be produced in the largest capital cities. Before the year's end there will appear several very elegant editions of the Coronation Mass.[6] The same editor, — Schuberth,[7] — has taken over the rights to the Gran Mass from the Vienna *City Press*, by buying up the other editions. He will soon publish the piano-and-voice score of this work, which has been more criticized than heard. In addition, I have been making several copyists and engravers moan, in Pest, Leipzig, and New York.

As a very pleasant diversion from my daily grind, I received a most charming note from Princess Metternich, who tells me of her "bold certainty" of seeing me soon again in Vienna. On this subject, Your Highness, allow me to take you into my confidence . . . something already mentioned in Rome: only at the moment when Your Highness judges it fitting and proper, shall I go to Vienna. To be displayed there now on posters, does not at all enter into my little personal program; — to put it otherwise, I am asking for no performance of my compositions in Vienna this winter, and if people play them, I prefer not to be present.

My sole claim would be to make a short visit there, with no other aim than to renew to Your Highness, the very humble testimonies of her very grateful servant

Pest November 30, '70.   F. Liszt.

LETTER 70

Your Highness,

You cause a divine beam of light to shine upon my psalm's[1] little hut.

It is one of those joys . . . poignant to the point of tears.

May the blessed angels thank you for it and delight your soul with their singing.

December 14, '70, Pest.   F L

LETTER 71

Your Highness,

M. Nohl[1] tells me that he has had the honor of being presented to Your Highness.

A few grains of that awkwardness and verbosity, reputedly
German, are blended in him with a good foundation of intellect,
study, and knowledge. In addition, people dispute with him for his
. . . Weimarian tendencies. Knowing that this last is scarcely an
opprobrious title in your eyes, I am venturing to solicit a little of
your kindness for the Beethoven Biographer; and I am charging him
to lay at Your Highness's feet the very humble testimonies of hommage

of your truly grateful servant

Pest, January 3, '71.   F. Liszt.

LETTER 72

Your Highness,

Your kind remembrance of the feast of St. Francis was very
sweet for me, and I thank you from my warmest "heart-felt memories."

Yesterday, Count Imre Szechenyi[1] told us of the splendid evening party at the *Augarten*, where M. Vogel[2] sang the springtime
of the *Nibelungs*.[3] I shall hint to Mme. Sach to ask him back again
in June for one of those Court Concerts that depend principally on
Her, and to which she understands how to give such an exquisite
tone. Furthermore, I shall set myself about faithfully fulfilling Your
Highness's commands concerning all possible "birds," naturally
including those nesting in button-hole (flowers).

In order to do justice to my obligations here, I shall still have to
remain about another twelve days. Out of a most *touching* sense of
charity, several lovely ladies are planning to raise a fund of a few
thousand florins for the benefit of the *day-nurseries*, depending
upon a satisfactory entertainment. They are arranging an amateur
show to be accompanied by a Concert for Tuesday, the 18th of
April, in the ballrooms of the magnificent Buda palace of my old
friend, Count Karatsonyi. Countess Rossi[4] will sing; your very
humble servant will play a little bit, etc., etc.; and afterwards I
expect to spend the last week of April in Vienna, and the months
of May and June in Weimar.

Happy Easter! "With unleavened loaves of sincerity and truth"
— forever, from Your Highness's

very grateful servant,

April 8, '71 Pest.   F. Liszt.

Dare I ask you to express my faithful testimonies of service to
Your most eminent brother-in-law? —

LETTER 73

I humbly beg your pardon, Your Highness, for my natural mis-
understanding. For a moment, Szechenyi's raptures carried away my
pen, which was returned to its stricter duties by your kind and indulgent lines. To continue: in addition to M. Vogel, M. Walter [1] is
coming to Weimar at my request. I hope that he takes notice of it;
and above and beyond his roles at the theater, and at the lyrical
evening party at the castle (which will take care of itself very easily),
we shall have a fine Concert, where M. Walter will sing my 13th
Psalm — which I do not wish to forget, since you so eloquently
heard it. Thank you also for the compliment rendered to the *Benedictus* — with Hellmesberger's glowing interpretation — at your
last evening party.

In learning about the great loss of Tegetthoff,[2] the first thing
that struck me was the sorrow you experienced from it. They are
saying to each other here that his sudden death was caused by the
extreme friendliness of Princess Lauri Schwarzenberg,[3] who tempted Teg. to go outside too soon. Some other persons even go so far
to suspect poisoning as probable.

In about ten days I shall come to the *Augarten*, to place at Your
Highness's feet the continually devoted affections of

your very obedient servant,

April 14, '71, Pest.   F. Liszt.

LETTER 74: *Preface*

That this correspondence is incomplete is indicated by a letter from
Liszt to Carolyne on November 29, 1871: "Poor Magne, how sad!
Write me about it. I wrote her a few lines yesterday . . ." (*L.M.* III,
No. 293). Marie's oldest son, Franz, had just died of diphtheria.

LETTER 74

Very grateful for the kind interest of Your Highness, I am allowing myself to inform her that my silly cold has improved slightly last night, and I shall probably be rid of it before the year's end.

Your very respectful
and truly devoted servant,

Saturday, December 30th.   F. Liszt.

LETTER 75

HORPACS[1] [engraved] — at the home of Count Imre Szechenyi —
November 8, '72.

Your Highness,

Your Highness's telegram came to me at Vienna shortly after October 22nd. It shall be for me one of those sweet angelic messages which enters the soul like a celestial ray of light.

I was granted several happy, quiet trips at Schillingsfürst.[2] Rietschel's bust of you presides over the salon, from whose five windows one may enjoy an extremely lovely panoramic view, rather analogous to that from the Villa d'Este. The Cardinal tenders me constant acts of kindness for which I have devout gratitude. Moreover, I appreciate to the utmost the princely charm of his bearing, and the indefinable intellectual and subtle aroma of his conversation.

The two new photographs of Schillingsfürst, which His Eminence has asked me to take to you, have been sent back to the *Augarten*.

I scarcely stopped at all at Vienna, and here I am now two leagues away from my birthplace, Raiding.[3] I visited there with Count Szechenyi and Mihalovich[4] last Monday, November 4th. I shall return to Pest next Monday, and I plan not to budge from the place until I go back to Weimar in the spring. As a result, I have excused myself to the *Friends of Music*[5] at Vienna, relating to my earlier promise to continue my Oratorio: "Christ." Last winter I thought that it was almost my duty not to decline their invitation; but it seems to me *at the least superfluous* to go on with it now, and in any case I prefer to take no part. In the same way, I shall take no part in the Concerts planned by Sister Mary, Princess Raymondine Auersperg,[6] who had the kindness to write me from Trieste inviting me to display my small talent as a pianist there for the benefit of her Dominican school. I answered her yesterday that I felt quite *paralyzed* and *disconcerted* by Concerts.

I hope soon to see Prince Constantine again in Buda, — and I beg Your Highness to believe me always, wholeheartedly, to be

Your very grateful and affectionate

servant,

F. Liszt.

LETTER 76

Your Highness,

In accordance with your kind permission, I am continuing with the Beethoven theme which Mosenthal first attacked. He wrote me eloquently, in July, that they were counting on me to furnish the pedestal for the new statue. I replied that I had done at Bonn in 1845 what they were now asking me to do again in Vienna; and to take the opportunity for such a repetition seemed to me dubious, in the light of my age and of the circumstances.

In all truth, for more than 40 years Beethoven's Symphonies have been performed unceasingly in every country. The same is true for his piano works: these were played a short while back in Vienna by Bülow and Rubinstein in such an admirable manner, that I could merely pick up the pieces they left behind. Furthermore, the hundredth anniversary of the birth of the Sublime Master was celebrated everywhere, in December, 1870, by musical festivals lasting several days; to continue these festivals for the occasion of M. von Mosenthal's *local* project, would be perhaps to risk too much the enthusiasm of the public, — a risk in which I prefer not to participate at all, for fear of succumbing myself.

Therefore, I take the liberty of begging Your Highness to pardon my coolness, and if the occasion presents itself, to *"make"* M. von Mosenthal "understand." Confidentially, I may add that, while being really grateful for the idea of placing my Beethoven-Cantata on the program, I hesitate to follow this path. At this time, the performance of the Cantata would be a dangerous and delayed compromise. It might have been done easily at the time of the "Anni-

150

versary Festival," the Committee asked me to conduct the "Missa solemnis" (which I finally accepted). But these Gentlemen feared by so doing to wound the potentates of "Criticism" — and I can only approve of their circumspection, as long as I am free to imitate it in turn.

To conclude, if already they are thinking of honoring the Art by another embellishment of one of Vienna's public squares, wouldn't there be a better way to do it than to erect a statue of Beethoven, in the style of the town of Bonn and 30 years later? Why not raise a collective monument joining together the five great musicians, *born in Austria*: Gluck, Haydn, Mozart, Beethoven, Schubert? — I submit this idea very humbly to Your Highness, for whom I remain perpetually,

her very grateful and faithful servant
F. Liszt.

November 28, '72, Pest.

M. von Bülow has just spent a few days in Pest; and during one of our intimate talks, I asked him if he had had the honor of seeing you recently. He confessed to me that he abstained from any trips to Vienna, and said this with a kind of systematic severity that scarcely surprised me, since I know of old his aversion for customary *obligations*. You may guess the observation I made to him with regard to the "Augarten"—In my old role as "friend of the truth," allow me to assure you that if B. neglected to come to your home, it was only out of a characteristic of *exaggerated* discretion; and he will hasten to atone for his error on the next occasion. Incidently, I am also warning you that Herbeck's merits and charms are appreciated no more by Bülow than by Wagner.

May I take the liberty, of asking you again to get my forgiveness from the kind "writer from Volhynia"? She sent me her composition last winter, the "Ave Maris Stella." I must admit, I could not feel sufficiently delighted to write to the author about it.

LETTER 77

Your Highness,

Excuse me for bothering you again about the Beethoven Monument. The Committee wrote me an extremely nice letter covered with signatures, among which shone those of Dingelstedt, Herbeck, Mosenthal. I am venturing to enclose a copy [1] of my answer so that Your Highness may be exactly informed of my stand in this case in which she has taken a certain interest.

Hoping that you do not disapprove of my reserve, I remain wholeheartedly,

your very obedient and grateful
servant

December 3, '72 Pest.   F. Liszt.

LETTER 78

Your Highness,

I shall immediately write M. Sach — who, by the way, reprimands me for the scarcity of my letters — and I'll try to persuade him to have M. von Saar's [1] Henri IV performed. Milford von Meiningen [2] has already given his favor to a Play where Gregory VII scarcely comes off well; I imagine M. Sach will scarcely show more orthodox scruples than his cousin, concerning such a big and controversial historical problem.

In order to proceed properly, M. Saar ought to send his tragedy to Baron von Loën [3] (the Intendant of the Theater), and write him a few *engaging* lines. Loën is a good fellow, and takes to heart the continuance of the traditional brilliance of the Weimar theater.

Your kind words concerning my answer to the Beethoven Committee calmed me. In stopping myself at the preamble to what I wrote Mosenthal in July, I do not claim to exclude myself completely from the affair; it is only that I feel neither the age nor the inclination to draw my sword. Others younger and more sound than I ought to take this chance to advance themselves; but supposing that I live a few more years, the right moment to *model me* will no doubt present itself. As for the collective monument of the five Austrian Musician-Geniuses, I dared risk the *idea* only in very humble confidence to Your Highness. If you don't altogether reject it, perhaps some day it too will have its happy moment. Schubert's very successful statue, in the *Stadt-Park*, doesn't seem to me to be a definite obstacle against the quintuple-monument: the chief difficulty rests in the composition of the group. To my way of thinking the place in the center belongs to Mozart, due to the universality of his genius; but how should the others be grouped and shown? May Zumbusch [4] be able to say "Eureka"! When I have the pleasure of meeting him again at Your Highness's, I'll ask him to sketch secretly the group, and I am counting on his design to get me your indulgence.

The tribe of musicians is unbearable; I've known it of old; excuse M. Breitner [5] for having proved it to you once more by his awkwardness. Rubinstein had recommended this young artist to me, and even paid the expenses of his trip from Vienna to Pest last winter. Since then Countess Dönhoff [6] has recommended him to me again and assured me that he is full of talent, — and his pockets are empty.

We've been loaded down with Music here. After Bülow, Mme. Schumann and Mme. Joachim [7] arrived; the *Florentines* are coming next week, and Hans Richter's [8] large Concerts (for Orchestra) are going their brilliant way every other week, amid great affluence and public approbation.

As for me, I only want to spend the quietest possible winter; I'm afraid of both the *cold* and the *heat outside*, and I'm much more comfortable in the temperature of my room. — If there is occasion for it in Lent, my ten fingers will contribute to a charity Concert (like the one of last winter); and I've also promised to arrange a *Vocal evening*, with piano accompaniment, for the honor and profit of Robert Franz. [9] To gather *comfortably* several thousand florins by means of Music isn't often as easy as you'd think.

Very sincerely, your very grateful
and completely devoted servant

December 10, '72.　　　　　　　　　　　　　　F L.

　　　Pest.
The copy of M. von Saar's tragedy has not yet arrived.

LETTER 79

Your Highness,
　　Your lines and Henry IV came to me together. I shall send this volume to M. Sacha tomorrow; and I shall write to him in the spirit

of your recommendations, without making it easy for him to guess from whom I borrowed them.

The chromatic and enharmonic scale of susceptibilities is quite familiar to me; M. von Saar may be assured that I shall do my best, and no false interval from Weimar shall come to wound his poet's ear.

Immediately upon M. Sacha's answer, I shall communicate it to Your Highness, for whom remains wholeheartedly

her very respectful
obedient servant

December, '72.   F. Liszt.
     Pest.

LETTER 80

Your Highness,

Ordinarily, M. Sach does not make me wait too long for his very kind missives. My letter, along with M. von Saar's book, ought to have arrived for him before December 15th, and up to now he hasn't answered me. If he delays still another week, I shall take the liberty of rewriting him about the same subject. In the meantime — as far as my little assertion relative to Your Highness is concerned — I shall allow myself to copy it right after the paragraph[1] concerning M. von Saar. As soon as the answer arrives, it will be sent to you, Your Highness, by your,

very humble and very grateful servant

January 5, '73.   F. Liszt.
     Pest.

LETTER 81

At last the oracle has spoken; here is his answer. His first words concern M. Luckhardt,[1] the well-known Viennese photographer, for whom I had insistently requested the gold medallion *with the ribbon*, as a reward for the *well-received* homage of my portrait. — Highly successful, they say. To explain further: you perhaps remember that my medallion by Rietschel had the honor of being placed, for the last fifteen years, near M. Sacha's writing-desk.

In order not to frighten the Pest post-office employees by my dealings with "foreign powers," I sent M. von Saar's book to the address of Count Wedel,[2] M. Sacha's secretary and the son of Countess Wedel who was the former chief lady-in-waiting to the Queen of Hannover. He answered me with the note that I am allowing myself to enclose to you, so that I might inform Your Highness completely and authentically of this petty *Weimarian* affair.

In truth, the performance of Hellwig's[3] Gregory VII, applauded *this winter* at Weimar, makes plausible the postponement until next season of M. von Saar's play, I will again recommend it to M. Sacha, at his home, this spring. However, it would seem fitting and opportune to me, if M. von Saar were to write a few words to Baron von Loën, the Intendant of the theater, and send him a "second" copy of his Henry IV and his Gregory VII.

I haven't said a word to Rome; and in order not to act like a "confidence man" (which wouldn't at all jibe with my old qualification as the "friend of the truth"), I shall abstain from mentioning anything about it in that direction. To compare Saar's drama with Kaulbach's *Arbnez* would seem to me a bit dangerous; but it is the prerogative of great minds to adventure and even to dwell in the highest regions of intellectual risk.

Please accept, Your Highness, the very humble testimonies of my most constant and devoted gratitude.

January 20, '73, Pest.   F. Liszt.

I have written recently a kind of a paraphrase of the *Szozat* (call) and of the Hungarian *Hymn*.[4] This patriotic selection will be performed here (by the Orchestra) before I leave, and I am allowing myself to dedicate it to Count Andrasy [*sic*], and to send it to him, printed.

LETTER 82

Your Highness,

I was able to grasp the imprint of your feeling in the enclosed *Song*. It has excellent musical quality; and if Riedel[1] will accept my praise, please be kind enough to transmit it to him, — particularly for the graceful melody in the lines:

> *"Like the shining of the sun,*
> *And the gently falling dew . . ."*

This comes again at the second stanza:

> *"Let yourself feel it everywhere*
> *Feel it night and day . . ."* [2]

I've added a small page of minor notes and changes to the manuscript. They ought to show you my intimate knowledge of the *song*, — and perhaps Riedel won't be displeased.

Mme. Nako never showed up here, from whence I leave my room as little as possible. *My* evening party, "for the honor and benefit of Robert Franz," has been announced for Sunday, February 23rd. I am venturing to send you the program, on which figure Mme. Semsey (formerly Countess Czaky) [3] and Countess Leo Festetics. The *"Szozat,"* dedicated to my illustrious patron Andrassy, will be performed in March; I'll be also incidentally acquitting myself for the debt of a Concert for the profit of various charitable organizations; and on April 2nd, (Saint Francis' Day), I shall be peacefully at my cousin's [4] home in Vienna, where I shall stay until Easter.

This year Mme. Sacha's birthday falls within Holy Week; consequently Their Highnesses will celebrate it among the family; — and I won't return to Weimar until mid-April.

There I will evoke M. von Loën's vainglory and "aesthetic sensibilities," regarding the tragedy of M. von Saar. I hope Your Highness will be pleased to relay my thanks to him, either verbally, or via the two enclosed lines.

February 6, '73. Pest.

Your very humble and truly grateful
F.L.

LETTER 83

Your Highness,

Careful discretion prevented me from sending you my congratulations by telegram the 18th of February; but I none the less celebrated this anniversary in my heart. For me, it is linked with the 8th of February.

Thank you for having so graciously received my little notes appended to Riedel's Song. His name is beginning to spread, thanks to your patronage; already he has pupils who are writing pretty *Songs* (among others Count Amadei,[1] my old friend Rosti's[2] nephew), and his have a good chance of being appreciated in good society. They conceal an attractive dreamy charm.

The *Szozat* and the Hungarian Hymn, dedicated to Count Andrasy, will be performed here by full orchestra in mid-Lent, and published immediately following. I shall write a dedicatory epistle to the most illustrious Count, and shall bring him his copy of this patriotic work to Vienna. I hope this may be said without lacking in necessary modesty, but success is predicted for it.

Enclosed is the program for the Sunday evening Concert, given for the honor and profit of Robert Franz. The Vienna *Vocal Academy* invited me to a Concert for the same purpose; I excused myself, since I find it is better to abstain from this type of production, so ill-advised at my age and in my condition.

Remenyi, back from Cairo for the last few days, said that the letter of recommendation Prince Constantine was so kind to give him was completely efficacious. The Khedive[3] showed himself as charming as he was munificent; and the splendid hospitality of His Highness came at a very good time for Remenyi, since as soon as he had "crowned the work of forty centuries with his personality and his violin" his wife prepared a paternal surprise here of almost-pyramidal variety, by bringing into the world twins of both sexes. —

Various obligations (including also a benefit Concert, under the auspices of Countess Anna Zichy)[4] are keeping me here until the end of March; but anytime from the first week in April on, I hope to renew my very humble and very grateful testimonies of service to Your Highness.

February 28, '73, Pest.   F. Liszt.

LETTER 84

[Vienna, April, '73.]

Delighted with your kind command, I shall come tomorrow with my cousin Eduard, at 5:30 — and remain forever,

Your very faithful servant

Friday.   F. Liszt.

LETTER 85

Your Highness,

M. Sach, having left last evening for Vienna, particularly expressed to me his desire to be well-received by Your Highness and by Prince Constantine. Knowing that you remember with affection those persons with whom you were formerly associated at Weimar, I gave Milord complete assurance; however, that seemed to him a little vague and too general. He desires something more specific — which one can only hope he may obtain. Allow me simply to indicate this slight *turn* to Your Highness, and to join to it the very humblest testimony of my most respectful gratitude.

May 21, '73, Weimar.   F. Liszt.

LETTER 86

Your Highness,

Upon his return from Vienna, M. Sach immediately told me how enchanted he was with your charming wit and your attractive salon. He is Lavish with his praise and hommage of you, and both are to be added to the huge floral display of the same variety, now decorating the "Augarten." —

Do you perhaps remember Dornburg,[1] so rich in roses? Yesterday the 55th birthday of M. Sach was celebrated there with the family. Except for the indispensable members of the Court staff, there was but a single guest, — your very humble servant — who is most proud to be writing you, at this very moment, on the old desk bearing Goethe's name, and from the same room formerly occupied by his Olympian Excellency.

Enclosed is the program for the performance of last evening's opera, "Erwin and Elmire": libretto by Goethe[2] and music by Duchess Anna Amalia.[3] It is perfect *rococo* and still admirable — if you look at it taking into account the sentimentality of its feelings.

Lassen played the orchestra part on the piano and will tell you the details about the performance next week at the "Augarten." There is no need to recommend Lassen further to you; but allow me to beg of you a favorable reception for Count Kalkreuth (Director of the Weimar "Art School"), who will have the honor of calling on Your Highness. Have you seen his landscapes at the exposition? They convey a breath of dreamy poetry, sad and calm.

Mme. Sach tells me that the marriage of her son with Princess Pauline von Sachsen (daughter of Duke Hermann, — living in Stuttgart) will be celebrated in September. Scheffel's[4] "Festival-Play"; "*Hail to the Bride*," with music by me, will have a place in the program of nuptial celebrations at the Wartburg. Thus I shall have a job to do right on the spot. I intend earlier to make a very humble visit to your most illustrious brother-in-law at Schillings-fürst (in the end of July); and I am awaiting a letter from Rome, in order to plan the rest of my time, until I return to Pest, at the latest on the 1st of November.

Believe me, Your Highness, to be forever

Your very grateful and faithful
servant
F. Liszt.

Dornburg, June 25, '73.

I shall return to Weimar tomorrow evening and stay there until mid-July.

LETTER 87

Your Highness,

You were kind enough to allow me to recommend M. von Wartenegg[1] to you. He will have the honor of presenting himself at your home, with the assurance that to him has been given some of your gracious concern for poets, by

your very humble and
grateful servant
F. Liszt.

Weimar, October 1, '73.

LETTER 88

Your Highness,

For me, the best part of Rome is that which links me to Your Highness. I feel it again keenly this time; and I shall allow myself to express this still more at the "Augarten," where to find you again in about ten days, is the humble hope of

your very faithful
servant
F. Liszt.

October 15, '73.
Rome.

LETTER 89

Your Highness,

Your very kind lines only arrived the moment I was leaving Vienna.

I don't know how to thank you enough for your continual favors; last Tuesday evening adds one more occasion for which I am truly and sincerely grateful.

Will you excuse a most involuntary error of omission that was also a privation for me? — I had merely a few hours to spend at the Exposition; M. du Sommerard[1] had not yet come; and I had to leave for Pest without giving him your note of recommendation. To this sin I add what may be a greater one: I am venturing to forward to you, enclosed, in its primitive stage, M. Nohl's *wish*. I am indebted to him for the favorable criticism he recently expressed in the "General Daily" and other places, about my Gran Mass and *Christ* Oratorio. Nohl will come here to hear this work again at the party on November 9th, and I want to be as helpful to him as I can. I am thus asking Your Highness if She would be so kind to accept the dedication of his new book, which he aspires to offer you.

Please receive kindly, Your Highness, my very grateful and devoted pledges of service

November 1, '73, Pest.   F. Liszt.

LETTER 90

Your Highness,

Count Albert Appony [1] has just told me that Baron Hoffmann [2] asked him to speak to me concerning a Concert. It is to be added to the program of the Vienna festival for the celebration of the 25th year in the reign of His Majesty the Emperor and King. [3]

I answered, that if they really wanted to invite me to this Concert, I would participate actively in it with all ten fingers out of a sense of duty and honor.

Hoping that Your Highness will find my answer a proper one, I have the honor to remain,

Your very obedient and most
grateful servant

November 14, '73, Pest.   F. Liszt.

LETTER 91

Your Highness,

The Vienna Concert is making progress, and it seems to be coming to something. Hoffmann and Albert Apponyi have sown the first seed for it; the sprinkling has taken the form of the telegram I am enclosing, so that Your Highness may be truly informed of it; and the buds will not be any later in appearing than this morning. I was talking with the committee, composed of His Excellency Baron Hoffmann, MM. Dumba, Klinkosch, [1] and the Burgomaster of Vienna, (so they say). They will determine the date and the arrangements for the above-mentioned Concert for the benefit of the "Kaiser Franz Josef Foundation"; and they will also try to make everything as pompous as possible, by convening the barons and retainers of the Philharmonic Society, the "Male Choral Society," etc.

My portion of the duty and honor here concerned will be to comply with the invitation — with the exception of a minor detail, intended doubtlessly to be obliging, but which seemed wise to me to lop off, as much out of modesty as out of prudence. M. Dumba suggested that I perform one of my symphonic compositions. I answered that *at this Concert* I had hoped only to figure at the piano by playing two long selections with orchestral accompaniment: the Schubert Fantasy (that might be called: "Travels") and a Hungarian Rhapsody.[2] This would be more pleasing to both the public and the critics, — and it would suit me better. Besides, I told M. Dumba to choose some new orchestral work by Brahms, Herbeck, Goldmarck[3] or someone else, in preference to the immortal Oberon[4] or Leonore Overtures.[5] These are always fixed stars on programs, and almost too brilliant for such an occasion.

Yesterday Prince Constantine paid me a very friendly call: I showed him the Burgomaster's telegram, and I'll hasten to give him the very simple and correct results tomorrow. I flatter myself that this will be equally understood by the public, and no one will be inconvenienced.

Please rest assured, Your Highness, that no absurd or *Dudinish*[6] whim will ever go through the brain of

your truly grateful and faithful
servant

November 26, '73.   F. Liszt.

Budapest.
I hope soon to talk to you again at Vienna about Weimar, and to thank you also for your kindness towards Wartenegg and Nohl. The latter has just been very badly treated by the "New Free Press"; but he can cheer up by reminding himself that those much better than he and I have often been treated worse.

LETTER 92

[Vienna, December, '73.]

Very happy to see you again at 5:30 — this evening — and I am completely at your service.
Sunday.   F. Liszt.

LETTER 93

[Vienna, December '73.]

I shall not fail to follow the way of the "best," which leads to the Augarten; until this evening, then,

Your very grateful servant

Tuesday.   FL.

LETTER 94

HORPACS [1] — January 26, '74.

Your Highness,

The papers announce that His Majesty the Emperor has been pleased to grant me a new honor. Since I know from what source this sort of honor stems, — beginning with the Iron Crown, continuing with my Hungarian nomination, — allow me, Your Highness, to come back to the same source and to place at your feet the testimony of my lively and perpetual gratitude.

F. Liszt.

Castle-life at the Horpacs' is most delightful. Countess Mariette Szechenyi,[2] (formerly Hoyos), and her husband, came last week; Albert Apponyi and Mihalovitch have rooms near mine; and our very kind hostess has asked Countess Dönhoff, whom we are awaiting, to return.

I shall be back in Pest before mid-February, where I shall stay until Easter.

LETTER 95

HORPACS February 1, '74.

Your Highness,

The length of the ribbon far exceeds my small virtues. Hence my sincerest gratitude and friendly thanks to Baron Hoffmann, since I shall have the pleasure of meeting him everywhere.

The "Polyphony of Musical Ideas"[1] is the property of Your Highness, who so kindly allowed me to give it to her in homage. This little book is no superfluous one, and is to be recommended for its ingenious method of placing the quotations under fitting titles: "The spirit and essence of music; Laws, Limits, Progress," etc. The worth of this wise methodology must be attributed to La Mara,[2] the pseudonym of Mme. Lipsius of Leipzig, Richard Pohl's sister-in-law, he who formerly was the literary laughing-stock of the *Mighty East* at the Altenburg. Do you know La Mara's "Musical Portraits"?[3] They make very pleasant and instructive reading. Berlioz, Wagner, and your very humble servant all received indulgence and absolution in them; Mendelssohn, Schumann and Franz were treated as befits their fame. This book didn't find the public indifferent, and a second edition has appeared. I have predicted to the author, that her "Polyphony of Ideas" will run to at least a dozen editions.

I'm being taught from Rome about the epic and dramatic, what Rubinstein calls "Ethos and Pathos." His idea of putting Ludwig's "Machabees"[4] into operatic form is a noble one. Would it result in a box-office success, — the only kind that counts today? No one wishes this for Rubinstein more than I. I confess, however, that the success of *serious* operas seems to me to be getting more and more unlikely. Offenbach[5] and his cronies (either disguised or not) are succeeding well. Wagner survives — and predominates — in the face of farces and platitudinous works. His genius alone gives sublimity to the theater. Therefore, speaking frankly, there is but one performance in which I am now interested: the *Nibelungs* at Bayreuth: at the same time that I think, come lean years or fat, good luck or bad, all self-respecting theaters should feel it their duty to perform *new* works, to be chosen with discernment. You remember this opinion of mine at Weimar, where I gave it full play, despite the public of that place.

M. Sach left me in '59, on the occasion of Wagner's Nibelungen; here is his last letter, like a sort of poetic digression — one of the kindest of its type. I shall delay my answer; since I am only able to offer him "roses from his own garden," and my apologies for not returning at all to Weimar for the whole year.

Countess Marie Szechenyi left here the day before yesterday. She'll stop for a few days with her family in Vienna, then return to Pressburg,[6] and thence to Rome (?) — Mme. Dönhoff has written a letter of condolence to Mme. Alexandra Szechenyi,[7] who answered her by a second invitation. This *second* one brings me back . . . to the 3rd Choirmaster. Rubinstein, Lassen, Doppler oughtn't to take *3rd place*. For that, *Sucher* [8] *has been discovered*. He is already quite well-fitted, almost too much so, for this job; his published works (The Woodland Maid, the Battle of Lepanto, etc.) show a strong talent, rather strapping, with fire, character and appeal. All of Sucher's artistic temperament seems to me to blend harmoniously with the Viennese *Concordia*: so well, indeed, that Hellmesberger's temporary dissonance will be resolved without too much trouble. The problem of which is to be "above" or "below" perhaps indicates an *increase in salary*.

I shall climb up to the lofty and pure *"Spring"*; my best fortune is there to contemplate the divine reflections of ideality.

your very grateful
F L.

LETTER 96

[February 1, 1874.]
Horpacs Monday evening.

Through excessive scrupulosity, which I beg Your Highness to pardon, I am adding this post-script to my letter of this morning. If they are seeking a 3rd Choirmaster *from elsewhere* than Vienna, M. Metzdorff [1] (actually in Brunswick) would perhaps be suitable. He has nice manners, plays the piano very well, and has conducted Concerts and operas with sucess in several cities. Herbeck probably knows him; and Mme. Moukhanoff [2] is very kindly acting as his patroness.*

A thousand humble pardons and respects.
F L.

LETTER 97

Horpacs February 16, '74.

Your Highness,
Receive these most respectfully fervent good-wishes on the eve of your birthday, as well as the perpetual testimony of my grateful attachment.

---

* It goes without saying that Metzdorff has written a large opera, and several symphonies.

I shall return to Pest tomorrow to remain there until Easter. Later I plan to take advantage of His Eminence's hospitality at the Villa d'Este, and there resume once more a few months of uninterrupted work — my sole means of rest —. Before I do that, I must make a courtesy visit to Monseigneur Haynald[1] at Kalocsa,[2] very near Sexard, where my very good friend Augusz is inviting me to reoccupy the dwelling he has prepared for me. . . . As for M. Sach's invitation, I am treating it as a valuable enigma, — not to be explained at all. Therefore, unless there are unforeseen changes, I'll go to Rome from Sexard (around the end of May), preferring not to get there too soon in order to stay there longer.

The Concert at Oedenburg[3] was a brilliant success; the same for the charming *post-soirée* at the Esterhazys'. Madame Dönhoff will give you an authentic account of it; she kindly came as far as Horpacs the day before yesterday, with the Szechenyis, Albert Apponyi, Mihalovitch, Lenbach, and Wartenegg.

I am delighted by your approbation of Zumbusch's *Beethoven-Monument*, and I sincerely wish it continuing successes in a growing *crescendo*. Semper,[4] Zumbusch, Makart,[5] Lenbach, Dingelstedt, Herbeck, and others are in Vienna as the *Augarten* representatives for art illustrations; may their task there be accomplished gloriously and to your satisfaction, and this is also part of the good-wishes for *February 18th*, from

your very humble and truly devoted
F. Liszt.

Thank you for remembering Hoffmann (von Fallersleben) so sweetly. He was never so great a poet, as he was at the *Altenburg*; and it is one of your noble acts, Your Highness, that you assured him of peaceful years in his old age. You did it with a persevering heartfelt charm that is rarer than any gift. In that, — and excuse the strange comparison, — you are like Napoleon III.

LETTER 98

[Pest]

Your Highness,

"Do good, and let others talk" certainly applies to our time, when a frightening epidemic of useless, evil words — spoken,

166

printed and repeated — rages about us. You were born with charity, Your Highness; and your primary quality is doubled by its practise. "Walk in happiness," as the Psalm says, — "go forth in happiness" — Neither the *"ashes"* of the devout brawlers, nor the pepper of the unbelieving cavilers, will spoil the Prince-Imperial's *"Goulash"* [1] on February 18th, or your excellent work for the "Relief-Kitchens."

Thank you for the newspaper knickknacks. The case of Naundorff's [2] 6 or 7 beneficiaries falls into the province of the so-called historical novel. Messire Favre wasted his Latin and good French eloquence thereon, with the same aplomb he wasted them against Bismarck. [3] But this time his illusions were less authenticated and more innocent than in '70: a simple matter of lawyer's fees, seasoned with a bit of vague royalist curiosity, leading to mere pettifogging and incidentally to scandal. Nevertheless, Henry V won't bother himself about it at all, vacillating as his legitimate chances of being *King of France* or of the French [4] (?!) may be.

Everything is happening (according to M. de Talleyrand) except for those things that don't happen at all. —

From the heights of *Naundorff* I descend to Nohl. His portrait, which so solemnly adorns the title-page of his book, nettled me; still more, the addition of the "in Vienna" to your Most Illustrious Name!! This is the most intolerable cretinism. Pardon him, I beg you, by remembering the other Altenburg cretins. He has many good qualities, and perhaps he will finally succeed in getting on his feet. To begin with, he fidgets with his legs; and his adversaries, who are top-men in the newspaper world and more blustering than he, are cutting his stilts from under him.

I have still to do some piano-playing here on March 4th and 23rd, for charitable reasons. Count Waldstein [5] has asked me to do the same thing in Vienna for the benefit of Princess Frederika Auersperg's convent. I am offering my very humble excuses, and shall practice my abstinence from the piano, as long as the Sister-Superior at the convent forbids her nuns the *Goulash* of the *"Relief Kitchen"* on Ash-Wednesday and all other fast-days.

With all my heart, your really grateful

February 27.   F. Liszt.

I've just written to your illustrious brother-in-law that I shall make use of his hospitality at the Villa d'Este, in May. If possible,

I should like to spend the rest of the year of '74 there. Before starting off for the Villa d'Este: a visit to express my gratitude, to Monsignor Haynald at Kalocsa; and probably a Concert at Pressburg (for the *Church Music Association*), where Countess Szechenyi is the chief attraction.

I'm adding two unedited letters to the "knickknacks" — no picture, and no need to read them.

LETTER 99

Your Highness,

I hope that Nohl won't be so idiotic to say, as did the cock in the fable: "the smallest grain of millet would be much more to my taste." [1] He, who would not understand your *pearl-idea* about the initials B.L.W. [2] to be added to the "*buttons*," deserves to crow on his own dunghill. Without buttons, initials, or ideas, Winterb.'s [3] pearl is his wife, — an extremely pretty *Russian* princess. She asked me, was there also any social life in Weimar? — My answer: "when you come there." Sacha Winterberger is up to his neck in debts, even as his brother was bravely riddled with wounds from the wars in '60 and '70. Please, Princess, don't send him a single Kreutzer. For him to stake *small amounts* by asking to borrow 350 florins from you, is really too stupid. Lassen settled the matter wisely the Bridoison [4] way: his way to think is not to know what to say. . . . If, however, out of extreme kindness you'd care to answer Winterberger, I beg you to do it along these lines: "Your best recommendation was from M. Liszt; since you want to conceal your course from him, I'll pay no more attention to the recommendation." —

The enclosed telegram from Rome, which came this morning, has affected me. It concerns a musical evening at Princess Wilhelmine Auersperg's, [5] both charitable and *productive*. After a long talk with her cousin Frederika, (preceded by several negative letters from me), I declared bluntly to the zealous Dominican, that in such circumstances, I finally saw but one possible "*compensation*," and this depended solely and exclusively on Your Highness's wisdom and orders, to which I shall be happy to submit wholeheartedly. Does the Auersperg affair seem to you wise or not? Is there a possibility that the small advantages will outweigh the inconveniences?

Please decide this question, Your Highness; if it is affirmative, I beg you to accept half the receipts for the "Relief Kitchen's" *Goulash*; because, in my humble opinion, it is imperative that the profits be divided. This is exactly what I explained, from A to Z, to Princess Frederika, who is coming to the Augarten tomorrow to seek your good favor and your decisive advice.

Please pardon your very obedient servant this new vexation.

March 11, '74.   F. Liszt.
     Pest.

I've been hearing M. Sucher warmly praised, from various sources.

LETTER 100

Your Highness,

Your answer makes me happy. I feared I was intruding, and you assure me to the contrary, in the most convincing manner. My sole regret is that *all* the little profit can't go right into the stove of the "Poor Kitchen's" Goulash; but since you generously approve of the share, the best would be to make it as simple as possible: two halves, one for Haking [*sic*],[1] the other for the Poor Kitchen. Such is my humble opinion, which I stoutly maintain, — and I shall write it categorically to Count Waldstein and to the Zealous Dominican.

If the date of March 31st (Tuesday) is set for the Auersperg evening party, I shall arrive at Vienna on the 26th, happy to get Your Highness's commands, and to obey them

as a very faithful servant.

March 15, '74, Pest.   F. Liszt.

How annoyed Dudin must be, since you shine so brightly by your absence! —

LETTER 101

Your Highness,

The day, the hour, the plans and arrangements for the Auersperg Evening concert depend entirely on the decision of Your Highness and of the little *Committee Director*, with whom you are being so kind to work. That is what I said from the start to Princess Frederika here. Consequently, if her cousin Wilhelmina and you, Your Highness, settle on April 6th (Easter Monday), I am at your service and shall arrive at Vienna next Tuesday around midnight. On the following day, April 1st, at the *Committee* meeting in the Auersperg Palace, we can easily decide about the program, according to the exigencies of time and place. Naturally we have to avoid offending the disposition of the potentates and petty meddlers of the day: the "newspapermen."

I am writing to Mme. Dönhoff, to ask her to select a piece not of my making: I'm afraid to smuggle in my writing via the piano, and I shouldn't care to implicate the gracious Countess.

Not knowing Mlle. Lutterotti [1] previously, I haven't dared write her, — all the more since I am neither the donor nor the arranger of Concerts, but merely a simple contributor to the Auersperg Concert's program at which I'll be very happy to applaud Mlle. Lutterotti. The same for my old "*Landgrave*" and fine compatriot Bignio. — [2]

Bösendorfer is a good friend of mine; he will intelligently follow the commands of Your Highness — one of whose most obedient and faithful confidents and servants I flatter myself to be.
March 26, '74, Pest.   F. Liszt.

The "Marling Bells" [3] are ringing in my ears; I shall lay their music at your feet next week at the *Augarten*.

LETTER 102

[Vienna]
Your Highness,

From the last note that Sister Raymondine wrote me at Pest, I expected to hear from her this morning to tell me what time the *Committee* was meeting, at the home of her Cousin Wilhelmina. I gather she must have forgotten me; it doesn't upset me at all, and I feel quite prepared to have myself forgotten still more in the whole affair. . . .

I shall have the great pleasure of seeing you again at 5:30, Your Highness, and renewing my very grateful pledges of service.

Wednesday noon, April 1st.   F. Liszt.

LETTER 103

Your Highness,

I am complying with the order from Rome to send you the enclosed article about the *relief-kitchens*, which are the Roman equivalent of the "Public Soup-kitchens." It is hoped that elsewhere the former do without the "mutual humiliations" as appetizers.

Allow me to thank you again, Your Highness, for the discreet and sure-handed guidance you lent to Princess Auersperg's musical evening; without your help it would have been a thankless job — a sort of bourgeois, clerical and aristocratic pot-luck affair, to which never to contribute is the wish of

your very grateful and most obedient servant

April 11, 74, Pest.   F. Liszt.

LETTER 104

[Pest]

No, certainly you are not *"like the majority"*; and you will always remain distinctly apart, lofty, and ideally pure in my mind.

Several passages in the letter from Rome have upset me, without surprising me: last October, I was told almost the same thing *orally*, so that my conscience caused me to drop a few hints to you. . . . I do hope that these frightful shadows will disappear, and that it will be given me to help bring about the return to Christian clarity and serenity.

Your answer had admirable restraint, worthy of the noble, tender daughter who understands how to be both a wife and a mother.

Sheet 2, (first page, last line) in the letter from Rome, read — in place of "saintly" — *loyally and with all my heart,* and you will *thereby* be happier.

Sheet 3, (end of page 3 and beginning of page 4) must be taken into serious consideration. You and your husband will find the most appropriate way to deal with the inauspicious decree of Civil Death rendered by the Petersburg Senate. Shortly before, Grand Duchess Maria Pavlovna spoke to me confidentially about the course of this sad business: "It isn't nice, but that's the way it goes; and I'm not strong enough to stop it"!

Sheet 4, (4th page, line 7). I wasn't able to make out the name beginning with M or N and ending with an H. Please be good enough to tell me, and also to *what* it applies. —

I was happy that you were kind enough to find the small sum satisfying, accruing to the Relief-Kitchens from the evening-concert at the Auersperg palace. Under those given conditions one could not have hoped for greater success.

Mme. Kaulbach will certainly have been very strongly touched by your affectionate remembrance. I, too, wrote her a few lines.

And that Talmudic Cassel! —[1] He has, since the Altenburg, figured as somebody once or twice, despite his get-up — and even at Berlin, so I am told. I don't know what *position* you'll invent for him at the Augarten, but I find it nice you remember him and act as his patroness.

When I returned from Vienna, I finally took care of my pestering grippe which forced me to keep to my room until now. Tomorrow noon I shall have the honor of accompanying Monsignor Haynald to Kalocsa and will spend the day in his beautiful archepiscopal palace. I'll bring Victor Hugo's '93[2] back to Pressburg on Saturday, and shall ask Mme. Dönhoff (who is probably coming to the Pressburg Concert Sunday morning, with Baron Hoffmann) to be kind enough to return these three volumes. I read them in their entirety with extreme interest.

Believe me, truly, to be with all my heart, your constantly grateful and devoted

Tuesday evening, April 14, '74.   F. Liszt.
        Pest.

A thousand thanks for Humboldt's *Preface*, from which I shall be so bold to make a revised edition for my own use and profit. If you can discover, without any bother, *in what year* this curious document was published, would you be good enough to tell me? I shall try to procure the German version for myself, which the Voss Journal[3] probably published at the same time as the French one.

LETTER 105

Your Highness,

My cold will end by becoming tired of my listless opposition to it, and it will leave me one of these days. I had hoped to find Mme. Dönhoff at Pressburg — where she was obliged to go to a Dinner given by her *boss*, M. von Schweinitz[1] — in order to ask her to send back Victor Hugo's '93 to you; and I offer you my excuses for having kept these volumes for two weeks. This, too, was a kind of *parasitism*: please be more indulgent to her this time, than is Hugo toward the "parasitical priest, judge, and soldier,"[2] whom he plans to wipe out right from the start!! —

You asked me for "definite information" about my trip to Sexard and my departure for Rome. The former has become quite unlikely: I still have to putter around here for at least two weeks to get the heavy backlog of my correspondence in order, send back a number of manuscripts with the proper polite comments, and correct copies and proofs of music for which editors are waiting. I dislike dragging this *dross* left over from the winter to Rome; hence I shan't start on my way much before mid-May, and allow me to write you the exact date beforehand. In the meantime, I heartily approve of the project for the breaking-up of the Number 89 Babuino Street[3] establishment, even if the attachés at the Embassy have to suffer looking for a new apartment. I've tried for several years without success to bring about this most desirable move. You're familiar with the attitude that held out against it: let's hope that it will soon weaken. . . . Basically I envisage the whole business from your point of view; and I take the liberty of repeating this to you, feeling it to be the only attitude that is at once resolute, fair, and conciliatory. Your observation — that one shouldn't "seek for ill-will, where one can't demand promptitude" — is the best working philosophy. I am also with you, in considering those "measures inopportune" which would aim at having that *barbarous* decree[4] revoked; since I like to hope that it has become obsolete anyway. However, unless I am mistaken, you attribute it wrongly to the preceding reign, that of Emperor Alexander. —[5]

As a change from my personal grievances, here are some more *miscellaneous* Weimariana. First, M. Sach's letter and telegram. He keeps setting April 13, 1824, as my pianistic debut,[6] despite my explicit protests. Also something else, not of the same brand: a simple *Prospectus*, seemingly very innocent, in which Weimar is linked with Hungary; but perhaps this will get me a *basket* at the Augarten (a too-literal translation from the German: "to get refused"). I implore you not to spare giving quite open encouragement, if you have the smallest inclination to do so, (since the subscription list may well be printed at the end of the book), to my old, discreet, hard-working, and most-deserving friend Steinacker.[7] He has confined himself to sending me *one* prospectus of his forthcoming publication, "*Hungarian Lyric-Poets*, etc." As an answer to him, I immediately sent 20 florins for my share; and I asked him to furnish me with several advance notices, that I might distribute them among my friends and acquaintances here, — something he didn't at all ask me to do. The Szechenyis, Apponyis, and others very kindly subscribed: I am sure that Steinacker, the former Altenburg poet, would be extremely touched and grateful by Your Highness's signature. Thus I am timidly venturing to lay the subscription list at your feet . . . while repeating once again my plea, that you only comply with my request insofar as it suits your own *personal* convenience. The simple *non-return* of the list would be sufficient to have me understand, without any further commentary.

From the bottom of my heart,
your very humble old servant
FL.

April 26, '74, Pest.

What a happy position you've chosen for Cassel! I now suspect him of receiving occult advice, more expedient and fruitful than that of the Talmud.

I wrote to Rome that I shall forward M. Sach's letter.

LETTER 106

Your Highness,

My date of departure is settled for Sunday, May 17th. If you have any commissions for me to undertake, please give them to me beforehand. I am delighted, "officiously," by the breaking-up of the Babuino Street house; and I hastened to telegraph and write them to sign the contract with Prince Orsini[1] for the new apartment as soon as possible. I know his wife, Mariette, Szechenyi's sister, slightly.

May the sweet angels bespeak my thanks to you — as well as to Steinacker.

For *simple information,* I am venturing to send you the enclosed letter from Klughardt,[2] with a footnote by

your truly and whole-heartedly grateful

May 7, '74   Pest.   F. Liszt.

LETTER 107

Your Highness,

Your charming sheets of writing-paper arrived this morning; I shall gladly deliver them on next Thursday, and am happy to hope that these same sheets will come to you as bearers of good tidings.

I am leaving this evening; and I shall stop only for one day in Florence at my good friend Mme. Laussot's[1] home, where I shall probably find Bülow.

At the beginning of June, I am settling down for the rest of the year at the Villa d'Este.

I allowed myself a small license concerning Prince Constantine and I hope you will explain it to him. Sexard wine has much in common with Burgundy;[2] since the latter is used at the Augarten, I would like to praise some of my compatriot's product there; and I'm taking the chance of sending a discreet sample — (from the finest vineyard, whose owner is my friend Augusz).

I hope it will not be a failure. As a recommendation, may I add that your brother-in-law, the Cardinal, likes it, and commonly has it served at Schillingsfürst.

With very humble and truly grateful acknowledgments

May 17, '74.   F. Liszt.
    Pest.

LETTER 108: Preface

Carolyne's *magnum opus, Les causes extérieures de la faiblesse intérieure de l'Eglise,* has been touched on in the Preface to Letter 61, and Note 1 to Letter 180 discusses the project at length. Liszt's letters to her abound in polite inquiries about the *Causes*, and occasionally he encouraged her by a hyperbolic outburst such as the following, which one feels to be a polite — if forced — piece of flattery: "With what virility and dexterity you present and develop, in a definitive way, the theses and hypotheses of Church politics, administration, organization, hierarchy, disciplines, and reforms! In all truth, you follow the line of St. Augustine, St. Bernard, St. Thomas, St. Theresa, St. Catherine of Sienna — and even a little that of Joseph de Maistre; for — and I hope this pleases you — you share with him the same militant and prophetic sense . . . you act as prophet of the future Church and of future social orders which will be placed under the kind protection of Catholicism." (*L.M.* IV, No. 344.)

Carolyne and her two secretaries, aided by a small hand printing-press in the Babuino house, showered Liszt with literally thousands of pages of endless theological discussion. The vague but always favorable criticism he wrote her in return would indicate that he gave her labors only a cursory glance, if any at all. When the Vatican finally interceded, in July 1877, and the Index banned the book's possession by the clergy, Liszt for the first time was worried and assumed a more active critical attitude in his admonitions to Carolyne. Since the volumes written up to that time had been privately circulated, the issue never became important. So far as Carolyne was concerned, the affair only served to whet her zeal and convince her that she was one of the glorious company of Church martyrs.

Liszt's principal worry was for Carolyne's health, as frequent references in the letters to Marie show. Any genuine analysis of Carolyne's condition was made impossible by her hypochondriacal state. The sole advice the musician was able to render was to caution her against excessive cigar-smoking and to recommend that she at least leave off her arduous duties to take a daily walk.

LETTER 108

Well, here I am at last settled down at Villa d'Este, a place I hold dearer than any other dwelling. I hope I may spend the rest of the year there, quietly writing my *Saint Stanislas*,[1] and continuing the "extras" of my musical labors. Your illustrious brother-in-law has indeed granted me a *favor* by allowing me to live here, where I can use my time comfortably to my best advantage and pleasure.

To do that, I merely have to stay in my room alone, in the company of my books, newspapers, and Music.

I have something on my mind to speak to you openly about, and to you alone, concerning M.² (permit me thus to use the old nickname, still so endearing to you). She is very tired, bowed down by her excessive work, troubled so badly by her eyes that she can scarcely read without effort; encumbered morning and evening with correcting proof, sickly, given to homeopathic doses, worried by the onset of a serious illness, extremely discontented with the two persons working for her, whom she scolds continually for their lack of brains and care: — to sum up, she is in a very distressing nervous condition.

She insists that she finish, without interruption, the 4th big book of her last work; "following that," she says, "I'll give myself one month of rest away from Rome." She hasn't left Rome for the past 14 years, and has stayed as if locked up in her room, and never leaves it for a walk. You know how incapable she is of accepting any ideas save her own; I don't dare risk suggesting anything to her, having so often failed. Up to now she hasn't picked out a place for her intended country holiday, and she talks vaguely of Sienna, Assisi, or of any small village whatsoever near Rome; but I'm afraid that it will be the same with this trip, as it is with all her plans for changing her residence. At the last minute she'll change her mind . . . and won't budge. The only promise I've obtained from her, is that she will come to Weimar next May. This *initial* success has given me hope again for the future.

To my perpetual litany of thanks in your praise and honor, I shall add today the names of Steinacker and of Sophie Menter, — both of them very deserving, although in two markedly different ways. As for Mlle. Adaiewski,³ she seems to me to shine in the style of those "*Flowery Devils*" (formerly banned from the Altenburg). You've displayed a discerning taste, in finding her Romances mediocre and her *orthodox* choruses more interesting; her Opera is even better, and in several aspects it possesses an original, engaging charm analogous to the "suspicion of a moustache" on the author's engaging little face.

Have you read Bülow's 2 remarkable articles (The Augsburg General Daily) about the performance of Glinka's⁴ opera, and the "*Festival*" Requiem of Verdi⁵ at Milan? The Italian and *Verdian* newspapers are anathematizing and blowing Bülow to shreds. He gets here next Monday.

With all my heart, your *serf*,

June 10, '74, Villa d'Este.   FL.

Please give my thanks to Prince Constantine, for the flattering reception of the *Sexardian* at the Augarten.

LETTER 109

Your letter came back to me yesterday at the moment when I had arrived here for the very Roman festival of Saints Peter and Paul. It was a lovely, sweet inspiration, worthy of your heart, to come unexpectedly to M.'s. I am deeply touched that you take me into your confidence, and above all by the trust that this betokens. Since you really value my opinion, I would say that it were better to put off your trip until a more opportune time. If this comes about during the course of this year (around St. Charles' day, for instance), I will take the liberty of telling you.

As for now, the "friend of the truth" has to advise you to wait: "Hoping, I have hoped!"[1]

I found M. virtually in the same condition, and not very good. At the doctor's orders, she has resigned herself for the last two weeks to walking an hour a day on the Pincio,[2] but she claims to feel neither better nor worse. The domestic difficulties, as well as others, continue. Before I return to the Villa d'Este (after tomorrow), I shall tackle again the ticklish notion of a country holiday, although it promises to remain very dubious.

Thank you for the program of tomorrow's Concert at Schoenbrunn.[3] It is as varied as it is well chosen, and shows the best musical taste as well as taste in general.

Herbeck's nomination to the Iron Crown delighted me extremely. This decoration should make him able to support more patiently Dudin's prolonged intrusion in the lodgings of the real Director of the Opera.

Wholeheartedly, your very humble and faithful

Sunday, June 28, '74; Rome.   F.L.

LETTER 110: *Preface*

Liszt's sole excursion into American literature was his use of Long-fellow's *Christus* for an oratorio. A remark in a letter to Carolyne dated December 2, 1873, should serve to establish his knowledge — or rather lack of knowledge — of English, and the statement also explains previous misspellings of Locke, Thackeray, and Disraeli. "I am singularly pleased by Longfellow's idea for poetic dialogue, where the Strassburg steeple plays the principal role. Please make me a gift of this poem, preferably with a German or French translation — for I am scarcely able to understand even vile prose in English . . ." (*L.M.* IV, No. 40.)

LETTER 110

Your Highness,

I am placing at your feet my music for the "Bells of Marling." May they sweetly tinkle near you! When I was writing the little enclosed sheet, I heard your voice; but how could I catch the angelic accent? Art is insufficient even for cleverer ones than I. If you have this song sung, allow me to beg you not to have it done by any *gentleman* whatsoever; I've indicated on the manuscript: for mezzo-soprano voice: it needs a woman to interpret its poetic dreaminess and tender melancholy.

For two weeks the casting of some other *bells*, a great deal heavier, has been keeping me busy. Longfellow's *Golden Legend*[1] furnished me with a text for a composition for Chorus, Orchestra, and Baritone, (Lucifer!) entitled: "The bells of the Strassburg Cathedral."[2] They are neither German nor French but truly Catholic, and they sing out the praises of God between Heaven and earth. — Perhaps I'll have this piece played (it lasts a good quarter of an hour), next winter at a Concert in Pest.

Nothing new to tell you about Rome, where I have just spent two days. The plan for the country holiday at Sienna seems to be abandoned, and the apartment-hunting is continuing limpingly with the same lack of success. You have the explicit information about the duenna — the housewife — sort of a white raven — who is so impatiently requested. I hope that you'll succeed in discovering her and sending her to Rome, well-versed and fortified by the instructions pertinent to her task.

Monsignor de Mérode's[3] sudden death has moved both the public and the press. The newspapers of the opposing parties are united in their praise of the nobility of his character, his initiative, the wealth of his philanthropy, his courage and ardent zeal in serving the Papacy, which he revered as the supreme expression of Divine stability, so necessary to the working-out of human progress.

Although one never could be certain of Mgr. Mérode, as one could be of Prince Eugène of Savoy,[4] he always said only what was necessary to say; the excesses of language habitual with the famous militant Churchman in no way were an obstacle to the outstanding brilliance of his memory. All this is consistent with my proper respect and regret for him. His funeral at the Basilica of St. Peter, last Monday, was extremely simple and almost stingy. His sister, Mme. de Montalambert,[5] was present; the Requiem, sung rather well by at least twenty unaccompanied voices seemed to me to be in good taste and exceptionally fitting.

I shall return to the "Bells of Marling," and pledge you once more wholeheartedly

my most grateful homage
F. Liszt.

July 16, '74 —
(Villa d'Este)

LETTER 111

Your Highness,

It is agreed, then, that your birthday is to be celebrated by both of us, with a single heart, at Rome on August 15th. As my knightly Vigil on the eve before, allow me to thank you for your kind letter. I shall order the little "Marling" bells, as well as all the big ones everywhere else, to peal out loudly in celebration — without hurting your ears too much.

I join to their ringing, the wish that you may keep your sweet and understanding affection

for
Your faithful
F.L.

Villa d'Este, August 12, '74.

LETTER 112

Upon returning yesterday from Tivoli,[1] I found that your mother has been bedridden for the past two weeks. She picked up the Roman fever this week, on top of everything else. She says that it isn't a pleasant sensation, although she has had no cause to worry seriously about it. She has had two doctors and is in an excessively weak condition. She doesn't attribute this to the fever, but rather to the turn taken by her chronic malady, due to the lack of attention she has had to endure for more than a year. Her real sickness comes from the open windows and the other neglects impossible to avoid with a pair of amateurs like Cesare and Mme. Emilie;[2] however, when the attack of fever came, Emilie took very good care of her both day and night. Your mother is now in such a weakened state, that a half-hour of conversation is too much for her. I thought I noticed that she was highly annoyed by the sea-baths you are giving your son. Write her in such a way as not to contradict her about anything. For her recovery, she needs much rest, silence, complete inactivity, and not the slightest emotional strain — and she shouldn't even be entertained. Your mother doesn't yet know how long she will be in bed, nor when she can write you; in the meantime, she wants to know if you received her letter and the St. Michael for Constantine's 8th of September. They brought her Communion on that day; and although she was suffering a great deal, she took it, nevertheless, and offered her prayers for your husband.

She will write you as soon as she is able.

Here is what your mother has told me to tell you. Allow me to add that I beg you *in no case* to start for Rome now. She is in no physical shape to stand any kind of emotional shock; such a thing might well bring about a recurrence of her fever, and we never know with a fever whether the danger is close or not.

September 14, '74.
Rome.

yours, very humbly
FL.

LETTER 113

Villa d'Este, October 26, '74.

To begin with, my return here must indicate M.'s convalescence to you; but her improvement is still only relative, and her nervousness is extreme. The least draft, the slightest noise make her suffer and irritate her. At each visit, I was careful to undergo a *quarantine* of several minutes in the antechamber, in order not to make the patient uncomfortable with the outside air. — Your telegrams and letters have greatly reassured her. She answered them with tenderness and eagerness. . . . Please pardon the delay of these lines; I was awaiting a second letter from Adelheid before giving you a complete account. Enclosed are the three. Adelheid[1] has also written in a charming way to M., who regards her with high favor, and she tells me that it would please her very much to see Adelheid again. Thanks to God and to you, I hope that M. will spend a quiet winter and spring. Adelheid will accompany her to Weimar at the end of June; there they will see what is to be done. No doubt a cure at Carlsbad or Eilsen will be necessary.

If Adelheid *stands the test*, she will return to Rome next winter ('75–'76). —

I suggest for now that you furnish Adelheid with a letter to Mme. Emilie, to whom you will say that Mlle. von Schorn is to take care of M.'s health, and Emilie is to consider her as *your* representative and is to follow her advice. This letter will avoid conflicts —always good to foresee. "A tonic is better than a remedy"! — Concerning Adelheid's housing, I talked *at length* with Mme. Tellenbach[2] and her extremely pretty cousin, the assistant *mistress of the house*. There is no doubt that Adelheid will be the recipient of their eager and delicate attentions. I shall wait for her at the station, and conduct her in triumph to the Tellenbach establishment on the Piazza di Spagna,[3] which is decorated with a handsome column in honor of the Immaculate Conception. In lieu of white hair, my grey and white hair will serve as stage-property for our friend's brilliant entrance into Rome.

My minor winter plans remain the same, Villa d'Este until the start of February; after that, Pest. Easter week, on the way to Weimar, I'll come to Vienna for two or three days, where this time I have nothing else to do except to get your instructions appertaining to *Rome*.

Wholeheartedly,
Your very humble and grateful servant,
FL.

M. Metzdorff wrote to me from Brunswick concerning Dessof's[4] vacancy. I had mentioned him to you rather favorably (without his having suspected it) after the Sucher incident; and I shall answer him, that he has only to please and be approved by Herbeck, that autocrat so bland in bowing out unsuccessful candidates . . . among whom Metzdorff is anxious not to be included.

Your charming *rondeau* on Weilen[5] and Mosenthal, Mosenthal and Weilen, amused me more than all the plays of the two poets together.

LETTER 114

Certainly, your telegram beamed brightly on the 22nd of October! This was the first day, after two months of illness, that M. reappeared in her *encyclopedic* room, decorated by its frightful paintings, lithographs and furniture more ostentatious than respectable. It is a room that has the advantage of being used, in turn, as a laboratory for her ideas, a place to hold her ethical, aesthetic, theological and transcendental lectures, a reception room, and a dining-room — for two. We celebrated St. Charles' day that way, chatting nicely about you and yours; following this, around 4 o'clock, we had some musical entertainment with *Mazeppa*[1] and the *Hungaria* (on two pianos — Sgambati[2] and I) at San Carlo al Corso,[3] in the large piano-store owned by M. Brettschneider,[4] whose name the Romans Italianize by cutting away both the *plank* and the *cutter*, and saying simply: Mr. Gustave.

M. wasn't able to be present at this session in her honor, because there were too many stairs to be climbed and the doctor forbade it; but she invited Emile Ollivier[5] there, his wife (a sensible person, it seemed to me) and M. and Mme. Keudell —[6] who are very gracious to me. I believe I already mentioned to you that M. Keudell is distinguished from his very honorable diplomatic colleagues by his very excellent and serious musical talent. He and Ollivier came to know each other a little better at M.'s the next day — something that ought not to upset the European *Harmony*.

I was called to Florence by a telegram and a letter from M. Sach. Friday and Saturday I stayed there as if *in Weimar*, blessed with the kind attention of Mme. Sach and her daughters. M. Sach definitely refuses to understand my settling-down any place but at his domicile. I've tried in vain to show him that I am honorably obliged to be tied to Pest, and that any negligence would render me contemptible. . . . He displayed deaf ear to all this, and didn't ameliorate his judgment: Weimar must remain my true and constant home. In order to relax this long and intimate conversation, I complimented M. Sach on the forthcoming visit of His Excellency Count Wilczeck; and no less, for the fine reputation of one of his subjects, the son of Professor Hildebrand of Jena — who is, they tell me, a sculptor of genius. Have you noticed two statues by him, in the Exposition at the Vienna *Hall of Artists*: one of a sleeping youth, another of one drinking? Those who know, insist that these are masterpieces.* Hildebrand is only 25 years old; he is now in Florence completing, for the Leipzig Museum, an Adam with the Apple, admired particularly by M. Sach, (both statue and apple together).

And what of our cautious Lassen? I was extremely surprised by his capricious intention to leave the Schiller and Goethe *Institute* (as my excellent, worthy friend Ziegesar called it). Fortunately for the *Institute*, the Vienna grapes only ripen when exposed to Baron Hoffmann's sun; and then they will fall right into M.J.'s [7] beak, he who is so well known as a capable and businesslike orchestra leader. As for the "Brunswicker," Metzdorff, I only mentioned him to you as a *possibility* in case of need. With no need arising, he would leave the scene without further ado. I do think, however, that he would be better able to get on with Herbeck than some others: he is easily handled, affable, very much aware of the London and Paris situations, plays the piano well, and understands both scores and singers. Consequently, he'd be suitable for Vienna.

You very wisely sent Mlle. Adajewski to graze at the Embassy of Holy Russia. Where the deuce can the straightforward singer and composer make her nest? Really, the absurdities of the artistic demi-monde go beyond belief!

I sigh for Adelheid, and I hope our Duino plot succeeds!

May the *Marling* bells sound out the very humble pledges of fealty of

your truly grateful

November 12, '74 —   FL.
   Villa d'Este.

* Formerly in Weimar they used to call Paul Heyse: "the young Goethe": today Hildebrand is the young Michelangelo. *We shall see.*

LETTER 115

Adelheid telegraphed me here, just in time for me to meet her at the station in Rome on Sunday. Let's hope that she shows herself all that we desire, and will be able to fulfill her rôle and her great promise. The first impression at the Babuino meeting was favorable. M. finds Adelheid has improved in her bearing and manners, shows good breeding and makes good conversation; in all truth, she is a frank person, straightforward, cordial, divested of any foolish pretense, free from equivocation, and with pleasantly good connections. I feel that her heart is in the right place so that she'll grow fond of M. — with a type of affection that will be both ardent and discreet.

M. is acquiring a doleful kind of health; and according to Adelheid, her condition and appearance haven't altered since the Altenburg. I shall be returning to Rome a few days before Christmas, and will then soon write you about the *rate of the recovery.*

Your dear letter informed me of the bad fortune at the Vienna "Temple of the Muses"; Herbeck has come to grief with a heavy deficit. This isn't surprising: with the singers' contracts now in vogue, the expensive scenery and costuming, etc., to do *good box-office business* becomes extremely hard. They say that M. von Hülsen [1] is always successful in that respect; and Dudin is bursting with pride at similar successes which Herbeck can't claim. What the deuce is he to do with this shooting-match? It would have suited him better to follow the Muse, rather than these backstage sirens. You thought so from the beginning of Herbeck's labors as a director, and unhappily for him you were only too right.

The overwhelming answer of the Minister "of pleasant Foreign Affairs" to the "anti-Confessional" diplomatic candidate, [2] is a meaningful *Sign of the times.* In the old days it was said in a free and easy way: religion is good for the people: today these clever ones demand it for high society. Nevertheless, the torrent of "Confessionlessness" is swelling, and the damages it wreaks are increasing. . . .

Thank you for remembering the "Bells of Marling" — and during my whole lifetime, I shall remain

your very grateful

December 10, '74, Villa d'Este.   F L.

I shall stay here until the end of January, and will get to Pest on the 9th or 10th of February.

185

LETTER 116

Your good, sweet wishes for the year '75 are coming true. M. is noticeably better. Adelheid is helping her greatly by instructing Emilie and Cesare in their duties, with much tact and concern. More than that, she fulfills her office of caring for Minette in the most perfect fashion; and her company has become very pleasant for M., who told her the other evening: "I really hope you stay a long time in Rome." I chatted afterwards in a friendly way with Adelheid, and begged her to delay leaving until the moment M. goes to Germany this summer, and then to accompany her on this trip. Since she has several scruples (very honorable ones), with regard to you, — as her temporary control stops in April, — please calm her, and assure her that I am not wrong about your kind disposition toward her. She deserves it, and has completely succeeded in endearing herself to M. —

Much to my sorrow, I must soon leave the Villa d'Este and my quiet little musical activity. I shall spend about two weeks in Rome, from the 24th of January to the 8th of February; and I'll get to Pest on the 10th — where Wagner's Concert has been announced for the 21st of February. Do you recall the one at St. Gall about 20 years ago? Wagner conducted the Eroica Symphany, and I the "Préludes" and "Orpheus."[1] Something analogous will now take place at Pest (and not elsewhere, no matter what the newspapers say); and since I've been asked in a most persuasive way to make my new "Bells" ring out, may they reverberate!

Right now, allow me to ask a confidential question. I am quite decided not to make an appearance in Vienna this winter, and I shall only stop there a couple of days after Easter, with no Concert whatsoever, when I go to Weimar. In the light of this situation, would you find it convenient if my daughter and Wagner pay a visit to the *Augarten*, or would it be better if they held off? Please reply *frankly* to the above, — unless you would prefer to be silent; and in that case I should advise my daughter not to venture making an ill-timed visit. Knowing your sensitive and fair understanding of complex affairs, I shall not ask you to pardon my query; and I remain with heart and soul,

your very grateful and
faithful servant
F. Liszt.

January 18, '75, Villa d'Este.

Antonio[2] is leaving tomorrow for Vienna and Rauden,[3] and I have just written your most illustrious brother-in-law how much I envy him his sprained ankle. A good injury to the foot, well-developed and lasting, which would merely prevent me from going out without making me interrupt my musical scribbling, would be singularly pleasing to me. It would garner me the satisfaction of quietly finishing my St. Stanislas here, which as yet has progressed but slightly. The "Bells," a short Legend about *Saint Cecilia*,[4] (verses by Mme. de Girardin)[5] and other urgent tasks, have stopped me from setting the Polish Saint to music, and I've only sketched out a few ideas.

My address at Rome:

Vicolo de' Greci[6] 43.

Madame Minghetti[7] has very cordially asked me to dine next Sunday. She is always prodigiously and brilliantly witty, and has the most charming affability.

LETTER 117

They say about eloquence, that it is as much a part of the listener as it is of the speaker. The same, and even more, holds true for Music. You listened very eloquently to my inadequate Faust-Symphony, and thus furnished the work with its best qualities. Such a listener awards the only prize that I covet, and your approbation exalts me to the serene region of the ideal — inaccessible to worldly discord.

Thank you for your sublime generosity; thank you, too, for the sweet sincerity of your answer to my last question. W.[1] will easily understand, that *intendantish* preoccupations would be incongruous at the Augarten; furthermore, these forgivable things form a chapter now belonging to the past.

The Wagner-Concert at Pest is announced for the 21st of February, and the one in Vienna for the 1st of March.

I shall still spend the party on the 8th of February here with M.; two days later, Pest will see

your truly grateful
and humbly devoted

February 1, '75, Rome.   F. Liszt.

LETTER 118

May there be a sweet and constant holiday in your heart, and all about you! Each year piles up the treasure of your lovely thoughts and good deeds; upon them heavenly blessings shall forever shine.

After having spent all day Monday, February 8th, with M. (fortunately pretty well recovered to her customary state of ailing health), I arrived here Thursday evening. The first news I heard was that the silverware and linen left behind in this apartment had been stolen. There were also several things of value, already recovered by the police, or so I am told.

Another piece of news which finds me more responsive: Wagner's Pest Concert will probably not take place. Seeing the hugeness of the expenses (3000 florins), Richter has declined to guarantee the sum of 5000 francs *clear* that Wagner had stipulated.

As for me, I have no other duty but to stay here as quiet as possible until Easter week when I plan to return to Weimar. I will first stop for a couple of days at Vienna. Please grant a half hour of *Roman* audience there

to your very humble and truly grateful

February 16, '75; Pest. F. Liszt

LETTER 119

[Vienna]

Arriving this morning, I am eager to see you, Your Highness. When will you allow me to call? I promised my cousin to celebrate St. Francis's name-day today with the family — from 3 until 7 (since after dinner there is to be some music). Later, or tomorrow, please command

your very humble
and ever grateful

April 2, '75. F. Liszt

Gussie [1] will take care of the verbal message.

LETTER 120

For many long years, you have continually displayed an intelligence vastly superior to any situation at hand. I flatter myself that I understand you well enough, to admire very sincerely the strong fidelity of your principles and convictions — which are of the highest sort. On important matters I am happy to remain in perfect accord with you; please continue to allow me to differ in some details of minor importance.

In no way does this take away from the deep feeling of respect and compliance enjoyed by

your very grateful and
religiously devoted

April 8, '75, Vienna.   F. Liszt.

LETTER 121

Having arrived here the day before yesterday in the evening, I was anxious to speak to M. Sach of your patronage for the Schiller monument at Vienna. He is all ready to contribute to it, and is only awaiting a few lines from your gracious hand to commence his munificence.

The performance of the "Christus Oratorium" at Munich was extremely satisfying. The public received the work well, and this makes my acceptance of the newspaper criticism easier.

Next Tuesday I shall be at Hannover, and the 2nd of May at Loo Castle,[1]

your very grateful and faithful servant
F. Liszt.

April 15, '75, Weimar (whence I shall return in mid-May)

LETTER 122

After his "supreme gift" of a "half a lock of hair" of Schiller, M. Sach is today sending you a welcome chicken accompanied by 100 Thalers. Confidentially, I suggested to him that he take about a hundred chances (at 2 florins each); but he preferred to come a little short of that, and felt that a Schiller Monument would be rather inopportune at Vienna — where, as he says, they have more need to cast cannon than statues. Furthermore, he was singularly annoyed to see Mme. Dudin among the patronesses: His Royal Highness retains a highly unpleasant impression of I don't know what play it was, they showed him at the *City Theater* at the time of the '73 Exposition. He refuses to grasp, despite my convincing explanations, that the magnificent Dudin's excessively-respectable "silly other-half" could make such a splash at Vienna.

The Schiller Monument brought forth your noble and touching fidelity to the attachments of your youth. M. Sach is hoping that you will give testimony of your choice here at Weimar, something that may evolve only too late.

In the meantime, let me make a "leg" (as the late Countess Theresa Apponyi[1] used to say) before the "Landlady of Styria."[2] Please be so good to tell me the name of your new summer home, for which I shall say the prayer for the Compline Service right out of my heart: "Oh Lord, visit this house; may Thy Holy Angels dwell there and spread Thy blessings."[3]

Would Adelheid really be "played out" at Babuino? Must I resign myself to this disappointment?

In her last letter, M. spoke to me of indiscretions followed by fever, and of Adelheid's "false standards." . . . Formerly, Cousin Eugene W. used to call me "the friend of truth": I accept the title, and so shall stay the rest of my life

your very humble and
truly grateful
FL.

May 20, '75, Weimar.

Yesterday I made a last try to get M. to return here this summer, as she had promised.

September 2nd, unveiling of Carl August's monument (an equestrian statue executed by Donndorf);[4] I'll be there. Before that, in the end of July or beginning of August, I am going to ask the Cardinal if he approves my coming to Schillingsfürst, — and I shall return to Rome before mid-September.

Concerning I don't know which poor tragedy, someone has said that it would be so simple not to write any tragedies at all. It seems to me to be no less easy to give certain gifts with complete good grace. Princes, above all, wouldn't lose anything they might have at stake; and without betraying my long-established feeling for M. Sach, I'm sorry that he didn't merely give in to my plan for the *Schiller Lottery*, at Vienna. . . .

Well, be patient with the ways and customs of Weimar, which are rarely in accordance with my very humble and more-or-less uncalled-for Artist's opinions.

Here at the Belvedere, some "august Visitors" (in the words of the late Baron Maltitz) will soon appear; on the 8th, 11th and 25th of June, a reception for Their Majesties the King of Sweden,[1] Queen Olga of Würtemberg,[2] and the Emperor of Russia.

On the 3rd of September, Carl August's party. His equestrian statue, sculptored by Donndorf (who had the previous honor of making your medallion), will be raised near the castle of Their Highnesses, my kind patrons.

After having been present and a contributor here, at the inauguration of statues of Herder, Wieland, Schiller and Goethe, I shall certainly be at hand for Carl August's.

Napoleon I.'s aphorism: "One should want to live and know how to die,"[3] has its complement in an older one of Frederick the Great's: "One must look to find one's pleasure in doing his duty."[4]

May *Friedstein*[5] be rich in blessings for You and Yours!

very faithfully, your
old, and truly grateful
servant
F. Liszt.

May 30, '75, Weimar.

Toward mid-September I shall return to the Villa D'Este for as long a time as possible. . . . If it were up to me, I wouldn't budge from the place except to be buried near by.

LETTER 124

Without counting a few days' mild illness, I was waiting for Adelheid in order to answer your very kind and friendly letter in a precise way.

She only returned yesterday, and tells me that she wrote the eve of her departure from Rome, — June 12th or 13th. Your message and telegram came at the height of her sickness; for that reason *alone* were her thanks delayed, and this in no way diminishes the sincerity of her truly grateful and devoted affection. When M. asks her to do so, she will gladly return to Rome. To my humble way of thinking, it would be better to delay a bit — until next spring — unless any determining factor occurs. As for now, Adelheid asks me urgently to protest against your excessive munificence: nevertheless, I am confiding to you the need for the continuation of these same bounties, and I have perfect faith in the exquisite tact of your kindness.

I hope that the "Quartet"[1] of colds is over, and that *Friedstein* will be a comfort to you.

This month "eminent visitors" appeared here: the King of Sweden, the Queen of Würtemberg, and the Emperor of Russia, (the day before yesterday). I had the honor to bow to Sweden and Würtemberg at the two musical evenings at the Belvedere. King Oscar is interested in a new Swedish opera, in which he has collaborated as the poet: they say this work, performed in Stockholm, will soon be given in Munich and London. Queen Olga, along with Their Highnesses of Saxony, was kind enough to enrich by her presence the "Musical Commemoration" for Marie Moukhanoff on June 17th. Enclosed is the program, composed exclusively of pieces by your very humble servant.

By order of M. Sach, the ballroom of the "Templars' Lodge"[2] was decorated that day with flowers, nicely arranged, encircling the admirable portrait of Madame Moukhanoff painted by Lenbach. Countess Coudenhoven[3] very nicely sent it to me at the painter's request. Cosima came for this *"commemoration"*; I was happy to give her your kind regards. She told me of Wagner's new dealings with Jauner. It would involve Wagner having a prolonged stay at

Vienna next winter, with the purpose of producing several of his works, under his direction, at the theater. Is this possible? —

Thank you from the bottom of my heart; and I remain

very faithfully your trusty old servant

June 29, '75. Weimar. F. Liszt.

LETTER 125

Mozart and Goethe had as their first name: *Wolfgang*. May Mozart's charming melodies and Goethe's Olympian serenity haunt your *Ocean Villa* at Wolfgang.[1]

Polyphony rules at Babuino Street. The latest letters to Adelheid are even bedecked with very pleasant flourishes. No matter how odd the plot of the new "Eckermann" [2] story may seem, it may finally be successful with Goethe's help.

Yesterday I wrote to His Eminence, Gustave, asking him when he would allow me to pay my respects to him at Schillingsfürst.

My little plans are: Wilhelmsthal, next week; Bayreuth, from August 3rd to the 15th; finally, Weimar, for Carl August's birthday on September 3rd. The equestrian monument of Carl August, (sculptored by your old Altenburg protégé, Dondorf, who since then has been working vigorously on the Great Monument of Luther at Worms—) will be unveiled at this time on the castle square.

Their Majesties the Emperor and Empress of Germany [3] will honor Weimar with their presence on September 3rd.

You know that the King of Spain [4] decorated M. Sach with the Order of the Golden Fleece. They say that Emperor William will be his brother-in-law's sponsor at the solemn ceremony of investiture of the golden chain.

The golden fleece brings me back to my silly sheep. . . . One out of a hundred thousand of this innumerable flock has settled down in Salzburg, near *Wolfgang*. He's directing the "*Mozarteum*" there, and a great many other musical events. Unfortunately he's written an opera, and considers it vastly superior to the "Free-Archer." . . . This work* has been met with enthusiasm at Co-

* entitled "Leonora," crammed full of popular stuff, including "The dead ride fast."

burg and Gotha, and the author is requesting a recommendation from me to be introduced to Your Highness. I stubbornly refused it (since each week he sends me a similar sollicitation); but I modestly propose M. Otto Bach[5] to you, Salzburg's *Vice-Mozart*, even as I recall with gratitude the kind favors formerly conferred at Vienna and Rome by his brother to

your very humbly
faithful and devoted
F. Liszt.

July 17, '75, Weimar

If you are so good to write me, please use the Weimar address up to the 10th of September.

LETTER 126: Preface

Liszt's trip to Bayreuth and the new *Festspielhaus* in 1875 reveals once more his open and unqualified admiration for Wagner's musical genius, and this letter echoes Liszt's more elaborate and detailed sentiments expressed in the letters written at the same time to Carolyne (cf. *L.M.* IV, Nos. 107–110). There is almost a pathetic note in Liszt's awareness of his friend's stature. The "Art-Work of the Future," which both had projected in the 1840's, now seemed to be achieved single-handed by Wagner's music drama; and Liszt — the Symphonic Poems, his unique contribution, left behind him — must have felt the *avant-garde* had moved ahead of him, and he was now safely placed in the Pantheon of the musicians of the dead and glorious past. The church music he composed in the 1870's and 1880's was cast in conventional molds, and certainly he realized that the times were out of joint for the musician who avoided secular and popular forms. The mild success of the *Graner Mass*, for example, was in no way comparable to the crowds of worshipers who flocked to Bayreuth; and Liszt the ex-virtuoso was scarcely the unassuming artist who could content himself with writing for posterity or eternity. In the world of art, where genuine admiration for a fellow worker is all too rare, Liszt's feeling for Wagner attests perhaps more to the real greatness of his spirit than do any of his other virtues.

Your inspirations are always full of the highest wisdom. I trust in them completely; and when you see fit to go to Rome, my deepest heart-felt wishes will accompany you. Perhaps the "friend of truth"[1] will meet you there, since he plans to take up his peaceful retreat again at the Villa d'Este on September 20th and to stay there at least six weeks.

Like you, I feel that the question of the Emilie-Cesare cabinet might be a menace demanding Adelheid's intervention next winter. She lately reassured me that she was well-disposed to resume her position as president of the *Babuino* Council, as soon as M. asks for her.

We are encircled at Bayreuth by the "Magic Fire"[2] of the "Ring of the Nibelungens." Only we do not sleep like Brunnhilde, but are dreaming wide-awake. "A pile of epithets is a poor style," said Pascal.[3] Hence I'm avoiding this — all the more since the most laudatory epithets such as admirable, wonderful, gigantic, unheard-of, sublime, all grow pale before the grandeur and beauty of Wagner's work, the "Nibelungen."

Would you allow me to express my strong desire that You be present at the Bayreuth performances next year? You know all about the actual preliminaries from the numerous newspaper articles, among which the one by Director Jauner shines. The truth is, that never has there been so much enthusiasm shown at rehearsals for any other work whatsoever. Here they've been going on for more than a month, twice a day: the singers, virtuosi, orchestra musicians, set-designers, technicians, costumers, — almost 200 persons are gathered here, — are all full of zeal, and they understand that something extraordinary and of the very highest order is taking place. Even the policemen who work at the gates are chiming in. One of them said yesterday to Mme. von Schleinitz:[4] "We are so happy that Your Excellency fills everything with such enthusiasm."

I congratulate M. Jauner for convincing Wagner to *get up* several of his works again for the Vienna stage. Besides his huge genius, Wagner has additional abilities in dramatic and artistic production, as well as in poetry, music, and stagecraft and all to the highest degree. Under his personal direction, the Viennese performances will gain noticeably in their tone and intensity of effect.

It is useless to add that I am not unaware of *the person* to whom the public owes this gift and M. Jauner his fortunate artistic results, as well as his financial success.

I hope to see your most eminent brother-in-law in mid-September at Schillingsfürst, on my way back to the Villa d'Este. The worldliness of Ragaz[5] would have distressed me; in the course of my dealings with the Cardinal, wariness and twilight — with no newspaper illumination — are much more attractive to

> your very humble and truly
> grateful servant.

Bayreuth, August 9, '75.   F. Liszt.

Have you already read Edouard Schuré's two volumes, called "The Music Drama"?[6] They are nobly written and conceived. A complete apology for Wagner's ideas and works, from Rienzi[7] up to the "Ring of the Nibelungs," is undertaken from the very beginning with great truth and with no touch of the polemical.

I shall be back in Weimar on the 18th of August.

LETTER 127

Rome, September 22nd, '75.

I was in a hurry to get back here, all the more so since I shall probably have to return to Pest in mid-November. Thank goodness M. is in fairly good health; no more of these doctors with their medicines, but she is now at her constant, prodigious intellectual labor, shown by her thousands of already printed pages, to which still thousands more are to be added. She has taken up her retreat again on the fourth story of the Babuino house. Mme. de Staël preferred the brook on the Rue de Bac[1] to the loveliest lakes and countrysides; M.'s are spread out on the rooftops. Fortunately she doesn't even bother to look at them, and she is happy to remain far above, in better regions, among the steep heights of Ideality.

Without daring to hint anything, I hope to see You at Her side at the right moment.

At her own instigation and expense, Adelheid is soon returning to Rome and Naples with one of her aunts, *"Frau Pröpstin."*[2] This chance combination doesn't annoy M., who has sincere affection for Adelheid. She exerted a happy influence on the *Emilie-Cesare* Cabinet, now operating in a fairly satisfactory way; in any case, it is most desirable that Adelheid stay on to complete her task as president of the Council. —

You were asking me about Bülow. I was troubled by his last letter in June. He was then at some village in the Tyrol, suffering strong physical and spiritual pain. How could it be otherwise, after such excessive work, fatigue, — and proud nobility? In this last respect, I know no artist who equals him; even his eccentricities, thought of as faults, arise from the highest aims, and are touched by the marks of honor and disinterestedness.

Despite his sickly state, I imagine that Bülow will go to New York shortly in order to fulfill a contracted engagement.

I plan to return to the Villa d'Este next Sunday. Much to my sorrow, some discreet reasons, which your most eminent brother-in-law will appreciate, kept me from making him a humble visit at Ragatz. He will grant me the occasion, I hope, next summer at Schillingsfürst.

May I be so bold to ask you to give the very kind Lady of the Manor at Duino,[3] the grateful and affectionate good wishes

of your very faithful and
obedient
F. Liszt

Perhaps I shall still stay here during next week. Please write: Vicolo dei Greci, 43, Rome.

LETTER 128

"With expectation I have awaited. . . ."

I haven't said a word about your arrival to M., but your most eminent brother-in-law alluded to it in his last letter. Fortunately it was simple for me to substitute one of his numerous nieces or cousins in your place.

You will find M. in a good state of health, and full of a vigorous and colossal aptitude for work. . . .

I shall come back to Rome on the 3rd of November; if you

arrive earlier, please send a telegram — "Tivoli, near Rome, Villa d'Este" — to your

very faithful and grateful

October 25, '75 — Villa d'Este.   FL.

LETTER 129

Nothing was said to me of the letter You mentioned.

I regret it from the bottom of my heart, and I will be careful never to allude to it with your mother. She knows my point of view, — different from her own, but conforming to yours, — concerning a situation I earnestly pray God to alleviate gently for both of you.

For that we need neither "lines nor sets" — but only the "*eventuality*." I hoped this could have happened this coming 4th of November. While I conscientiously acquiesce to your momentary renunciation and obedience, I pray for good results during the coming year.

your very humble and faithful

November 2, '75 — Villa d'Este.   FL.

LETTER 130

Once more, I knew nothing about the letter that now troubles me so much. It has not been mentioned since, and I shall be careful not to bring it up. To heal certain sores, it is better to be silent than to babble.

The 4th of November was spent quietly. In the morning, Your Mother asked me to take Communion with her at the altar of The Heart of St. Charles, at the church of San Carlo al Corso. Formerly the Pope used to visit it in state each year, on the Holy Cardinal's name-day.

Your most illustrious brother-in-law sent M. the nicest telegram and bouquet; also a letter, from which several lines written in fine humor were read to me. As for your letter, it wasn't shown me; but I know that it made a very good impression with its quotation from the thaumaturge, Prince Alexander Hohenlohe,[1] and the legend of Aquila of Philippi.[2]

From morning until evening there followed numerous congratulations and calls: among others, Adelheid came. She has written you
and will soon return to Germany in the company of her aunt, "Frau
Pröpstin von Stein." She may come back to Rome in a year (without
the aunt), and I still think that she would fit perfectly the delicate
and complex task of presiding over the "*Study*" at Number 89
Babuino Street.

Until my return to Pest in mid-February, I shall stay here quietly
writing a few pages of Music. M. admonished me roughly for my
false interpretation of the textual demands of the *St. Stanislas* Oratorio: as a result I must sadly postpone the completion of this work.
I have written about a third of it: the two others are awaiting your
wise counsel and the salutary help of a poet, since two or three
passages in the middle and end of the libretto in its present form
would be the ruin of better music than my own. If only Mosenthal
weren't elsewhere occupied, he might easily help me out of this fix.

Next April, allow your very humble and truly grateful F.L. to
chat about it, "academically," at the Augarten.
November 9, '75 — Villa d'Este.

LETTER 131

I am often reproached for writing too seldom and too little; I
hope that You won't accuse me of the opposite. Your last lines
calmed me again so well, that I couldn't delay thanking you from
the bottom of my heart.

May all the maternal "wounds," with their accompanying procession of misunderstandings, disappear: this is my humble prayer
to the Holy Father.

A (rather mediocre) poet has pompously said:

> "*And pale Famine, and the frightful plague*
> *Cannot equal the evils and the various troubles*
> *Sown by misunderstandings in the Universe.*" [1]

It is simply a matter of understanding each other well, — it
would seem much the easiest. . . .

I am very happy about your nice meeting with Cosima.

Between *Antonio* and *Tasso* there is nothing basically irreconciliable; as for the form, it will present itself, without too much effort, at the opportune time. —

I applauded M. Grünfeld[2] at the "Augarten," and assured him that he would be an imbecile to seek his fortune away from here, at Vienna.

I shall come to the "Augarten" to seek your kind and very helpful aid promised me for the *St. Stanislas*; and you will decide for me how to end this *Oratorio*. I have had to hold its completion in abeyance, due to a difficulty with the text which Mosenthal will know how to remedy.

Your very humbly
grateful and faithful servant

November 26, '75, (Villa d'Este)   FL.

LETTER 132

Without any deception, I was not a party to the enclosed letter and to the charming lines that explain it with revealing sweetness. The day before yesterday M. spoke to me about the W.'s[1] dinner at the Augarten, where Dududin[2] looked ("the perfect image") of the complete Arch-Duke or of the Most Super-Serene Highness.

Most humbly and from the bottom of my heart, I thank you for your helpful part in the affair. "Swans and ducks" pay you homage; accept this calmly, since you are the Phoenix.[3]

Merry Christmas. I am spending it here, "lonesomely." The saying goes: "Pine-cones at Christmas, fires at Easter." — I am enjoying the pine-cones now in the nice sunlight at the Villa d'Este, and I shan't worry about the fires until toward mid-February, in Budapest.

Now and forever,

Your very grateful and faithful
F. Liszt.

December 24, '75 (Villa d'Este)

LETTER 133

Budapest, February, 17, '76.

My first lines from here are to celebrate tomorrow, and to give you very humble testimony, once more, of my faithful attachment.

It would be sweet for me to be able to show it still more. Furthermore, certain of your virtues and of the continued loftiness of your spirit, I have the firm hope that God will augment the gifts He has given to you and yours. May they increase from earth to Heaven!

My stay at the Villa d'Este was concluded by two days of good conversation with Cardinal H. His coming to Rome, no matter what the comments were, was most fitting. It was neither any sort of a risk nor a blunder. Without displaying any adroitness, he nonetheless excels at it all the more.

Your approval of the landscapes M. Onken[1] painted of the Villa d'Este and its neighborhood delighted me. I am interested in this young painter's success, and hope that he may merit your patronage.

Dudin's Baronetcy coincides exactly with the centenary of the *City Theater*. It'll be nice to call D. "my dear Baron," and I shall always retain my old feeling of true affection for him. His virtues are of a more unusual type than are his faults, and to my way of thinking far outnumber the latter.

I shall stay here until the 2nd of April; on the 7th I'll be at Weimar. Before anything else, I hope to renew my keen and constant gratitude to you, at the *Augarten*.

F. Liszt.

LETTER 134

You left a fine impression of charm behind you at Weimar. M. Sach spoke to me about it, and we sang your praises together. —

Next Sunday, July 9th, baptism of M.S.'s grandson — born the morning you left here. They say his name will be William. Emperor Alexander will come the night before and spend the day at the Belvedere. Toward mid-July, Their Highnesses will take their country holiday, as usual, at Wilhelmsthal; in August M.S. will be present at that prodigious art-event, the performance of the "Nibelungen Ring" at Bayreuth.

When the Seville Cathedral was built, the Canonical Council ordered the Architect to design it in such a way that posterity would say: the architect and the Council must have both been mad to dream of accomplishing such a monument![1] Such a program would scarcely be in line with the economical demands of constitutional and representative government (which, no doubt, has other more necessary advantages); but it does conform rather well to the *concept* of Bayreuth, so attractive to me for these many long years.

I shall probably be in Rome (or at the Villa d'Este) from the end of September until the 4th of November; but from the 15th of November on I shall certainly devote myself entirely to my new duties at the Budapest *Academy of Music*.

Forever and always, with wholehearted and deep gratitude,

Your very humble old servant

July 2, '76   Weimar.   F. Liszt.

M. von Saar's *"Stories"* and his *Drama* have been favorably received here; — and M. von Loën is quite prepared to have Saar's drama performed during the next theatrical season.

LETTER 135

The visit you told me about, will be very pleasant for me. I shall write to Madame Lauchert[1] tomorrow, asking her permission to come and pay my sincerest respects to her at Gotha. I have remembered my friendly relations with her husband with much happiness; if she receives me at all graciously, I shall be very grateful. My special and very original friend, Felix Lichnowsky, once took me to Rauden. Since then, rather special circumstances have kept me bound to the Hohenlohe-Schillingsfürst family, to whom I remain modestly and faithfully devoted. The *"friend of the truth"* (as your Cousin Eugene so amusingly called me), will never forget what he owes to Prince Constantine for his comfortable stay in Budapest and to Cardinal Gustave for the enviable retreat afforded by the "Villa d'Este." Tired as I am of living, still I can never cease being grateful to my benefactors.

Here, everyone is away. M. Sach is making a *royal* progress (to Neustadt,[2] etc.): Mme. Sach is undergoing a solitary rest-cure, with the sea-air (minus the baths) at Helgoland. The *heirs-apparent* are at Ettersburg. All remember your presence with pleasure, and have lately spoken to me of it.

I shall see M.S. at Wilhelmsthal before the end of the month, and shall tell him again that M. von Saar's drama ought to be given here during the course of next winter. If you'd care to write him a few lines occasionally, they would embellish still more the "favorable dispositions" of which M. von Saar may be certain. To assure him of these without delay would seem desirable to me, since this would simplify his dealings with the Intendant, M. von Loën. The latter will accompany M.S. to Bayreuth: and the new aide-de-camp, Prince Wittgenstein,[3] (Emile's brother) will be there fresh for his new position. I shall probably have the pleasure of meeting him at Wilhelmsthal next week, They tell me he has had a rather *animated* career in Austria and Bavaria. . . .

Monsignor Haynald did me the honor of stopping a few hours at Weimar on Friday. He was coming back from his cure at Ems, and on his way to one at Töplitz. Archduke Albrecht[4] and the Emperor and Empress of Germany favored him with their attentions at Ems — and Empress Augusta bestowed a beautiful gift upon him for the Sisters at Kalosca.

Yesterday my good friend Hans von Bronsart told me again how touched he was by his kind reception at the "Augarten."

I shall be present in spirit at the Mass of the good Capuchin Fathers at Friedstein: and "Sursum corda"[5] I remain

your very humble and faithful

July 16, '76, Weimar.   FL.

I am staying at Bayreuth from the 1st to the 30th of August.

Adelheid has been at her cousins' the Steins (*in Meiningen*) for the past two weeks, but she will also come to Bayreuth before mid-August.

LETTER 136

Your Highness,

The warm memory you keep of me shines like a lucky star over my past and future.

Many thanks for the telegram which arrived here Saturday evening.

At Szegszard[1] I only leave Augusz's house to go to Mass; usually this is at a new church built in the Gothic style between 1864–'68 under Augusz's direction. It is dedicated to the Archangels Michael, Gabriel, and Raphael, whose nicely sculptured figures of painted wood, done by Schönfeld[2] (of Vienna) after the devotional manner of the old masters decorate the three altars. I pray there in spiritual communion with the praiseworthy and much-beloved author of the "Friendship of the Angels."

The tone of her last letters is one of sweet moderation.

Last winter I interviewed Emilie's successor at the home of Madame Lindemann,[3] who has resignedly spent her last years in bed. Her personal maid has had good recommendations: let's hope that the results will be to M.'s satisfaction —

It appears that Wagner is expected at Rome, and they are preparing a *reception* for him and his "Lohengrin," and a concert is to be directed by my young friend and disciple Sgambati — the most *prominent* pianist and musician in Rome.

Cosima wrote and telegraphed me from Sorrento, but without mentioning the Roman trip to me. This apparently would cause no trouble at all at Babuino Street, especially in my absence.

I shall spend the approaching All-Saints' Day and All-Souls' Day at Kalosca (near Szegszard), at Milord Archbishop Haynald's, — and on November 3rd, back in Budapest for the whole winter, will be

your very humble
and very faithful servant
F. Liszt.

October 28, '76 — Szegszard.

LETTER 137

I wholeheartedly agree with your happy inspiration from Rome. If it wasn't able to produce all the desirable results with one stroke, at least a few have been outlined; several of the harsh aspects and much of the "bitter prejudice" have disappeared. You have truly accomplished a Good Deed.

As for the whole situation, you know that for many years I have been completely on your side, never having doubted for a moment either your clairvoyance or your good qualities; and among the latter your filial affection has stood out in the first rank. It has not been for me to lose my way among "imaginative whirlwinds" or "conjectural labyrinths"; I maintain, however, a constant, firm faith in the "balm of your thoughts" and the Christian charity of your spirit.

M. didn't breath a word to me about the "excommunication Bull." An old Roman proverb goes: "The Pope affirms and cancels his Bull." Let's hope that things will take this turn now, and that Emily's thefts don't provide a prolonged *casus belli* against the *Hohenlohes!* —

You have evidently seized upon, along with M. von K.,[1] the best way to avoid troubling M. with the unpleasantness ensuing from Emily's trial . . . an affair best made no business of Rome's.

My plan is to arrive at Babuino (*without warning*) during Holy Week. Please keep my surprise a secret. In mid-March it would be hard for me to avoid the boring chore of a Concert for the Vienna Beethoven Monument; I shall probably perform the E-flat Concerto[2] at the "Friends of Music," (the same one I played to the satisfaction of the Bonn* critics in 1845) on the 18th of March, 1877. After this required pleonasm, which will keep me 3 or 4 days at Vienna, I shall go from there to Rome.

Several newspapers have me making a trip to England and Holland: not at all. I shall remain here quietly until mid-March, teaching a dozen pianists of both sexes at the new Academy of Music. Part of my instruction consists of telling them that several hundred of their profession are already "in excess" in this world of "*concerts*" and harmony trimmed with dissonance (see Gortchakoff's recent dispatch). Although I've written a great many dissonances in Music, I'm happy never to have come up against them in real life, at the homes of the few persons to whom sincerely devoted, remains

your truly grateful
and very humble

November 20, '76 — Budapest.   F L.

LETTER 138: *Preface*

The "disgrace" to which Liszt refers remains a mystery. The pronouncement issued by the Vatican against Carolyne's book did not appear until July 1877 (cf. Preface to Letter 108; also Letter 180, Note

* at the time of the inauguration of the Beethoven monument.

1); and certainly the failure to be appointed to either the directorship of the Sistine or Lateran Choirs could not be considered as a "disgrace."

Since letters were "temporarily lacking" at the Augarten from Rome, we may assume that relations between Marie and her mother were still strained, and Liszt was hard at work at his role of mediator and arbiter. His interest in Ferdinand von Saar's play and its possible presentation by the theater at Weimar is another indication of the effect advancing age had upon Liszt. More and more he contented himself with acting as general cultural adviser at Weimar, Rome, and Budapest, and the earlier rigors of musical composition were on the whole supplanted by the more genial duties of instructing the many piano students who made their pilgrimage to the master's house at Weimar.

An amusing footnote to Liszt's new capacity as pedagogue is found in Sitwell (*Liszt*, pp. 286–293). Apparently the charms of the other sex still had appeal for the aging lion. Carolyne at one point became alarmed — after the information was given her by her faithful scout, Adelheid von Schorn — by the successive and extraprofessional attentions he devoted to Baroness Olga Meyendorff, Amy Fay, and the fiery "Cossack" Olga Janina. The latter pupil even threatened to kill both herself and Liszt, in a melodramatic scene at Budapest that must have reminded him of the Romantic days of the 1830's and 1840's. Liszt succeeded in calming her, however, and returned to Rome soon after for spiritual consolation and the chastening advice of Carolyne.

LETTER 138

The best crops are grown slowly. "With expectation I have awaited. . . ."

As for me, I have had to submit to the hardest *Roman* disgrace of the past dozen years. It defies all logic but is none the less real, just like the famous "wrath of the Hohenlohes" — tempered by kindness in the Cardinal and in your husband.

Since letters from Rome are temporarily lacking at the *Augarten*, allow me to forward the last one that came here yesterday. To clarify it further, I added a small previous page by Cosima. M. von Keudell was wonderful to the Wagners in Rome.

I shall write M. Sach tomorrow and remind him of his promise to have M. von Saar's drama performed this winter at Weimar. In view of the temporary cool relations between Prince Constantine and his cousin Georg von Meiningen, it would be better not to approach the latter, and instead to go *all the way* with Sach; all the more so, since he has already taken a stake in the affair. When he answers me, I'll send you his letter; and I will take the liberty of requesting two lines to be written to Loën, to revive his zeal.

The "Beethoven Monument" Committee wrote me again yesterday morning; I shall now play at the Vienna Concert in mid-March.

Your very humble and truly grateful

December 7, '76, Budapest.   FL.

LETTER 139

[Budapest]

Here is the letter from M.S., to whom I hadn't written since I left Weimar. The reproach made to me by a deputy in the House here, that I live more in Weimar than in Pest, provided me with the excuse to remind Sach of several art projects in his domain. There is the Bach monument (at Eisenach) that they ought to turn over to Donndorf, who has already made a nice sketch of it; the *Wagner Association* that they have so prudently neglected to found up to now . . . and finally and above all, M. von Saar's drama. S.'s answer to me should indicate his favorable attitude to you; and if you now would be so good to write a few lines to Baron Loën, the production of the play would get on swimmingly.

For a long time at Bab.,[1] they've been claiming to get everyone and everything "in line," and in *their* way. Unfortunately, too often people go about this in an odd manner: either they cut off the feet of others or their own. My faith in personal infallibility doesn't extend to the point of thinking this method extremely expedient, and I'm not even quite convinced that the Duchess of Maine[2] was altogether right, when she said to Mme. de Staal: "Humph, child, I'm the only one I see who is always right." Nevertheless, this cult of the *Infallible I* numbers such a large quantity of apostles and martyrs of both sexes (without speaking of the common herd of the faithful), that one is almost ready to believe it true.

I presume you have more recent letters from R.[3] than the two I enclose, where he uses Dante's verb: "to be prolonged into the future." [4] My petty measure of wit and talent doesn't allow me to bestraddle winged-horses . . . and I restrict myself to the middle-region of "daily demands," while at the same time I sincerely admire those few elect who climb much higher and are able to soar.

You have always been a *noted critic* (in the sense Spontini[5] meant it) of my modest efforts. Thank you from the bottom of my heart for the beautiful commentary on the Beethoven Cantata. I only learned of its performance from a preliminary letter of Richter's, most obliging — to whom I sent my thanks and quasi-apologies by way of an answer.

Several telegrams have arrived inquiring about my health. It may be that a few newspapers have mentioned my fall — not as composer, but a simple fall while getting out of a carriage. The damage was minor: I had to stay in my room several days. I shall have recovered before Sunday.

Very faithfully, your
very grateful
FL.

Tuesday, December 26, '76 —

I don't know who it was asked me yesterday, if I'd read a story by Wirth[6] (?) entitled "Artist and Princeling." They say it refers to the novel by your sister-in-law, Mme. Lauchert. Up to now I merely know the title, and I'm still not sure if they quoted it exactly. If the tale comes out in favor of the heroine, I shall read it: otherwise *no*.

PART THREE

1877-1886

LETTER 140

The Aunt of Madame George Sand[1] used to say to her: "There is nothing in this world worth the trouble of being repeated: not even M. de Buffon!"[2] This wise sentence notwithstanding, I am taking the liberty of rewriting, on your behalf, my *Roman*[3] lines of today. Last week I wrote more categorical ones, with the sketch of the four cardinal points that take me away from Rome.

Surprisingly enough, they were answered with complete kindness and sweetness.

Very faithfully, your
very humble and grateful
FL.

January 23 '77 — Budapest.

LETTER 141

I was talking to you yesterday about a favorable answer. Here's another one, by which I am dismissed. I neither accept it nor protest against it! . . . persons like myself (as the late Prince Hohenzollern[1] used to say) only take orders from themselves.

In the enclosed letter, the first two pages deal with young Prince Boris Czetwertinski.[2] He is playing the Nabab at Pest, losing a hundred thousand florins at card at the Club, they say, and spending several hundred thousand florins fixing up an apartment in the house of one of the Count Karolys. Considering M.'s former friendship with the old Boris Czetwertinsky, I asked her if she knew anything about young Boris, whom I have not had the pleasure of meeting.

M. also handed me a letter from Léonille Wit.[3] . . . where M. thanked her for a quotation (a prayer) from the Imitation of Christ. This, it seems, has contributed to forcing Léonille more than before into the bosom of Our Holy Mother the Church. The quotation is more than thirty years old * but it was piously reaffirmed on New

---

* perhaps the translation of Saint Pius's relic at Sayn was effected, as a result of the quotation —

Year's Day, '77, and I have read Léonille's recent letter of dignified gratitude. Unfortunately M. no longer feels me deserving enough to tell me what chapter and verse of the *Imitation* contains the prayer. In any case, I shan't immediately borrow my friend Zaluski's [4] "mouse-colored" top-coat. . . .

Your most humbly faithful

January 24, '77, Budapest.   F.L.

LETTER 142

Due to several details, quite to the advantage of Constantine, "who has hit upon the right idea," I shall not send you the rather tempered letter of January 28th from Rome. It has been intimated to me to warn you that the answers by telegram will stop: if you write on the occasion of February 8th, you will receive a real letter as an answer. Here is the literal quotation:

"I have promised you, that after having stopped writing to my daughter, I shall answer the letter she will write to me for the 8th of February. Otherwise I would have limited myself, as I have since her departure, to answer her by telegraph. . . .

For many years now, I have come to the conclusion that the Carthusians and the Trappists are still really chatterers. . . .

Excuse this extravagance by
your most humbly
faithful and grateful

February 1st, '77   Budapest.   FL.

LETTER 143

The incredible letter from Rome stuns me. The one that arrived for me at the same time has a more temperate tone, and it will confirm you in what you already clearly know: which is, that for years I have been objecting to these false flights of the imagination that lead to such deplorable results.

In this turn of affairs, a good spell of silence would seem to be necessary. To sound the note of the Penitential Psalms would scarcely be suitable. As you so aptly noted, you can't claim to repent of sins which, in the depths of your soul, you don't believe you have committed; and "humility is too holy a virtue to be hypocritically employed."

Thus we must content ourselves temporarily with the first verse of the 39th Psalm (which is not one of the penetential psalms): "*With expectation I have awaited. . . .*"

The same letter, (from the 2nd to the 8th of February), mentions twice a difficulty pending in Rome. It may be that Audisio's[1] book will mark the beginning of the censuring of that anonymous work, unpublished but already rather well-known, entitled "Concerning the Inner Causes for the Outer Weakness of the Church."[2] This will not be a thunderclap, but it will be painfully annoying. I wish now that the authoress hadn't laid herself open, and that I hadn't neglected to warn her in time, several months before the start of the Council in 1869.[3] Since then, M. has proved to me that I was pusillanimous and foolish: I wasn't able to combat her arguments, and I contented myself with the humble wish that I should like to see her wonderful intelligence and great knowledge employ themselves in less arduous regions than that of transcendental theology, and prophecies joined with disquisitions concerning the politics and administration of the Church. To my way of thinking, *lay* Catholics should have nothing to do with this "galley,"[4] which is well-provided with the advice and tactics of the venerable College of Cardinals and aided by the glorious chorus of bishops and the thousands and thousands of doctors, preachers, advisers, rowers, and scriveners.

For these *lay* Catholics, (who are neither members of the Chamber of Deputies, nor of the House of Lords, nor professional journalists, nor in the employ of any government whatsoever), the wisest stand to take is the devoted conformity of silence, with respect to the problems that Our Holy Father the Pope will infallibly resolve, aided by the inspiration of the Holy Spirit.

Keep your indulgence for your
worried and most
constant servant

February 14, '77.   F.L.
Budapest.

March 31, '77, Bayreuth.

And I too, Your Highness, fall today into the role of your petitioner!

Wagner asks me to beg Prince Hohenlohe to grant several weeks' leave to Richter — who would then be commissioned to direct the last rehearsals of the Wagner Concerts at London — and to ask his help for the 6 Concerts themselves announced for the fortnight of the 7th to the 22nd of May. I therefore am venturing to beg you to intervene favorably, with my request (enclosed here) to Prince Constantine. For his own part, Richter will have the honor of personally presenting a similar request to His Highness, supported by a letter from Wagner.

You know that Standhartner [1] and M. Jauner have saddled me with a commission, concerning the complete performance at Vienna of the tetralogy, "The Ring of the Nibelungs." Wagner is now not at all inclined to deal with the Opera directors: the obvious proof, is that he declined the twenty-thousand Mark letter of credit brought him by Richter the day before yesterday, as a premium from M. Jauner for the "Nibelungs." When I spoke to him, however, of the supreme good-will that the Emperor so kindly displayed toward his work, he answered me immediately in tones of real emotion:

"As soon as His Majesty will be so good to convey me his desire to see my Nibelungs performed at Vienna, I shall comply most respectfully, and then place my work at the disposal of the Imperial Theater."

Wagner repeated the same answer to me the following day, and explained himself to Richter in a similar manner. I wrote this to Standhartner, adding that preferable intermediary for His Majesty's wish ought actually not to be Director Jauner.

My last letters from Rome were sweetly temperate. Schubert was rightly inspired by his "Faith in Spring." [2] I pledge myself to it, and remain.

your faithful old servant
FL.

Next Wednesday I shall be back in Weimar.

LETTER 145

April 7, '77   Weimar.

After having spent a very pleasant day at the Duke of Meiningen's, I returned here Wednesday evening. At my first interview with M. Sach, I put him back on the track of M. von Saar's Drama. Milord again assured me that the performance would soon take place.

Baron Loën turned his back to the "Devil's temptings" of the Intendancy of the Frankfurt theater, (enhanced by a salary of 6000 Thalers, a free house, and some other eventual remunerations). Loën is loyally staying at Weimar in accordance with Mme. Sach's wishes, and he is lured by the latter's *ticklish* strategy.

Tomorrow, the 8th of April — Mme. Sach's birthday — we shall have a Gala performance of Brüll's[1] "Golden Cross." I told Loën yesterday that in Vienna they were right to follow this pretty opera by the charming "Coppelia"[2] ballet.

In answer to my letter from Bayreuth, I received several pages this morning, among which I take the liberty of enclosing this one for you.

Your very humble faithful
F L.

Dom Pedro II is expected here next Saturday. They are giving the two parts of *Faust*[3] in his honor.

LETTER 146

August 22, '77 — Rome

Not knowing where to send a telegram to Your Highness on the 15th of August, I didn't send one; but I celebrated your birthday, nonetheless, with my whole heart. Indeed I even did this twice: in the morning at the Bayreuth church, and in the evening at Schillingsfürst, in the "*drawing room*" decorated by your photograph and Prince Constantine's.

Your most illustrious brother-in-law has very sensibly enlarged the Schillingsfürst gardens; they will stretch out from the castle to the schoolhouse founded by Him and directed in an *exemplary*

2 1 5

fashion by the very respectable Benedictine Sisters.* The establishment is going so well, and has already acquired such good repute, that soon they will have to consider adding a second house.

I only stopped for a half-a-day at Munich. Semper was my neighbor at the Hotel *Marienbad*. He still shows the consequences of his serious illness, which the baths and the bad Reichenhalle [1] food have not yet been able to drive out of his system. To amuse himself while convalescing, he made a series of daily trips around Belgium; and he will participate, as if rightfully invited, in the splendid *Rubens Festival* at Anvers. Lenbach will be there, too. His magnificent portrait of Andrassy is almost completed: I was struck by the noble similarity, at once real and historical. The illustrious Count really has the look of grandeur and intelligence that becomes him: his fine Hungarian costume, with the Ribbon of St. Stephen, enhances the effect; and the painter has taken advantage of an old cameo (an opal, so Lenbach said to me) with a picture of Jupiter which shines as a clasp at his *"Chin."*

Arriving here Sunday, I found M. in that state of sickly health she's had for so many years. Nevertheless, from the moral and intellectual point of view, she keeps all her imperturbable courage and her *"noble-mindedness."* †

Cardinal H. intimated to me that I ought to crave an audience with the Holy Father. I shall obey: consequently, I can only enjoy the kind hospitality of the Villa d'Este for next week.

Without any diminution,
your very faithful
and truly grateful servant
F.L.

LETTER 147: *Preface*

An interesting eyewitness account of Liszt during the fall of 1877 may be found in Mrs. Winthrop Chanler's *Roman Spring*, where the author describes the gathering that took place on the musician's sixty-sixth birthday on October 22 — a little over a month after this letter to Marie was written. The description rendered by Mrs. Chanler — called

---

* There, 25 girls are raised, taught, fed, lodged, and taken care of.
† This is always sublime, but rarely within the comprehension of the ordinary public.

by Henry James "the only truly cultivated woman in America" — reminds us how closely the concept of the seemingly dead past is related to the problem of generation. To read her book, as well as *Memory Makes Music*, is to see once more the value of the anecdotal method of history. She also makes pertinent comment concerning Liszt's ordination and *l'affaire Wittgenstein*. "It was often said that he became an abbé so as to escape from marrying the Princess" (*Roman Spring*, p. 82).

LETTER 147

I was completely ignorant of what Clelia[1] wrote Gussie; but in Spiridion's[2] letter, mailed to Friedstein yesterday, the *Clelia* paragraph was of my making — consequently exact. At the same time that I find it rather odd that "the Romaness"[3] has entered into such dealings with Gussie, it would seem to me you would be perfectly and wisely nice if you'd care to send her 100 Lire. More than that would be excessive.

Returning here Wednesday, we spoke continually of you to M. She plans to write you before the end of the month. Will you expect her letter, or will you write her first? Without meddling in things which are unhappily so delicate, I can assure you that *now* a few lines from you to her would be welcome.

It goes without saying that I shan't breath a word about the *Clelian* correspondence: out of an excessive sense of precaution I even burnt immediately the first page of your yesterday's letter. When I can't be of service, I at least try not to be of harm.

All sorts of misinformation about Wagner is filling the newspapers. The one about the *ribbon* attached to the *Playhouse Society*[4] Medal is one of the silliest. It may be that a few owners of this medal, ribbon-fanciers like so many fellows that one meets, asked Wagner if they might wear it as a buttonhole decoration. This would suffice to spread the stupid story about, of a new and purely-imaginary Bayreuth decoration. . . . As for the rest, the serious business at Bayreuth isn't in the bad shape that everyone delights shouting about. Without a doubt, there is a big deficit (more than 120000 Marks) to meet: they are setting about to correct this as soon as possible.

I'll be back in Budapest around mid-November; and as for the past 7 years, I'll spend the winter there.

Your truly grateful and
faithful servant

September 16, '77, Rome.   F L

Ernesto Coratti,[5] recommended by Gussie, came to see me yesterday. He works at the piano with one of my pupils (at the Saint Cecilia High-School); another of his teachers told me that he was very talented, and I shall try to be pleasant to him.

Would you be good enough to remember me kindly to your neighbor in the Friedstein valley, M. Dumba?

LETTER 148

Your Highness,

On this blessed date of your birthday,[1] I placed the humble pledge of my faithful regards and memories at your feet. May they have been welcomed by your angelic kindness, and this hommage remains for me at once a great honor and a personal consolation.

Before returning to Weimar, I shall spend, as usual, the first week in April at my excellent cousin's[2] in Vienna. I hope to see you then, and once again voice my unalterably devoted gratitude.

February, Budapest, '78.   F. Liszt.

They are not at all tired of me here, and I am existing peacefully happy, without any taste for unnecessary travels.

LETTER 149

The best thing is to content yourself with a tender and *genuine* telegram, and to accept the letter as a cross to bear — and one of the saddest ones ever. I pray God to remedy this affliction for both sides.

M. explained to me why she went into such heavy mourning for Pius IX. First, in 1861, an act of justice by the Holy Father; later, a miracle. The act was tempered by prudence, and the miracle not the less so. Since I am scarcely exclusively a part of the Roman camp, I refused to argue; at the same time I was convinced that M. was wrong. There is no doubt about the great nobility and sublimity of her feelings. If there is, mixed within these, some sort of emphasis and an increasing taste for a completely historical *attitude* which I find hard to understand — well, it's not up to me to watch over her.

I was quite wrong concerning the paragraph about the letters to Andrassy. In order to have M. avoid certain embarrassment, I told her last fall that they were saying in Pest and in Germany, that she was writing to Bismarck, Andrassy, Mme. Eugénie,[1] etc. With such a person, however, neither warnings nor political dithyrambs filled with forewarnings are effective.

Let's let Leo XIII[2] (whom I did not have the honor to meet when he was Cardinal) take care of the running of the business of the Church, guided by that inspiration lasting until the end of time — the Holy Spirit. Lay members, not being rulers, have only to be silent and obedient. —

I come back to the Old Testament and the Maccabees. No one wishes Rubinstein all imaginable success more than I; he deserves it by his supreme talent and his praiseworthy, tireless efforts. . . . Excuse him for displaying a kind of dignity he previously lacked at the *Augarten.* He probably suspects that you lack enthusiasm for his genius. For my part, I can't see the value of any other serious *operas* save those of Wagner. Evidently (from the box-office receipts), they are a happy necessity all over the world. Rubinstein's error, as I had already told him in Weimar — ('55) — consists in refusing to recognize the obvious fact, that Wagner's works are justly predominant in Germany. The criticisms that are made of them diminish neither their value nor the public's curiosity. This last point is a decisive one; since the criterion of theatrical success is only to be found in the cash-box, and this is sustained by the affluence of those who are curious. Thus, up to the present Rubinstein has had no luck in that direction, except at Berlin, where the Maccabees was fairly well supported. A very gifted artist who has rare dramatic feeling (what M. de Voltaire called the "devil in the body")[3] — Marianne Brandt[4] — contributed noticeably to the success of the Maccabees in Berlin. I don't know whether Vienna has an actress-singer of this variety.

Thank you wholeheartedly for what you were so kind to tell me, and I am constantly and forever

your very humble and
truly grateful servant
F. Liszt.

February 24, '78 — Budapest.

Count Ghéza Zichy[5] has planned a Concert by Walther[6] and Mottel,[7] here in mid-March.

LETTER 150

Amid the happy little family of Pest concerts, there are the usual snakes — and frogs — in the grass. My friend Gheza Zichy certainly can't help it. He arranged Walter's concert for the best; the new songs of Rudi Lichtenstein,[1] the "Bayreuthian" who performed the day before and the day after, would have delighted us. But alas — "blond" Riedel's 50 florins, plus the hotel expenses and several *extras*, spoiled everything. At present, Gheza Zichy has to concern himself exclusively with his brother's and his wife's mourning. Upon first hearing about the death of Countess Alexander Zichy, (formerly Karatsonyi), I thrashed all the persons who spoke of poisoning. Alas, I was mistaken! Morphine did its work; the suicide had been premeditated for two years; Countess Adrienne effected it with lavish courage and singular grace.

A few days earlier, she had piously taken Communion; and they say that in order not to bother the future sleep of her husband, she took the mattress away from their conjugal bed and had it carried into another room. . . . There, she expired.

Funerals follow one upon the other this year, and are not too much alike; after Victor Emmanuel,[2] Pius IX; and yesterday there was the Archduke Franz Karl.[3] Those who live ought to prepare themselves for dying, and accustom themselves to seeing others die, — young and old. For my part, I find that my life has lasted too long . . . but I shall leave off with this funereal tone, and recommend a young pianist to you who bursts with youth and talent — Mlle. Martha Remmert.[4] She has already been recommended to you by your sister-in-law, the Duchess of Ratibor, and I will only add that she has worked very *hard* at Weimar and Pest. Mme. Sachotte[5] favors her with her patronage; and at *Graez* castle, at the Lichnowskys,[6] she has succeeded very well in giving lessons to the Countess.

During the first days of April I hope to renew my old pledges of service to you, at the *Augarten,*

with sincere and perpetual
gratitude
F. Liszt.

March 12, '78 — Budapest.

LETTER 151

Martha Remmert has both talent and good looks. I have ventured to add a word to the recommendation of your sister-in-law, the Duchess of Ratibor; and thank you for having favored the Concert of the "blond-tufted Naïad" by your presence and your "infinite train of an indefinable blue" kind of accompaniment.

She does not plan to stay in Vienna, and I am not at all encouraging her aspirations to glory. Bad singers are able to find good engagements, since theaters are everywhere necessary. It's another thing for pianists of both sexes: 99 out of a hundred are at least superfluous, if not downright pests. One of their wittiest rivals said to me yesterday: "There ought to be Massacre of St. Bartholomew for us"!

An ex-pianist, also named *Martha,* — now the Reverend Mother Superior of the Sisters of the Annunciation — spoke to me of the charming reception you had in Vienna. She will return to Bucharest tomorrow; and she seemed to me very capable of fulfilling, with neither awkwardness nor exaggeration, the mission of evangelical charity with which she is charged.

Next week, at the *Augarten,* I shall place my humblest and most faithful testimonies of service at your feet.

March 28, '78   F. Liszt.
Budapest.

LETTER 152

Would you allow me, Your Highness, to solicit your kindness once more? It is a matter of the particule *de* ("*von*") to be joined to the name of one of my best friends, who had no other fault than that of being almost too constantly prodigal with his noble work for the advantage of the Vienna artists and public. I am taking the liberty of asking you to interest yourself in this DE, in Bösendorfer's favor, and to mention it as something at once kind and equitable to Prince Constantine. He, Bösendorfer, hinted his wish to me about two or three years ago, without reminding me of it since: I honor as best I can his discreet silence, while confiding my request to Your great kindness.

I shall be back in Weimar around the 20th of June, where they are to celebrate the 25th year Jubilee of the Grand-Duke's reign before mid-July. In August I hope to return to the Villa d'Este.

Everywhere and forever,
Your very humble
and most grateful servant
F. Liszt.

May 1st, '78 — Weimar.

LETTER 153

[Weimar, mid-May, 1878]

Your Highness,

After Vienna, I spent a week in Bayreuth at Wagner's. His genius is not at all waning: on the contrary, he climbs with *Parsifal* [1] from the sublime to the miraculous, for which the first-act music and a third of the second act is completed. There only remains to write the orchestration, — a rather long job but an easy one, since the chief instruments for it are already established within the context of the present score for piano and voice.

Wagner has entitled his *Parsifal* "a Festival-Play for the Consecration of a Stage." Up to the present people have not become accustomed to seek a "Consecration" for the theater. This tentative effort is therefore all the finer; and perhaps that which now seems still impossible for the art, will not always be so.

Returning here on the Wednesday of Holy Week, I found Mme. S. [2] in better health than last year, and very happy with her stay in Constantinople. Monsieur S. keeps himself always in the cheerful and lively frame of mind with which you are familiar. In honor of the King of Sweden, [3] there was a small *select* concert at the castle. His Majesty is very much interested in a young singer from his country, Mlle. Frieberg. [4] She aspires to the fame of her

222

compatriots Lind and Nilson;[5] Mme. Viardot has given her lessons, and she will soon make her debut here. At our old barracks of a theater at Weimar, whose interior has been passably fixed up by M. de Loën, Madame Materna[6] has just brilliantly appeared as Ortrud, Elizabeth, and Armide.[7] Sunday they will again give Saint-Saëns' opera *Dalila*,[8] which obtained the highest-quality success at its first performances this winter. For my part, I retain a kind of prejudice against Biblical subjects in the opera. Since Méhul's *Joseph*,[9] there has been no lasting success in this genre: even the *Moses* of the great Rossini[10] is only kept alive in concerts by the famous Prayer. The *warriors'* duet, sung by Rubini[11] and Tamburini,[12] which formerly delighted the public throughout Europe, has almost disappeared, and so has the delicious Trio, so much applauded: "Mi manca la voce." Nevertheless, my bias against Biblical operas does not make me unjust when I consider the very great talent of Saint-Saëns, whom I admire and esteem.

This evening I shall see *Rheingold* again at Leipzig, and tomorrow *Walküre*. Baron Loën promises us *Rheingold* here at the end of May. I will then be in Paris, because Minister Trefort[13] and Count Jules Szapary[14] (President of the Hungarian Exposition in Paris)[15] are anxious to send me there as the *Hungarian* member of the International Jury at the Exposition. I would not know how to decline fulfilling such an honorable post, notwithstanding my extreme fatigue from trips, either short or long, which my *triangular* existence (as Wagner calls it) between Pest, Weimar and Rome inflicts upon me. [The conclusion of this letter is missing.]

LETTER 154

Your Highness,

I was on my way to Paris, when the telegram arrived at Hanover telling of the delay for the 13th class of the International Jury (Musical instruments), to which I belong out of patriotic Hungarian reasons.

Returning here, I found your very kind letter and Dingelstedt's *scenario* for *Saint Stanislas*. You have approved of it, and I find it perfect. There remains to perfect it poetically and musically. Despite my estrangement from the theater, I make no objection at all to the staging, with costumes and sets, of the "Stanislas" Oratorio. If the poet considers this style more suitable, I put myself on his side.

Appended herewith, I am taking the liberty of sending you the autograph of *Scenario*, (with minor annotations concerning the role of *Christina*, and the desirable economy for the choirs of angels).

Would you be so kind as to return his manscript to Dingelstedt, accompanied by my letter of really sincere thanks?

The "state secret" that caused Mme. Sach to "bear a grudge against Vienna" is unknown to me; consequently I shall not at all betray it. I merely know that She has a definite predilection for her son-in-law, Prince Reuss.[1]

M. Sach spoke to me again about M. von Saar, with some intention of wheedling and *establishing* him at Weimar. I explained the corollary distinctly to him; and I have been ordered to obtain the photograph of the poet, Saar, for S. — he is cousin to the military husband of my cousin Marie, whom you know.

Tomorrow morning I shall be in Paris; and I shall return here on June 20th, owing to the "Erfurt Music Festival," at which the "audience of kings"[2] of Napoleon I.'s time will not convene. Enough to say that the "General German Music Association" has been proceeding in an honorable fashion, in no common way, for more than 20 years. People will take more note of it later on.

"Faithfully and constantly"
your most humbly grateful

June 8, '78 — Weimar.   F. Liszt.

The temperature in Rome seems to be moderate.

LETTER 155

Your Highness,

Thanks to your forbearing coöperation with the St. Stanislas, I am getting confident about the success of the work. Dingelstedt seems to me to have well comprehended the characters and the situations: his highly experimental skill will take care of the rest. At the very first I was frightened of the scene where King Boleslaw kills the Holy Bishop; but this crime is historical, and provides dramatic motivation for the madness and the final repentance of the King.

I shall thank Dingelstedt again, and will try not to spoil his poem by dull Music.

M. Sach is extremely well-disposed toward M. von Saar. He spoke to me of him yesterday in such a way as to make me think that the "Court of Muses" will offer him a footstool. It goes without saying, that You were not mentioned in my conversation with M. Sach on this matter. The talks go on — soon to come to a conclusion, I hope.

I only spent 9 days in Paris, due to the Erfurt *Music Festival* in which I had promised to participate.* Your sister-in-law, Princess Chlodwig, (whom I barely knew) gave me a cordial welcome; her son Philip [1] possesses a very agreeable baritone voice, and is charming the Parisian salons with the Schumann and Rubinstein *Songs*.[2]

I had to do a little piano-playing at Princess Caraman Chimay's [3] in honor of the Countess of Flanders,[4] and Her Grace Marshal MacMahon's [5] wife. The Chimays were some of my best connections in Rome some twelve years ago. We even arranged a Concert with them under the aegis of Monseigneur Hohenlohe at the Barberini [6] Palace, for the hospital of the "Benevolent Brotherhood" at Tivoli. —

I'm staying here until the end of the month, and toward mid-August I shall return to Rome and the Villa d'Este,

your very grateful and faithful

July 1, '78 — Weimar.   FL.

A thousand thanks for each of your very kind lines and for the postscript about the Coronation Mass, performed in the Castle chapel. I beg you occasionally to tell Hellmesberger of the remembrance I retain of his admirable interpretation of the *Benedictus*, at the time of the solemnities of the coronation at Buda.

Weimar will be festive from the 9th to the 12th of July, in order to celebrate her sovereign's 25 years of rule. If M. von Saar could get there, it would be opportune. When I am still more convinced of M. Sach's *resolution*, I shall take the liberty of writing to you about it.

* Bülow and Bronsart principally attracted me there.

Your Highness,

The numerous and brilliant parties at Weimar during this month of July had their conclusion yesterday, the 34th birthday of the Grand-Duke-Elect. At the Belvedere, dinner for about twenty persons; following that a ball and supper for more than 60. Their Royal Highnesses will stay at the Belvedere until mid-August — after the wedding of Prince Henry of the Netherlands. They will betake themselves from Berlin to The Hague.

Last week the Reuss's went to Vienna; Princess Marie [1] is holding her salon and German court there, with approbation and indubitable success. Her father, M.S., spoke to me again about M. von Saar, and I hope that he will conclude setting him up here comfortably next winter. In the meantime, I forwarded Saar's photograph, (sent by my cousin), to S., who treasures and particularly praises Saar's "*short novels.*" You may find a chance to have him presented to Princess Marie Reuss; by this channel he can quietly navigate toward the port of Weimar, where I wish him safely to anchor. Henry VII [2] continues to be on very good terms with his mother-in-law, without whom there is no security in these parts.

The nomination of your brother-in-law, the Cardinal, as Archpriest of the Basilica of Santa Maria Maggiore seemed to me to be a wise and favorable thing. Among other advantages, it guarantees him a dwelling worthy of His Highest Eminence at the *Canonica*; and it thus exonerates him from the expensive boredom of the largesse that a bishopric, even a suburban one, would have occasioned. Pius IX said: "St. Peter's vessel is guaranteed, but not so the crew." Cardinal Hohenlohe has his sea-legs, and runs his ship perfectly.

My news from Babuino is quite peaceful: at the end of August I will be in Rome and the Villa d'Este. I shall probably not return to Budapest before January.

Adelheid Schorn is not crippled, and has written to you.

On the 15th of August at Bayreuth, as a prisoner of love, you will be entertained by

your very humble and grateful

August 1st, '78 — Weimar. F L.

I've been showing off with the charming anecdote about the Shah of Persia,[3] ("very silent"), accompanied by the gesture of decapitation — about which the humanitarian Minister Glaser[4] ought to be extremely amazed. Too bad the miserly Shah discredited the proverbial "oriental luxury."

I'm listening to the bells of "Marling" and like Gussie, seeking the "blue spots" on the horizon!

LETTER 157

[Budapest]

Your Highness,

The best part of my religious compositions is the emotion evoked by them in a few fine souls. Your lines concerning the Coronation *Mass* are the most precious of rewards for me: they have also led me to make an exception to my rule of not appearing in public activity. In this regard, several flattering proposals have again recently arrived to me from London, Aachen, and Berlin. I excused myself on account of my age and for other very solid reasons; nevertheless I did not answer negatively to Bösendorfer's *prelude* — in case the Vienna "Friends of Music" show themselves favorably inclined toward the *Gran Mass* and perform it at the end of March or on the first Sunday in April — since I ought to be back at Weimar on Easter.

Yesterday, at last, I wrote my very sincere and grateful thanks to Dingelstedt. His *Stanislas* seems to me to be a huge success, rich in beautiful scenic and Musical effects. Nothing would be more agreeable to me than to compose immediately this dramatic Oratorio; but a very considerable obstacle presents itself. . . . I shall venture to confide it to you confidentially at Vienna. Perhaps I shall succeed in removing the obstacle, in the fall, at Rome.

Count Charles de Linanges recommended the pianist Herrmann[1] to you. I haven't heard him for many years; but he then seemed to me to deserve marked attention. One of the wittiest pianists, Madame Raab,[2] told her colleagues here at Budapest Music Academy: "We are decidedly many too many: there ought to be a St. Bartholomew's massacre among pianists. Without one we shall all perish."[3]

Let us make an exception of Count Geza Zichy, my most well-wishing friend; he is brilliant at the piano with his left hand alone. Sardou[4] asserted in Paris that Zichy, "with one arm, plays four-handed." This was proved once again splendidly here at his Concert the day before yesterday.

With constant and complete gratitude,

your old and very humble servant

January 26, '79.   F. Liszt.

I am told that Saint-Saëns will come to Vienna and Pest at the end of February. I venture to recommend him particularly to you, as the best musician I know of all France and Navarre.

LETTER 158

Your Highness,

You have a charm bred of compassion. Profoundly moved by the real and delicate kindness of your last letter, I am reproaching myself for not going to Vienna as soon as the sad news reached me. Petty affairs kept me here; had I arrived the following day, it would only have been in time to accompany my beloved Cousin[1] to his last earthly dwelling. My soul remains in communion with his.

You know that I've accepted (most exceptionally) to conduct the Gran Mass at Vienna on the 8th of April. This work has been more criticized than comprehended; perhaps it will now receive fewer unfavorable attacks than formerly. . . . The favorable action of the "Society of the Friends of Music" has assured me about the success of the performance. Zellner writes me that Madame Gomperz[2] will be good enough to sing the Mezzo-Soprano, for which I am very grateful. The other 3 Solo parts will be filled by Madame Kauser[3] and Messieurs Walter and Rokintansky.[4] Furthermore, I have asked to add the *Gradual* from the Coronation Mass to it, which Hellmesberger will set off to advantage. As an *Offertory* there will be the "Beatitudes." This piece, as yet unknown in Vienna, has been sung several times without displeasing the public at Leipzig, Weimar, Berlin, Pest and even in Rome. Bignio will carry it off well.

What you've told me about the "Twilight of the Gods" is quite in accord with my own feeling. A powerful, continual gale impels the Tetralogy of Wagner's Nibelings toward the summit of Sublimity. They may not easily be grasped, but who cares? Great works of human genius carry their own absolution within themselves.

My letters from Rome are full of sublime things; before them I kneel with devotion, even while I stay in this area governed by the way of the poor world, which is not that of the Thrones, Dominions, Powers, and other Archangels! . . . My humble attitude in this regard is the same one you have known for the last fifteen years.

On this Tuesday, the 18th of February,

for you and yours with all his heart, will pray
your old faithful servant
February 15, '79.   F. Liszt.

The same mail is bringing you the "Bells of Marling." I shall put a separate copy at your feet in Vienna; and I'm sending you the notebook I received yesterday, only in order to forestall any other indications from someone else.

LETTER 159

I hope, Your Highness, that Count Wilczek isn't displeased with me. Not having found me the morning of the day before yesterday, he was kind enough to return in the evening at the very same time that I was going to his house. He told me that he will soon be called to Rome by a meteorological convention: I profited by this unexpected transition in order to touch upon the *Rome affairs.*

Without any doubt, the true and natural solution would be a peaceful settlement: but the Roman weather conditions are scarcely favorable . . . and after fruitless observations, many times reiterated, during the last ten years, there only remains for me to pray urgently to the "Good Angels" that they fulfill their benign roles.

A happy meeting with Wilczek on the stairway of the *Hungaria* Hotel afforded me the pleasure of seeing him once more, the day before yesterday in the evening, at Geza Zichy's. I shall accompany *this* Zichy tomorrow evening at Klausenburg,* and he will reaccom-

* capital of Transylvania —

229

pany me to Vienna in the first week of April. Our friendship is of the highest order, quite exempt from the calculations and the pleasures of the vulgar.

Very faithfully,
your very humble
F. Liszt.

March 8, '79, Budapest.

P.S. Saint-Saëns was here. He is worth still more than his great reputation.

LETTER 160

Your Highness,

To keep you completely in touch with my correspondence with Countess Andrassy, I am taking the liberty of sending you her two letters, enclosed, and my answer to the last one.[1] The latter was suggested to me by a line from your very kind letter: "A joint endeavor might be arranged in one of our homes. . . ." In this case, both my hands are at your feet; but as I wrote Countess Andrassy, it's hardly suitable for me to play the piano again in Vienna, either at the theater or at any kind of ordinary Concert hall.

Would you have the willing kindness to chat about it with Countess Andrassy, and then tell me what I should do to show my devoted service?

I shall be at Vienna, (the Schottenhof), on the 2nd of April and stay there until the 9th. It doesn't seem to me convenient to get embroiled in the Szegedin[2] Concert, at Their Majesties' silver-wedding celebration; therefore, if the Concert in question is to take place, it should be put before the performance of the Gran Mass ("For the eve of a festival. . . .") or on the day after, the Wednesday of Holy Week. — This would perhaps be better, owing to the ticket sales.

As for the Program, there's no need of either Orchestra or Chorus; consequently it can be arranged very easily, and I'll willingly take care of 3 or 4 selections.

The parallel you make between Doré[3] and St. Saëns is striking in its aptness and sensitive appreciation: I am sorry that St. Saëns hasn't had an opportunity to come to the *Augarten*. I have held him in great esteem and sincere friendship for a number of years.

Your very grateful old servant

March 29, '79.   Budapest.   F. Liszt.

LETTER 161

Your Highness,

I subscribe wholeheartedly to your admirable solution of the little question of the Szegedin Concert.

Please let me know on Wednesday morning (at the "Schotten-hof"), at what time you would allow me to submit the concert program to you. I should like Madame Gomperz to contribute her fine talent to it.

As for the details of the arrangements, no one could effect them better than my good friend, M. Bösendorfer.

Very humbly, your
old faithful servant

March 31, '79, Budapest.   F. Liszt.

You will determine the *date* of the Concert with Countess An-drassy, whenever you find it opportune.

LETTER 162

[Vienna, April, 1879]

Very happy to see you again, I shall come exactly at 1 o'clock.

Your trifling servant

Wednesday.   FL

LETTER 163

[Vienna, April, 1879]

Your Highness,

In order to save room, it will probably be necessary to modify the program we sketched this morning. The accompaniment for the Psalm by Harp, harmonium, and Violin would eliminate at least 8 or 10 paid seats, and without this accompaniment, the Psalm would lose much of its effect.

Tomorrow at one-thirty, there will be a meeting with Mme. Gomperz about the program, at Countess Andrassy's.

Dare I beg you to take part? Without any doubt at all, you will find the idea *"appropriate"* to the occasion for the Concert planned for next Monday.

Your very humble
and most obedient

Wednesday evening.   F Liszt

LETTER 164: Preface

Liszt reached a higher stage in his ecclesiastical career on October 12, 1879 — exactly one month after this letter to Marie — when, through the good offices of Cardinal Hohenlohe, he was appointed a Canon of Albano. (*L.M.* IV, No. 258.) That he was aware of certain adverse criticisms of his new role is apparent in a letter to Carolyne on July 18 in the same year, and his comments are also of interest in revealing Liszt's youthful leanings toward the priesthood. "You better than anyone know my absolute lack of ambition for an ecclesiastical career. When I took minor orders at the Vatican in 1865, at the age of 54, the idea of practical advancement was as far from me as possible. I was merely following, out of the simplicity and uprightness of my heart, my youthful penchant for Catholicism. If my early fervor had not been tempered by my good mother and my confessor, Abbé Bardin, it might well have led me to the seminary in 1830 and later on to the priesthood." (*L.M.* IV, No. 250.)

LETTER 164

My prayers for you weren't lacking on this 15th of August, and they always respectfully accompany you. I was again present at our poor little Weimar church on Assumption Day, where our fine old priest, Hohmann,[1] celebrated the Mass. The lovely altar-carpet embroidered by your mother decorated the foot of the altar, and the Celebrant of the Mass has a very special regard for you — rightfully so.

I stayed at Wilhelmsthal from the 16th to the 20th of August, where Elsi [2] gave me a bit of news about you; following that, I spent about ten days at *Wahnfried*.[3] With *Parsifal*, Wagner climbs still higher on that mysterious Jacob's Ladder with which art links heaven and earth.

You knew that the performance of *Parsifal* has been postponed until '81. Next winter, Wagner, Cosima, and the children will spend their time at Posillipo,[4] from mid-January until the end of April.

I met Princess Auersperg (the "proprietress" of our concert, shared between the "poor-relief" and the zealous Dominican of "Haking") and the Princess Imperial [5] of Germany — at Lenbach's Munich studio. Do you know his much-praised portraits of Angeli? [6] Lenbach will doubtlessly also have the honor of painting His Imperial Highness. Up to now, he seems to me to have succeeded wonderfully with Andrassy, Bismarck, Moltke,[7] Döllinger,[8] Mme. Moukhanoff, Mme. Minghetti, and others — all more or less fortunate models.

I arrived at Rome Thursday, and Sunday at the Villa d'Este, my tent of seclusion for the past ten years.

M.'s *speed of recovery* appears rather good to me. She continues to work at length; her great work is developing more and more, and will reach at least 15 fat volumes. Dante's words: "*to be prolonged into the future*," [9] has definitely become her motto: —

O.[10] (allow me to use this abbreviation, as I do for the S.'s at Weimar) is busying himself with the present situation. Leo XIII values and honors him; the rest will take care of itself. Thus, His Eminence is climbing the ticklish heights with a sure foot. . . .

I am even more grateful for his constant favor and friendly interest. In this regard, I'll repeat a neologism for you, coined by Don Marcello,[11] who once said to me: "With you, the Cardinal isn't at all *voluble*." Nor are my deep-seated feelings for you *voluble*; and it is truly and whole-heartedly that I remain your faithful, very grateful, old servant.

September 12, '79 —   F. Liszt.
        Villa d'Este.

A sincere admirer of Andrassy, I hope that the Austro-Hungarian monarchy will not dispense with his intelligent services. For who could represent it as Minister of Foreign Affairs, with so much capacity, nobility, good presence, and a spirit at once old and new? Only Andrassy could know how to display all this with such pertinence.

Have you seen Mme. Sach in Vienna?

I plan to stay here until Christmas, save for a few trips to Rome and my devotions at the Albano [12] Chapter.

I shall return to Pest during the first week in January.

My address in Rome: 65 Babuino Street.

LETTER 165

October 1st, '79 —
Villa d'Este.

After due thought, I have decided not to warn M. about your filial undertaking; but I have just spoken about it to Your most illustrious brother-in-law. He thinks, as do I, that your visit to Rome is secretly wished for by M., and it will produce the desired effect. Carry out, then, with devout confidence, the inspiration of your heart, and the Lord's blessing be upon all upright souls.

If I may be of any small assistance with the preliminaries to the performance of Othon III,[1] please tell me; and bank upon my thoroughness. Bronsart will certainly be eager to do justice to your recommendation, and M. Sach likewise . . . "with uneven step," like the young Julius in the wake of Pious Aeneas.[2] To my humble way of thinking, you would be of service to M. Edler, if you *first* would write to Meiningen, even if you have to leave Weimar until later.

M. and Madame Sach and Elsi are going to take a few weeks in Biaritz; upon their return, they will spend a little time in Paris.

In the hope of seeing You soon in Rome, I shan't make these lines any longer, and I simply put at your feet the testimony of my deep gratitude.

F. Liszt.

Speaking confidentially, it may be possible that your brother-in-law will be away from Rome for about two weeks after the 15th of October.

Your Highness,

    I never succeed in making people understand that they oughtn't to ask me to recommend them either to Cardinal Hohenlohe or to his brother. I am bothered by letters about this continually; they go into the basket, — except M. Jäger's,[1] which I enclose and place humbly at your feet — and beg you to decide whether it would be opportune to mention it to Prince Constantine.

    Did Bronsart reply affirmatively to M. Edler? Plays and Operas are abundant in every country — even in Rome. They are announcing here several new operas for this season: *Hero and Leander* by Bottesini,[2] (the Paganini of the Double-Bass); a young Italian composer's *Sardanapalus*,[3] etc. The theater is like a big greasy pole at a carnival, where only a happy few succeed in getting the silver dish. I wish Mottl good luck for his *Agnes Bernauer*, now in rehearsal at Weimar.

    In the Musical section of the Journal of Debates (Saturday, December 13th) Reyer[4] reproaches the large German and French theaters for not yet giving Berlioz's *Taking of Troy*. It is the sequel to that extraordinary work: *The Trojans at Carthage*, which barely enjoyed about twenty performances at the Paris Lyric Theater, on the condition that they were cut. Reyer also mentions the genesis of the *Trojans* at Weimar, discusses M. Sach's autograph letter to Emperor Napoleon III, and quotes Berlioz's remarkable dedicatory letter to M. in its entirety.

    This reminder will be nice for her; since she has always retained her former predilection for Berlioz, about whom a former Minister wisely said: "His is no commercial talent." Wagner, too, deserves not to be classed among the latter; however, the commercial vicissitudes of the theater have set him up in a handsome fashion.

    On the 15th of January, back in Budapest will be

your very humble and grateful old servant

December 19, '79:   F. Liszt.
   (*Villa d'Este*)

Your Highness,

There are such peremptory reasons for not hiring M.J.[1] in Vienna, that I am asking you to hold his letter as if it never arrived. Do not speak of it to Prince Constantine — who, on the other hand, is doubtlessly very well-informed in this matter.

For the sake of Bayreuth, I yielded in a most *exceptional* way to this letter, whose superfluousness I foresaw. Balzac called Toqueville a "Monobible";[2] it would seem as if J. were a "Mono-actor." That sort of business used to be a success in Italy: for instance, there was the famous Tenor, Moriani,[3] who made a brilliant career of perpetually singing nothing but Gennaro and Edgardo.[4]

It seems to me that Edler is wise to take up with warmth Bronsart's cause. Among the Intendants I've known, he is almost the only one who is concerned with a dramatic work for the *sake of pure art*. Loën prefers protecting authors who are worth a newspaper article for him, where the praises of his Intendancy and the forever-radiant glories of the Weimar theater are sung. M. Sach gives a ready ear to this line, but he becomes absolutely deaf when it is a matter of risking himself or spending a little bit of money.

I am happy with the good reputation Mottl has already acquired at Weimar, and wish him complete success elsewhere.

I replied to Geza Zichy that I couldn't imagine the notion or the occasion for a *Liszt Concert* at Vienna this winter. For me to venture into it casually would be a blunder. I am thus awaiting for fuller information, which I'll be given in about two weeks at Budapest. Time enough then to think of a program, if it is to take place. The vision of Ezekiel[5] would be revolting to all the reigning critics; I don't know whether I'll ever risk showing "these dry bones" at a public Concert. It's only 50 or 60 slow measures; but they are frightful, and move in a progression of dissonant chords such as have never been written before. I may show my "Bells of Strassburg" (words by Longfellow) to Zellner and Hellmesberger. They've only been heard once before in Pest, at Wagner's express desire, at the occasion of a Concert he conducted in '74 or '75; and they are totally unknown elsewhere. The performance is easy and lasts about 20 minutes. You need a Chorus and Orchestra, also a *strong* Baritone for the role of Satan. There is no conceivable allusion to the extant political situation at Strassburg: [6] there is merely the struggle of the demons with the angels, and the final triumph of the latter.

With heart and soul
your deeply grateful and
faithful servant

January 1, '80 — (Villa d'Este)   F. Liszt.

We had a brilliant Concert yesterday at the Villa d'Este (for the poor-relief). Your most illustrious brother-in-law will tell you all about it.

I shall leave Rome for Pest on the 10th of January.

LETTER 168: Preface

Liszt's remark about the "new Royal Academy of Music" reminds us that he was appointed as its musical head in November 1875. Contrary to the popular notion of his being the great Hungarian nationalist composer, an interest in Hungarian music and culture came quite late in his career. A brief scanning of the catalog of Liszt's works reveals that his first composition with definite Hungarian characteristics was a little-known *Hussitenlied* published in 1841; a *Marche héroïque à la hongroise* appeared in 1844; and the famous *Rhapsodies* came out between 1851 and 1854. The only symphonic poem of the twelve which was based on Magyar themes was the *Hungaria* (1856). The *Coronation Mass*, performed in 1867, was Liszt's single major attempt to incorporate Hungarian melodic material in a choral composition, and a few small orchestral and vocal pieces written during the last thirty years of his life comprise the remainder of his nationalistic music.

The relatively minor part played by Hungarian elements in the musician's background and personality and his inability to speak the language with fluency has been discussed in the Foreword. It is difficult to find a satisfactory explanation for Liszt's belated interest in things Hungarian. The Magyar aristocracy had lionized him as one of their own when he had played in Budapest late in 1839; the shaky state of Hungarian culture was hospitable to his creation as a kind of national hero; and Magyar society, never famed for its intellectual or aesthetic eminence, was anxious to find at least *one* Hungarian artist it might flaunt in the face of Viennese condescension. The failure of a projected Hungarian patent of nobility to materialize (cf. Sitwell, *Liszt*, p. 95) may have altered Liszt's incipient patriotism. Perhaps his feelings — to employ modern psychological jargon — underwent a period of latency. Certainly the 1848 Revolution in his native land found him apathetic to the successes of either liberalism or reaction, and one looks in vain throughout his correspondence for any indication that he was aware of the developments that were taking place. In later life he knew many of the prominent Hungarians who were active politically both during and after 1848, but his sympathies never went much further than the personal plane. One may best describe them as being vaguely and indiscriminately nationalistic.

Liszt did, however, write one ambitious literary work which treated the problem of Hungarian and Gypsy music: *Die Zigeuner und ihre Musik in Ungarn* (1861). With its dubious scholarly pretensions and highly speculative investigations into such fields as the origins of the "folk-epic" and the Gypsy race, the book makes fascinating reading — if one can bear with Liszt's alternately lyrical and neo-Hegelian prose. It illuminates many of Liszt's attitudes concerning art in general, even as it presents facets of the musician's character hitherto neglected by biographers.

The opening pages of this 400-page opus deal with the folk-epic and "Nationale-Poesie"; and since they simply recapitulate all the Romantic ideas on the subject, Liszt's theories represent no original thought. After a brief discussion of the nomadic, nonintellectual, and primitive aspects of Gypsy culture, Liszt makes an analogy to the Wandering Jews. To any admirer of Liszt, the anti-Semitism that follows is appalling; and the sole hint of Liszt's attitude in this correspondence was his dislike of Lessing's *Nathan der Weise* (Letter 12, Note 11). Briefly, Liszt describes the entire Jewish race as sullen, servile, cruel, and the avaricious inhabitants of cities alone — all in contrast with the Gypsies. Jewish music, with Mendelssohn and Meyerbeer as examples, is overintellectual and weakly imitative. Finally, the menace of Jewish world-revolution can be avoided only by deporting the race back to their beloved Jerusalem — an act Liszt hopes may be effected without bloodshed.

The transition from this violent and disturbing polemic is made when Liszt compares the Jewish respect for law, interpreted as a craven acceptance of social bondage, with the Gypsy love of individual freedom. The remainder of the essay is an analysis of Gypsy-Magyar cultural interrelationships and the general outlook of the two races, which Liszt tends to merge into a unity. Liszt hails the "poetical Egotism" of the Gypsies (p. 73) and their close, naïve, and primary relation with nature. "For city-dwellers and factory-workers, nature remains a closed book. . . She sings to the poet in his heart; offers him privately all the indescribable sweetness of her sublimest secrets. . . Among robbers, smugglers, wild thieves and pirates there are many examples of the powerful magic worked by nature. . . And a similar attitude may be discovered in wild societies, such as the mad love of nature possessed by the Gypsies" (pp. 85–86).

Added to his uniqueness as a special votary of nature, the Gypsy "would enjoy his passions completely, fully, on every occasion and forever" (p. 97). He lives in a state of luxuriant and hedonistic idleness; envied, hated, and hence persecuted by a bourgeois and materialistic society, he is the true and the natural nobleman. Liszt describes a young Hungarian Gypsy fiddler, one Sarai Joszy (who looks very much like pictures of the young Liszt), whose contempt for a debilitating civilization is matched only by his fatal attraction for women.

Liszt goes to some length to differentiate between the *real* Bohemia of the Magyar Gypsy and its false and effete counterpart in Western Europe — the world of Rodolphe and Mimi, and the world Liszt himself knew so well during the 1830's in Paris. Curiously enough he mentions George Borrow, the author of *Lavengro* and *Romany Rye*, as one of the few *Ausländer* who penetrated into the Gypsy soul — an ability Liszt ascribes to the English love of nature and freedom. And it is these two cardinal affections that produce the ruling characteristic of the Gypsies: their claim to fame lies in their virtuosity. For the virtuoso, says Liszt, is no mere mediator between a creative artist and his audience. "He is not the passive instrument that reproduces the feelings and thoughts of others and adds nothing to them. . . The virtuoso is quite as much a creator as the author himself; for he must virtually possess the same passions with which he is entrusted to let glow the full brilliance of their fresh phosphorescence" (p. 332).

The Gypsy with his violin — for Liszt stresses the place of instrumental music — gives birth to his race's folk-epic by playing the music that lies mute within its collective soul. From here it is but one short step to the definition of a "virtuoso" such as Liszt himself, who represents the meeting of civilization and barbarism, the cultured and the primitive. Indeed, when Liszt comes to discuss his *Rhapsodies* we see how neatly he fits himself into the framework of his ideas. The word "rhapsody" he relates to its original Greek meaning, and hence to the epic itself — and his task has been to transmit these musical-epics of the Hungarian Gypsies to the West via the piano.

The ideas in this essay, sketched here with a necessary bevity, certainly have little absolute value. Their provocative quality lies in another area, that of almost unconscious self-revelation. What Liszt has defined is really himself, and *Die Zigeuner* is actually one of those rare documents — part spiritual autobiography, part idealized conception of what one artist dreams *the* artist should be. The descriptive is blended with the normative in a starange unstable combination.

(References were to Volume VI of the *Gesammelte Schriften*, ed. Ramann. There is also available an English translation of *Die Zigeuner* by Edwin Evans: London, 1926.)

LETTER 168

Your Highness,

I am very comfortably ensconced for the winter at the Hungaria Hotel. It's my third or fourth temporary set of lodgings in Budapest during the past ten years. I am very pleased with them, since my superb official quarters at the new Royal Academy of Music are not yet dry. My ten piano students of both sexes come to work three times a week at the *Hungaria*; three or four are distinguishing themselves.

Count Geza Zichy and Bösendorfer have been insistently speaking to me of a Concert planned for Vienna. If they definitely decide to give it, I am suggesting one of the first days of Holy Week as a date, and this is the program:

1. Mass [1] for men's voice, (with organ). It was performed once under Herbeck's direction at Vienna, at the Church of the Augustinians, about 25 years ago.

2. "The Ideal" [2] (or "Hungaria"?) — Symphonic tone-poem.

3. "The Bells of Strassburg," for Orchestra, Chorus, and a strong Baritone in the role of Satan.

(This composition, based on Longfellow's *Legend*, is as remote from politics as is the Strassburg Cathedral itself.)

Each of the three numbers of my program lasts, at the longest, from 25 to 30 minutes. —

The "Mozart Week" in Vienna seems to me to be in excellent taste. I'm sorry not to have been able to profit from it: and I would have liked to see, no less, the performance of Grillparzer's "The Waves of the Sea and of Love" — so full of grand passion's sublime lyricism.

Both Dudin's hands are happy and well-exercised: his left isn't lacking in any dexterity. I wish him well with his title of Excellency, out of good old friendship: without it his insomnia would give him no peace.

M. Edler can count on Bronsart's effectual good-will.

Of all my old former friends, Joachim is the *only* one with whom it has been hard to keep up. He is playing here tonight. I shall willingly applaud him; because to my way of thinking, he has stayed the classic chief of all contemporary violinists for the past thirty years.

To get back to Hero and Leander: [3] Mihalovitch has written and published a brilliant symphonic poem of the same name (dedicated to my daughter, Cosima), and Bottesini has written an opera to be performed in Rome this winter. It has already been a success at other Italian theaters.

The difficulty is to make the amorous hero swim nicely in music. [4]

Your very faithful and
truly grateful servant

January 23, '80 — Budapest.   F. Liszt.

LETTER 169

Your Highness,

Your sad worries are over; I am taking the liberty of continuing to thank you, and to write you about all sorts of inconsequential items.

The Concert dedicated to me by Viennese "Friends of Music" has been settled for Tuesday, March 23rd. The evening before, a general rehearsal. I shall be there, and will stay at the *Schottenhof* for about ten days. There is also the question of an evening party at Bösendorfer's of the "Wagner Association," on Wednesday, March 24th.

The evening party ought to be quite inoffensive: unadvertised, free, and with limited invitations. My Symphony, or rather my sketch of a Symphony for Dante's "Divina Comedia," would make up the program — done without orchestra, since I've dissuaded the "Wagner Association" from going to any expense for any one of my works. Thus, if the above evening-party takes place at Bösendorfer's, they'll hear the Dante Symphony on two pianos; and one of them will be played by your very humble and very grateful old servant

March 12, '80 — Budapest.   F. Liszt.

LETTER 170

[Vienna]

Your Highness,

My eagerness to return to your house made me forget completely, last night, that Tuesday from 7 to 9 o'clock, I am to be taken up with a Concert. The enclosed program indicates my obligation to hear it from beginning to end. Fischer the organist, (from Dresden), is a talented, worthy musician; he has come to Weimar several times, and I also knew in Weimar and Rome his colleague for the same Concert, Baron Alexander von Kieter.[1]

Would you allow me to come to the *Augarten* on Wednesday at 6 o'clock (the evening before I leave)?

Very respectfully and
with constant gratitude
Friday evening.   F. Liszt.

LETTER 171: *Preface*

Liszt's "old affectionate relations with S." remind us that he and the Grand Duke Carl Alexander remained close friends until the musician's death in 1886. Their correspondence during the 1861–1869 period has been mentioned earlier, when Liszt in a rather coquettish fashion avoided any direct answer to Carl Alexander's entreaties that he return to Weimar. But after the musician took up his residence at the Hofgärtnerei, the letters simply reflect the long, intimate relationship of two old friends. The sole possible note of mild disagreement between them was Liszt's new attachment to Budapest, which was gained somewhat at the expense of his Weimar affiliations. In 1874, for instance, the two cities wished to fête the artist on the occasion of the fiftieth anniversary of his concert début: Liszt extricated himself from embarrassment by declining both invitations. (Cf. *Briefwechsel*, No. 136 and No. 137.)

It is interesting to note that the Grand Duke never lost his grand idea of making Weimar once again the cultural center of Germany and even

Europe, and there is a certain pathetic quality in his reiterated statements of the city's past glory. A letter written to Liszt on November 10, 1876, is illustrative of his attitude: "The duties of Weimar toward Germany are well known. They are the natural and inevitable consequence of her past, Weimar's past. This past ought to govern the present in order to prepare the future." (*Ibid.*, No. 152.)

After listing the various achievements enjoyed by Weimar under his reign, the Grand Duke concludes: "these details are merely one detail within a larger whole, for which Weimar bears the responsibility not only toward Germany, but toward the entire civilized world." One feels that Liszt was much more cognizant of the nineteenth-century cultural shift than was his royal patron, who still regarded himself in the line of Louis XIV, Frederick the Great — or even his own grandfather, Goethe's benefactor. Whether it was a mistake to remain in Weimar is a question that Liszt never settled in his own mind, and we find him posing this rhetorical question in a letter to Carolyne as late as September 1882: "Why am I at Weimar? Is it an error, a mistake, or folly? Perhaps all three at once!" (*L.M.* IV, No. 352.)

LETTER 171

Your Highness,

Thanks to your constant kindness, I hope soon to busy myself with the St. Stanislas *Oratorio*, and to complete it. One of Rome's patrons — sweet, sympathetic St. Philip of Neri[1] — used to be interested in this type of composition: he accorded them a place in his Church and even provided them with its name. I shall evoke his protection for my work, that it may be a worthy testimony of Catholic art and of my deep Polish feelings. Your daughterly affection will understand my purpose.

I tried, with Elizabeth, to glorify Hungary musically; now my job is to do the same with Poland via the Bishop-Martyr, Stanislas.

The alterations in the *Oratorio* text, done by M. Edler, are effective improvements, as much for the poetry as for the Music. I am very pleased with them and beg You to thank Edler, at the same time asking him to complete his entire labor before the end of September. My own will not be delayed: I shall attend to it at the Villa d'Este, and plan to bring it to a happy end in less than a year, since about a hundred pages are already written. . . .

Enclosed is the first page composed yesterday, for the initial line:
"Woe is us! Sorrow's cup is full to the brim!"

Without a transition, I am skipping to the ribbon. My best chance is with the Duke of M.[2] I'll see him again at Liebenstein[3] in the month of August: do me the favor of telling me beforehand the title of the work Edler is to send to His Grace.

I shall recommend again to Bronsart and others, that his drama be performed.

My old affectionate relations with S.[4] continue. His sister, the Empress,[5] spent a day here. She was nice enough to tell me very kindly that she would see me again with pleasure at Baden-Baden, where I shall go next week for the "Musicians Convention" — from May 19th to the 23rd. Following that, I'll come back here and stay, as in preceding years, until mid-July.

The 2 parts of *Faust*[6] were given 3 times this season. The public flowed in with such numbers that the box-office couldn't answer the demands for Tickets; a rare embarrassment for Weimar! At the last performance (May 1st), I had the honor of being admitted into the Royal Box during the intermission, after the 4th Act; the German Prince Imperial favored me with a few kind words.

Perhaps Dudin will bring about his old project in Vienna of staging the two parts of *Faust*, which he brilliantly sketched out in his *lecture* at the "*Concordia.*" He has a sure hand for success; I am not at all surprised at his opportunistic success in dealing with the constant changes of regime in the Viennese theaters. Dudin wouldn't know how to suffer detriment from them, and Excellence naturally accrues to him.

Mottl's *Agnes Bernauer* succeeded nicely, and even more so did the composer. He charmed the court and city with his really stunning Wagnerian performances. Everyone praised him, applauded him, lionized him; S., however, hasn't made up his mind to nest his pet-bird in the brave young artist's buttonhole. This failure annoyed me; I had hoped that Mottl would keep lasting memories of Weimar, — and he really deserves to be decorated.*[7]

The new Mazurkas by Countess Gizycka[8] (Loulou) seem to me to be very pretty. She was nice enough to play them for me last Friday in the "Court Nursery," but she flew away to Dresden on

* Among the best lines arising out of Molière's wonderful genius, is: "A plague on misers and those who are stingy!"

the same evening. Her *Schumanian* cult, strongly excusable, took her to Bonn on May 2nd, on the day of the unveiling of the Schumann monument executed by Donndorf. You already know a few medallions and the equestrian statue of Carl August done by him. He is also doing the statue of Bach for Eisenach.

Speaking of monuments designed for great Artists, I don't know any comparable to that of Beethoven in Vienna. The City and the Sculptor, Zumbusch, can legitimately be proud of it.

ever new gratitude

May 12, '80 — Weimar. F. Liszt.

I am praying for your dear, sick, loved one.

LETTER 172

Your Highness,

The first fifteen pages of the new, definitive version of St. Stanislas, which you were so kind to send me, satisfy me completely. Thank you again, and I shall compose the music for them at the Villa d'Este this fall. So that my work be not interrupted, would you please ask M. Edler to finish his part, and to do it in the same style which was so successful in the first two scenes? It would certainly be better to start the King's speech with

"Welcome, valiant knights and lords" etc.; rather than "Noble knights, I have invited you, etc." *

Formerly, people never looked at *libretti* very closely; today more care and poetic rapport have become necessary, particularly for *Oratorios*; for they lack the advantages of the setting, decorations, costumes, and all the theatrical business. So let's carry out, without any rigamarole, a noble and disciplined alliance of poetry and music. The vulgar overlapping of one being merely near the other is no longer tolerable.

Our *Stanislas* ought to glorify the Bishop-martyr, the Catholic Church, and Poland, without stooping to the presentation of antiquated ideas. —

* And the same is true for Edler's numerous and excellent modifications and improvements.

When Milord G.[1] returns to his Duchy of M., I shall have the honor of visiting him and recommending a decoration for Edler. —

Bronsart, a perfect gentleman, can be taken on his word.

To my sorrow, I was away from Weimar when M. Weilen came there. Yesterday, Milord S. explained his annoyance to me about this ribbon-wearing crew. I answered him that it wasn't always the best of taste to be niggardly and caviling in that respect. A little graciousness becomes a Prince, particularly if they guard themselves against excesses which lead to ridiculous and absurd practices.

Your advice to Weilen to write a biography of Grillparzer [2] is certainly the best he could have.

Could the remarkable historical study about "Peter the Great's Son" in the Revue des deux Mondes (May 1st and 15th), signed Eugene Melchior de Vogüé,[3] have come from the pen of Vogüé, ambassador at Vienna? There is nothing more praiseworthy than its conclusion: "the time seems to be at hand when in most human relations, those who are wise will say increasingly: 'understand,' and less and less: 'judge.'" The Gospel commands us to do this.

Very humbly and
grateful with all my heart
F L.

June 11, '80 —

At Weimar, where I shall stay until the end of July. From mid-August until January: Rome.

LETTER 173

Your Highness,

I am with you spiritually on your pilgrimage at Einsiedeln.[1] Thank you for your very kind lines from Axenstein.[2] The last time I saw again the lake of the four cantons, rain and hail fell thick and fast accompanied by thunder-claps. It was that day when in '67, I went to seek out Wagner at Triebschen, where he was finishing that serene and wonderful work, "The Master-Singers." [3]

Supreme serenity still remains the Ideal of great Art. The shapes and transitory forms of Life are but stages towards this Ideal, which Christ's religion illuminates with His divine light.

S.'s birthday (June 24th) was celebrated, as it was last year, at Dornburg with the family, and with 7 or 8 of his devoted subjects attached to the party. When I returned here, I found Bülow — of all persons the least devoted. I spoke to him, in a discreet aside, about the affair in Hanover, where Mme. von Bronsart's hat and slippers played such a role. Bronsart indubitably belongs to that élite company of most honorable and distinguished men; my old friendship for him stays the same, without any "reservations."

M. Edler will get on perfectly with Bronsart. Chance always plays a great part in any success; I wish Edler's drama the best luck, and I am begging the author not to trouble himself with finishing a definitive text for the St. Stanislas Oratorio. The first two scenes will take me at least two months to compose and score; hence, if I receive the 3 other scenes — which I sincerely hope You read before with Edler — around Christmas, it will be perfect timing.

In order to avoid pointless discussions, I shan't speak to M.[4] of the subsequent text or Music of the *Stanislas*. When the work is ended, I shall place it very humbly at her feet.

I am being kept here until the end of July. Around the first days of August, I'll visit the Duke of M.[5] at Liebenstein — and from there return to Rome.

Your very grateful,
faithful old servant

July 30, '80. Weimar.   FL.

LETTER 174

Your Highness,

I spoke yesterday to Duke G.[1] about M. Edler — his drama, and his personal merits.

It would be wise if Edler sent his printed works directly to G. (Meiningen) without delay, and I could tell G. of the favorable interest You have taken in them.

In the letter accompanying this message, I am asking E. to name me, as the intermediary, to the Duke.

Very grateful thanks for the continuation of the St. Stanislas text. I shall soon set it to music, at the Villa d'Este, and I hope to finish the whole work by next year.

> With faithful gratitude,
> your very humble old servant,

August 22, '80 — Meiningen.   F. Liszt.

A week from today I shall be back in Rome.

LETTER 175

Your Highness,

The last sheets of the Saint Stanislas have arrived for me. I am extremely pleased with each of the six scenes and with the whole effect, concluded so well by the Krakow hymn. From the start to the finish of this Oratorio text, the two great *strains* of the Catholic religion and of Poland are nobly upheld according to my wishes. The Bishop maintains his holiness; the King never grows contemptible, although his fit of passion drives him almost to transgression; and the *voice of the people* expresses their role of suffering and hope blended with patriotism and piety.

May my composition do credit to your benign concern!

I am taking the liberty of asking you to convey to M. Edler my enclosed words of thanks. Due to your letter, the Duke of M. is highly disposed in his favor; Her Highness told me at Liebenstein that She will gladly take an interest in Edler's works; and that accomplished gentleman Bronsart will certainly not fail to have her fulfill her promise.

I found Your most illustrious brother-in-law back here Saturday, in perfect health and in the most agreeable frame of mind. At my respectful request, he himself wishes to order the armchair you are intending for M. A well-known upholsterer will take care to fix the piece in such a way to deserve every praise. On the 4th of November, I will write you of the complete success of your gift.

I shall see the Wagners again a week from now, at Siena, where they will spend several weeks. Some grumbling doctors recommend that Wagner take a rigorous cure at Gräfenberg,[1] (Silesia), but perhaps he will think otherwise.

From the 1st of October until Christmas I shall work here, with all my might, on the Saint Stanislas,

Your very grateful
old servant,
F. Liszt

September 10, '80 —
Villa d'Este.

The letters of a Bachelor of Music, which the *Westermann* Review announced, are an old affair, published in the year '35 in the Paris Musical Gazette, and now translated into German.[2] When the 1st volume of my biography by L. Ramann[3] appears, I will venture to send it to you. The author is excessively benevolent towards me.

Your gracious "joint" telegram came to me in mid-August at Wilhelmsthal.

LETTER 176

Your Highness,

Upon my return Saturday evening, I thought to find your most illustrious brother-in-law here; but he is going to be at his Episcopal residence at Albano for several weeks. I wrote him yesterday; and since he had the kindness to order and supervise the construction of a piece of furniture intended to decorate your mother's salon, I copied in my letter to the Cardinal the pertinent passage from your letter — the one clearly indicating the difference between an arm-chair and a small cot. The latter will be put in the room at Babuino on Thursday morning, November 4th. I am sure that M. will be nice and comfortable on it. Insofar as her exorbitant work and her sad worries permit, she is quite well and looks in good health; and she never stops writing about the Good and the Best with an all-consuming passion.

Wagner's health has recovered. I just spent about ten days with him, at *Torre fiorentina,* a charming and princely villa near Siena. Cosima and the five children are in good health. They will spend the month of October at Venice and will return in mid-November to "Wahnfried," at Bayreuth. *Parsifal,* most sublime of all, may be considered as finished. The piano and voice score is written and copied; there remains to put the orchestra score down on paper. It is now ready and already vibrating in Wagner's head; but he seems anxious to go on neither with this work nor with the performance. As for me, I can only consider that he is right not to hand *Parsifal* over to the present theatrical repertory, and to demand thoroughly exceptional terms for such an extraordinary work.

Certainly, Count Daniel de Charnacé [1] is the grandson of the Countess d'Agoult (Daniel Stern). I haven't seen his mother again, Claire d'Agoult, for about thirty years; and I know her only from a few letters, very remarkable in their wit and sensibility, to Cosima with whom her friendship dates from way back and remains constant.

The good favor of the Duke of Meiningen seems to me to deserve even more appreciation, seeing that several of his associates take the opposite stand.

I am jealous of Minister Unger's good fortune at Friedstein, and remain perpetually,

your very humble and truly grateful

Monday, September 30, '80 —　　　　　　　　　　F. Liszt.
(Villa d'Este)

M. Edler's excellent lines have arrived. I will thank him for them, when our St. Stanislas shapes up.

Mottl's nomination as Kapellmeister at Carlsruhe gives me real pleasure.

LETTER 177

Your Highness,

After reading Saar's poem: "the loud voices of the day are silent," [1] I immediately sang it: there only remained to write down the enclosed notation, which I place very humbly at your feet. It is for *Alto* voice, with the nice notes:

(the "si" enters only for the last note, "Night")

My secret wish would be that Madame Gomperz will be kind enough to let you hear this *song*. —

Don Marcello Massarenti[2] most obligingly took care of your present for November 4th. The object seems to me to have been perfectly carried out; it costs nearly 90 Austrian florins. On the evening of the party its happy success will be forthwith described to you by

your most grateful
and faithful servant
F. Liszt.

October 20, '80 —
   (Villa d'Este)

LETTER 178

Your Highness,

Despite its good appearance and its comfortableness, the gift for the 4th of November was a complete failure . . . scarcely estimable. I am a little sheepish about it: all the more so since I counted on its being half-successful.

M. is writing to you that she doesn't expect to be treated like a *"paralytic"*; and that even when sick, she is always well enough to do without cots — already 3 samples remain, without being used, in her rooms. That reminded me of a nice remark of Cardinal Antonelli's,[1] (who was scarcely lavish with them): "It's a little bit like that, but not entirely so."

Your favorable first impression of my Saar song gave me the greatest pleasure. I hope that Madame Gomperz will confirm this with her magic voice, where "the gleaming purple trembles . . . in the heaven's waves" —

Your very grateful and
faithful servant
F. Liszt.

Nov. 7, '80, (Villa d'Este)

I immediately settled the upholsterer's bill with 200 Italian lire. The simplest thing would be to send them directly to me in 80 Austrian florins.

If the *Friends of Music* at Vienna have my Dante Symphony

and the 13th Psalm played at the end of March or better in April (Holy Week), I will come there. I would not like to leave Budapest suddenly, since I must be back by mid-January. At my age, unless one is a minister, one has to limit and economize one's travels.

LETTER 179

Your Highness,

I've just spent three days in Rome. M. is bedridden, and predicts that she will stay the same until the month of February. Happily she can work without respite. The last chapters of her new volume satisfy her; her frame of mind is quite calm, except in the matter of the poor service of her help and their ineptitude in fulfilling the simplest offices. We spoke again about the *Cot* in a friendly way: perhaps Your most illustrious brother-in-law will profit by it at Saint Mary's or at Albano, since M. has the idea of favoring him with this delightful piece of furniture on his birthday (February 26th). Thank you for the 80 florins received last week. It was only half-successful; certainly no defeat. Complete success will come later. To be patient and to live is one and the same thing.

Since my retirement from the Weimar theater, I am quite removed from all theatrical affairs, in every country. I even don't remember having made any kind of pronouncements concerning the change in direction of the Vienna Opera, and I scarcely know the influential people there — with the exception of Dingelstedt — to whom I wish all possible *Intendantish* luck. The generous graciousness of the Emperor toward Dingelstedt's daughter is worthy of the genuine good-will of the sovereign.

I am leaving the responsibility of his unfavorable judgment about M.J.[1] to my good friend Bronsart. I can neither reproach nor condone it, due to my ignorance of the case with which it deals.

The Revue des deux Mondes doesn't get to me at the Villa d'Este. Of Lanfrey,[2] I have only read his history of the Popes. It was written from the free-thinking point of view, as an attempt at a fictional impartiality of a kind. For my part, since I am a respectful

Catholic I only ask for the subjection commanded by the perpetual authority of the Holy Apostolic Roman Church.

With all my heart,
your very humble and grateful servant

December 12, '80;   F. Liszt.
(Villa d'Este)

Too many interruptions have prevented me from going ahead with the composition of the Saint Stanislas Oratorio. I hope to finish it within a year. Edler's text is highly successful, and it is perfectly adapted to the musical demands of the work.

I will remain here or at Rome up to the 6th of January, and I shall return to Budapest on the 15th of January.

LETTER 180

Your Highness,

Excuse me for having delayed thanking you by letter for your very kind lines. I can only inform you from Rome of the continual sickly state of your mother. She stays almost constantly bedridden, but works without respite at her great, historic, monumental, administrative work — destined to prepare and bring about the final triumph of the Catholic Church.[1] One can only bow before such a labor — in ten volumes, at least. I have learned from competent judges that this great work will mark the era. My ignorance keeps me from the heights of ecclesiastical and worldly politics: I would not even know how to venture an opinion thereon. As I said to the late Princess Metternich forty years ago, the business of this world belongs to diplomats and to bankers: my vocation is to make Music as well as I am able.

Music will come along in Budapest — in a few years. Things appertaining to it are still too skiddy there — one might almost say stuck in the mud.

Princess Marcelline Czartoryska[2] will speak to you about her *Ruthenian* Concert; it's almost like a price-raise over Princess Raymondine Auersperg's *Dominican* Concert, with the difference that Princess Marcelline plays the piano admirably, and will dominate the whole program. I will gladly provide the accompaniment for it

— if the opportunity provides itself at Vienna at the start of next April. It must be without street-corner billboards, for I bore my cross of pianistic publicity at the Beethoven Concert. —

Hence the Ruthenian Concert can only be a *salon affair*, — with 3 or 4 thousand florins, at the most, for gate-receipts. I explained my attitude to Princess Marcelline last Sunday, at Budapest.

Your very humble
and truly grateful servant

February 2, '81, Budapest.   F. Liszt

LETTER 181

[Undated; probably mid-March, 1881]
Your Highness,

Please vouchsafe to excuse the delay of my very grateful thanks for your kind lines. The Ruthenian concert doesn't interest me, beyond a feeling of respectful courtesy due to Princess Marcelline Czartoryska. In all truth, I thought that the execution of her musical project would be put off until Doomsday, since it seemed still more difficult than Haking's Dominican Concert patronized by Princess Raymondine Auersperg. For my own part I would much prefer it if they finally left me with a little peace. Tiring the public is the hardest and the most ungrateful of all fatigues.

However, if you have the kindness to intervene I have no doubt as to its success; and I put myself at the command of Princess Czartoryska to accompany her in the Chopin Concerto [1] — which she plays admirably — at a second piano. She will add to it several Mazurkas and perhaps two or three Dumkas [2] of Countess Gizycka-Zamoizka, very fitting for this evening party.

We hope that Madame Gomperz will agree to participate in the program. An invitation shall be made to Madame Hanslik [*sic*] [3] to sing a few songs. With Hellmesberger and a cellist of his choosing, we shall perform together the Beethoven Trio dedicated to Archduke Rudolph. [4] The arrangement of the program, according to the tickets, has been left to me. Beethoven ought to open and Chopin close it, under M. Czar's bediamonded fingers. —

It goes without saying that my name, as pianist, can no longer be displayed on any kind of a poster.

You hit upon it magnificently, concerning the place of the salon concert in question. Its real title remains: "To the overthrow of spirituality in Galicia."

Your very humbly, obedient
F. Liszt.

LETTER 182

Your Highness,

My small hopes that the *Galician* concert would come to nothing have disappeared. I am resigned to it; and above all I thank you with full gratitude for your effective solicitude, without which my superannuated piano-playing would be too much.

Bösendorfer is sending me the preliminary version of the Program for the 9th of April. I hope that Madame Gomperz will be so kind to add Saar's song, (dedicated to Your Highness), to it, and also a song by Countess Gizicka-Zamoiska. She will decide with Mme. Gomperz on the choice.

In suggesting to Bösendorfer to invite Madame Hanslick, I was displaying my customary quality: impartiality. People have made great use of this in respect to me, and to my detriment. In this case, Hanslick and Her Highness Marcelline Czartoryska are in complete agreement. For them and for a great many others, I can only remain a celebrated pianist. All the worse for me, if my idea differs from theirs. Happily that doesn't at all do away with ordinary social politeness.

I shall belong to Count Geza Zichy from the 3rd to the 7th of April. We will go together to Pressburg and Oedenburg. Monday, (April 4th), I'll be in Vienna to plan the coming Viennese programs with Bösendorfer. Please be so kind, Your Highness, to tell me at what hour on Monday evening you will allow me to talk to you about the Galician Concert.

Your very humble and
grateful servant
March 30, '81 — Budapest.   F. Liszt

I will take up my former residence at the Schottenhof in Vienna, for a week, starting with the 8th of April.

LETTER 183

Your Highness,

Due to the trip to the village of Raiding tomorrow morning, I shall only be able to get back to Vienna tomorrow evening after nine o'clock.

I am eager to call on Baron Conrad [1] Friday morning, and to put myself at the command of Princess Marcelline Czartoryska.

Bösendorfer is taking care that the program for the Saturday evening musicale is properly printed the night before.

with unchanging gratitude,

Oedenburg, Wednesday April 6, '81. F. Liszt.

LETTER 184

Your Highness,

It gave me great pleasure to see Gustchen again. Thank Heaven all the news is favorable about Friedstein and you and your family.

My silly accident,[1] from which I expected to be recovered in a week, is still dragging along. Next Wednesday I will continue with the warm baths at Bayreuth, followed by sweat-baths — according to the doctor's orders.

I shall have returned to Rome before the 10th of October.

A big secret to tell you today. Probably you already know it. The Intendant of the Weimar theater, Baron von Loën, aims to succeed Dingelstedt; and he has some fear of not being warmly received by Prince Hohenlohe, to whom Loën — unknown to M. Sach — wishes to confide his secret. You know Loën, with his affable manner and his understanding of the ways of the theater and the Court. He is now going to Vienna at the invitation of a writers' convention. I beg you, therefore, to ask Prince Constantin to receive him in a good frame of mind, and afterward to do as little or as much for him as the Prince wishes.

At the Wartburg, Loën's and his wife's ancestors stand around in heavy suits of armor: I, a poor devil, without armor. I am grateful to the living Loën's for the friendly attitude we have mutually displayed each other here for the last twelve years.

With all his heart, your most
grateful old servant

September 12, '81 — Weimar.   F. Liszt.

LETTER 185

[Vienna]

Between the hours of four and five, to the Augarten will come your

most devoted servant

Friday   F L.

LETTER 185a

Heartfelt gratitude
October 22, '81.   F. Liszt

LETTER 186

Your Highness,

Your old servant never went by your birthday without remembering your constant kindness towards him. He often reminds himself of it, and he prays God to lavish His blessings upon you and your family; but my idiosyncrasy against letters and telegrams increases from year to year. For that I reproach myself, hoping that you will grant me your indulgence.

The artistic event this winter, which put all ranks of Budapest society into a flutter, was Munkacsy's[1] *Christ before Pilate*: even more, the presence of the painter, who was entertained, pampered, glorified, and exalted to the utmost. If, indeed, there may have been an excess of patriotism, that were still better than the sterile convenience of a lack of enthusiasm or of open disparagement. All in all, Munkacsy showed great spirit, — simple, grateful, and with that touch of inner pride that behooves a great artist. A little like Napoleon I telling his august sovereign-hosts at Erfurt that at the start of his career he was a second lieutenant, Munkacsy recalled his beginnings as a poor carpenter. I am told that amidst his brilliant success he is occasionally overwhelmed by profound melancholy.

From Holy Wednesday until yesterday, I have enjoyed the very gracious hospitality of Cardinal Haynald at Kalocsa. His Eminence has displayed the most flattering kindness to me for the last fifteen years. This he ostensibly demonstrated while presiding at my Jubilee, at Budapest, for 50 years as an artist, and he vouchsafes to continue his kindness to me without any break. Your most illustrious brother-in-law is in the same category: his last letter informs me that he has suspended his dealings with M., due to too sharp a harangue which he received as a New Year's present.

I shall be in Vienna on Saturday or Sunday, but only for a couple of days, since this occasion I am very pressed for time. I ought to arrive at Brussels on the 27th of April, (for the occasion of a great performance of the *Elizabeth*, sung for the first time with a French text); and I have promised to spend the preceding week at Weimar.

With all my heart,
your very grateful,
F. Liszt.

Shrove Tuesday, '82 — Budapest.

LETTER 187

[Vienna, April 1882]

Your Highness,

Tomorrow evening I shall be at the *Schottenhof*, and I had planned to leave from there on Monday. But since you are so kind to ask me for that day, it goes without saying that I will come. If you have a free quarter-of-an-hour on Sunday or Monday afternoon, I beg you to indicate the time you will allow me to "call."

your very grateful
F.L.

Friday morning.

LETTER 188

[Vienna, April, 1882]

Pohlig,[1] the Weimar pianist par excellence, left Vienna several days ago. I am sorry for him that he missed the chance of being introduced to you, and of providing the *Augarten* with his distinguished talent this evening. I am none the less grateful for the kind invitation that you asked me to give him.

With my humblest respects

Monday morning.   F.L.

LETTER 189

Your Highness,

Here is my modest "Christmas Tree," [1] for 2 and 4 hands.

I offer it most modestly to you for your Court pianist [2] at the *Augarten.* —

Most humble and truly grateful

April 29, '82, Weimar.   F Liszt

Tomorrow evening I shall be at Brussels and then back here on the 10th of May — until the end of June.

LETTER 190

Your Highness,

Strongly vexed by a delay on the part of my old Weimar bookbinder, Hens, I shall not be able to send you my *"Christmas Tree"* (for 2 and 4 hands) for about ten days; when I return to Weimar.

Very humbly
your grateful

May 1st, '82 — Brussels.   F Liszt.

LETTER 191: Preface

Letter 191 contains the first reference to Liszt's growing infirmity. By 1882 he had reached the age of seventy-one; and a long and active life, complicated by years of erratic and wearing artistic activity and the constant state of "vagabondage," was beginning to exact its toll. A hard fall on the steps of the *Hofgärtnerei* in 1881 marked the actual commencement of his physical decline (cf. Sitwell, *Liszt*, p. 344), and according to observers, he aged rapidly after the accident. Although he persisted in refusing to play the piano in public except for an occasional benefit, he was still engaged in conducting his own choral and orchestral compositions. The demands made upon him as a teacher at Weimar — for this was the period when his pupils included such later virtuosi as Moszkowski, de Pachmann, Sgambati, Godowsky, Rosenthal, Mottl, Scharwenka, and Busoni — must have been tremendous.

LETTER 191

Your Highness,

When your very kind lines came to me (at Weimar), I was suffering from a twitching of the nerves that kept me from writing for a week. I waited for an hour of relief — which I only found today — in order to thank you at length for your continual favor. The remembrance you guard of the improvisation about the "cradle," performed at the German ambassador's at Rome, touches me keenly. I finally finished scoring the symphonic poem based on a remarkable sketch of Michel Zichy's,[1] entitled "From the Cradle to the Grave." [2] It seemed natural to put an exciting movement between the two: "the fight for life," ("The struggle for existence"). The whole thing is now being printed, and you will hear it for full orchestra next year at Vienna, as well as my *second* "Mephisto Waltz." The Bilse [3] orchestra recently performed it not without success, at Berlin.

I would have most willingly gone to Salzburg for the occasion of the performance of my Hungarian Coronation Mass which, they say, was most satisfactory. But after my musical excursions to Brussels, Friburg, [4] (Brisgau), Baden, Zürich, — from the month of May to July — and following that my two trips to Bayreuth, I really needed a little rest.

Your most illustrious brother-in-law honors me greatly, when he shelters my bust by Ezéchiel beneath the shade of the Schillingsfürst park. This same bust is now being exhibited in Paris at Goupil's,[5] the supreme promoter of painters' and sculptors' reputations.

Despite some adverse criticism, I predict Ezéchiel's final success, particularly in America. M. de Joukowski,[6] (son of the tutor and friend of the late Emperor Alexander II), has recently made a large portrait of your humble servant — intended for the wealthy piano manufacturers, Rish and Mason,[7] in Toronto, Canada.

J.'s portrait succeeded so well, that M.S. asked him for a repeat performance at the Weimar Museum. It shall be done here soon, where I am staying until New Year's Day in a princely fashion at the Wagner's. The beautiful Vendramin [8] palace used to belong to the Duchess de Berry; her son, the Duke della Grazia,[9] inherited it, and he very graciously rents out the large entresol — extremely spacious, and containing about fifteen rooms with salons — to Wagner for one year and at the very modest sum of 6ooo francs. I am benefiting from it, and I have just sent my humble thanks to the Duchess della Grazia.

Wagner lives in seclusion with his family at Venice; he abstains from either making calls or receiving callers. I shall try to copy him in this measure to the best of my ability, despite my lack of practice.

The S.'s showed the kindest, most affable, and affectionate friendship for me, the day before the eve of my departure from Weimar. He had returned from Biarritz and Paris; she from her lovely Heinrichsau [10] estate — (Silesia) The curing of her serious illness — (diphtheria) — is progressing so-so, for she was still only able to subsist on oysters and meat-broths.

The Reuss's were present at the two last little dinners (for 7 to 8 persons) to which Their Highnesses had invited me. Conversation turned on the usual themes; there was also an artist, an *extraordinary* pianist, by the name of d'Albert.[11] Richter introduced me to him in Vienna last April. Since then he has worked at Weimar, without interruption, under my tutelage. Among the young virtuosi, from the time of Tausig, — Bülow and Rubinstein naturally remain the Senators and Masters — I know of none of a more gifted as well as of a more dazzling talent than d'Albert. Although he is scarcely 18, M.S., on my suggestion, called him the Weimar "Court-pianist."

After the two performances of his *Maccabees*, which he conducted at Leipzig with a great deal of success, Rubinstein came to spend half a day with me at Weimar. He returned to Petersburg and will stay there for the winter, composing many a work and directing the large Orchestral Concerts, etc., and Oratorios.

I shall certainly not neglect to spread about Riedel's songs, who is now firmly established in Brunswick. At the "Music Festival" of the "General German Music Organizations," whose honorary president I am, I shall find a singer next year capable of showing the worth of these *songs*. I would be obliged if you would send them to me. Riedel is like a Court-Chamberlain of Brahms', and this will not do him any harm.

Cosima and her daughter Daniela retain their affectionate memories and regards for you.

With all his heart, your
ever-grateful
F. Liszt.

November 24, '82 —
Venice, Vendramin Palace.

From Rome: rather nice and less-severe letters.
Before the middle of January, I will return right to Budapest from here.

LETTER 192

What an admirable discovery, Your Highness, and how grateful I am to you for telling me of it! Thus we have found the conclusion for our St. Stanislas. I looked for it in vain until now. King Boleslaw II, whom I would not want to disparage, since he was a brave warrior, ought to sing his "out of the depths" as a penitent at the Ossiach [1] convent in Carinthia — according to the recent historical and archaeological findings. To end it, he will cry out softly the "Holy Poland," as if an interjection. The chorus then starts and ends it. I have already written the *Out of the depths* and the *Holy Poland*: also the two preceding polonaises, — the one strongly lugubrious, the other triumphant.

There remains to compose the great scene of the miracle and the resurrection, where the owner of the field acquired by St. Stanislas is called as witness. This scene will conclude with the murder of St. Stanislas, committed by the king. As the text of the Oratorio has already been sent to Pest, I shall take the liberty of writing to You from there about how I hope the climax may be achieved, while at the same time I send You the manuscript. Your friendly poet will only have a job of 15 or 20 verses to do. . . . It is better not to put the murder in the church, but rather immediately following the miracle of the Resurrection. Musically, the church scene would call for a pompous prolixity which should be avoided. Between the crime and the penitence at the Ossiach convent, I will put an orchestral interlude telling of Boleslaw's pilgrimage.

I only wrote to M. saying that I would work again at the Stanislas, which is perfectly true; and yesterday she telegraphed me her pleasure. I carefully refrained from speaking to her about the historical discovery, and the new trend in the text of the Oratorio. *Please be so kind* not to confide in her, lest you arouse in her observations from now on superfluous; since my stand is absolutely taken. On the 4th of November I hope to place the completed score at her feet. Before that, I shall try out, probably at Weimar, the 2 Polonaises, the "Out of the depths" and the "Holy Poland." —

Thank you for the picture of the beautiful statue of "God's Great Pauper" — St. Francis of Assisi, by Alonso Cano.[2] It will adorn the edition of my "Canticle of the Sun"; my feeling, however, about St. Francis, is otherwise. I should not like such an austere face for him (like St. Francis of Paul, or Saint Bruno), nor the clasped hands — but rather stretched out, begging for the stigmata and the "Great Pardon!" — I spoke of this to M. de Joukovski, who is in the process of painting a St. Francis for a Capuchin church near Siena. He is of my opinion, and I hope that he will succeed in bringing it to life in his painting.

The large portrait of your very humble servant that he painted at Bayreuth and Weimar has met here, as at Weimar, with no ordinary success. Passini [3] and other painters and connoisseurs have given it serious praise. I am attached by a strong friendship to Joukovski. Personally he is very much of a gentleman, and not at all boring.

I suppose that Daniela wrote to you about the Venetian performance of Wagner's unpublished Symphony,[4] composed in 1832, and then performed a single time at Leipzig. On Cosima's 45th birthday, Christmas Eve, Wagner wanted her to hear his juvenile and robust Symphony; and he himself directed the orchestra, which he had do five preparatory rehearsals. The pretty Fenice hall and the adjoining grand salon were gayly illuminated. In a third room a buffet was held for the members of the orchestra, (more than 50 persons). A general *no-admission* for the public, and particularly for the journalists for whom W. has taken a dislike, including his warmest partisans. . . . Thus the audience consisted of the 7 members of the family; then the governess, the tutor, the vice-director of the Orchestra, the President of the Music Academy, Count Contin,[5] who had lent the hall, — and Joukovski, who has virtually belonged to the family for the last few years at Bayreuth, Palermo, Siena, and Venice.

Wagner is writing a very witty letter to his editor Fritzsch [6] (Leipzig) on the subject of this *special* evening. It will appear in the next Number of the same Fritzsch's "Weekly Musical Sheet," and it will certainly be reprinted by other journals. Next to Bismarck, Wagner is the person who is most in the public eye.

I have become the most complete stay-at-home. Wagner is still a more thorough one, and he calls on nobody; his wife succeeds with great difficulty in persuading him that he must, however, make a pretense of rubbing up against a few human-beings at infrequent intervals, even if they are very unpleasant. His bitter and ironic exclusiveness is related to his supremely absolute genius. In such a most extraordinary case, to reproach him would be to make a mistake.

There is no possible mistake with H. Riedel. At the next "Tone-Artists' meeting," his agreeable songs will figure on the program; and if before that I can find a singer in Budapest capable of interpreting them in a suitable and successful manner, I shall ask Riedel to present them in private and in public recitals.

I have seen Princess Theresa Hohenlohe [7] again as well as your nephew Philip, the Schillingsfürst "heir-apparent." He sings Heine's "3 Grenadiers" [8] in an impressive way — in the two versions, by Schumann [9] and Reissiger.[10]

The very charming Countess Dönhof stopped here for three days and left for Rome yesterday. Her marriage with Lenbach is merely a sneering remark of mediocre fabrication.

On Sunday evening at Budapest will arrive your old and faithfully grateful

January 11, '83 — Venice.   FL.

LETTER 193

The humblest tokens of my constant gratitude are always at your feet, Your Highness. I reiterate my sincere expression of them on this, your birthday.

In the near future I shall indicate a few minor modifications to be made to the text to the author of the St. Stanislas poem, and I will allow myself to ask definitive advice from you, verbally.

Considering the startling archaeological discovery concerning King Boleslaw, (at a convent near Klagenfurt),[1] my St. Stanislas Oratorio is drawing to a happy conclusion. —

A young sculptor of great talent, who has worked in Zumbusch's studio, has made a statue of me commissioned for the new big Budapest theater. It is to be opened in October, '84, according to the command of His Majesty the King of Hungary. He is a native of Hungary, by the name of Strobl,[2] and your husband honors him with his favor.

A surprise in the line of sculpture [3] is being prepared for you for February 16th, but I shall be very careful not to tell you about it ahead of time.

Your most devoted servant
F. Liszt.

February 14, '83 —
  Budapest.

LETTER 194: *Preface*

"Cosima's state of health" is a reminder that Wagner had died at Bayreuth on February 13, 1883 — three weeks before this letter was written to Marie. Liszt had been staying with the Wagners at the Vendramin Palace in Venice for almost two months, and he departed an exact month before the sudden death of his son-in-law. Cosima had even pressed her father to take up his residence with them. Both Liszt and Wagner realized that despite their mutual affection and musical admiration, such a household would have been impossible — and certainly Carolyne, never a Wagnerite, would not have allowed it.

Letters 194 through 198 are also of interest since they reveal Liszt's careful method of composition and the reliance he placed on Marie's efficacious aid. Curiously enough, Marie must have devoted herself to dramatic composition during at least one part of her life. Although Liszt never alludes to any play written by Marie, an entry in Roenneke (*Dingelstedts Wirksamkeit*) indicates that a play of hers, *Freund Granet*, was performed at the Weimar Theater during the 1858–59 season.

LETTER 194

Your Highness,

The person recommended by Countess Giziska, M. Richard Heuberger,[1] will be very well received, with or without any florid *counterpoint*. If the composer were to delay in arriving, and were not to take a keen interest in getting to know Budapest, he might spare himself two-thirds of the trip. Saturday, March 16, and the following day, Palm Sunday, I shall be at Pressburg. They are giving *Elizabeth* there. I no longer have any interest in it, since its success has already been sufficiently established in various countries. Nevertheless, since the *Church Music Society* of Pressburg has several times displayed its good-will towards me by performing the *Gran Mass* and other compositions of mine without my presence, I am anxious this time to present them with my personal compliments.

I will spend Holy Week here, (or at Kalocsa?), and as usual return to Vienna during the first days of April. I shall then again be so bold to ask your advice and help for *St. Stanislas*. It is impossible for me to work on it in Budapest, due to the rain and hail of letters that descends on me from everywhere. No matter how parsimonious my answers may be, they take me many hours each day....

When you have approved, (as I hope), the short but important change in the St. Stanislas text, I shall reapply myself to the work; and I plan to finish it around Christmas.

With continued acknowledgements of most devoted gratitude

March 6, '83 —   F. Liszt.

Budapest.

Yesterday's telegram from Bayreuth assures me that Cosima's state of health is nothing to worry about.
She is keeping herself in complete seclusion.

LETTER 195

[Pest]
Monday, April 2, '83.

Your Highness,
This time my stay in Vienna will be very brief.
I shall arrive tomorrow evening, and will leave Saturday morning to be at Weimar on the 8th of April — the Grand-Duchess's birthday.
Therefore, I am taking the liberty of asking you to come to a hearing of the *St. Stanislas* on Wednesday or Thursday. Will you be so kind to indicate the time (Schottenhof) to your very humble and most grateful servant?

F. Liszt.

LETTER 195a

(Vienna, April 4, '83.)
This evening, at 8 o'clock, Your Highness, a reading at the Augarten — the *definitive* Stanislas. Thursday, tomorrow, I am completely at your command. In perpetual gratitude,
Wednesday.   F. Liszt.

I am returning to Weimar Friday evening.

LETTER 196

[Vienna, April 5th or 6th, 1883]
It will be better to dispense with all the conspirators in the *St. Stanislas* Oratorio. These Gentlemen are too hackneyed in the theater, and I am anxious to avoid anything botchy for my work.
It will probably be necessary to add a few verses to the first air

267

sung by the Bishop's Mother, in order to give more scope to the sole character-part in the Oratorio.

The eternal conflict between Church and State is brought out strongly by Stanislas and Boleslaw; the intermediate role of the chancellor seems necessary to me, even for the Music.

Let's cut out the tedious excommunication scene without any scruples; let the king cut the bishop to pieces at the cemetery immediately after Petrovich's resurrection. If the body of critics condemns this historical transgression, at least the public will ratify it.

After the death of Stanislas, Boleslaw's penitential pilgrimage, (orchestra alone), is to end at the Ossiach convent where the king sings the "Out of the depths" and joins with the chorus in the "Holy Poland."

The finale, without any "cream-puffs!" —

FL

LETTER 197

Please excuse my insistence, Your Highness, but I am preoccupied with the idea that the St. Stanislas Oratorio can only succeed under your aegis and with you presiding over the completion of the text.

Since M. Edler's corrections are concerned only with the defective versification of the preceding version, and do not touch on the distribution of the scenes, I thought it would be more convenient for you to read the libretto as it was before. I have noted the modifications on it that seemed to me necessary: principally; the murder of the bishop, *at the cemetery*, after his brief apostrophe to the King: "Behold here the arm of God, forever upraised to avenge the Truth!"

Down with the conspirators who impede the simple movement of the work, and a few more verses for the *Mother's* air (in the first scene): that's all!

Now it is a matter of your intervention. Please ask M. Edler to print a copy of his *entire text* on about twenty pages, 1, 3, 5, 7, etc. — leaving 2, 4, 6, 8 — etc. empty.

For the last scene, (Ossiach) — already completely composed

— there is no other text needed, except the *Out of the depths* and the *Holy Poland*.

With very humble and real gratitude

April 6, '83 — Vienna.   F. Liszt.

If I receive M. Edler's manuscript at the end of May, I shall set to work right away. I hope to have arrived at a happy conclusion by Christmas.

LETTER 198

Marburg, May 1st, '83.

Eureka! — that is to say that you, Your Highness, have found it.

I benefit thereof and am more than satisfied, — delighted — with the poetic and vigorous text of M. Edler, where your indications take on a suitable shape. Hence, no more hesitation or fruitless research: I shall compose the St. Stanislas Oratorio — with the definite assurance of its success. The work has consistency and will bravely show itself thus.

How can I show you my appreciation for the happy solution afforded my lengthy tribulations with St. Stanislas? I will succeed better in Music than with syllables. At last due to your efficacious intervention, behold the plot and the text that I need, — with neither theatrical banalities nor extravangaza.

Please be so kind again, Your Highness, to convey my two enclosed words of thanks to M. Edler.

Marburg [1] is bedecked with flags and is quite festive for the celebration of the 600th anniversary of St. Elizabeth's church. For this occasion, my "Legend" will be performed here tonight. Tomorrow I am setting off for Leipzig for the "Tone Artists' Conference," whose honorary president I have the honor to be. As usual for about the last twenty years, we shall have 5 or 6 concerts of programs rich with new compositions.

Before mid-May back again in Weimar, (and there remaining for several months), will be

Your very humble and really grateful
F. Liszt.

LETTER 199: Preface

A hiatus in this correspondence is again indicated by a letter to Carolyne written on December 16, 1883, where Liszt mentions the sad death of Marie's second son, Prince Wolfgang: "I have written a few words to Magne — the sad fate of the living is to see those who die!" (*L.M.* IV, No. 385.)

LETTER 199

Your Highness,
I come to you on this anniversary, to renew my constant gratitude and my most respectful attachment. To them I join the wish that Your Highness may condescend to keep her good-feelings for me; she will ever be for me one of Providence's most precious gifts, and a tender gleam of the Ideal.
February 17, '84.   F. Liszt.

LETTER 200

[Vienna, March or April, 1884]
Unless Your Highness has another engagement, her most humble servant will present himself at the Augarten today at one-thirty.
                                                   With constant gratitude,
Monday morning,   F. Liszt.
            Schottenhof.

LETTER 201

[Vienna, 1884]
Your Highness,
I forgot to tell you yesterday of an invention by Bösendorfer which appears excellent to me. This is the *Octavier* piano; there is only a single example of one completed; will you allow me to have it carried to the Augarten to show it to you this evening?
No answer will mean "yes."
                                        Yours, with a contrite heart
Wednesday morning.   F. Liszt.

Bösendorfer's new piano takes up no more space than do the old grand pianos.

LETTER 202

[Vienna, April or May, 1884.]
Certainly I am your most delighted and *most devoted servant*. Gussie will present you my compliments. Chlodwig's sons are expected, along with yours.

Completely at your feet,
FL

LETTER 203

Beginning tomorrow at 2 o'clock, to the Augarten will come,
Your very faithful servant
Monday.   FL.

LETTER 204

[Weimar]
What are your orders for today, Your Highness?
If Wednesday evening was poor, might not tonight be successful at the "Hofgärtnerei?" [1]
Please be so kind to notify your very humble
Monday morning.   F. Liszt.

LETTER 205

The pleasant memories you retain of Weimar, Your Highness, touch me keenly. Since the year of '47, I have become as if imbedded here. It is a heartache to me, that Your mother does not condescend to return. I can only yield to certain fixed ideas.

Naturally M. and Mme. Sach were very sorry not to have seen you this time. When you come, it is a continuation of the "Ideal Ones" for the *Altenburg*.

271

Our 25th anniversary of the "Tone-Artists' Conference" succeeded very well. Gracious Countess Gi.[1] (Loulou) already has told you about it.

I am adding, that the "Holy Poland"[2] — at the instigation of Countess Schleinitz, and Mme. Meyendorff,[3] in agreement with M. Sach — was repeated at the next day's concert.

By Pentecost of '85 I hope to have finished the score of St. Stanislas. I write slowly — cross out three-quarters, and then do not know whether the fourth part can stand by itself.

Your most humbly grateful

May 30, '84 — Weimar.   F. Liszt.

LETTER 206

Your Highness,

I hope to catch a glimpse of you during the 2 or 3 days at Vienna, — from next Tuesday to Thursday; but I don't wish to wait until then, to thank you wholeheartedly for your very kind telegram of yesterday, which was extremely touching for

your constant and very grateful servant

October 23, '84 — Weimar.   F. Liszt.

LETTER 207

Your Highness,

It is consoling for me to find your mother in better health than I had thought, and also in a much better frame of mind than she was formerly. We were able to chat without a hitch about subjects that previously had been more-than-painful. The busts of Constantin and of Do.[1] are well-placed in the salon: the first near the writing-table, slightly in the shadow: the other near the piano, not too much in the light.

The 25th volume of the "Causes"[2] — an immense work of a fierce fourteen-years' labor — is being courageously completed. After the last page is printed, the author at (long) last intends to rest next summer, and even to take a trip around Italy in little daily stages — Assisi, Siena, Pisa, Florence, Bologna, Venice, etc., etc.: *mirabile visu!*

Naturally your mother disapproves strongly of His Eminence [3] and his giving up the Bishopric of Albano. This didn't seem to me to be a renunciation of dignity for something less worthy and more fruitful.

For today, His Eminence has invited Ambassador Keudel to dinner, and also the envoy Schlözer,[4] — perhaps the only person whom the papers continually mention, in order to do nothing more than that to him

Your very humble and grateful

Rome, December 17, '84.   F. Liszt.

LETTER 208

On the anniversary of the blessed day of your birth, Your Highness, I again place at your feet the very humble testimony of my faithful gratitude.

As I grow older, I keep only my dearest memories, and my hopes for Divine mercy.

February 14, '85 — Budapest.   F. Liszt.

LETTER 209

Like Beethoven, Your Highness, You understand how to make mediocre themes interesting. Your *variations* on M.S. are delightful, and they make the finest *counterpoint.* He himself wrote to me a few friendly lines from Vienna. For more than four months our correspondence had come to a standstill; and I thought that he was being cool to me after my last letter in October, when I begged him not to ask me to do any more unnecessary writing. He answers me now with generosity and assures me of his *"pertinacity,"* to which I remain reverently devoted. My forty years of service and good offices at Weimar bear witness to my good will. S. recognized this when he told others and repeated to me: "Liszt has never given me bad advice, nor selfish advice, either."

Thus I shall go on, modestly, and with complete consistency.

What should one think of M.'s projected trip for next summer? Will her 25th volume be finished? Might not two or three supplementary volumes keep her in Rome? — I give up any prognostication.

In about two weeks, to renew his most grateful homage, will come to the *Augarten*

your very humble
March 23, '85, Budapest.   F. Liszt.

LETTER 210

A very humble request, Your Highness. What hour tomorrow would you care to receive your very grateful servant?
Tuesday, April 14, 5 o'clock (Schottenhof)   F. Liszt.

LETTER 211: *Preface*

Complaints about the failing condition of his sight appear increasingly in letters to Carolyne from 1885 until Liszt's death. In June 1886, his physicians recommended that he undergo an operation to remove a cataract on his left eye. He declined, however, on the grounds that he was too old.

The brevity of the last thirty or forty letters in this correspondence shows that writing was difficult for him, although actually — except for a slight enlargement in the size of his handwriting — the calligraphy in these same letters remains much the same as it was from the start.

LETTER 211

Your Highness,

To my long litany of thanks for your good-deeds, is added a little stanza that corresponds to your very kind last letter.

As for her health, your mother is at *her* best — despite the prodigious activity and the extreme ardor of both the intellect and heart of the persevering patient, who only departs from her sublimity by her compliant amiability.

I have seen your most illustrious brother-in-law (in a pleasant expectant mood), both here and at the Villa d'Este —

You mentioned Albert Apponyi to me. No one has better brought natural abilities to fruition by study than has he, and he is a noble soul.*

My eyes are still getting weaker: my memory too, with the exception of that of my heart — described by a deaf-and-dumb person as "gratitude." This I place constantly before your feet
November 19, '85 —   F. Liszt.
    Rome.

LETTERS 212–215: Preface

The four letters to Marie that bring the correspondence to a close were written during 1886: Letter 215 is dated April 3rd, and Liszt died at Bayreuth on July 31st. It was the year of his final great tour, and the aged lion — the last Romantic musician — was once again heard on the concert stage. A triumph in Paris was followed by two weeks in England in April. Sir Alexander Mackenzie conducted *St. Elizabeth* for a huge and enthusiastic audience. There were immense state dinners and private receptions; and Liszt played for Queen Victoria at Windsor Castle on April 8th — an occasion that must have reminded him of an earlier performance, when as a child prodigy he performed for George IV, in June 1824. London was succeeded by Antwerp, Paris, Weimar, and Luxemburg. It was the train ride in a drafty coach from there to Bayreuth that gave Liszt his fatal chill. He insisted on seeing *Tristan* given at the *Festspielhaus*, despite the protests of his doctor; and the *Liebestod* of the two stage lovers served as a musical prelude to his own death exactly one week later on July 31, 1886. Carolyne survived him by a scant six months and died in February 1887. Like a faded and somewhat literary Isolde, she carried out the last act of their own drama.

> *So stürben wir, um ungetrennt,*
> *Ewig einig, ohne End',*
> *Ohn' Erwachen, ohne Bangen,*
> *Namenlos in Lieb' umfangen,*
> *Ganz uns selbst gegeben,*
> *Der Liebe nur zu leben.*

* I am only sorry that Apponyi could not be more on Andrassy's side in politics.

LETTER 212

Your Highness,

This time I will have but three days to spend at Vienna: from next Friday to Monday.

Please be kind enough to let me know at what time, at Your Highness's, your very grateful old servant may present himself *Sunday, March 7, '86 —*   F. Liszt.
Budapest.

LETTER 213

[Vienna, March 11, 1886.]

A thousand thanks, Your Highness.

Today, punctually at 6 o'clock, to Your home will come

your old servant
Friday morning.   F. Liszt.

LETTER 214

Although it may be a bit late, I have just written to the Chairman of the Committee, M. Aubry,[1] asking him to invite Mademoiselle Olga de Lagrenée[2] to fulfill the kind role of Lady Patroness at the festival on March 25th. I hope that she will graciously accept. An *incident* about which I haven't spoken to you, Your Highness, nearly made a failure out of the performance of the Gran Mass at St. Eustace's.[3] As a result I have abstained from any meddling with it, for about a week.

Humbly and with perpetual
gratitude
March 15, '86 — Vienna.   F. Liszt.

Standhartner gave me reassuring news last night about Princess Reuss's recovery.

I left two calling-cards at the German Ambassador's.

Standhartner also told me that at Prague they will soon give the

Barber of Bagdad, which had a fine success at Munich. Princess Reuss had some idea of having this very witty and subtle work heard at her Home, with piano accompaniment.

LETTER 215

April 3, '86. Paris.

In comparison with the poor reception and pitiful performance of the Gran Mass in '66, this time it made a good impression — even twice in one week — something almost without antecedents for a piece of Church music.

The *Préludes, Tasso, and Orpheus*, were warmly applauded at the Colonne and Lamoureux Concerts.[1] So was the Concerto, brilliantly played by Planté.[2]

With perpetual gratitude,
F. Liszt.

NOTES AND BIBLIOGRAPHY

Notes

Letter 1

1. Marie was born on February 18, 1837.

2. Carolyne's principal Polish estate. Woronince was in Podolia, a district of southwestern Russia bounded by Volhynia to the north, Kiev to the east, Bessarabia to the south, and Galicia to the west. Sitwell describes the estate in *Liszt* (London: Faber & Faber, 1934). "The chateau of Woronince would seem to have been built early in the last century upon vaguely classical lines. It had great avenues, ornamental canals, and woods with long rides out through them" (p. 157). Liszt's last letter to Carolyne from Woronince is dated November 10, 1847; his first to her from Weimar was on February 4, 1848 — the same day he wrote this letter to Marie.

3. Prince Eugene zu Sayn-Wittgenstein. Before leaving Woronince, Liszt stopped at a Mr. Hauser's to inquire about a lamp ordered by Carolyne for her nephew, Eugene.

4. Evidently one of the horses at Woronince.

5. Marie's English governess, who went to Weimar with the two princesses. She was kept and pensioned by the Wittgensteins; and in a letter to Carolyne from Adelheid von Schorn, Miss Anderson was described as living with the family as late as 1860.

6. There are no other references to these names, which may have belonged to friends or playmates of Marie at Woronince; or perhaps they are characters from stories.

Letters 2a, 2b, 2c

1. Liszt.

2. Marie.

3. Racine, *Andromaque*; Cléone to Hermione. Liszt omits the question mark which belongs after the last line.

Letters 3a, 3b

1. Marie.

2. Carolyne's residence at Weimar. It was "a house on a small knoll on the other side of the Ilm, on the road to Jena," built by Oberstallmeister von Seebach (cf. Letter 23), and the Princess bought it soon after her arrival at Weimar. Cf. Adelheid von Schorn, *Das nachklassische Weimar* (Weimar: Kiepenheuer, 1911), vol. II, p. 34.

Liszt stayed at the *Hotel zum Russischen Hof* when he came to Weimar before 1848. Upon returning from the Russian tour, he settled at the *Erbprinz* near the marketplace and shortly after moved into one of the wings of the Altenburg. His mail — particularly messages from the Court — continued to go to the Hotel, since his liaison with the Princess was regarded with disfavor by most of Weimar society. Schorn comments on the small number of callers at the Altenburg during 1848 and 1849. (Schorn, *Weimar*, I, pp. 117 and 250; *L.M.* I, Letter 25).

281

There is an excellent description of the Altenburg in Wilhelm Bode, *Das Leben in Alt-Weimar* (Leipzig: Haessel, 1922), p. 89.

3. Marie.

4. Marie.

5. Carolyne.

6. This may be a nickname for Mme. Gross, who wrote children's stories under the pseudonym of Amalie Winter and who headed a literary salon in Weimar.

7. Liszt. The reference is to the line of Merovingian rulers who earned the title of the "Do-Nothing Kings."

Letters 4a, 4b

1. Marie.

Letters 5a, 5b, 5c

1. Liszt had just moved from the *Erbprinz* to the Altenburg, and apparently Marie was ill when he wrote this note.

2. In these early letters, Liszt somewhat archly refers to *Bon Bozé* (Polish: *Bog*, vocative *Boze* — God) when he invokes the deity to watch over Marie. We have translated this *passim* as "The Good Lord" or simply "God."

3. Nickname for Miss Anderson.

4. In Zoroastrianism, Ahriman was the late Persian designation for evil or the principle of evil; Ormazd was the Parsi form for the chief deity in Mazdaeism — the opponent of Ahriman.

5. Also spelled Goullon — a doctor at Weimar.

Letter 7

1. A musician in the Weimar Court Orchestra (cf. *L.M.* I, No. 56). This is possibly Anton Wilhelm von Zuccalmaglio (1803–1869), whose pseudonym was Wilhelm von Waldbrühl. He contributed to Schumann's *Neue Zeitschrift für Musik* and collected German folk songs.

2. Peter Cornelius (1824–1874), who joined Liszt at Weimar as one of the members of the *Neudeutsche Schule*. His opera, *Der Barbier von Bagdad* (1858), was to embody the principles of the Liszt-Wagner musical doctrine. Unfortunately it received only a single performance. As did Wagner for the *Ring*, Cornelius turned to the norse *Eddas* for the theme of another unfinished opera, *Günlod*. He is remembered principally for his songs, and among these is *Ein Ton* — for years a staple of *Lieder* recitals. Cornelius was also an amateur poet: several of his verses, written for various birthday parties of Princess Marie, may be found in Schorn's *Zwei Menschenalter*, pp. 53 ff. He once described himself in the following quatrain:

> *Ich bin ein blasser Lisztianer,*
> *Bis zum letzten Ton und Hauch;*
> *Berlioz-Wagner-Weimaraner,*
> *Ein Cornelianer auch.*

3. This was the *Club Neu-Weymar*, the informal literary-musical association headed by Liszt to which most of the Weimar musicians and *literati* belonged. One of his aims was to restore to Weimar the glory it formerly possessed under the cultural aegis of Goethe and Schiller; and he hoped it was to become the operatic center of Europe and the focal point of what Wagner was later to call the "Art Work of the Future." Cf. Marion Bauer, "The Literary Liszt," *Musical Quarterly*, vol. XXII, no. 3 (July 1936).

Letter 8

1. The doctor at Eilsen, where Marie and her mother were taking a cure. Marie was also recovering from an attack of typhus. (*L.M.* I, No. 54).

2. "An absolute ruler, unlimited by law or constitution."

3. Mux or Moux, Liszt's pet dog at the Altenburg. Two of Liszt's nicknames for Marie were also "Moux-Furet" and "Moux-Blanc."

4. Hermann Becker, Liszt's servant, called "Pan Lapin(e)." He may have been related to the actor and magician Heinrich Becker, mentioned by Eckermann. Cf. *Gespräche mit Goethe*, ed. Beutels (Leipzig: Diederichs, 1902), February 26, 1824.

5. Posen or Poznan, capital city of the Polish district that bears the same name. It is approximately 170 miles west of Warsaw.

6. Probably a reference to the Great Exhibition at London in 1851.

7. The children of the Grand Duke.

8. Carl Alexander (1818–1901).

9. Carl Friedrich, the Grand Duke.

10. Baron Ziegesar, who succeeded Hans von Spiegel as Intendant of the Weimar Theater in July, 1847.

11. Unidentified.

12. St. Jakobskirche am Jakobsplan.

13. Marie's tutor.

14. Constanz von Fritsch, Chief Lady-in-Waiting to the Grand Duchess.

15. An opera composed by Joachim Raff (1822–1882), one of Liszt's musical disciples at Weimar from 1850 to 1856.

16. A bass who sang at Weimar.

Letter 9

1. The Grand Duke.

2. Marie.

3. Winged horse.

4. Miss Williams and Mrs. O'Brien, two Englishwomen who lived intermittently at Weimar.

5. Possibly Szerdahely, a Hungarian musician and pupil of Liszt.

6. Alexander Winterberger (1834–1914), organist, pianist, and one of Liszt's pupils.

7. Former owner of the Altenburg, who sold it to Carolyne in 1851.

8. Cf. Letter 8, Note 15. The movement mentioned by Liszt may be from one of Raff's eleven symphonies.

9. The *Andante* from Beethoven's A minor Quartet, Op. 132: "canzona di ringraziamento in modo lidico offerta alla divinita da un guarito."

10. Marie.

11. Daniel Liszt, son of the composer and Countess d'Agoult. He was born in Rome in 1839 and died in Berlin in 1859.

12. Marie.

13. Liszt's parentheses. Marie's birthday was February 18.

1. The Grand Duke.

2. Liszt's secretary.

3. Probably the brother of Ulysses Stock (cf. Letter 9, Note 8).

4. That is, the rooms belonging to Liszt and Marie — "Les Bessons."

5. The Weimar Theater. The original building stood from 1779 to 1825; in the latter year a new edifice was erected on the same site, and it was one of Weimar's showplaces until it burned in 1907. Many of Goethe's and Schiller's plays were performed at the Theater, and its importance is high in the history of German drama. The shift in repertory already mentioned, from drama to opera, began there early in the 1840's.

The Theater received a certain amount of international fame in 1864, when a large Shakespeare Festival was held for several weeks. This led directly to the founding of the *Deutsche Shakespeare-Gesellschaft* in April 1864. Cf. Leonhard Schrickel, *Geschichte des Weimarer Theaters* (Weimar: Pause, 1928). A complete list of the repertory of the Theater from 1857 to 1867, including opera, ballet, etc., may be found in the Appendix to Rudolf Roenneke's *Franz Dingelstedts Wirksamkeit am Weimarer Hof-Theater* (Greifswald: Adler, 1912).

6. Hans Feodor von Milde (1821–1899), who with his wife Rosa (1827–1906) sang at the Theater for many years. He was the first Telramund in Wagner's *Lohengrin* (1850); she, the original Elsa. Schorn (*Zwei Menschenalter*, p. 51) quotes a poem written by Cornelius to celebrate their wedding.

> *Mit Ruhm bedeckte sich ein Künstlerpaar,*
> *Vereint im Leben und im Reich des Klanges. . .*

7. Lortzing's opera, *Zar und Zimmermann* (1837) — the story of Peter the Great.

8. Probably *I Capuletti ed I Montechi* (1830) by Bellini.

9. *King Alfred.* Cf. Letter 8, Note 15.

10. A Leipzig bookseller.

11. This issue contained Liszt's article on Chopin. The *Revue* was founded in 1829 with Mauroy and Ségur-Dupeyron as directors. In 1830 the *Journal des Voyages* was incorporated with the *Revue*; and in 1831 — the year that marked the magazine's real entry into French letters — the editor François Buloz took over its direction. Sainte-Beuve, who became literary arbiter for the *Revue*, wrote some 144 articles for it between 1831 and 1849; and among its contributors were Vigny, Hugo, Planché, Musset, George Sand, Balzac, Chateaubriand, Mérimée, and Stendhal. In 1835 Pierre Leroux and the *Revue Encyclopédique* joined the *Revue des Deux Mondes* — a movement indicative of the journal's political concern, and in this case of the prominence of the whole Christian Socialist tendency, in which Liszt took an active part.

Beginning in 1831, the *Revue* published musical articles and reviews, and one of its leading music critics was Ange-Henri Blaze de Bury. It also treated the fine arts; and later, supplements were added discussing the annual *Salons* held at the Louvre. Cf. *La Revue des Deux Mondes: Cent Ans de Vie Française* (Paris: Hachette, 1929).

12. Carolyne. This is probably a reference to the leading figure in Molière's *L'Avare*; although it seems strange that Liszt, who was partially dependent upon Carolyne's bounty, would hint at her miserliness.

13. Hungarian sculptor.

14. Joseph Joachim (1831–1907), one of the most famous nineteenth-century violinists, who stayed at Weimar from 1849 to 1853 as concert-master for the orchestra. He later broke from the Liszt-Wagner circle when he became a close friend and musical admirer of Schumann and Brahms. Paul Bekker, in "Liszt and his Critics" (*Musical Quarterly*, July 1936), discusses Joachim's shift in allegiance and attributes it in part to the influence of Clara Schumann. There is also a letter from Joachim to Clara Schumann in 1855, where the violinist says of Liszt: "One can hear the lies in every note and see them at every moment." Cf. *Letters*, trans. Bickley (London: Macmillan, n.d.) Many of Joachim's letters to Liszt may be found in La Mara, *Briefe hervorragender Zeitgenossen an Franz Liszt* (Leipzig: Breitkopf & Härtel, 1895–1904).

15. Unidentified.

16. A game close to pinochle, played by from two to four players with a pack of twenty-four cards. The aim is to acquire sixty-six points and this is achieved by making combinations called "marriages" and by possessing certain counting cards as tricks.

17. Probably Friedrich August Johann, Freiherr Vitzthum von Egersberg, who had the title of *Obermundschenk* (Honorary Cup-Bearer) at the Weimar Court.

18. Town in southern Schaumburg-Lippe, near Bückeburg, Osnabrück, and the Belgian border — famous for its baths.

19. Capital of Prussian Saxony, on the Gera River. Erfurt is roughly halfway between Gotha and Weimar, east of the latter.

Letter 11

1. Raff's *King Alfred*.

2. Rosa Agthe (1827–1906), wife of Feodor von Milde.

3. The Grand Duchess Maria Pavlovna.

4. Ziegesar.

5. Unidentified.

6. Identity uncertain; possibly a cook at the Altenburg.

7. Unidentified.

8. Liszt is referring to Goethe's *Faust*, Part One ("Studierzimmer"), when Mephistopheles enters as a poodle.

> *Sei ruhig, Pudel! renne nicht hin und wider!*
> *An der Schwelle was schnopperst du hier?*

9. Ange-Henri Blaze de Bury (1813–1888) literary and musical critic and brother-in-law to François Buloz. The family name was actually Castil-Blaze, with no particule; and he should not be confused with his brother François Henri-Joseph (1784–1857), a minor critic and even less-renowned composer. Ange-Henri B. visited Weimar in 1839 and was a great admirer of Goethe as well as of Arnim, Brentano, and other members of the German Romantic School. Liszt is alluding to his second trip to Weimar in 1851. Blaze de Bury was music critic for the *Revue des Deux Mondes* from

1833 to 1873. Three of his major works were *Les Salons de Vienne et de Berlin* (Paris: Lévy, 1861), *Les Écrivains modernes de l'Allemagne* (Paris: Lévy, 1868), and *Musiciens Contemporains* (Paris: Lévy, 1856). Curiously enough, none of these three books mentions Liszt. This omission, particularly in the last volume, seems too obvious to be accidental. By 1856 Liszt was almost as well known as a composer as he had been as the youthful virtuoso. Bury treats several minor musicians who today are forgotten, and who are barely included in even the most generous musical encyclopedias. It may be that they had a falling-out of some sort. There is no other reference to Blaze de Bury by Liszt.

10. Prince Carl von Hohenzollern-Sigmaringen (1801–1883) and his wife Antoinette.

Letter 12

1. In the Roman Church calendar, the Feast of Saint Francis of Paula falls on April 2, the day on which the Saint died in 1507.

2. A Russian dish composed of small pieces of beef rolled and fried in rice.

3. Buckwheat (Russian).

4. One of Liszt's many names for the Wittgensteins, mother and daughter.

5. Tamino's aria in Act I of Mozart's *Magic Flute* (1791).

6. The famous nineteenth-century Norwegian violinist (1802–1894) and pupil of Spohr and Paganini. Bull toured England, the Continent, and the United States. Liszt knew him at an earlier date: there is a letter from Liszt to Bull, written April 1, 1840, in La Mara, *Zeitgenossen* (I, p. 20).

7. Louis Kossuth (1802–1894), the Hungarian journalist and statesman. At the time of this letter, Kossuth was in exile. He had spoken on March 3, 1848 — the eve of the revolution in Hungary — in the House of the Estates at Budapest, and demanded that the Hungarian Parliament vote for complete separation from the Austrian Empire. Later when he commanded the revolutionary armies, the South Slavs and the Slovaks fought against him on the side of Franz Josef, and Kossuth was defeated.

8. The reference is to the son of Zeus and Antiope. Amphion played so well on his lyre that the stones of Thebes moved into place of their own accord when the city was being built.

9. Director and actor at the Court (*Hofburg*) Theater in Vienna.

10. Goethe's play in two parts, completed 1808 and 1831.

11. Hugo's Romantic drama, completed in 1827, best known today for its revolutionary, manifesto-like *Préface*.

12. G. E. Lessing's drama (1779). The play still stands as one of the great pleas for religious tolerance. Liszt's violent attack upon Lessing and his play is interesting, since it is revelatory of his shaky dramatic taste and his Catholic and Romantic dislike of the Enlightenment.

13. Probably Stock.

14. It is difficult to see what Liszt is making of the potpourri of classical references.

15. Doubtlessly Zeiss. Cf. Letter 8, Note 13.

16. Pierre-Louis Ginguené (1748–1816), French writer and politician. Ginguené was sympathetic to the Revolution in 1789, although as a moderate he was later imprisoned under the Terror. From 1799 to 1802 he was a member of the *Tribunat*. Among Ginguené's critical works were the *Lettres sur les "Confessions" de J. J. Rousseau* (1791) and the *Coup D'Oeil rapide sur "le Génie du Christianisme" de Chateaubriand*. His chief scholarly work was an unfinished literary history of Italy, published 1811–19.

17. Jean-Charles-Léonard Sismonde de Sismondi (1773–1842), Swiss historian, economist, and aesthetician. Of biographical interest is his relation with Mme. de Staël. Among his books on economics were the *Nouveaux Principes d'Économie Politique* (1819) and the *Étude sur l'Économie Politique* (1837). His largest works were the *Histoire des Républiques Italiennes au Moyen Âge* in sixteen volumes (1803–18) and the *Histoire des Français* in thirty-one volumes (1821–44). From the literary point of view, Sismondi's greatest contribution was *De la Littérature du Midi de l'Europe* (1813), a document that ranks him as one of the leading theoreticians of European Romanticism. Liszt may be referring to this book, since he mentions Sismondi and Ginguené together.

Robert Bory in *Une Retraite romantique en Suisse* (Geneva: Sonor, 1923) mentions that Sismondi called frequently at the salon kept by Liszt and Marie d'Agoult at Geneva during 1835.

18. It has been impossible to locate this quotation in either the index to the Goethe *Jubiläums Ausgabe* or in several other concordances to Goethe's works.

19. Goethe.

20. Pet names. The last two refer to unknown persons.

Letter 13

1. Baron Nicolaus Josika (1796–1865), Hungarian novelist. He lived at Brussels as a political refugee from 1850 to 1864.

2. A small town in Schaumberg-Lippe, about thirty miles west of Hannover.

3. Ferdinand, Freiherr von Beidenfeld, a German writer then spending some time at Weimar. He was the author of *Sagen, Märchen, Kriegsscenen, etc. aus Spanien* (Weimar: Voigt, 1836) and *Feldzug der Oestreichen in Italien* (Weimar: Voigt, 1849).

4. Julius Elkan, appointed *Hofbankier* to the Weimar Court in 1833.

5. Possibly Marie.

6. Queen Marie-Amélie de Bourbon-Naples (1782–1866), widow of Louis-Philippe who died in 1842. She had been living in exile, chiefly in Claremont, England. Schorn (*Zwei Menschenalter, passim*) mentions that the Queen was staying at Eisenach in 1848.

7. A city about forty-five miles west of Weimar.

8. Princess Helena von Mecklenburg-Schwerin, who married Queen Amélie's oldest son, the Duc d'Orléans, in 1837.

9. Edouard Genast (1797–1866), singer, actor, onetime director of the Weimar Theater. He and his wife Karoline Genast are mentioned several times by Eckermann as friends of Goethe. Genast's play *Florian Geyer* was performed at Weimar during the 1858–59 season. Schorn (*Zwei Menschenalter*, p. 296) quotes a letter from his daughter, Emilie Merian-Genast, to Eduard Lassen written in 1871 which includes an interesting description of Liszt's portrait, and is indicative of the attraction Liszt possessed for both painters and women: ". . . the deepest expression of his soul is reflected in the eyes; I have never seen such a portrait which so intensely stares at the observer, so that one cannot look away."

10. Carl Friedrich, the Grand Duke of Weimar.

11. Ziegesar.

12. Evidently Raff had been to the Prussian Court at Potsdam.

13. Raff's opera, *King Alfred.*

14. Charles Kingsley's novel, *Alton Locke, Poet and Tailor,* was published in 1850. The book must have had peculiar interest for Liszt for its exposition of English Christian Socialism and the Chartist Movement, since it was only ten years before that Liszt had been a disciple of Lamennais, and had thus shared in a parallel Continental intellectual movement. It would be fascinating to know, for example, if Liszt had read Chapter IX — "Poetry and Poets," Chapter XL — "Priests and People," or Chapter XLI — "Freedom, Equality, and Brotherhood."

Letter 14

1. Probably Richard Talleyrand.

2. Marie was now fourteen years old.

3. Eduard, Ritter von Liszt (d. 1879), a half brother to Liszt's father. An eminent Viennese lawyer and jurist and the author of many works on legal theory, he later became *Generalprokurator* at Vienna.

4. Ziegesar.

5. La Lectrice, ou Une Folie d'un Jeune Homme, by Jean François Alfred Bayard (1796–1853). Bayard was a popular French dramatist and the author of many comedies, melodramas, and assorted potboilers. He also collaborated frequently with Scribe.

6. Author unknown.

7. Ernst Raupach (1784–1852), German dramatist. His earlier writings reflected a childhood spent in Russia. Later his historical dramas and comedies were popular on the Berlin stage, and the former genre included a *Hohenstauffen* series and a *Cromwell* trilogy. Raupach represents the continuation of the line of Iffland and Kotzebue. Indeed, he displayed the same literary fecundity as did Kotzebue — one hundred and seventeen plays, sixteen alone dealing with the history of the Hohenstauffen dynasty. *Cromwells Ende* was performed at Weimar during the 1857–58 season; Raupach's *Vor Hundert Tagen* was staged there in 1861.

8. Carl Friedrich.

9. Liszt's predecessor as *Hofkapellmeister* at Weimar — a vigorous opponent of Wagner, Liszt, and the "New Music."

10. In view of Liszt's liaison with Carolyne, this is a curious nickname for her.

11. Beethoven's opera, first performed in 1805. The text was by Sonnleither, based on Bouilly's story — and this, in turn, had been inspired by the famous *Lenore* ballad by Bürger.

12. Viktor Nikititch Panin (1800–1874).

13. Fanny Lewald-Stahr (1811–1889), novelist and poetess. She had been affiliated with *Junges Deutschland* in the late 1830's; and many of her novels, such as *Clementine* (1842) and *Jenny* (1843) have affinities with Gutzkow's *Wally*. She also wrote huge historical novels — *Prinz Louis Ferdinand*

(1843) is an example — and later she became associated with the literary salon of Varnhagen and Rahel von Ense in Berlin.

Fanny Lewald married the writer Adolf Stahr in 1847. One of her later books was the lengthy novel *Von Geschlecht zu Geschlecht* (1864–68), where the older aristocracy was criticized at the expense of the new rising bourgeoisie. In *Zwölf Bilder nach dem Leben* (Berlin, 1888), Fanny Lewald wrote an excellent description of Liszt in the 1850's: "When he looked about him, he seemed to appear as a man to whom the world belonged; and who was born to this role, so that it suited him naturally. His head possessed so much nobility that he . . . had as much influence upon sculpture as did the classical beauty of the Countess d'Agoult."

Many of Fanny Lewald's letters to Liszt are included in the La Mara *Zeitgenossen* collection.

Letter 15

1. The tapestry-makers.

2. Leipzig music publishers. Härtel was a partner in the publishing house of Breitkopf & Härtel.

3. Private joke between Liszt and Marie.

4. Marie — "Quint-Quatorze."

5. *Charivari* was the satiric journal founded December 1, 1832, by Charles Philipon, which attacked the July Monarchy with much wit and brilliance. Among its contributors were Louis Despoyers, Altaroche, Laurent Jan, and later Daumier.

Letter 17

1. A town in Brunswick, about 110 miles southwest of Berlin.

2. Unidentified.

Letter 18

1. A long-threaded and rather coarse wool velours, often used for recovering furniture.

2. This is the house referred to by Wagner as the "Escher Haus," and Wagner commented on Liszt's delight at seeing how well Wagner was living in Zürich — an interesting footnote to Liszt's fastidiousness and elegant taste. Cf. Richard Wagner, *Mein Leben* (Munich: Bruckmann, 1914), vol. III, p. 63.

Wagner's relation to Liszt was central to the development of their theories about art in general. He first met Liszt in Paris in the late fall of 1842. They were introduced by the poet Laube, a member of *Junges Deutschland*. The two musicians saw each other again in 1848 at Vienna and Weimar; in the interim, Liszt had been active in getting Wagner's early operas performed — *Rienzi, Der fliegende Holländer*, and *Lohengrin. Tannhäuser* was given by Liszt at Weimar in 1849, its second performance after the initial presentation at Dresden. Wagner fled to Weimar and the Altenburg in May 1849, after he had been involved in revolutionary affairs at Dresden. He often spoke of his "betrayal" at Chemnitz, although Wagner's escape from that town was more ludicrous than heroic.

Between 1849 and 1853, Liszt was most ardent in espousing Wagner's cause; the latter was a refugee in Switzerland, and Liszt went to great effort to keep the German public aware of Wagner's works. He undertook a similar task in France, through his secretary Belloni. Liszt and Wagner met again at Zürich in 1853, and it is to this reunion that Letter 18 alludes. They spent a happy week discussing music and contemporary politics, and the writer Georg Herwegh was with them much of the time. All three climbed one of the local mountains; and Wagner describes how "Liszt had the happy notion to drink a toast of brotherhood [*Brüderschaftstrunk*] to me, from the three streams of the Grütli." (Cf. *Mein Leben*, vol. III, p. 63.)

For a more complete study of the Liszt-Wagner relationship, consult the *Briefwechsel zwischen Wagner und Liszt*, ed. E. Kloss (Leipzig: Breitkopf & Härtel, 1910).

3. Carolyne.

4. Countess Louisa Bathyany, *née* Zichy.

5. Georg Herwegh (1817–1875), German poet best known for his patriotic and political lyrics, such as *Das Lied vom Hasse* — "Wir haben lang genug geliebt, und wollen endlich hassen" — and *Aufruf*, both from the *Gedichte eines Lebendigen* (1841).

Herwegh actually played an abortive military role in the 1848 Revolution. He was head of the German Democratic Society in Paris as an exile. In March 1848, he and an organizer named Hecker mustered a "Legion" of some four thousand men, and planned to invade southwestern Germany from Alsace with this republican army. The move failed, owing to internal dissension and to the Baden government's last-minute withdrawal of support. (Karl Marx, who was cognizant of the operation, viewed the "Legion" as a manifestation of bourgeois-military reaction, and was vehement in his opposition!) Herwegh went to Zürich as an exile soon after, and it was there that Wagner met him in 1851. Veit Valentin describes this aristocrat with Communistic leanings as a "dreamer, egocentric and over-sensitive, bored by practical details, always at high-tension, alternately dreaming and silent and then violent and inclined to be despotic about trifles." *(1848: Chapters of German Unity*, trans. E. T. Scheffauer, London: Allen & Unwin, 1940, p. 227.)

6. Franz Friedrich Appolonius (1795–1870), Baron von Maltitz, amateur poet and novelist and the Russian Minister to Saxe-Weimar and to Dresden. His play, *Des häuslichen Zwistes Jahrestag*, was performed at Weimar in the 1857–58 season.

7. Dr. Christian Bernhardt von Watzdorff, appointed *Staatsminister* at Weimar in 1852.

Letter 19

1. Marie was confirmed on the eve of leaving for Carlsbad with Carolyne, and she chose St. Francis as her patron.

2. Unidentified.

3. Weimar was in the bishopric of Fulda.

4. Christine Wilhelmina Planer (1809–1866), who married Wagner in 1836 and was separated from him in 1866.

5. No painter named Händl has been located, and Liszt certainly is not referring to the composer Handel. (In Liszt's *Années de Pèlèrinage, Première Année; Suisse*, the first composition is *La Chapelle de Guillaume Tell*. It was written in 1852.)

6. The Ducal residence at Weimar.

7. A resort in the Rhineland.

8. Devrient (1801–1877) was director of the Carlsruhe Theatre.

9. Count Charles de Linange, who married Carolyne's niece, Elizabeth zu Sayn-Wittgenstein.

10. A Mayence music editor and publisher.

11. Wagner's opera, first performed at Weimar under Liszt's direction in 1850.

12. First performed under Wagner's own direction in 1845. Liszt played the overture at Weimar in July 1848. He conducted the whole opera there on February 16, 1849. This was the work that first brought Wagner to the attention of the French public and artists. It caused Baudelaire, for example, to write that highly provocative essay, *Richard Wagner et 'Tannhäuser' à Paris*, after the opera was produced there in 1861. Cf. Georges Servières, *Tannhäuser à l'Opéra en 1861* (Paris, 1895) for a complete account of the artistic and political *ambiance* surrounding the production.

Pauline Metternich, who had met Wagner through Liszt at Leipzig, suggested to Napoleon III that *Tannhäuser* be given. A political issue soon arose involving the Jockey Club cabal, Court intrigue, and even the famous Countess Walewska who was jealous of Princess Metternich. The Republicans objected to the work as a symbol of the invidious Court and Napoleon III and Pauline Metternich; extreme French patriots regarded it as an example of German infiltration; orthodox French musicians were scandalized by Wagner's innovations.

13. Niece of the composer, and the soprano who sang the role of Elizabeth in the first performance of *Tannhäuser*. She was famous for her range of three octaves and two notes.

14. Albert Wagner (1799–1874), Richard's brother.

15. This projected collaboration never came about.

16. Franz Wille, a Hamburg journalist and political refugee in Zürich.

17. Heinrich Heine (1797–1856). Except for a single trip back to Germany in 1843 which led to the writing of *Deutschland, ein Wintermärchen*, Heine was an exile in Paris from May 1831 until his death in 1856. A letter by Heine about Liszt, sent to the *Revue Musicale* in 1838, provoked Liszt into writing the seventh of the *Lettres d'un Bachelier ès Musique* (July 8, 1838). The two artists were friends for a short time; but Liszt's Romantic extravagances were too excessive for Heine to let pass without a display of his biting wit. An amusing and vitriolic article by Heine appeared April 25, 1844 (cf. *Werke*, ed. Elster, vol. VI, p. 441), scarcely flattering to the musician. In the La Mara *Zeitgenossen* (I, p. 68) one may read Heine's apology, written just *before* the article came out. Evidently he had just asked for tickets to a concert by Liszt and felt that some excuse was in order. "I have already written a first article [i.e., about Liszt] that I would like to send to you *before* your second concert, and there may be something in it that may not please you; hence it seemed proper that I speak to you first. Your friend, H. Heine."

18. *Prometheus*, Liszt's symphonic tone poem, was composed in 1850 and published in 1856. Apparently the manuscript had been mislaid.

19. Baron Talleyrand, French ambassador to Weimar.

20. Carl Friedrich died July 8, 1853, and was succeeded by his son Carl Alexander (1818–1901), who married Sophie Wilhelmina of the House of

Orange. Vehle (*Der Hof zu Weimar*, p. 341) makes interesting comments about Carl Alexander. "Despite his good intentions, Carl Alexander was not liked at his Court and was definitely disliked by his people." The new Grand Duke seemed most at home with "wandering scholars and artists," and Vehle as a good Weimar *Bürger* found this trait of Carl Alexander's as disquieting as he did the Duke's distaste for Weimar as a residence. "He preferred the seclusion of the woods at Ilmenau."

Letter 20

1. The hotel in Carlsbad at which the two princesses were staying.

2. Ziegesar.

3. Baron Charles Olivier de Beaulieu-Marconnay, who succeeded Ziegesar as Intendant of the Weimar Theater in 1853. Liszt, who had been happy with Ziegesar, found Beaulieu increasingly difficult; and a series of petty disagreements finally culminated in Liszt's resignation in 1858. Schrickel (*op. cit.*) cites a letter from Beaulieu to Liszt, written in 1852, where the new Intendant even complained of excessive noise during the performances in Parterre-Loge VI — the Wittgenstein box!

4. Unidentified.

5. Ludwig Ernst von Hopfgarten, appointed *Oberjägermeister* in 1852 at Weimar.

6. Hans Karl Ottobald, Graf und Herr von Werthern-Beichlingen, *Oberkammerherr* at the Weimar Court.

7. Franz, Graf und Herr von Beust, *Hofmarschall* at Court.

8. Talleyrand; cf. Letter 19, Note 19.

9. A small town northwest of Weimar on the Ettersberg, the hill mentioned frequently by Eckermann as a place where he and Goethe discussed birds.

10. Talleyrand's servant.

11. This could be either Dumas *père* (1803–1870) or Dumas *fils* (1824–1895), since the younger writer had already published his first play, *La Dame aux camélias*, in 1848. In any case, Liszt's mention of the passage from Dumas must have been verbal since it does not appear in any letter to Carolyne. There are two letters from Dumas *père* in the La Mara *Zeitgenossen* collection (vol. I, pp. 22, 67).

12. Eduard Reményi (1830–1898), pseudonym for Eduard Hoffmann, the Hungarian violinist and friend of Liszt who later became closely associated with Brahms and the opposing school of music. It has been said that Reményi was the inspiration for Liszt's essay, *Die Zigeuner und ihre Musik in Ungarn*. Liszt dedicated the *Benedictus* of the *Coronation Mass* (1867) to Reményi.

13. Benjamin Disraeli (1804–1881), Lord Beaconsfield. His novels before 1853 were *Vivian Grey* (1826), *The Young Duke* (1830), *Contarini Fleming* (1832), *Alroy* (1833), *The Rise of Iskander* (1835), *Henrietta Temple* (1837), *Venetia* (1837), *Coningsby* (1844), *Sybil* (1845), and *Tancred* (1847).

14. William Makepeace Thackeray (1811–1863). These *Vorlesungen* doubtlessly refer to the *English Humourists of the Eighteenth Century*, a series of lectures Thackeray gave in London during 1851 which were published in 1853.

15. Princess Alix Montmorency (1810–1853), wife of Ludwig Talley-rand-Périgord, Duc de Sagan et Valençoy.
16. Eighty miles southwest of Weimar.
17. The town in Hungary where Liszt met Marie and her mother in April 1848, after they had left Woronince.
18. Jules Michelet (1798–1874), the French historian. *Jeanne d'Arc* was part of a larger *Histoire de France*, of which the first six volumes appeared in 1846.
19. Frédéric Morin (1823–1874), historian, philosopher, opponent of Napoleon III. Morin was arrested several times for his continued defense of the Church versus the State in France. *Saint François et les Franciscains* (Paris: Hachette) appeared in 1853.
20. The following passages were copied out of the "Bibliothèque des Chemins de fer" edition of Morin's text. Liszt, who seems to have had a penchant for misquotations, was fairly accurate in this instance. In the original, there is an exclamation point after the first verse; all the "Mon Dieu's" are spelled with a small *m*; there is no dash after the second verse; in the fifth verse, the word is "frère" and not "père"; the last verse should read "la terre, qui *nous* soutient." The translations naturally follow Liszt's errors. Cf. Morin, pp. 38–39.
21. This last excerpt from Morin may be found on p. 61. Except for the omission of a comma after "cellule" and the replacing of a small *d* by a large one in "Démon," Liszt copied it correctly.

Saint Francis always had great attraction for Liszt: the first of the *Deux Légendes* for piano (1866) is *St. François d'Assise prédicant aux Oiseaux*, and it will be remembered that Liszt eventually entered the Franciscan order.
22. This book has not been identified.
23. Probably Carolyne's servants.
24. Unidentified.
25. Henri Wieniawski (1835–1880), Polish violin virtuoso, famous to-day for several violin concertos. He taught for many years at Brussels.

Letter 21a

1. Ernst II, Herzog von Sachsen-Coburg-Gotha, the author of the opera *Diana von Solange*, libretto by Prechtler. This was performed at Weimar during the 1858–59 season.
2. Wilhelm von Baden, of the House of Hohenzollern.
3. Approximately twenty-five miles east of Weimar.
4. A colored servant was lent to Liszt when he stayed at the Ducal Palace at Gotha.
5. Rossini's opera, originally called *Almaviva*, written and produced in 1816 and based on the play by Beaumarchais.
6. Ira Aldrige (1805–1867) was a Negro tragedian and protégé of Edmund Kean. Born in America, Aldrige made his début at London in Othello in 1826. He toured the Continent for several years from 1852, and was a great success in Germany, where he acted for three years. Adelheid von Schorn mentions that Aldrige performed as Othello in Weimar on December 16, 1852. She also comments on the bad speech he interpolated into the last act (*Das nachklassische Weimar*, vol. I, p. 304).

Letter 21b

1. Charles III of Parma, who married the daughter of the Duc de Berry and was assassinated on March 27, 1854 — four days before this letter was written.

2. A city in Tuscany on the Serchio.

3. The Duc de Berry had been killed in 1820.

4. Becker, Liszt's servant (cf. Letter 8, Note 4).

Letter 22

1. Liszt twice wrote piano compositions dealing with Venetian gondolas: he transcribed Rossini's *La Regata Veneziana* from *Les Soirées musicales* in 1838; and one of his last works was *Le Lugubre Gondole*, composed at the Palazzo Vendramin in Venice in 1883, just before Wagner's death.

2. Henry of Nassau and Orange (d. 1879).

3. Probably Haydn's *The Seasons*, the oratorio written in 1800, based on the poem by James Thomson.

4. Johannes Verhülst (1816–1891), a pupil of Mendelssohn. He became director of the *Maatschappij tot bevordering van toonkunst* at Rotterdam in 1848.

5. Gustave Hippolyte Roger (1815–1879), a French tenor.

6. Karl Johann Formes (1816–1889), a German bass.

7. Johann Baptist Pischeck (1814–1873), a Czech baritone.

8. Jenny Bürde-Ney (1826–1886), a German dramatic soprano.

9. Beethoven's sonata for piano and violin, Opus 47 — the inspiration for Tolstoy's story, *The Kreutzer Sonata*.

10. Donizetti's opera, *Lucia di Lammermoor* (1835), based on the novel by Scott.

11. Pedro II (1825–1891), Emperor of Brazil and grandson of Francis I of Austria.

12. Liszt refers to a confusing political situation. The ministerial difficulties had to do in part with the growing problem of the Church and the State in Holland. This had been aggravated by certain measures taken by the Liberal Minister of Internal Affairs, Thorbecke, and the result was additional dissension between Catholic and Protestant elements in the country. In the elections of June 1854 — a month before Liszt wrote this letter — the formation of a new cabinet was left to Thorbecke's successor Van Hall, a Conservative. To the troubled domestic scene was added the possibility of Holland's involvement in the Crimean War, which now threatened to become a general European struggle.

13. Amalia, who was of the House of Sachsen-Weimar-Eisenach before her marriage to Prince Heinrich von Nassau-Orange. The King was Wilhelm III (1817–1890).

14. Liszt is alluding to the Crimean War, already in progress at this date.

15. Ferdinand Hiller (1811–1895). Pianist-composer, friend of Mendelssohn, and famous in his day as an interpreter of Beethoven.

16. The Dutch painter and sculptor Ary Scheffer (1795–1858) represents the line of Delacroix. His earlier works reflected the popular *genre troubadour* of the 1820's and 1830's, and the bulk of his painting was concerned with the Middle Ages and with Christian and religious scenes. Henri

Focillon (*La peinture au XIXe siècle*, Paris: Renouard, 1927, p. 215) says of him that Scheffer was a manifestation "of that semi-Romanticism which led to nothing for lack of vigor, lack of poetry in expression, and above all for an excess of literature." A partial list of his most famous paintings is appended, principally to indicate the direction of his interests and to show the similarity of Scheffer's tastes and Liszt's: *La Mort de Géricault*, 1824; *Faust*, 1831; *Lénore*, 1830; *Le Larmoyeur*, 1834; *Francesca da Rimini*, 1855; *Mignon*, 1838; *Le Roi de Thulé*, 1838; *St. Augustine et Ste. Monique*, 1849; *Les Rois Mages*, 1841; *Ode de Pétrarque*, 1826; *Mazeppa*, 1839.

Scheffer also illustrated Thiers, *Histoire de la Révolution française* (1834) as well as an edition of Béranger's poems published in 1834. He painted five portraits of Liszt during 1839. Schorn mentions (*Zwei Menschenalter*) that one hung in the music room at the Altenburg; Bory says (*Une Retraite Romantique*) another is at the Geneva Music Conservatory. In 1855, Scheffer did one portrait each of the Wittgensteins, mother and daughter. Paintings of other persons appearing in this correspondence include Lamennais (1845), the King of Holland (1840), Pauline Viardot (1840), Tamburini (1839), and Prince Adam Czartoryski (1850). Scheffer also painted Dickens in 1855, when the writer made one of his brief trips to the Continent.

Scheffer first heard Liszt play in 1825 at a salon held by Louis-Philippe in Paris. The pianist introduced the painter to Countess d'Agoult in 1839, and Liszt was also instrumental in bringing Scheffer and Lamennais together in 1845. Cf. Marthe Kolb, *Ary Scheffer et son Temps* (Paris: Boivin, 1937). Despite his immense popularity in the mid-nineteenth century, Scheffer's paintings are today almost forgotten — or at best, cited by critics as examples of the flamboyant, grandiloquent and essentially bad taste of a bygone age. The final irony is that he is perhaps most remembered as the father-in-law of Ernest Renan.

17. A Rotterdam art-collector and patron of Scheffer.

18. The governess to Liszt's three children in Paris.

19. Octave Tassert (1800–1874), a French lithographer and painter, admired by both Théophile Gautier and Charles Baudelaire.

20. Hughes Félicité Robert de Lamennais (1782–1854), French religious writer and one of the most fascinating figures in the nineteenth-century movement to reconcile Christianity and the democratic social tendencies. His chief work was the small but very significant book, *Paroles d'un Croyant* (1833).

Liszt's interest in social and humanitarian problems appears to date from the late 1820's and early 1830's. He sketched out a *Symphonie Révolutionnaire* in 1830, for example, only to rewrite it as the *Héroïde Funèbre* in 1857. Liszt met the Saint-Simonian and political theorist Père Enfantin in 1830, and it is possible that Liszt may have joined the *Phalanstère de Ménilmontant* in Paris. Cf. Julien Tiersot, "Liszt in France," *Musical Quarterly*, vol. XXII, no. 3 (July 1936). His meeting with Lamennais was, however, of much greater importance. They were introduced early in 1834 by Ortigue, editor of the *Quotidienne;* and it is evident that Lamennais' idea of the regeneration of art as a means toward social amelioration found an enthusiastic reception with the musician. The result was the short-lived periodical *Le Monde*, established in 1837 with Lamennais as editor, and

Liszt, George Sand, Charles Didier his contributors. The nature of this scarcely orthodox group made any lasting collaboration impossible, and their joint activity was complicated by Liszt's intricate relations with George Sand and Countess d'Agoult. Sainte-Beuve, who knew the group intimately, made several amusing, polemical statements about them. He said of George Sand, Liszt, and Lamennais — "There is a touch of buffoonery about this *pas de trois*, danced in public with the utmost gravity" (*Nouveaux Lundis*, Paris: Lévy, 1869; vol. XI, p. 365). In that most vindictive book *Mes Poisons* (Paris: Plon, 1926, p. 106) the earlier critique is expanded. "The coterie of George Sand, Lamennais, Liszt, Didier, etc. (with the exception of the naïf Lamennais) is a pile of affectations, vanity, pretension, pomposity, showiness of every variety; a veritable *plague* when one considers the worth of their talents."

Liszt stayed with Lamennais at La Chênaie (Chesnaye) for three weeks during May 1834. His letters to the philosopher are full of Romantic, youthful extravagance and admiration: in one letter addressed to the *cher père* he says, "It is apparent . . . that Christianity in the 19th century, that is to say the whole religious and political future of humanity, is in your hands!" and in another, "I love you from my very bowels [du plus profond des entrailles]." (These letters from Liszt to Lamennais may be found in *Le Porte-feuille de Lamennais* (1818–1836) ed. G. Goyau, Paris: La Renaissance du Livre, 1930, pp. 140–142). Sainte-Beuve also describes Liszt accompanying "the philosophic meditations of the priest-poet on his piano." (Sainte-Beuve, *Correspondance Générale* ed. J. Bonnerot, Paris: Stock, 1935, vol. I, p. 478.)

21. This passage occurs in the *Paroles d'un Croyant* (Paris: 1834, 7th ed., chap. XXV, pp. 115–118). It may well be that this was the same edition used by Liszt. Except for minor errors in punctuation and the customary frequent omission of accent marks, Liszt copied it accurately.

Letter 23

1. Alexander von Humboldt (1769–1859), the German geographer and scientist, brother to the philosopher-statesman Wilhelm von Humboldt. He was educated at Freiburg and Göttingen. In 1799 he started his many voyages of exploration by a trip to South America, and it may be said that he was the first who raised geography to the level of a science. Humboldt did extensive work on climatology, terrestrial magnetism, the nature of ocean currents, and vulcanism. He represents the transition between the eighteenth-century methodology of Linnaeus and Buffon and that of Darwin. In his metaphysical interest in a "life-force" his writing is reminiscent of Goethe, with whom he was acquainted.

2. A reference to pre-Socratic speculations about the "Music of the Spheres."

3. Georges Frédéric Cuvier (1769–1852), French biologist, geologist, and comparative anatomist, who later became Inspector General under Napoleon I and a Peer in the Restoration. One of Cuvier's chief works was *Le Règne animal* (1813). As an early pre-Darwinian evolutionist, he was partner in the famous academic feud with Geoffroy de Saint-Hilaire, who had such a strong influence on Balzac's scientific conception for the *Comédie Humaine*.

4. Wilhelm von Kaulbach (1805–1874), one of the most popular and prolific German mid-nineteenth century painters, leader of the "Munich School," and at one time Court painter for Ludwig I of Bavaria. He painted many canvases in the sentimental-domestic genre, but Kaulbach's chief fame was based on huge historical tableaux such as the *Hunnenschlacht* and similar patriotic and highly idealized works. Of the Munich School, Focillon (*op. cit.*, p. 112) says they were "passionately idealistic; and since they were guided by a *mystique*, they treated the art of painting only as a means of thinking."

5. Ernst F. A. Rietschel (1804–1861), German sculptor who executed the Goethe-Schiller monument at Weimar in 1852. He later did a medallion of Liszt.

6. Ludwig Ferdinand Schnorr von Carolsfeld (1789–1853), a Viennese painter known principally for his landscapes. Two examples of his work appear in that excellent collection of Austrian painters by Bruno Grimschitz — *Maler der Ostmark im 19. Jahrhundert* (Vienna: Schroll, 1940) — *Chamonix mit dem Mont Blanc*, a mysterious moonlit scene foreshadowing Böcklin; and *Die breite Föhre nächst der Brühl*, a charming, sentimental sylvan landscape complete with a romantic young couple and happy peasants.

7. Johann W. Schirmer (1807–1863), German landscapist strongly influenced by Poussin and Claude Lorrain — a transition figure, midway between Romanticism and Naturalism.

8. Director of the Royal Museum in Berlin.

9. Felix Bartholdy-Mendelssohn (1809–1847), whose setting for the 114th Psalm (1839) was for eight-part chorus and orchestra.

10. Mme. Fritsch. Cf. Letter 4, Note 2.

11. Unidentified.

12. Possibly Frédéric Sorel who came to Weimar in 1822 as Carl Alexander's tutor. Sorel's geological interest brought him to the attention of Goethe, and Sorel translated that writer's *Metamorphosen der Pflanzen*. He also worked with Eckermann on a later edition of the famous *Conversations with Goethe*.

13. Liszt's *Faust Symphony* was completed in 1854 and first performed in Weimar on September 5, 1857. It was not published until 1861. Ramann (*op. cit.*) says that Liszt's inspiration for the composition came from his hearing Berlioz's *Damnation of Faust* in 1846. Certainly the legend always had great attraction for Liszt, and he wrote several other miscellaneous pieces that have their origins in the Faust theme: the *Mephisto Waltzes* (1881) and *Mephisto Polka* (1884) for piano, a piano transcription of Gounod's *Faust Waltz* (1868), songs from Goethe's *Faust*, and even an early *Chorus of Angels* from the same play (1849). Tiersot (*op. cit.*) mentions that when Gérard de Nerval (1808–1855), French poet and first translator of Goethe's *Faust, Part I* into French, came to Weimar to see the first performance of *Lohengrin*, Nerval and Liszt planned to compose an operatic version of *both* parts of Goethe's huge drama, and Dumas *fils* was to be a collaborator. Unfortunately plans for this amazing triple artistic endeavor never reached fruition. There are no references to Nerval in any of Liszt's writings. There is, however, a letter from Nerval to the musician

dated October 8, 1850, but it contains nothing about *Faust*. (Cf. La Mara, *Zeitgenossen*, vol. I, p. 143.)
    The *Faust Symphony* — scarcely a symphony in the classical sense — is in three parts: *Faust, Gretchen,* and *Mephistopheles.* It concludes with a *Chorus Mysticus:* the final lines from *Faust, Part II* — "Alles Vergängliche ist nur ein Gleichnis . . . Das Ewig-Weibliche zieht uns hinan."
    14. It is difficult to understand what Liszt means. There is no other evidence that he planned to write other musical works based on Schiller or Petrarch, and certainly no more symphonic poems. There are of course the *Tre Sonetti di Petrarca* for piano, but these were written before 1848. The only piece of Liszt's that concerns Schiller is the *Künstler Festzug* written for the Schiller Festival in 1859, four years after the date of this letter.
    15. Ugolino della Gherardesca, who appears in the *Inferno,* Canto XXXIII, in Dante's *Divina Commedia* (within the ninth circle of the second ring or "Antenora," reserved for those who betrayed kinsmen).
    16. Cf. Letter 3a, Note 2.
    17. Summer residence of the Grand Duke.
    18. Cf. Letter 10, Note 17.
    19. Possibly a town near Elkerhausen in Hessen-Nassau, or Elkenrath in the Saar.
    20. Richard Pohl (1826–1896), composer and musicologist and one of the leading theoreticians of the Liszt-Wagner school. Pohl contributed articles to the *Neue Zeitschrift für Musik.*
    21. Wife of the Weimar comedian, Heinrich Marr (1797–1871), who was known as "Sangali."
    22. Prince de la Tour d'Auvergne-Lauragais, French ambassador to Weimar.
    23. The *Club Neu-Weymar.*
    24. Adolf Fischer (1827–1893), organist.
    25. Franz Kugler (1808–1858), art historian.
    26. Possibly Carl and not "F." Eggers (1787–1863), a Dresden painter of historical and religious scenes.
    27. Heinrich Hoffmann von Fallersleben (1798–1874), German poet and author of *Die Wacht am Rhein.* His early poems had been intensely patriotic; indeed, *Die Wacht* was written when the poet Becker's verses ("Sie sollen ihn nicht haben, den freien, deutschen Rhein") were answered by Musset's *Le Rhin allemand,* and Fallersleben entered the literary, nationalistic battle. Like Herwegh and Freiligrath — whom Fallersleben most resembled as a poet — his liberal stand in 1848 led to difficulties, and he was exiled from Prussia for his excessive patriotism and radical tendencies.
    In 1854 Liszt obtained for him the job of editing the *Weimarisches Jahrbuch* for the Grand Duke. The project collapsed in 1857, when Carl Alexander lost interest. In 1856 Fallersleben was made a member of the *Neu-Weimar Verein* — an appointment he apparently took with much seriousness. Although he and Liszt remained close friends, Fallersleben's last remarks about the musician were tinged with bitterness. "Sir Abbot now has better things to do than to chat with his old friends." Cf. Fallersleben, *Mein Leben* (Berlin: Fontane, 1893; vol. VIII, p. 220).
    28. Ludwig Rellstab (1799–1860), Berlin novelist and musicologist, and the author of one of Liszt's first biographies.

29. Karl August V. von Ense (1785–1858), the Berlin writer who with his attractive wife Rahel (1771–1839) maintained a salon in the 1820's which became the focal point for the later German Romantics — Heine, Eichendorff, Grabbe, Alexis, etc. He first heard Liszt play in December 1841, and described how he became faint after the experience. (Cf. Varnhagen von Ense *Tagebücher*; Hamburg: Hoffmann & Campe, 1870; vol. I, p. 385.)

Varnhagen introduced Liszt to the indefatigable Bettina von Arnim — who with his wife was another famous bluestocking of the day; and in the La Mara *Zeitgenossen* collection there are over a dozen letters from Bettina von Arnim to Liszt, mostly highly philosophic speculations about the nature of music. It will be remembered that she found Goethe unreceptive to these same ideas in her *Briefwechsel* with that great man. Varnhagen von Ense's reaction when Liszt took preliminary steps toward obtaining lay orders in the Franciscans is amusing and worth citing. "One might recommend other outlets for his spirituality. The whole thing is a joke." (*Tagebücher*, XIII, p. 312.)

For more detailed information about the Varnhagen salon, cf. Otto Bedrow, *Rahel Varnhagen* (Stuttgart: Greiner & Pfeiffer, 1900), Chapter XII.

30. Hans von Bülow (1830–1894), conductor, composer, pianist, and pupil of Liszt. Bülow came to Weimar in 1852. In 1855 Carolyne made arrangements with Bülow's mother in Berlin that Hans take Liszt's two daughters under his instruction. In 1857 Bülow married Cosima. The marriage broke up in 1867 when she went off with Wagner, whom she later married. Cf. La Mara, *Briefwechseln zwischen Liszt und von Bülow* (Leipzig: Breitkopf & Härtel, 1898).

31. An example of Liszt's misquoting. He was thinking of a famous letter of Mme. de Sévigné to Mme. de Grignan, August 9, 1671: "When you succeed in loving me as much as I love you . . . my little ones would have to be thrown into the bargain; they are all my heart's delight [mes petites entrailles, *not* mes petits boyaux], and it is this excess of tenderness that I have for you."

32. Carl Werdern (1806–1893), Berlin Professor of Philosophy.

33. Count Sandor Teleky, Minister of the Hungarian Revolutionary Party under Kossuth in 1848. He agreed to return to Hungary from exile if he would abstain from his liberal tendencies, and soon after committed suicide.

34. Kaulbach. Cf. Note 4.

35. Adolf Bernhard Marx (1795–1866), composer and music theorist. He was later codirector of the Stern Conservatory in Berlin.

36. Probably a nickname for Bernhard Cossman, first 'cellist of the Weimar Orchestra.

37. Wilhelm Taubert (1811–1891), Berlin pianist, conductor, and composer.

38. Von Bülow.

39. Weimar.

Letter 24

1. Friedrich Preller (1804–1878), Weimar painter and protégé of the Grand Duke. He was known for his scenes from the *Odyssey*, and Preller's works reflect that curious type of German pseudo neo-classicism so popular

in the 1830's and 1840's — for which Goethe's influence was certainly responsible to no small degree. Focillon (*La peinture au XIX* *siècle*) places Preller in the "Nazarene" school — the result of German artists' "Sehnsucht nach Italien" and their frequent studies in Rome.

    2. Carl Tausig (1841–1871), virtuoso pianist and pupil of Liszt from 1855 to 1859. Tausig is best known today for his technical studies and his edition of Clementi's exercises — the bane of all piano students — *Gradus ad Parnassum.*

    3. Prince Casimir Lubomirsky, musical amateur and friend of Liszt. Cf. *L.M.* I, No. 85, for mention of his wife Zeneida Lubomirska.

    4. Unidentified.

    5. The *Scherzo, March,* and B Minor *Sonata* were all written in 1854. The latter is one of Liszt's largest compositions for piano, and it is considered by many critics to be his finest. Sitwell (*Liszt,* p. 208) says that with this piece Liszt felt he was redefining the whole sonata-form, but that most of his friends and pupils — and all of his opponents — found it dull and empty. Brahms is said to have fallen asleep when Liszt played the *Sonata* for him; and this act was, as one might expect, the beginning of their enmity.

    6. The object of this mediocre anagram was Daniel François Esprit Auber (1782–1871), French musician and prolific writer of *opéras comiques* and *opéras bouffes.* The dramatist Scribe provided Auber with several libretti. Auber represents the tradition of Boïeldieu, Hérold, and Adam; his most famous work was *Fra Diavolo* (1830), adapted by Hollywood in the mid-1930's as the film, *The Devil's Brother,* with the comedians Stan Laurel and Oliver Hardy.

Letter 25

    1. Talleyrand.

    2. Dante, *Divina Commedia,* "Inferno," Canto II, Stanza 11, lines 79–80.
        "tanto m'aggrada il tuo comandamento,
        che l'ubidir, se già fosse, m'è tardi."

Letter 26

    1. Small town in Saxony between Halle and Weimar.

Letter 27

    1. Liszt's three children.

    2. A mineral-spring resort in the district of Eger, Bohemia.

    3. Ulrike von Pogwisch. When Maria Pavlovna came to Weimar from the Russian court in 1804, she brought with her Countess Ottilie Henckel von Donnersmarck as her Chief Lady-in-Waiting, who died in 1851. Her daughter Frau von Pogwisch, Lady-in-Waiting to Duchess Louisa, had two daughters. The first, Ottilie, married Goethe's son August. The second was Ulrike, to whom Liszt is referring.

    4. Hector Berlioz (1803–1869). The trio of Liszt-Berlioz-Wagner must be viewed as an entity if any one of the three musicians is to be understood; and the influence of Berlioz on Liszt's music — and on his temperament — was of the greatest importance. There are a large number of letters from Berlioz in the La Mara *Zeitgenossen* collection.

The musical career of Berlioz began with his award of the coveted *Prix de Rome* in 1830, although he had already written a number of youthful, radical compositions. One of his first successful orchestral works was *Sardanapale* (1830), inspired by Byron's play. His famous, extravagant courtship of the English actress Harriet Smithson inspired the *Symphonie Fantastique*, and Liszt was present at its first performance on December 5, 1830. Among Berlioz's overtures were *Lear*, *The Corsair*, *Waverley*, *Les Francs Juges*, *Rob Roy*, *Le Carnaval Romain*. His operas included *Benevenuto Cellini* (produced by Liszt at Weimar in March, 1852), *Béatrice et Bénédict* (1862), *Les Troyens* (in 2 parts, completed 1858). He also wrote miscellaneous orchestral works and oratorios: *Harold in Italy*, *Le Damnation de Faust*, *Roméo et Juliette*, *L'Enfance du Christ*, and several *Te Deums* and choral pieces including the interesting *Chant des Chemins de Fer* (1846).

Berlioz's first Weimar concert was in 1843, on his first German tour. Liszt later organized "Berlioz Weeks" in 1852 and 1855 — for an eyewitness account of the earlier, cf. Schorn, *Das nachklassische Weimar* (vol. I, p. 304 f.). Both Liszt and Carolyne encouraged Berlioz to undertake his ambitious setting for Books II and IV of Virgil's *Aeneid*, and all three discussed the work at length when Berlioz stayed at the Altenburg during February, 1856. He completed *Les Troyens* two years later. Tiersot (*Liszt in France*, p. 292 f.) says that Liszt and Berlioz drifted apart, and the rift was due chiefly to Berlioz's dislike — and possible jealousy — of Wagner. Certainly Berlioz never shared Liszt's all-out enthusiasm for his friend. "When I hear or when I read certain pieces by this coarse master, I restrain myself by grinding my teeth with force until I can get home; and there, alone, I deflate by cursing." (La Mara, *Zeitgenossen*, II, p. 32.) The letter Liszt mentions is not to be found in any existing collection. For the most comprehensive study of Berlioz, cf. Jacques Barzun, *Berlioz and the Romantic Century* (Boston: Little Brown, 1950).

5. Unidentified.

6. Liszt.

7. Maltitz. Cf. Letter 18, Note 6.

8. Liszt's son.

9. Victor Hugo (1802–1885). *Le Rhin: Lettres à un Ami*, published in 1842, were actually a series of letters written by Hugo between 1838 and 1840. The Left Bank of the Rhine had become a political issue with the determination of the population as Prussian or French the key element. Hugo's work reflected his desire to enter an active political career — and to be chosen to the *Académie Française*. He succeeded in both, and his appointment to the latter took place in 1841.

Hugo met Liszt during the early 1820's in Paris. Tiersot (p. 286) mentions that Hugo actually studied piano with the musician for a short period, but no reference to such activity has been found in the correspondence of either man. In view of Hugo's acknowledged lack of musical sensibility, I consider any musical studies most unlikely. The two compositions for which Liszt was indebted to Hugo are *Après une Lecture de Dante; Fantaisie quasi Sonate* (1848: from the *Années de Pélérinage, 2ᵉ année*) — based on Hugo's poem of the same title written August 6, 1836 and included in *Les Voix Intérieures* (1837):

Quand le poète peint l'enfer, il peint sa vie,
Sa vie, ombre qui fuit de spectres poursuivie . . .

and the symphonic Poem, *Ce qu'on entend sur la Montagne*. This piece was composed for piano in 1840 and scored for orchestra in 1849. The inspiration was Hugo's verses dated July 27, 1829, included in *Les Feuilles d'Automne* (1831). Liszt also composed some curious musical compositions from 1870 to 1875 — *Musical Recitations*, intended to be played while a monologist declaimed poetry. One of these was to a poem by Hugo, *Le Juif Errant*.

10. Cf. Letter 60.

11. There is no other reference to Milton's poem in the correspondence of Liszt. The attraction possessed by Milton's Satan for early and mid-century artists is well known. It seems strange that Liszt, prolific as he was, should have passed Satan by.

12. Evidently Countess d'Agoult's scornful appellation for Carolyne.

13. City in Saxony.

14. Liszt's Piano Fantasia on Meyerbeer's *Le Prophète*, composed by Liszt in 1841.

15. Unidentified.

Letter 28

1. St. Ouen (609–683), archbishop and chancellor at the court of Dagobert I, and patron saint of one of Rouen's churches.

2. Prince Kamiensky, a cousin of Carolyne.

3. Suburb outside Weimar.

4. Weimar doctor.

5. Possibly the daughter of Gustav Schmidt (1816–1882), an orchestra conductor.

6. Marie's dancing teacher.

7. Rosalie Spohr (1829–1881), a harpist virtuoso greatly admired by Liszt. She was wife of Graf Xavier von Sauerma and niece of the musician Ludwig Spohr (1789–1859).

8. Otto Roquette (1829–1894), German poet and dramatist who wrote the libretto for Liszt's oratorio, *Saint Elizabeth*. Roquette was in 1855 teaching German and history at the Blockmann Institute in Dresden. His chief poetical work was the long narrative poem *Waldmeisters Brautfahrt* (1851). He also wrote a "Künstlerroman," *Heinrich Falk* (1858), and a history of German literature, and became a professor at the Darnstadt *Polytechnicum* in 1869.

9. Completed 1862 and published the same year. Cf. the above note.

10. Liszt's symphonic Poem based on Dante's *Divina Commedia*, completed and published in 1856. It is in three parts — *Inferno, Purgatorio, Paradiso* — and concludes with a chorale ending in the *Magnificat*.

11. Liszt's daughters, Cosima and Blandine.

12. Blandine.

13. Mme. Patersi. Cf. Letter 22, Note 19.

14. The novel by Marie d'Agoult which portrayed in more or less fictional form the story of her great romance with the musician. Liszt is thinly disguised in the book as the painter Geurmann Regnier and Marie d'Agoult becomes Vicomtesse Nélida de Kervaëns. *Nélida* was started in

March 1844, and the authoress showed it to Herwegh for criticism. The first printing was done without her name (Paris: Moussin, 1846).

15. Pen name of Marie d'Agoult.

16. Unidentified.

17. Vitzthum.

18. Weimar.

Letter 29

1. Anton Rubinstein (1830–1894), considered by many to be Liszt's only peer as a virtuoso. He met Liszt when Rubinstein had just arrived from Russia in Paris in 1840, a child prodigy, and Rubinstein was Liszt's pupil for a short time. He was a prolific composer in the line of Mendelssohn; and Rubinstein's opera, *Die Kinder der Heide*, was given at Weimar during the 1861–62 season.

2. *Les Préludes* was written and first performed in 1856, and it is today probably the most often played of Liszt's orchestral compositions. The inspiration supposedly came from Lamartine's *Méditations Poétiques* (1820). The Concerto referred to is in E Flat, for piano and orchestra (sometimes called the "Triangle Concerto") and was not published until 1857, two years after this letter.

3. *Tasso, Lamento e Trionfo* (1856), the second of Liszt's twelve symphonic poems. Liszt later wrote an epilogue: *Triomphe Funèbre de Tasso*, published in 1863.

4. This must be the setting Liszt made for the *13th Psalm*: tenor solo, chorus, and full orchestra. It was composed in 1855, published in 1863.

5. Friedrich Wilhelm IV of Prussia (reigned 1840–1861) and his wife, Elizabeth of Bavaria.

6. Leopold Damrosch (1832–1885), originally a musician attached to the Weimar orchestra. Damrosch later went to Breslau and then to New York in 1871, at the invitation of a choral society, which he made into the Oratorio Society in 1873. In 1878 he was instrumental in founding the New York Symphony Orchestra.

7. August Goltermann (1826–1890), court 'cellist at Schwerin.

8. Alfred Jaell (1832–1882), virtuoso pianist, popular for his concert paraphrases, *grands galops brillants*, and similar displays of pianistic pyrotechnics.

9. Identity uncertain. Possibly the son of the minor composer E. A. Wendt (1806–1850).

10. Richard Wüerst (1824–1881), composer, critic, and professor of music at the Kullak Conservatory in Berlin. Wüerst was editor of the *Neue Berliner Musikzeitung* from 1874 to 1875.

11. The author of this line has not been identified, but the editor suspects Goethe.

12. Hans Bronsart von Schellendorf (1830–1913), pianist, composer, and pupil of Liszt. He was appointed Intendant of the Hannover Theater in 1867.

13. Christian Rauch (1777–1857), Berlin sculptor who was one of the most popular of his day, and who exercised a strong influence on the work of the North German sculptors. Rauch met Canova and Thorvaldsen at the home of Alexander von Humboldt (cf. Letter 23, Note 1) in Berlin; and later, like so many German artists in the century, spent much time in Italy.

Today he is perhaps best known for several busts of Goethe — all executed in that mixture of neo-classic and contemporary style that marked the taste of the second quarter of the century. He was also commissioned by Ludwig II of Bavaria, Wagner's patron, to furnish statues for that mad monarch's *Walhalla*. Among Rauch's students were A. Wolf, Rietschel, and Kiss.

Letter 30

1. Eduard von Liszt (cf. Letter 14, Note 3).

2. Simon Löwy, a Viennese banker.

3. Eduard Hanslick (1825–1904), the leading Viennese music critic at this time. He wrote articles for the *Weiner Zeitung* in 1849, the *Presse* in 1855, and was made professor at the University of Vienna in 1870. He later became one of Wagner's — and hence Liszt's — chief musical opponents, and attacked the music of the *Neu-Deutsche* school in his reviews. Cf. the Introduction to this correspondence.

4. Liszt's *Messe de Gran* or *Graner Mass* for soloists, chorus, and full orchestra, composed in 1855.

5. No Mass written for the Church at Fôt has been located.

6. The Károlyi von Nagykárolyi family was an old Hungarian family, famous as patrons of the arts. While no Stepan Károlyi of prominence has been found; Aloys, Graf von Károlyi (1825–1889), was Austro-Hungarian ambassador to Berlin and London after the formation of the Dual Monarchy in 1868 and present as delegate at the Berlin Conference of 1878; Arped von Károlyi (1853–1934), an art historian, became Archives Director at Vienna; and Michael Károlyi was President of the Hungarian Republic for five months in 1919.

7. Prince Richard von Metternich-Winneburg, son of the famous Austrian statesman Klemens von Metternich. Prince Richard became Austrian ambassador to Napoleon III in 1859 after the Peace of Villafranca and the Italian War. His wife Pauline was a patroness of Liszt, both in Vienna and at the Paris Embassy. She herself was a musical amateur and played four-handed pieces with the composer. It was at her home in Paris that Liszt performed for Napoleon III, who made the unfortunate remark, "How well, *maestro*, you imitate thunder!" Liszt apparently took the remark with fairly good grace; but the comment of the soon-to-be-deposed emperor scarcely raised him in Liszt's eyes, who already resented the anti-Papal activity of Napoleon III. Saint-Säens, Gounod, and Wagner were also favored by Pauline's patronage. Her temperament made it difficult for her to retain the artists she lionized as friends; and Liszt alone remained faithful after she had fought with Wagner and many others. He played for her as late as 1881.

8. Rossini's opera, written for the Carnival of Venice in 1823.

9. The Congress of Verona was held in October 1822, when the major European powers discussed Greek and Spanish internal affairs.

10. Karl Franz Brendel (1811–1868) edited the *Neue Zeitschrift für Musik* from 1844 until 1856, and he was a strong defender of the *avant-garde*. Hebbel called Brendel "the flag-bearer of the music of the future." (Hebbel, *Briefe*; Berlin: Behr, 1906; vol. VII, p. 245.)

11. Khevenhüller.

12. A member of the family famous as music patrons; one of her ancestors had been Haydn's benefactor. At one point the Esterhazy family even desired to buy Liszt's birthplace at Raiding to give to him. The original title of Baron Esterhazy-Galantha went to Miklos, first Count of Frakno (1583–1645), and the title of Prince was granted to the sovereign branch of the family in 1712.

13. A Hungarian music patroness.

14. Clara Schumann, *née* Wieck (1819–1898), the most eminent woman pianist of the nineteenth century, married Schumann in 1840. She had made her début as a pianist at Leipzig in 1832. The concert mentioned by Liszt was given by her six months before Robert Schumann died on July 19, 1856. Although she and Liszt cooled in their relationship, there are many letters from her to him in the La Mara *Zeitgenossen* collection, all cordial in their tone. Bekker (*Liszt and His Critics*) says that Liszt gave Schumann's rarely-performed opera *Genoveva*, based on a play by Tieck, at the Weimar Theater.

15. Salvatore Marchesi, Cavaliere de Castrone (1822–1908), and his wife Mathilde (1826–1913), voice teachers at the Vienna Conservatory. Rossini, always a wit, considered her to have one of the few Italian women's voices that did not sound "as if it were a question of the capture of the barricades."

16. It was at Lichnowsky's castle that Liszt and Carolyne rejoined each other after her departure from Woronince. He was later killed in Frankfort during the 1848 Revolution.

17. Young Hungarian noblewoman and musical amateur.

18. Giacomo Meyerbeer (1791–1864), whose real name was Jakob Liebmann Beer. A pupil of the curious charlatan-musician Abbé (Abt) Vogler made famous by Browning, Meyerbeer became one of the leading operatic composers of the 1824–1849 period. He also directed the first performances of Wagner's *Rienzi* and *Der fliegende Holländer*. Goethe admired his music greatly, although today it seems sentimental, vulgar, and bombastic. (Cf. Eckermann, *Gespräche mit Goethe*, January 25, 1827 and February 11, 1829.)

19. Alexander von Villiers, secretary to the Saxon Legation at Vienna.

20. Franz-Josef of Austria.

21. A Viennese society woman.

22. Count Schlick, a petty *Hofburg* official.

23. Prince Alexander Gortchakoff (1798–1883), Russian diplomat. He was Minister for Foreign Affairs in 1856, and in 1862 he became a Vice-Chancellor of the Russian Empire.

24. Possibly Liszt's servant Becker.

25. A minor Hungarian sculptor.

26. Josef Kriehuber (1800–1876), a Viennese painter who began his career doing chiefly military and peasant scenes. Kriehuber soon became popular as a society portraitist; and one of his better-known works was a *Matinée bei Liszt* — a tableau with the pianist at his instrument, surrounded by an elegant audience grouped in respectful positions.

27. Eduard von Liszt.

28. Cognac. It may be that Liszt had been tippling to the displeasure of Carolyne, but there are never any references by his contemporaries to his drinking excessively.

Letter 32

1. I.e., the Feast of St. Wenceslas; a holiday in Prague.

2. Liszt's ninth symphonic poem, published in 1856.

3. Leopold Alexander Zellner (1823–1894), musicologist and editor of the *Blätter für Theater, Musik, und Bildende Kunst* at Vienna from 1855 to 1868. He wrote *Ueber Liszts Graner Festmasse* (1858).

4. Curate of the Pest *Stadtpfarrkirche.*

5. The Cardinal Primate of Hungary.

6. Winterthür, in the canton of Thurgau, Switzerland, near Zürich.

7. Probably Carolyne.

8. Kostenecka, Marie's wet-nurse.

9. Probably Grosse, a trombone player from the Weimar Orchestra who often traveled with Liszt.

Letter 33

1. Carolyne, who was suffering from rheumatism.

2. Kassel, in Hessen-Nassau, southwest of Göttingen.

3. Probably either the theologian Johann Tychsen Hemsen, author of *Anaxagorus Clazeomenius* (1821), *Der Apostel Paulus* (1830), and *Die Authentie der Schriften des Evangelisten Johannes* (1823); or the critic Wilhelm Hemsen, author of *Schillers Ansichten über Schönheit und Kunst* (1854).

4. Louis Spohr (1784–1859), violinist, minor composer, and choirmaster at the Court at Kassel.

5. Unidentified.

6. Meyerbeer's opera, first performed in 1836.

7. John Locke (1632–1704). Liszt's misspelling ("Loke") was a common one for French nineteenth-century writers.

8. Joseph de Maistre (1754–1821), author of *Les Soirées de Saint-Pétersbourg* (1821), opponent of the French Revolution and the eighteenth-century *philosophes*, and ardent defender of Church and Monarchy.

9. Étienne Bonnot de Condillac (1714–1780), empiricist and sensationalist philosopher, author of the *Traité des Sensations* (1745), and the disciple of John Locke. It would seem as if Liszt were confused and had coupled the wrong pair of teachers and pupils.

Letter 34

1. A musical amateur in Aachen, at whose house Liszt was staying.

2. City in northeast Westphalia, south of Detmold and east of Lippstadt.

3. Patron saint of Paris (422–512), whose shrine and relics are now at St. *Étienne du Mont.*

4. Unidentified.

5. There was a Grecian Temple in the park at Weimar, and possibly Liszt is referring to this building.

6. Velasquez (1599–1660), the great Spanish painter of the Counter Reformation.

7. Sebastien Érard (1752–1831), creator of the first French piano in 1777, who founded a firm of piano manufacturers in 1786. In 1809 Érard invented the original repetition-action grand piano.

306

8. August Karl Eduard Kiss (1802–1865), Berlin sculptor.

9. Suermondt.

10. This may be Christian Beuth, head of the Berlin Weaving Institute, or possibly Johann Christian Beuthe (1817–1878), a porcelain painter from Meiningen.

11. Turanyi, conductor of the Aachen Orchestra.

12. François-Joseph Fétis (1784–1871), Belgian musicologist, whose major contribution to musical scholarship was the *Biographie Universelle des Musiciens* (2nd. ed. 1860–65, 8 vols.; supplement by A. Pougin, 1878–80).

13. Jenny Lind (1820–1887), the famous opera and concert soprano known as "The Swedish Nightingale." She made her debut in opera in 1838. P. T. Barnum brought her to America in 1850 along with General Tom Thumb, and she later became Mme. Lind-Goldschmidt. The concert mentioned by Liszt was the *Niederrheinische Fest* held at Aachen during Whitsuntide, 1846.

14. "Mme. Sacha," the Grand Duchess, was born Sophie-Wilhelmina of Orange. Her grandfather was Wilhelm I of Holland, who married the Countess d'Outremont after his abdication in 1840, since his people objected to this second match with a Belgian and a Roman Catholic.

15. Probably Michael Brand (1814–1870), Budapest musician who wrote under the name of "Mosonyi" and composed mainly Hungarian patriotic songs and marches. In 1857 Liszt had intended to perform Brand's opera *Maximilian* at Weimar, but the plan was dropped when Brand refused to make any changes in the score.

16. Ludwig Friedrich Bischoff (1794–1867), founder and editor of the Cologne *Niederrheinische Musikzeitung.*

Letter 35

1. Berlioz's Oratorio in three parts, composed from 1850 to 1854.

2. A bass at the Weimar Theater.

3. Probably Karl Schneider (1822–1882), lyric tenor.

Letter 36

1. In the north corner of the Rhineland near the Dutch border.

2. Small city south of Braunschweig, east of Hildesheim, southeast of Hannover.

Letter 37

1. One of the priests at the Aachen Cathedral.

2. Liszt wrote a number of marches for orchestra, among them the *Huldigungs Marsch* for the Grand Duke of Weimar (1858) and the *Künstler Festzug* for the Schiller Festival (1859).

3. Prague soprano.

4. Agathe was the heroine in Carl Maria von Weber's (1786–1826) opera *Der Freischütz*, written in 1820 and first performed in 1822.

5. Josef Kehren (1817–1880), a Düsseldorf painter, known for his religious panels, church frescos, and Biblical scenes.

6. Alfred Rethel (1816–1859), an Aachen painter, also the author of religious works. Two of his better paintings were *Les Suisses avant Sempach* (1834) and *La Justice* (1836).

7. Liszt's handwriting is here difficult to decipher, and the word may be "Ark." In that case, the man is doubtlessly Friedrich Ark (1807–1878), the city architect of Aachen from 1839 to 1878 and the builder of the Rathaus.

8. Unidentified.

9. Liszt's designation for his friend, the painter Kaulbach.

10. Cyprian (ca. 200–58), Bishop of Carthage, one of the early Church martyrs.

11. This is a strange remark by Liszt, since — according to the Roman Catholic Catechism, unchanged after the Council of Trent in 1566 — there are *seven* precepts of the Church.

12. The myth of Sisyphus concerns the King of Corinth who for betraying Zeus — or possibly for deceiving Pluto — was eternally condemned to push a huge rock up a high hill in Hades, only to have it forever roll down again.

13. Cosima Liszt, at this time married to Hans von Bülow.

Letter 38

1. François-René de Chateaubriand (1768–1848) wrote his *Mémoires d'Outre-tombe* from 1803 — although he gave as dates at various times 1809 and 1811 — until 1844. They were first edited and published by Girardin in 1849 and 1850.

2. Cf. Chateaubriand, *Mémoires*, ed. Giraud (Geneva: La Palatine, 1946), vol. II, p. 59. "J'étais mon propre obstacle et je me trouvais sans cesse sur mon chemin." Liszt alludes to one of the most exciting passages in the book, the scene where Chateaubriand describes himself walking in the countryside outside Ghent in Belgium and hears the sounds of the battle of Waterloo (June 18, 1815). Then, after the confusion of the conflicting rumors has cleared and victory is assured for the Allies, he is left to speculate on his ironic fortune: his monarchist convictions had made him a supporter of Louis XVIII, whose weaknesses were all too evident.

3. Unidentified.

4. An Aachen doctor, treating Liszt.

5. Unidentified; possibly either the minor German novelist Otto Müller (1816–1894) or the equally little-known poet Wolfgang Müller (1816–1873).

6. Justus Liebig (1803–1873), the German scientist who established one of the first real chemical laboratories at Giessen in 1826.

7. Probably Mannheim, a Frenchman who invented a type of slide rule ca. 1850.

8. Robert W. Bunsen (1811–1899), a science professor at Heidelberg who invented the burner now called after him.

9. Hoffmann von Fallersleben.

10. Albert Hahn (1828–1880), musicologist and conductor who founded the journal, *Die Tonkunst.*

11. The martyrs Amor and Viator have a Feast Day celebrated at Saint Amour (Cevenna) on August 9.

12. The roles of Liszt as Lear and Marie as Cordelia are difficult to visualize. Perhaps the composer was casting Cosima and Blandine as the two other less-devoted daughters, since he was having minor altercations with them at this time. The lines from *Lear* are from Act V, Scene 3.

Letter 39

1. Probably the *Mass in C* (1807).

2. A composition by Bronsart for orchestra.

3. Christian Möhr (1823–1888), a Cologne painter who specialized in religious *tableaux.*

4. Director of music at the Aachen Cathedral.

5. Viennese tenor.

6. Possibly Winterberger.

7. Unknown.

8. Halévy's most famous opera. First performed in 1835, with libretto by Scribe.

9. A Cologne professor who accompanied Marie and Carolyne on a trip down the Rhine as archeological tutor and guide.

Letter 40

1. Either Alfred Meissner (1822–1885), a minor German poet and novelist, or August Meissner (1801–1886), a Cologne painter of equivalent fame.

2. Robert Pflughaupt (1833–1871) and his wife Sophia (1837–1867), both pianists and pupils of Henselt. They lived in Weimar 1857–1862 and were two of Liszt's most devoted disciples.

3. Unidentified.

4. Wife of Graf Anton von Prokosch-Osten, Austrian diplomat and at one time ambassador to Greece, later to Turkey.

5. The Court at Constantinople. The official diplomatic designation was the "Sublime Porte."

6. Liszt is playing on the names of the movements in his symphonic poem, *Tasso.*

7. Pierre Martinien Tousez, called Bocage (1797–1863). A leading French actor in Romantic drama, Bocage made his debut in 1821 at the *Comédie Française.* He later played in melodramas at the *Porte-Saint-Martin* and became director of the *Odéon* in 1845. Bocage played the principal roles in Dumas' *Antony* and *Le Tour de Nesle* and he was hailed as one of the most intelligent actors — and certainly one of the most passionate lovers — on the contemporary stage. Heine described him as being as handsome as Apollo. Bocage was a close friend of George Sand and appeared in dramatizations of several of her novels, including *François-le-Champi* (1849).

Letter 41

1. April 2, Feast Day of Saint Francis.

2. Probably Liszt's *Mass* for four male voices, published in 1848. It may also be the *Graner Mass.*

3. The *Katholische Kirche* at Budapest, in the Belvaros section of the city and off *Franz-Josef Strasse.*

4. Karl Beck (1817–1879), Hungarian poet and novelist, author of a long novel in verse: *Janko, der ungarische Rosshut* (1844). Liszt apparently considered writing a musical setting for the work and then later gave up the idea.

5. Salomon Mosenthal (1821–1877), dramatist and librettist, who was

309

collaborating with Beck. Two plays by Mosenthal were given at Weimar: *Deborah* (1858) and *Die deutschen Komödianten* (1862).

6. In Silesia, west of Breslau and north of the Riesengebirge.

7. Graf Guido Karatsonyi von Beodra, *Geheimer Rat* at the Austrian Court and a wealthy Hungarian magnate.

8. Count Leo Festetics, who was actually no great friend of Liszt and who plotted against the performance of the *Graner Mass* in 1856. He was also an amateur composer.

9. Johannes Brahms (1833–1897) first heard Liszt play at Hamburg. They were introduced soon after by the violinist Joachim, and Brahms stayed at the Altenburg for six weeks in 1849. He appreciated Liszt as a pianist but was well aware of the virtuoso's limitations as composer. By 1860 the German world was split into two groups: the Wagner-Liszt *Kreis* and their opponents who gathered around Brahms. Part of Brahms's later antipathy came from Schumann's earlier influence, but Brahms also resented what he felt to be the unhealthy effect of Berlioz on Liszt; and he tended to see Liszt's theories as a movement away from pure German music (despite Liszt's claims to writing Neo-German art) toward a weak cosmopolitanism.

A major reason for their disagreement was of temperamental origin. The modest, self-effacing, and rather witty Brahms deplored the histrionics of Liszt and his followers. Liszt's musical influence on Brahms, however, is undeniable. Brahms's Hungarian Dances are cousins to the Hungarian Rhapsodies of Liszt; and Brahms also profited from Liszt's earlier experimentation with the technical device of "rhythmical transformation" — a method of developing thematic material.

10. Marie.

11. Karatsonyi.

12. Ofen was the German name for Buda (Budapest).

13. Music publisher in Wolfenbüttel.

Letter 42

1. Friedrich Wilhelm, Fürst von Hohenzollern-Hechingen (1801–1869), musical amateur and patron of Liszt and Berlioz. He maintained a small private orchestra on his estate at Löwenberg.

2. Felix Draeseke (1835–1913), German composer and Liszt-admirer who wrote articles on the "New Music" for the *Neue Zeitschrift für Musik*.

3. Unidentified.

4. Daniel Liszt.

5. Carolyne (literally, "one who is fond of the arts").

6. Agnolo Bronzino (1503–1572), Florentine painter.

7. Giovanni Antonio de Lodesanis (1484–1539), Florentine painter.

8. Carlo Cignani (1628–1719), Bolognese painter.

9. Caspar de Crayer (1584–1669), Flemish artist.

10. Probably Liszt means Polymedes, Greek sculptor (sixth century B.C.) thought to come from Argos.

11. Giovanni Benedetto (1616–1670), called "Il Grechetto" — a painter from Genoa.

12. Moritz von Schwind (1804–1871), one of the leading Vienna and Munich painters from 1840 to 1870, and a pupil of Schnorr von Carolsfeld.

Popular and prolific, he worked in all genres. Focillon (*La peinture au XIXe siècle*) classes Schwind among the group of sentimental landscapists (already discussed) whose paintings exhibited all the *Biedermeier* virtues, and who depicted life as quiescent, sweet, and comfortable.

13. Liszt's fourth symphonic poem, *Orpheus*, published in 1856.

14. Ferdinand Laub (1832–1875) who succeeded Joachim as first violinist in the Weimar Orchestra.

15. Liszt arranged Schubert's *Divertissement à la Hongroise* for piano, published in 1846.

16. Joseph Dachs (1825–1896), pianist and pupil of Czerny. Dachs later taught at the Vienna Conservatory.

17. Perhaps Mux (Moux) was a Dachshund.

18. Liszt's use of this phrase, so often associated with diplomatic affairs, makes it interesting to speculate about any *ententes cordiales* in 1858. The Franco-Italian alliance was in the air; but unfortunately for our purpose, Cavour did *not* have his famous meeting with Napoleon III at Plombières until three months after this letter was written.

19. Eduard von Liszt.

20. Carl Haslinger (1816–1868), Viennese music publisher, composer, and friend of Liszt.

21. Either Albert Franz Doppler (1821–1883), flute teacher at the Vienna Conservatory or his younger brother Karl (1825–1900), also a flautist and the transcriber of Hungarian folk tunes.

22. Zellner.

23. Archduke Joseph of Austria (1776–1847), son of Leopold II, Palatine (Vice-King) of Hungary.

24. Archduke Stephan von Habsburg (b. 1860).

25. Liszt's oratorio, *Die Legende der heiligen Elizabeth*, completed and published in 1862. The work was based on a book written by Otto Roquette.

Letter 43

1. Bunzlau, a town in Upper Silesia, west of Breslau.

2. Fürst von Hohenzollern-Hechingen.

3. Max Seifriz (1827–1885), violinist and music director at the Prince's estate of Löwenberg. Seifriz later became *Hofmusikdirektor* at Stuttgart.

4. City in Upper Silesia, west of Bunzlau.

5. Street on which Cosima and Hans von Bülow lived in Berlin.

6. Unidentified.

Letter 44

1. Intendant of the Court Theater at Gotha.

2. Liszt's handwriting is difficult to decipher here, but the second word is no doubt "Courier."

3. Ernst II, Herzog von Sachsen-Coburg-Gotha (1817–1893). Several of his letters to Liszt are in the La Mara *Zeitgenossen* collection.

4. Franz Dingelstedt (1841–1881), German poet, novelist, and playwright. He first met Liszt in 1845 and in May 1857 was invited to come to Weimar as Intendant to succeed Beaulieu. His initial production, a *Festspiel* given in September 1857, was a great success. The Theater was reorganized on a firmer financial footing. More important — unhappily for

Liszt — the drama, which had taken second place in favor of Liszt's operas, now was revived to restore to Weimar the old glory of the Goethe-Schiller era.

Liszt had been happiest with Ziegesar, an Intendant who was happy to let Liszt go his own way. Beaulieu gave Liszt more opposition. With Dingelstedt, whose ego was a match for Liszt's, it soon became open warfare. The money allotted for music was diminished, and the climax came when Liszt wished to produce the opera *Der Barbier von Bagdad* by his disciple Cornelius on October 30, 1858. The opera was given, marked by Dingelstedt's noticeable lack of coöperation. Liszt resigned as opera director soon afterward, retaining only his job as concert director. This too he relinquished on August 14, 1861.

Liszt's conduct throughout the professional quarrel was impressive, since he displayed no personal rancor or jealousy. Dingelstedt wrote him in January 1859, saying that although they had differences, he hoped that these would in no way imperil their friendship. There can be no doubt that Dingelstedt was a brilliant, even daring director. Under him, the Weimar Theater incorporated ideas prevalent at Paris, Berlin, and with the Meiningen players.

5. Gustav H. G. zu Pütlitz (1821–1890), Berlin poet, novelist, and playwright; later appointed *Kammerherr* and *Hofmarschall* at the Prussian Court. Pütlitz wrote great quantities of *vers de societé* and dramas that were an unfortunate amalgam of Kleist and Scribe. A contemporary critic, speaking of Pütlitz and his colleague Rodwitz, said:

> "*Gegen diese abgehärmten,*
> *Diese Mondscheinnachtverschwärmten*
> *Pseudo-Dichter Epigonen . . .*
> *Diese lahmen Jambenzimmerer,*
> *Zahmen Dithyrambenwimmerer.*"

At least five of Pütlitz's plays were given at Weimar: *Das Testament, Badekuren, Wilhelm von Orangien, Liebe in Arrest,* and *Das Schwert des Damokles* — all between 1858 and 1866. In 1873, Pütlitz was made Intendant of the Schwerin and Carlsruhe Theaters.

6. Intendant of the Hannover Theater.

7. Eduard von Tempeltey (1832–1919), minor poet, dramatist, and Cabinet Minister to the Duke of Coburg. He wrote the libretto for Redern's opera *Christina* in 1860.

8. Otto Prechtler (1813–1881), Austrian lyric and dramatic poet, friend and admirer of Grillparzer. Prechtler's poems appeared from 1844 to 1871; he also wrote a long verse epic, *Das Kloster am Traunsee* (1847) and a lyric drama, *Die Kronenwächter* (1844). He was author of more than thirty libretti — among them *Diana von Solanges* (cf. Letter 21, Note 1) with music by the Duke of Coburg-Gotha.

9. Friedrich W. Kücken (1810–1882), composer and conductor at Stuttgart; arranger of Thuringian folk tunes.

10. Meyerbeer's opera (cf. Letter 33, Note 6).

11. Verdi had written twenty-one operas before this date, including *Rigoletto, Il Trovatore,* and *La Traviata.*

12. It is possible that Liszt may have been thinking, when he used this phrase, of the Congress of Paris in 1856. This took place at the close of the Crimean War, when England, France, and Austria banded together against Russia on the Turkish question.

13. Baron von Lüttichau, Intendant at the Dresden Theater.

14. In Sachsen-Meiningen on the Werra River, south of Gotha and southwest of Weimar.

Letter 45

1. Castle near Löwenberg, owned by Prince von Hohenzollern-Hechingen.

2. Hohenzollern-Hechingen.

3. Ludwig I, King of Bavaria from 1825 to 1848. He was forced to abdicate in favor of Maximilian II.

4. A lake and a town south of Munich where Ludwig had one of his many royal residences.

5. Wilhelm, Herzog von Brunswick (1809–1884).

6. Ludwig II, Herzog von Hesse-Darmstadt (1777–1848).

7. Ludwig's mistress was the famous dancer-adventuress Lola Montez, born Gilbert (1818–1861). Ludwig later made her Gräfin von Landsfeld over the protests of his scandalized Ministers. Heine's verses, directed at the King of Prussia, are amusing (*König Ludwig an den König von Preussen*, from *Letzte Gedichte*, 1853–56):

> "*Stammverwandter Hohenzoller,*
> *Sei dem Wittelsbach kein Groller;*
> *Zürne nicht ob Lola Montez,*
> *Selber habend nie gekonnt es.*"

8. François Lenormand (1837–1883), French archaeologist and Assyriologist, who undertook extensive excavations in Greece, Calabria, and the sites of ancient Assyria.

9. Pius IX, born Giovanni Mastai Ferretti (1792–1878), who became Pope in 1842. He inherited all his predecessor's administrative and political problems. When the 1848 Revolution swept over the Papal States, Pius IX fled to Gaeta, to be restored only by French aid. In an attempt to redefine the status of the Church, he issued, among other statements, the papal bull *Ineffabilis Deus* concerned with the Immaculate Conception (1854); the *Syllabus of Errors* (1867); and the controversial *Doctrine of Papal Infallibility* (1870).

10. The Crimean War (1853–1856). Cf. Letter 22, where Liszt also voices disapproval of Christian nations allied with pagans.

11. Revelation 13:1.

12. Count Alexandre Walewski (1810–1868), illegitimate son of Napoleon I and the Polish countess Marie Walewska. In 1855 Napoleon III made him Minister of Foreign Affairs, Minister of State from 1860 to 1863; and a Duke in 1866. Walewski, an Austrophile, was generally hated by the many Hungarian exiles in Paris during the 1850's and 1860's.

13. This might be any member of the artist family, from the time of Francesco Bassano (ca. 1470) to five generations later.

14. Marco Antonio Franceschini (1648–1728), Bolognese painter.

15. David Vinkeboons (1578–1629), Dutch painter.

313

16. Either David I (b. 1582), David II (b. 1630), David III (b. 1638); or Julian I (b. 1572), Julian II (b. 1616).

17. Meindert Hobbema (1638–1709), Dutch landscapist.

18. Rosa (1615–1673), the Italian painter, engraver, poet, and musician. His works were extremely popular with the Romantics; Keats and Shelley, for example, refer to him frequently. Cf. Liszt's *Canzonetta di Salvator Rosa* in the *Années de Pélérinage, 2ᵉ année.*

19. The Bakhuijzens were a family of eighteenth-century Dutch painters, best known for their sketches of animals and flowers.

20. The Ruysdäel family was another Low Country family of painters, early and mid-seventeenth century.

21. Or Andrea d'Agnolo (1486–1530), Florentine painter.

22. Called "Il Guido" (1575–1642), Italian painter, engraver, and sculptor.

23. Francesco Francia (ca. 1450–1517), Bolognese painter and goldsmith.

24. Jacob Philipp Fallmerayer (1790–1861), historian and antiquarian. *Fragmente aus dem Orient* appeared in 1845. His role as a Liberal in the Frankfort Parliament (1848) forced him to flee to Switzerland for several years.

25. Adolf Zeissing (1810–1876), German aesthetician and pupil of Hegel, who found in the "Golden Section" the answer to the most perfect aesthetic shape. His theory had been anticipated as far back as Luca Paciola's *De Divina Proportione* (1509). Zeissing developed the idea in *Neue Lehre von der Proportionen des menschlichen Körpers* (1854), *Aesthetische Forschungen* (1855), and *Der Goldne Schnitt* (1884). A disciple of Zeissing, G. T. Fechner, attempted to define the "Golden Section" as rectangle with the proportions of 34:21!

26. Liszt's spelling of "Deutsche" (*Teutsche*) is reminiscent of some of the writings of Görres, Fichte, Vater Jahn, during the Wars of the Liberation when German Nationalism ran high.

27. Franz Lachner (1803–1890), Munich composer, conductor, and counterpoint teacher.

28. Paul Louis Heyse (1830–1914), German novelist and dramatist. From 1854 to his death he lived chiefly at Munich, where he and the poet Geibel shared the leadership of the *Münchener Dichterkreis.* Maximilian II granted Heyse a stipend which was continued by Ludwig II.

Despite his friendship with Ibsen, Heyse was a strong opponent of the Naturalistic movement in literature; and he resented what he considered its debasing aspects. He is best known for his *Novellen,* of which he wrote about one hundred and twenty, including the famous *L'Arrabbiata.* Adelheid von Schorn met him at Munich in 1874, and she mentions that Carolyne knew him well. At least three of his plays were produced at Weimar: *Die Sabinerinnen* (1858), *Elizabeth Charlotte* (1860), and *Hans Lange* (1864).

29. No libretto with this title has been located. Moritz von Schwind painted *Die Sieben Raben,* which received much notice at the Munich International Exhibition of 1858; and it may be that Liszt was considering this painting as musical inspiration. *Die Sieben Raben* is the sixteenth of the Grimm brothers' *Kinder und Hausmärchen.*

30. Meyerbeer's opera, *Le Pardon de Ploermel* (*Dinorah*, in Italian), written and produced in 1859.

31. Unidentified.

32. Liszt was awarded the decoration of the Iron Crown of Hungary in April 1859.

33. Leipzig.

Letter 46

1. Ahasuerus appears in the Old Testament in the Books of *Esther* and *Ezra* — a figure who caught the fancy of such Romantics as Eugène Sue, Goethe, and Victor Hugo, who saw him as the symbol of the Wandering Jew.

2. Julius von Kolb, amateur pianist.

3. Karl Bärmann (1839–1913), Munich pianist and pupil of Liszt. He taught in Boston from 1881 until his death.

4. Heyse, who was a student at Bonn until 1850, went to Italy in 1852. *Thekla*, an epic dealing with the legend of the Apostle Paul and Thecla, was written in Florence that year.

5. The Grand Duke of Saxe-Weimar.

6. Emmanuel Geibel (1815–1884), leader of the "Munich School" of German poets and perhaps the best representative of German poetry from 1848 to 1870. Maximilian II invited him to Munich in 1852 as an honorary university professor, and Geibel stayed there until his death. Although he wrote several tragedies — *König Roderich* (1843), *Brunhild* (1858), *Sophinisbe* (1869) — and an epic, *König Sigurds Brautfahrt* (1846), his chief production was vast quantites of lyric verse, collected in the *Juniuslieder*, *Neue Gedichte* (1857), and *Spätherbstblätter* (1877).

Tennyson is the best English equivalent of Geibel, and certainly the latter was uncrowned poet laureate of Germany. His style was eclectic; like most of the *Epigonen* he reworked all the Romantic themes, and his verse technique is essentially that of Goethe, Heine, Lenau, and even Hölderlin. An example of his patriotic poetry is *Durch tiefe Nacht* (1845), and one of his finest lyrics is *An die Musik* set to music by Robert Franz:

> "*Nun die Schatten dunkeln,*
> *Stern an Stern erwacht . . .*"

There are no references to Liszt in Geibel's collected works.

7. Dingelstedt.

8. Handel's oratorio, composed in 1746.

9. Marie's portrait was done by Kaulbach. Cf. Letter 23, Note 4.

10. A letter from Liszt's mother was included in the envelope sent to Marie.

11. A letter from Dingelstedt was also forwarded by Liszt to Marie. It includes a set of occasional verses dedicated by Dingelstedt to Liszt, as well as a toast drunk to the composer by one R. Gottschall (1823–1904), a minor writer and literary historian.

Letter 47

1. The *Brandenburg-Hof*, where Liszt stayed during this trip to Berlin.

2. Franz Kroll (1820–1877), pupil of Liszt. He taught piano in Berlin after 1849, and edited Bach's *Well-Tempered Clavichord*.

3. The doctor who tended Daniel Liszt at Berlin.
4. Eduard Hildebrand (1818–1869), Berlin landscape painter.
5. Possibly Philipp Schmitz (1824–1887), a Düsseldorf painter.
6. Unidentified.
7. The second part of Liszt's oratorio, *Christus*, published in 1866.

Letter 48

1. Liszt's forty-eighth birthday.
2. Pauline Viardot (1821–1910), famous French opera-singer and sister of the singer Malibran. She sang the leading roles in such operas as Gounod's *Sappho* and Meyerbeer's *Le Prophète*, and enjoyed the same sort of fame in Parisian literary circles as did Lola Montez in political ones.
3. Berlioz's opera in two parts. (Cf. Letter 27, Note 2.)
4. Austrian politics in 1859 was in a state of confusion. The Crimean War had left the country with acute financial problems, and the Franco-Austrian War in Italy was about to begin.
5. The newly-married couple soon moved from this residence to the *Augarten* in Vienna.
6. Alexander, Freiherr von Hübner (1811–1892), member of the Committee of Fifty at the Frankfurt Diet in April 1848 — the group that desired a federation with Austria, and failed to obtain their aim. He was later Richard Metternich's predecessor as Ambassador to France. In 1868 Hübner became Austrian Minister at the Vatican.
7. Probably Karl, Graf von Grünne, First Adjutant-General in Austria until 1859.
8. Franz Falliot, Graf von Crenneville, who succeeded Grünne as Adjutant-General from 1859 to 1867. A political and military reactionary, he favored a Prussian-Austrian alliance and was a member of a military commission whose aim was to effect that end in 1861. Yet in 1866, he was one of the Austrian generals who clamored for war with Prussia.
9. Johann von Herbeck (1831–1877), former lawyer who turned to music and became conductor of the Vienna *Männergesangverein* and later of the *Hofoper*.
10. After the Liszt-Dingelstedt schism, Hoffmann von Fallersleben felt that the Weimar Theater had no more future. Hence in May 1860 he acceptd the job as librarian at Schloss Corvey offered to him by the Duke of Ratibor-Hohenlohe. Liszt was instrumental in obtaining the position for the poet; and in the La Mara *Zeitgenossen* Collection, there are many letters from Fallersleben to Liszt expressing his gratitude.
His interest in the *Club Neu-Weymar* never flagged. When Liszt finally left Weimar, this — coupled with the earlier demise of the Grand Duke — meant the end of an era for Fallersleben. His letters praising Liszt, Marie, and Carolyne are charming and full of genuine affection. "The Altenburg was for me a sanctuary full of sunny spring days." Cf. *An Meine Freunde*, letters ed. Gerstenberg (Berlin: Ehbock), *passim* and p. 317.
11. Viktor von Ratibor-Hohenlohe (1818–1893), brother-in-law to Marie after her marriage.

Letter 49

1. St. Petersburg, where Marie and her husband had gone to call on the Czar.

2. A reference to Liszt's refusal to reaccept the musical direction of the Weimar Theater.

Letter 50

1. Liszt's son Daniel (b. 1839 in Rome) was vacationing at his sister Cosima's in Berlin when he fell sick. He died December 13, 1859, two days before Liszt arrived.

2. Detskoje Selo, formerly Zarskoje Selo ("Czar's Town"), south of St. Petersburg, and for one hundred and fifty years the summer residence of the Russian royal family.

3. Liszt hoped that the good reception granted to the Hohenlohes by the Czar might aid the possibility of Carolyne's divorce.

4. Alexander Kotzebue (1815–1889), son of the famous German dramatist August von Kotzebue. His artistic renown came from his paintings of battle scenes. An officer in the Russian army, he resigned in 1837 and was appointed Court painter by Alexander II.

5. Raphael (1483–1520) painted this work at Pérouse in 1505.

6. Probably Okraszewski, Carolyne's lawyer engaged in attempting to obtain her divorce.

7. Weimar.

8. Wagner's opera, *Der fliegende Holländer*, composed in 1841 and first performed at Dresden in 1843. The *Spinnelied* is sung in Act II by the heroine, Senta, and a girls' chorus. The work was given at Weimar during the 1864–65 season.

9. At first sight this would seem to be the conference held at the end of the Crimean War, but that affair preceded this letter by three and a half years. More likely Liszt refers to a less famous meeting of diplomats after the Franco-Austrian War of 1859, which terminated a month before this date.

Letter 51

1. The death of Daniel.

2. Constant von Wurzbach, Ritter von Tannenberg (1818–1893), Viennese poet and historian. After a youthful career as army officer, he was appointed Director of Archives in the Ministry of the Interior.

3. The church Liszt refers to was an edifice erected on the site of an older church attached to the medieval monastery of Irish Benedictine monks. The square facing it is still called the *Schottenhof.*

4. Eduard von Liszt.

5. Eugenio Terziani (1824–1889), pupil of Mercadante, composer of operas and masses.

6. Liszt's orchestration was published in 1859; the second edition in 1871.

7. Heinrich Schlesinger, Berlin music publisher and son of the founder of the firm. An opera by Schlesinger, *Mit der Feder*, was given at Weimar in 1861. His brother, Maurice (1787–1871), is known to scholars of Flaubert, since he served for the model of Arnoux in *L'Éducation Sentimentale.*

8. Liszt's piano transcriptions of the Chopin *Songs* were published in 1860.

9. Edouard Lassen (1830–1904), pupil of Liszt, director of the Weimar Orchestra after Liszt's resignation. Liszt gave his opera, *Landgraf Ludwigs*

Brautfahrt, at Weimar in 1857; and Lassen's *Frauenlob* was performed there during the 1859–60 season.

10. The original two lines of the Hohenlohe family were Hohenlohe-Neuenstein and Hohenlohe-Waldenburg; the Oehringen line started with Philipp von Hohenlohe-Oehringen-Ingelfingen (d. 1781) in Würtemburg.

Letter 52

1. Maria Pavlovna died June 23, 1859.

2. Rudolf von Mülinen, secretary at the French Embassy at Weimar. His chief bid for fame seems to be that he hurt himself jumping over a ditch at the Trianon in order to display his zeal before Franz-Josef, when the Emperor visited France in October, 1867.

3. A reference to Franco-German relations, which already were strained by 1860.

4. Intendant at the Berlin *Hofoper*.

5. Name of the hall in Cologne where regular symphony concerts were given.

6. Leopold Schefer (1784–1862), German poet, novelist, and musician. From 1804 to 1845 he managed the estates of his friend Prince von Pückler-Muskau (that whimsical, Byronic dandy). Like Goethe and Platen, Schefer was interested in Oriental verse-forms — the *ghazel, pantoum*, etc. A trip to the East 1816–1821 gave him material for *Hafis in Hellas* (1853) and *Koran der Liebe* (1854). He spent the last years of his life in Russia.

Letter 53

1. Wagner.

2. Tenor at Weimar.

3. Wagner's *Tristan und Isolde*. The play was written at Zürich in 1857 and the score was completed by August 1859. Von Bülow conducted the *Prelude* in March 1859. The first performance of the entire work was given under his direction in Munich in 1865.

4. In Czechoslovakia, province of Mähren.

5. (Brno) southwest of Olmütz, southeast of Prague.

6. Auber's opera, *Gustave IV, ou le Bal Masqué* (1837), text by Scribe. Verdi's better-known work, *Un Ballo in Maschera* (1859), was based on the same libretto.

7. The libretto of one of Mme. Ingeborg von Bronsart's four operas: *Die Göttin zu Säis, Jery und Bätely, Hjarne*, and *Die Sühne*.

8. Nickname for Liszt.

Letter 54

1. Marie's birthday.

2. Johannot (1803–1852), French etcher, lithographer, painter, and next to Gigoux the leading illustrator of his day. Between 1830 and 1835 he illustrated works of Hugo, George Sand, Sue, Vigny, and Balzac.

Letter 55

1. Beethoven's *Sixth Symphony* in F, first performed in 1808.

2. Suburb south of Vienna.

3. Small river near Vienna.

4. Possibly a "Mr. Landsberg" — a musician at the Vatican whom Liszt met in 1853.

5. Prince Wilhelm von Preussen, appointed Prince Regent after Friedrich-Wilhelm IV was officially declared mad in 1858. He governed until 1861.

6. Austro-French relations at this time were unfriendly. The war which started in April 1859 — marked by the bloody battles of Magenta and Solferino — had been concluded by the Peace of Villafranca in July. But by January 1860, the two countries were embroiled over the Roman question.

7. Marie had just sent Liszt two diamonds in a setting.

8. Either the women's chorus (Act I, Finale) in Mendelssohn's unfinished opera, *Die Lorelei* or the *Vintage Chorus* for men by the same name. Both were composed in 1840, Opus 98. The *Vintage Chorus* (or *Song*) was published in 1847.

9. Ernst II.

10. Allusion to Constantin's position at the Austrian Court.

11. *Brandus, Dufour & Cie*, music publishers founded in 1834.

12. Meyerbeer.

13. Meyerbeer.

14. Wagner.

Letter 56

1. Marie sent Liszt a crown of laurel on the Feast of Saint Francis.

2. The *Akousmata* of the Pythagorean sect contains no references to the shade of the laurel.

3. Louis Daguerre (1787–1851) perfected his invention in 1839.

4. Liszt's birthday.

5. Okrazewski.

6. Ferdinand David (1810–1873), violinist and professor at the Leipzig Conservatory. Mendelssohn's *Violin Concerto* was dedicated to David.

7. Albert Niemann (1831–1917), Berlin opera singer famed for his *Heldentenor* roles in Wagner's operas. He sang in the first performance of *Tannhäuser* at Paris, in 1861.

8. Liszt's work was published in 1862. He wrote four *Mephisto Waltzes* for piano between 1860 and 1885; this was Number One.

Letter 57

1. Eduard Beurmann, editor of the *Frankfurter Zeitung* and author of *Ludwig Börne als Charakter in der Literatur* (1837).

2. Cf. Hoffmann von Fallersleben, *Mein Leben*, vol. VI, p. 152.

3. It has been impossible to find this remark of Frederick the Great.

4. The castle near Eisenach, built ca. 1123. It was at the Wartburg that Elizabeth of Hungary, who inspired Liszt's oratorio, became betrothed at the age of four. Duke Carl-Alexander restored the Wartburg, and Moritz von Schwind painted frescos for the *Sängerhall*.

5. The Grand Duchess.

6. Stanislaus, Graf von Kalckreuth (1820–1894), Austrian landscapist. He was invited to found an Art Academy at Weimar in 1859, and he was the director from 1860 to 1876. Ramberg was appointed there to teach historical painting, Lenbach and Corräder for portraiture, and Böcklin (Hitler's favorite nineteenth-century painter) for landscape painting.

7. Artur-Georg, Freiherr von Ramberg (1819–1875), one of the leading members of the Munich School of painters. He undertook such tasks as illustrating Goethe's *Hermann und Dorothea* and Voss's *Luise*. Ramberg came to Weimar in 1859 and painted frescos for the Ducal Palace while a member of the newly-formed Academy. He also painted frescoes for the *Lutherhalle* at the Wartburg.

8. Franz von Lenbach (1836–1904), Munich painter whose 4,000-odd canvases are scattered throughout most of the museums of Europe. Focillon (*La peinture au XIXᵉ siècle*) discusses Lenbach's heavy, intense style, which he sees as the result of the unhappy and ill-digested influence of Spanish and Italian art on German painters. Lenbach's portraits of Bismarck (1879) and Pope Leo XIII may be cited as examples of the tendency of mid-century German painters to spend too much time in museums.

9. Karl von Piloty (1826–1886), Munich historical painter and teacher. Piloty's *Nero auf der Trümmern Rome* was hailed by contemporary critics as the triumph of historical painting. Perhaps Focillon's comment best sums up the Munich group: "Upon every German artist of this period, even those who were occasionally gifted with genius, was superimposed a terrible and candid Philistinism." (Focillon, *La peinture au XIXᵉ siècle*, vol. II, p. 116.)

10. Conrad Corräder or Corradi (1813–1878), known for his highly-sentimental, bourgeois-bucolic Swiss landscapes.

11. The new Weimar Art Academy.

12. Opera by Kauer, given at Weimar in the 1857–58 season. Schrickel (*Geschichte des Weimaren Theaters*, p. 187) calls *Saale Nixe* a "popular folk-play with singing and dancing, written by Hensler von Vulpius" — who may have been related to Goethe's wife, Christiane Vulpius.

13. Opera by the popular poet-painter-musician Rost (d. 1860). Three other works by Rost were given at Weimar: *Landgraf Friedrich* (1857), *Ludwig der Eiserne* (1859), and *Berthold Schwartz* (1864). It is interesting that an opera with a similar title (*Der letzte Zauberer*) was performed at Weimar on June 8, 1869 — music by Pauline Viardot, French text by Turgenev and German text by Pohl. This piece of curious collaboration was first given at Turgenev's villa at Baden-Baden in the spring of 1868.

14. Christian Friedrich Hebbel (1813–1863), considered by many critics to be the leading German dramatist of the nineteenth century. Hebbel's first play, *Judith*, (1840) was given at Weimar in 1857. Although he wrote lyric poetry and *Novellen*, the drama was his chief interest. Among his other plays were *Maria Magdalene* (1844), *Herodes und Mariamne* (1850), *Agnes Bernauer*, the first performance of which directed by Dingelstedt, took place at Weimar on September 18, 1852; *Gyges und sein Ring* (1854); and the three parts of a *Nibelungen* drama, completed in 1860, and given at Weimar in 1862.

Hebbel was introduced to Liszt by Dingelstedt in June 1858. He stayed at the Altenburg in December 1858, and again in February 1861. Liszt greatly impressed Hebbel. The writer was grateful for the musician's patronage, but more than that, Liszt's temperament and apparent heroic stature caught Hebbel's attention. There is a description of a musicale at the Altenburg, where Hebbel tells of Liszt's hair waving as he played with titanic power, and Marie turned pages reverently (cf. Hebbel, *Briefe*, vol.

VI, p. 159). Hebbel seemed fascinated by Liszt's magnetic ability to attract disciples: "I cannot, as a layman, pass judgment on Liszt's music; but he has gathered a circle about him, such as I have never seen on this earth." (*Ibid.*, p. 175.) The departure of Liszt from Weimar was for Hebbel, as for Dingelstedt, a symbol of the decay of a once-great cultural center. He said, in a letter to his wife, that had he, Liszt, and Wagner stayed at Weimar, it might have been a "moonlight" after the noontime glare of Goethe and Schiller. But Hebbel also realized that the elegant, restricted Court Theater was finished, and that the future for a dramatist lay in the bourgeois, commercial stage. Berlin replaced for him the confines — pleasant as they may have been — of the small comic-opera Grand Duchy.

15. Town in the Saar near Saarlouis.

16. Robert Prütz (1816–1872), Stettin poet, dramatist theorist, and historian. Although a Radical Democrat, Prütz took no part in the 1848 Revolution; and a grateful Conservative government made him Royal Professor at Halle as his reward. *Die Deutsche Literatur der Gegenwart* was written 1848–53, published 1859.

17. Karl Gutzkow (1811–1878), Berlin novelist, playwright, leader of the *Junges Deutschland* movement — the group of young republican writers including Börne, Laube, Grabbe, and Heine. It lasted from 1833 (when Gutzkow coined the phrase) until 1840. Repressive measures, dissension within the group, and a new wave of patriotism tended to break down their international socialistic aspirations. The "Three Graces" of *Junges Deutschland* were Rahel Varnhagen, Bettina von Arnim, and the "martyr" Charlotte Stieglitz. Much of the new ideology was concerned with female emancipation (cf. Gutzkow's novel, *Wally*, 1835).

His plays were *Uriel Acosta* (1846) — *Die Saddukäer von Amsterdam* was a first draft, produced at Weimar in 1861; *Das Urbild des Tartüffe* (1845: Weimar, 1860); *Werner, Richard Savage,* and *Zopf und Schwert.* Several letters from Gutzkow to Liszt are in the La Mara *Zeitgenossen* collection.

18. Gustav Freytag (1816–1895), German novelist and playwright. He edited a liberal weekly, *Die Grenzboten,* for twenty years; and although a Prussian nationalist, he was a consistent opponent of Bismarck. The Duke of Sachsen-Coburg-Gotha was his patron in later life, as was the Prussian Crown Prince.

His plays are mostly forgotten: *Graf Waldemar* (1847) was staged at Weimar in 1865. A book about dramatic theory, *Technik des Dramas* (1863), is of more value. But Freytag's novels, particularly *Die Verlorene Handschrift* (1864) and *Soll und Haben* (1855) brought him fame. The latter is reminiscent of Scott and Dickens; it marked, however, a step in the direction of realism and a genuinely middle-class point of view, away from the endless soul-searching of the traditional *Künstlerromane.* There is one letter from him to Liszt in the La Mara collection.

19. Franz Grillparzer (1791–1872), leading Austrian playwright of the early nineteenth century. Like Tieck and later Hofmannsthal — his Viennese compatriot — Grillparzer shows the influence of Calderon and Lope da Vega. His first play, *Die Ahnfrau* (1817), a Romantic fate-tragedy, was followed by the trilogy, *Das goldene Vliess,* completed in 1820. These three plays, as well as *Des Meeres und der Liebe Wellen* (1831) and *Sappho*

321

(1818) were classical in their outlines. Both *Die Medea* (from *Das goldene Vliess*) and *Sappho* were performed at Weimar in the 1861–62 season.

20. Garibaldi left Genoa on his Sicilian Expedition on May 6, 1860. After landing on May 11th he defeated the Bourbon troops of Francis II at Calatafini on the 14th. The day this letter was written, Garibaldi entered Palermo in triumph.

Letter 59

1. Hebbel.

2. Mme. Kalergis, *née* Countess de Nesselrode, friend of Liszt and Wagner. Her second marriage was to Count Moukhanoff.

3. In 1827, when Liszt was barely nineteen, he fell in love with Caroline de Saint-Cricq, daughter of Charles X's Minister of Commerce and Industry. She later married. Liszt apparently never forgot her, and even left her a small item in his will.

4. City in southwest Saxony, south of Leipzig and southwest of Dresden.

5. Unidentified.

6. Clara Schumann.

7. Von Bülow.

8. Unidentified.

9. Léon Escudier (1821–1881), Paris music publisher and writer of musical biographies. Escudier founded *La France Musicale* in 1838 with his brother, Marie Escudier.

Letter 60

1. Liszt's tenth symphonic poem, written 1859 and published 1886.

2. Liszt's eleventh symphonic poem (1856), inspired by Kaulbach's painting.

3. Probably the *Künstler Festzug*, written in 1859 for the Schiller Festival at Weimar.

4. This reference to Pascal has not been located.

5. Clodwig von Hohenlohe-Schillingsfürst (1819–1901), Marie's brother-in-law. A member of the Bavarian *Reichsrath* in 1846, he became Bavarian Minister of Foreign Affairs in 1866 for Ludwig II. Actually Wagner was influential in having him chosen, since Ludwig II was far more concerned with opera and his many castles than with politics.

While a Catholic, Hohenlohe was opposed to the Pope's Bull of Infallibility (cf. Letter 45, Note 9); and he encouraged Döllinger in his rebellion against the Roman Church. Hohenlohe also supported Bismarck's anti-Papal measures. From 1873 to 1880 he was ambassador at Paris. Hohenlohe succeeded the unpopular Manteuffel as Governor of Alsace-Lorraine, and the height of his political career was the appointment as German Chancellor (1894–1900). Hohenlohe's advanced age suited the young German emperor perfectly: Bismarck had been the "dropped pilot," and the new monarch wanted the executive power for himself.

6. The Passion Play at Oberammergau started 1634 in Garmisch, Upper Bavaria.

1. Residence of Marie and her husband, Konstantin von Hohenlohe-Schillingsfürst, after he was appointed *Obersthofmeister* at the Court in Vienna. The Augarten is in the Leopoldstadt district of Vienna, northwest of the Prater and northeast of the Hofburg.
2. Evidently, Liszt was planning to dine at the British ambassador's.

Letter 62

1. Graf Fürstenberg, Intendant of the Vienna *Hoftheater*.
2. Graf Ferdinand von Beust (1809–1886), Austrian Chancellor whose chief accomplishment was the establishment of the Dual Monarchy of Austria-Hungary (November 14, 1868). Originally a Minister in the government of Saxony, he left its service for that of Austria after 1866. The "Monarchie bicéphale" was pleasing to the Hungarians; the Austrians, who regarded Beust as a foreigner, were naturally angry. In 1869, Beust — still thinking in anti-Prussian terms — tried to arrange a Franco-Austrian alliance, but the project failed, owing to Franz-Josef's objection to the French abandonment of the Pope at Rome. Beust also incurred the hostility of the Austrian pro-Vatican group, because he disapproved of the political-theological pronouncements of Pius IX in 1864 and 1870.
3. Probably Baron Karl August von Reisach (1800–1869), Archbishop of Munich and Freising, and one of the delegates at the Bishops' Conference at Würzburg in 1858.
4. Hietzing, District XIII of Vienna in the western part of the city. This includes Schönbrunn.
5. Baron Anton Augusz (1807–1878), Hungarian statesman, musical amateur, and friend of Liszt.
6. The Metternich estate near Vienna.
7. Emile Palleske (1823–1880), writer and actor. Palleske played chiefly at the Weimar and Berlin theaters after 1851. As author, he wrote a book about Schiller and one play, *Oliver Cromwell* (1857).
8. Johann-Georg Leitert (1852–1901), pianist and pupil of Liszt.
9. Ludwig Bösendorfer (1835–1918), son of Ignaz Bösendorfer, who started a Viennese firm of piano manufacturers in 1828. *The Konzertsaal Bösendorfer* was inaugurated by Bülow in 1872.
10. Liszt's arrangement for two pianos of Beethoven's Sonata No. 8, Op. 13, in C minor. The transcription was written between 1845 and 1851.
11. Sophie Menter (1846–1918), pupil of Tausig, Bülow, and Liszt. She married the violinist Popper in 1872 and taught at Saint Petersburg.
12. A collection of twenty-one pieces, Op. 9.
13. Either Liszt's transcription for piano of *Gretchen am Spinnrade* (Schubert) or the *Spinning Chorus* from Wagner's *Fliegender Holländer*. Both were written in 1862.
14. Johann Graf von Willczek (1837–1922), Viennese musical amateur, painter, and polar explorer.

Letter 63

1. Boileau, *L'Art Poétique*, Chant I:
   "Enfin Malherbe vint, et, le premier en France,
   Fit sentir dans les vers une juste cadence."

323

2. Ernest Hébert (1817–1888), Grenoble painter and pupil of d'Angers. He was known for his portraits of women and children. His first exhibition was at Paris in 1839. One of his most popular paintings was *La Sventurata*.

Letter 64

1. The scene is reminiscent of Liszt's own fable written twenty years earlier for Marie — *Les deux Roses.* Cf. Letter 6.

2. Liszt's *Soirées de Vienne,* nine waltzes for piano, were written in 1852 and based on Schubert's *Waltzer und Ländler,* Op. 18; *Waltzer,* Op. 127; and *Valses Sentimentales,* Op. 50.

3. Fifteen pieces for piano, Op. 15.

4. This pastiche of literary allusions combines references to the *Odyssey* and to the *Divina Commedia.*

5. From this point on, Liszt employs this appellation for Marie's brother-in-law, Cardinal Gustav-Adolph, Prince von Hohenlohe-Schillingsfürst (1823–1896). Like his elder brother Chlodwig, later the Chancellor, Cardinal Gustav shared the view of those German Catholics who with Döllinger protested against the pronouncements of Pius IX in 1864 and 1870. Bismarck wished Gustav to be Prussian representative at the Vatican in 1872, but Leo XIII — successor to Pius IX — protested on the grounds that the family was inimical to the Papacy. The Cardinal, who resided at Rome, was given the Church of Santa Maria Maggiore. He was later instrumental in negotiating the treaty between Bismarck and the Pope that ended the *Kulturkampf.*

W. R. Thayer (in "Cardinal Hohenlohe — Liberal," *Italica,* Cambridge; Riverside Press, 1908) says that Hohenlohe counseled the Pope *not* to leave Rome in 1870, and that he continually stressed the necessity for the Papacy to resign itself to a loss of temporal power. Consequently he was disliked by most of the Vatican party, particularly the Jesuits; and his admiration for the Italian Liberal Minister Crispi almost cost Hohenlohe his cardinalate. Thayer also states that Hohenlohe was for a while considered as a possible candidate for Pope. Primo Levi (in *Gustavo Adolfo, cardinal principe,* Rome, 1896) even hints that Hohenlohe was poisoned by his enemies, but I have never seen this accusation made by any other responsible writer.

His friendship for Liszt was long and untroubled, and lasted until the musician's death in 1886. He later became reconciled with Carolyne, who at first would have nothing to do with the Hohenlohe family since she felt they all opposed her match with Liszt. There are several of her letters to the Cardinal in Schorn, *Zwei Menschenalter* — plaintive in tone when she discusses her unfortunate life; scholarly and in the "bluestocking" vein when she debates theological matters.

6. Cardinal Hohenlohe's residence at Tivoli, outside Rome, where Liszt subsequently lived at Hohenlohe's invitation. It inspired three piano compositions by Liszt: the two *Cyprès de la Villa d'Este* and *Les Jeux D'Eaux à la Villa d'Este,* numbers 2, 3, and 4 of the *Années de Pélérinage, 3e Année* (pub. post. 1890). An indirect description of the villa appears in Maurice Baring's *The Cat's Cradle* (London: Heineman, 1925), p. 393: ". . . that stiff, prim garden with its avenues, its yew hedges, and formal beds, and ponds, and little Greek temples, and its stone ornaments, has be-

come an enchanted place. It is all overgrown and wild — and like the palace of the Sleeping Beauty of the Wood. It reminds me of the Villa d'Este."
7. Priest attached to the court of Napoleon III and Empress Eugénie. He was her confessor, and originally a Jew converted to a Carmelite. Merimée said, "The Empress is virtue incarnate, but she has a scoundrel as a confessor." Richard Metternich and others at Court claimed that Bauer collaborated with Napoleon III on a brochure (anonymous) about the Italian question, full of scurrilous references to Pius IX. In 1870 Bauer went to the Front with the French ambulance corps. He wrote one amorous, lurid novel. Gesztes (in *Pauline de Metternich*) sums up his career: "After the debacle and one love-story, he became unfrocked and a free-thinker." Cf. Jules Wogue, "Un aumônier israélite," *Mercure de France* (Paris, July 1936).

Letter 65

1. Liszt's apartment near the Church of San Francesco a Ripa, across the Tiber from the Palatino. He lived there before moving to the Villa d'Este.
2. Liszt's use of the future tense is confusing. His only known *Beethoven Cantata* was written for a festival at Bonn in 1846.
3. Also known as the *Stadtkirche* on the *Herderplatz* at Weimar.
4. Possibly Seckau in Upper Styria, Austria.
5. Gustav von Hohenlohe.

Letter 66

1. Fortuné Layrand (1834–1912), French portrait painter who did two oils of Liszt in 1869 and 1870.
2. Duchess Adele Castiglione-Colonna (1836–1879), who, when Liszt knew her, was living in a cloister and was painting. Her earlier career was more active. In 1860, Cavour sent her to act as a *femme fatale* with Napoleon III (she was then known as "la bellissima contessa") in order to curry that susceptible monarch's favor for Italy against Austria. She was successful: her small house near the Royal Palace was convenient for his visits. She fought Countess Walewska for Napoleon's attentions; and her triumph was an appearance as *Salambô*, Flaubert's exotic creation, at a ball in the *Tuileries*, in March 1863.
3. Vinnie Ream (1847–1914), American sculptress from Wisconsin. Two of her popular works were statues of Farragut and Lincoln in Washington, D. C.
4. Concerto No. 1 in B Flat, Op. 19.
5. Liszt's Concerto No. 1 in E Flat, 1857.

Letter 68

1. Rome was indeed the seat of important historical events in 1870. Napoleon withdrew his troops in August; the Republican Army under Cadorna attacked the Vatican troops, and entered the Vatican City on September 20. Pius IX was forced to disband the Papal forces, and the ultimate result was the "Law of Guarantees" of May 13, 1871, which defined the relations of Church and State in Italy.
2. Nikolaus Dumba (d. 1900), wealthy Viennese musical amateur and Wagnerite.

325

3. Joseph Unger, Viennese lawyer, musical amateur, and Minister without Portfolio in the Austrian government.

4. Baron Felix Orczy (1835–1892), director of the Budapest National Theater, president of the Budapest Music Festival Committee, husband of the authoress of *The Scarlet Pimpernel*, etc. née Countess Emma Vass von Czege-Szent-Egyed.

Letter 69

1. Wagner.

2. Félicien César David (1810–1876), French composer. An ardent Saint-Simonist in his youth, David went to the East in the 1830's to spread the new doctrine. His chief success was the opera *Lalla-Roukh* (1861), based on the Moore work. Gesztes mentions (in *Pauline de Metternich*) that he was *chef du claque* at the Paris *Opera* in 1861 when Wagner's *Tannhäuser* had its stormy performance there — and that Wagner threw David from the hall.

3. Franz, Freiherr Kuhn von Kuhnenfeld (1817–1896), Austrian General and Chief of Staff of the Hungarian Army fighting in Italy in 1859 and 1866. At this date, he was Austrian Chief of Staff.

4. Melchior Longay (1822–1884), appointed Minister of Finance by the Deak government in Hungary on May 21, 1870. Longay had the singular ability to stabilize the chaotic monetary system of the Hungarian half of the Dual Monarchy.

5. Graf Jules Andrassy (1823–1890), Hungarian statesman who fought with Kossuth in 1848 and who, like Teleky, Batthany, and Karolyi, was forced into exile in Paris soon after. Their hope was that Napoleon III would do for Hungary what he had undertaken in Italy; and the years 1849–1867 were filled with schemes to embroil France in Austro-Hungarian complications. The formation of the Dual Monarchy ended the period of expatriation for most of the former insurgents. Andrassy returned to Hungary after Solferino, accompanied by his wife who was known for "the whiteness of her skin and the redness of her political opinions." (Gesztes, *Pauline de Metternich*, p. 234.) Andrassy succeeded Beust as Chancellor of the Dual Monarchy.

6. Liszt's patriotic choral piece, based partly on Hungarian folk tunes (1867).

7. Julius Ferdinand Georg Schuberth (1804–1875), head of a music publishing firm with branches in Hamburg, Leipzig, and New York.

Letter 70

1. Probably Liszt's *Psalm CXVI*, for piano and chorus, published in 1871.

Letter 71

1. Ludwig Nohl (1831–1885), Heidelberg musicologist who published a Beethoven biography (1864–1877) and edited the Mozart and Beethoven letters. He wrote *Beethoven, Liszt, und Wagner* (1874) and *Wagners Bedeutung für die nationale Kunst* (1883). The former work asserted that Wagner and Liszt were continuing the tradition established by Beethoven, and it is this controversial thesis that Liszt calls "Weimarois."

Letter 72

1. Szechenyi (1825–1898), Austro-Hungarian diplomat and musical amateur. The family were prominent in Hungarian politics and as patrons of the arts from 1629, when the title was granted. Count Imrey S. was secretary to the Austrian delegation at the *Bundestag* in Frankfort from 1852 to 1854. As a friend of Bismarck, he worked diligently for Prusso-Austrian unity during his term as Austrian ambassador at Berlin (1878–1892). His father, Count Stepan Szechenyi (1791–1860) had been a patriot in 1848 and an exile in consequence. Both father and son followed the Deak program of political moderation, in contrast to the radicalism of Kossuth.

2. Probably Heinrich Vogl (1845–1903), Wagnerian tenor who sang the role of *Tristan* in Wagner's opera for many years at Bayreuth.

3. Siegmund's "Winter Winde wichen dem Wonnemond" from *Die Walküre*, Act I. *Die Walküre*, first of the trilogy of *Das Ring des Nibelungen*, was completed in 1856 but not performed in its entirety until 1870 at Munich. Vogl (see above) sang the role of *Siegmund*.

4. Marie Rossi, daughter of the singer Countess Henrietta Sontag-Rossi (1806–1854).

Letter 73

1. Gustav Walter (1834–1910), *Liedersinger* and tenor at the Vienna Opera.

2. Admiral Wilhelm von Tegetthoff (1827–1871). In the Prussian-Danish War (1864) he was commander of the Austrian North Sea Division, and with the Prussians beat the Danes at Helgoland. Tegetthof defeated the Italians at Lissa and helped avenge the somewhat shattered Austrian honor after Sadowa. Under the Dual Monarchy he became *Marine-Ober-kommandant*.

3. Wealthy Viennese patroness of the arts.

Letter 75

1. Town southeast of Wienerstadt, in the province of Sopron in Upper Austria.

2. Seat of the Hohenlohe-Schillingsfürst family, southwest of Nürnberg, Bavaria.

3. Small town near Oedenburg and Eisenstadt in Hungary, and Liszt's birthplace. His father, Adam Liszt, moved there to be steward on the Esterhazy estates one year before Liszt's birth.

4. Edmund von Mihalovich (1842–1929), Hungarian composer and conductor. A piano pupil of Bülow, he succeeded Liszt as head of the Budapest *Landesmusikakademie* (1887). Mihalovitch became a *Geheimrat* in 1918.

5. The Vienna *Friends of Music* was founded in December 1812. From 1850 to 1890 it was conducted by Hellmesberger, Herbeck, Rubinstein, Brahms, and Richter. Allied to it were the *Conservatory* (founded 1817), and the *Singverein* (1858). Originally the concerts were held at the hall *Zum roten Igel*, and in 1870 the organization moved to the *Musikvereinsgebäude*.

6. Princess Raymondine von Auersperg, who joined the Dominicans after being Lady-in-Waiting to Archduchess Sophia von Hapsburg.

Letter 76

1. Carolyne. Volhynia (Wohlau) is probably the district in southwestern Russia, north of Podolia, bordering Galicia and Poland.

Letter 77

1. Liszt's letter to the Committee is not included, although it does not appear in any other collection of his correspondence. In it he declines their invitation. Of possible interest is the quotation of Lucretius, since this is one of the few citations in Latin that appears in his writing. "Et quasi cursores vitae lampada tradunt" ["And like runners they hand over the torch of life"]. *De Rerum Natura*, Book II, line 79.

Letter 78

1. Ferdinand von Saar (1833–1906), Austrian dramatist, poet, and playwright. His plays were either historical dramas or in the line of Scribe and the popular "well-made play." Saar's *Novellen* are worthy of more serious attention. In the collections *Novellen aus Oesterreich* (1897) and *Schicksale* (1889) he portrayed the problematic relations of the Austrian upper and middle classes; and in this sense, Saar is a forerunner of that artist of Viennese disintegration and decay, Artur Schnitzler.

There are several letters from Saar to Liszt in the La Mara collection. *Kaiser Heinrich IV*, "a German tragedy [*Trauerspiel*] in two parts" — *Hildebrand* and *Heinrichs Tod*, was written between 1862 and 1864 and published 1865–66. It was never staged, however, since censorship prohibited the appearance of a Pope in theatrical performances.

2. Georg II von Sachsen-Meiningen, who succeeded to the title in 1866. His main interest was the theater; and he appointed the young, imaginative Karl Grabowsky to succeed Bodenstedt in 1870. The reforms of the Meiningen Theater were in the direction of complete realism — even to the extent, in one play, of having a dead horse on the stage! Ludwig Chronegk, also a radical producer, was made *régisseur* in 1866. The Meiningen Players began their famous tours in 1874 (Berlin); their final performance was at Odessa (1890) after they had toured all the major European cities.

The Duke entered into a morganatic marriage with one of his actresses, Ellen Franz, and gave her the title of "Helene, Freifrau von Heldburg." She supervised productions, while the Duke himself did much of the scene-painting. Both Antoine of the French *Théâtre Libre* and Stanislavski of the Moscow Theater were strongly influenced by the work of the Meiningen group.

3. August, Freiherr von Loën (1828–1887), one-time Court Chamberlain to the Duke of Dessau and Intendant of the Weimar Theater after Dingelstedt left in 1867.

4. Gaspard Zumbusch (1830–1915), Austrian sculptor and professor at the Vienna *Kunst-Akademie* in 1873. Zumbusch did a portrait and several busts of Liszt.

5. Ludovic Breitner (1855–1925), pianist and pupil of Liszt and Rubinstein.

6. Countess von Dönhoff, wife of the First Secretary of the Prussian Embassy at Vienna. She later became Countess von Bülow, wife of the German Chancellor.

7. *Née* Amalie Weiss, a singer, who married Joachim.

8. Hans Richter (1843–1916), conductor of the Pest National Theater Orchestra, 1871–1875, and later of the Vienna Court Opera. Richter was one of the first conductors of Wagner's music dramas.

9. Robert Franz (1815–1892), German *Lieder* composer. He wrote approximately 350 compositions. Liszt wrote a short sketch of Franz's life (1872) and also transcribed twelve of his songs for piano (published in 1875). Among the lyrics set to music by Franz were Heine's *Lotusblume*, "Der Tod, das ist die kühle Nacht," "Leise zieht durch mein Gemüt," and *Der Runenstein*; Eichendorff's *Die Nachtigallen*; and Lenau's *Schilflied*.

Letter 80

1. The paragraph copied by Liszt may be found in La Mara, *Briefwechsel zwischen Liszt und Carl Alexander* (Leipzig: Breitkopf & Härtel, 1909), no. 130, pp. 153–154.

Letter 81

1. Unidentified.

2. Successor to Beust as *Hofmarschall* at the Weimar Court.

3. Unidentified.

4. Hungarian national airs, orchestrated by Liszt in 1872.

Letter 82

1. Hermann Riedel (1847–1913), *Lieder* composer, best known for his songs for Scheffel's *Trompeter von Säkkingen*. Riedel wrote one opera, *Der Ritterschlag*.

2. The author for these verses has not been found. They are not from Scheffel's *Trompeter von Säkkingen*.

3. Hungarian amateur singer.

4. Eduard von Liszt.

Letter 83

1. Unidentified.

2. Possibly a young man Wagner met while canoeing on the Danube in 1863. Cf. *Mein Leben*, II, 851.

3. Ismail (1830–1895), Khedive of Egypt (1863–1879). His extravagance was noted; and he and his brother Mustapha made frequent trips to Europe where they attempted to spend the immense wealth accrued from the mismanaged Egyptian finances.

4. Mother of the pianist Geza Zichy.

Letter 86

1. Small town east of Weimar, northeast of Jena. Goethe went there often: cf. *Eckermann* June 15, 1828; November 11, 1828; and March 9, 1831. The castle overlooked the Saale Valley and the mountains.

2. Goethe wrote this *Singspiel* (1774) at Frankfurt, along with *Claudine von Villa Bella*. He revised it in 1787 with the help of his musician-friend Kayser.

Actually the two versions are separate compositions. The first, called "Ein Singspiel" is in verse, has four characters, and is divided into two acts with scenes. The second, *Erwin und Elmire*, has the same number of persons, but two have different names. It is called "Ein Schauspiel mit Gesang," has no divisions into acts and scenes, and is a mixture of prose and verse. The later play contains the poem *Das Veilchen* set to music by Mozart:

"*Ein Veilchen auf der Wiese stand,*
Gebückt in sich und unbekannt."

3. Grand Duchess of Saxe-Weimar (1739–1801) and grandmother of the reigning Grand Duke. Two of her other plays were given at the Weimar Theater while Liszt was there: *Der Majorateserbe* (1857) and *Der Landwirt* (1861).

4. Josef Viktor von Scheffel (1826–1886), German poet and novelist who followed the legal and diplomatic professions. *Der Trompeter von Säkkingen*, written while the author lived at Capri, was immensely popular, and was later made into an opera by Viktor Nessel. Scheffel's humor suggests that of E. T. A. Hoffmann, whom he greatly admired. Scheffel represents the last phase of German Romanticism with his love of the medieval past, student-wanderings, and so forth. *Ekkehard* (1885) was a long novel incorporating all these elements. *Gaudeamus: Lieder*, was a collection of student songs gathered by him. There is also a correspondence published between Scheffel and Duke Carl Alexander.

Letter 87

1. Unidentified.

Letter 89

1. Edmond du Sommerard (1817–1885), French archaeologist who completed the work started by his father, Alexandre du Sommerard (1779–1842): *Les Arts du Moyen Âge*, and *Paris: Hotel de Cluny et Musée de Thermes* (1877). The younger Sommerard was also author of *Les Monuments historiques de France* (1876).

Letter 90

1. Graf Albert Apponyi (1845–1933), Hungarian statesman and leader of the Opposition in the Chamber from 1872 to 1899. At Versailles in 1920 Apponyi was one of the ardent defenders for Legitimist and national rights. He was a good friend of Liszt when the musician came to Budapest in the 1870's, and in Apponyi's memoirs there are excellent descriptions of musical evenings (cf. *Erlebnisse and Ergebnisse*, Berlin: Keil, 1933).

Liszt's patriotism and strong attachment for Hungary is evident in a letter to Apponyi written December 7, 1874 (*Erlebnisse*, p. 68): "A point of honor, which none understands better than do you, binds me to Hungary — our Fatherland." Apponyi's appraisal of the musician is fair: he felt that Liszt had weaknesses that were the temperamental failings of any virtuoso, but that essentially his character was warm and generous. "Envy and ungraciousness were unknown feelings for him" (p. 70). But despite a personal attachment for Liszt, Apponyi felt that Wagner was the greater musician.

2. Baron Leopold von Hofmann (1822–1885), Austrian Finance Minister 1875–1880. He later became Intendant of the Vienna Court Theater.

3. Franz Josef succeeded to the throne in 1848.

1. Unidentified.

2. Fifteen of Liszt's *Hungarian Rhapsodies*, most popular of his piano compositions, were first published from 1851 to 1854. He added four more, written 1879–80, in 1886. A twentieth *Rhapsody* is still in manuscript, unpublished, at the Liszt Weimar Museum.

3. Karl Goldmarck (1830–1915), Viennese composer, best known for his *Sakuntala Overture* (1865).

4. Opera by Carl Maria von Weber (1826). The text was by Planché, based on Wieland.

5. Beethoven's opera *Leonore*, begun in 1803, given in 1805, and later known as *Fidelio*. The three overtures were No. 2 (1805), No. 3 (1806), and No. 1 (1807).

6. Dingelstedt.

Letter 94

1. The name "Horpacs," here and in Letters 95, 96, and 97, is engraved on the letterhead.

2. Wife of Denis Szechenyi and sister-in-law to Count Imrey Szechenyi.

Letter 95

1. A volume published by La Mara in 1873: "a collection of remarks by distinguished musicians concerning their art."

2. Pseudonym for Ida Marie Lipsius (1837–1927), the musicologist who devoted most of her work to studies of Liszt and editions of his letters. She was made Royal Professor on her eightieth birthday, in recognition of her scholarship. Her books were written from 1862 to 1918. It seems particularly ironic that Liszt's first two references to this patient woman, who adored Liszt with a passion similar to that of Marie d'Agoult and Carolyne Wittgenstein (or with the scholar's equivalent) should both be misspelled!

3. La Mara's book, *Musikalische Studienköpfe* (1862–82).

4. Otto Ludwig (1813–1865), German novelist and dramatist. His early training was musical; he wrote a "Liederspiel," *Die Geschwister* (1837), and an opera, *Die Köhlerin* (1838). A stipend to study with Mendelssohn at Leipzig was used instead to pursue the novel and drama. Ludwig's play *Der Erbförster* (1850) made him famous, and it is one of the outstanding examples of early German dramatic realism. In theme it is similar to Hebbel's *Maria Magdalene* and Hauptmann's *Einsame Menschen*. His best-known novel was *Zwischen Himmel und Erde* (1855). He also left behind at his death a vast number of unpublished notes and sketches — notably the *Shakespeare Studien*.

Ludwig wrote three versions of *Die Makkabäer: Die Makkabäeren* (1850), *Die Mutter der Makkabäer* (1851); and *Die Makkabäer* (1852), produced in Vienna. Hans Sachs treated the same story — *Die Machabeer* — set to music by Handel (1776), as did Zacharias Werner in *Die Mutter der Makkabäerin*.

There is one letter from Ludwig to Liszt in the La Mara *Zeitgenossen* collection.

5. Jacques Offenbach (1819–1890), born Eberst, the leading nineteenth-century light-opera and operetta composer. Offenbach went to Paris from

Cologne in 1833. His first work was performed in 1853, and during the subsequent twenty-five years he wrote over ninety pieces for the French stage. These included such favorites as *La Belle Hélène*, *La Fille du Tambour-majeur* (1874), *Orphée aux Enfers* (1858), and *Les Contes d'Hoffmann* (post., 1884).

6. Pressburg or Bratislava, then in Hungary, now a Czech city due east of Vienna in the Carpathians.

7. Probably the wife of Imre Szechenyi.

8. Joseph Sucher (1843–1908), conductor at the Leipzig *Stadttheater* in 1878, *Hofkapellmeister* at Berlin in 1888. Both he and his wife (*née* Rosa Haslbeck) were known for their Wagnerian roles, she particularly at Bayreuth for her portrayals of *Isolde* and *Sieglinde*.

Letter 96

1. Richard Metzdorff (1844–1919), piano teacher, conductor, and composer, whose opera *Rosamunde* was given at Weimar in 1875.

2. Marie Moukhanoff — Kalergis (1822–1874), *née* Countess Nesselrode. She was a great friend of both Wagner and Liszt.

Letter 97

1. Ludwig von Haynald (1816–1891), professor of theology at the Gran Seminary and later Archbishop of Kalosca (1867) and Cardinal (1879). He was also an amateur biologist.

2. Town south of Budapest, west of Szeged.

3. Oedenburg (Sopron), city in Hungary south of Vienna and west of Budapest.

4. Gottfried Semper (1803–1879), architect. Semper restored the *Hofburg* at Vienna, and other Imperial buildings.

5. Hans Makart (1840–1884), Austrian painter whose *forte* was historical subjects, portraits, and allegories. Makart was a pupil of Rubens at the Vienna Academy and later of Piloty at Munich. In 1879 he was appointed professor at Vienna. Focillon says of him: "Never did anyone make so much fuss about being a master, and never was anyone so far from being one" (*La peinture au XIXᵉ siècle*, II, 119).

Letter 98

1. One of the four Hungarian dishes made with paprika, along with *pörkölt*, *tokány*, and *paprikás*.

2. Karl-Wilhelm Naundorff (d. 1845), one of the most famous and persistent of nineteenth-century royal imposters. A wooden clockmaker of Polish-Prussian extraction, Naundorff announced with much fanfare, at Luxemburg in 1830, that he was "Louis-Charles de Bourbon, Duc de Normandie" — or Louis XVII, the unfortunate Dauphin. He came to Paris in 1833, and for a short while enjoyed the favor of some Legitimists until his fraud was exposed.

3. Jules Favre (1809–1880), French lawyer and Deputy who became Minister of Foreign Affairs on September 4, 1870, after the collapse of the Second Empire. He met Bismarck (September 15) at Ferrières to attempt to mitigate the harsh peace imposed by the Prussian Chancellor; and Liszt's remark refers to Favre's lack of success. He saw Bismarck again on January

22, 1871, at Versailles to negotiate the final peace settlement. Under the Ministry of February 17 Favre was again made Minister of Foreign Affairs; and during the insurrection of the Commune he gave strong support to Thiers' suppressive measures.

4. The Comte de Chambord, Duc de Bordeaux and grandson of Charles, was the Legitimist pretender to the French throne after the fall of Napoleon III. His stubborn refusal to accept the tricolor jeopardized Monarchist chances in 1871, when success might have been possible. In November 1873 the Austrian diplomat Frohsdorff, acting as intermediary, suggested to Marshal MacMahon that he play Ney to Chambord's Napoleon-landing-at-Elba. When the upright Marshal refused to accept this dubious political role and declined even to see the Count, the plan failed. Chambord left France to complete his forty years of exile.

5. Graf Waldstein, director of the Vienna Art Association and descendant of Beethoven's friend and patron.

Letter 99

1. Cf. La Fontaine, *Fables:* "Le Coq et la Perle" (No. XX).
2. Allusion to Nohl's book, *Beethoven, Liszt und Wagner.*
3. Winterberger.
4. Cf. Beaumarchais, *Le Mariage de Figaro*, Scenes 6 and 14. Don Guzman Brid'oison, "le juge ordinaire, le lieutenant du siège," whose name is synonymous with pomposity, says frequently: "La forme, voyez-vous, la forme. . . La forme, la-a forme!"
5. Wife of the Chamberlain at the Austrian court, cousin to Frederika Auersperg.

Letter 100

1. Ober- and Unter-Hacking, two small suburbs of Munich.

Letter 101

1. Unidentified. She may have been related to Heinrich Lutter (1858–1887), student of Liszt and Bülow and later accompanist to Joachim.
2. Unidentified.
3. Marling is a small village in the Austrian Tyrol and the Sarntaler Alpen, south of Innsbruck and southwest of Salzburg.

Letter 104

1. Unidentified.
2. Hugo's novel, *Quatre-vingt-treize*, written 1872–73 when the excesses of the Commune were still fresh in Hugo's mind. It was his last novel: its thesis, if it may be said to have one, is the triumph of Revolution over institutionalized religion. Published in 1874, it was received with only mild enthusiasm; and the later dramatized version of '93 by Paul Meurice enjoyed no better success.
3. Journal begun by Leopold Voss (1793–1868), Leipzig publisher who printed many of Wagner's compositions.

Letter 105

1. Hans Lothar von Schweinitz (1822–1901), German ambassador at St. Petersburg, 1876–1893. He was instrumental in carrying out Bismarck's

policy of keeping Russia neutral during the diplomatic intrigues of the 1880's. Schweinitz engineered the Russo-German treaty of 1881 and the so-called "Reïnsurance Treaty" of 1887 — the latter when relations between the two countries were threatened by new Franco-Russian amity.

2. This quotation has not been located in Hugo's '93.

3. Literally, "baboon street," residence of Carolyne in Rome. The avenue is south of the Monte Pincio, running between Piazza di Spagna and Piazza del Populo.

4. The St. Petersburg decree depriving Carolyne of civil rights as a Russian citizen.

5. Evidently Nicolas I (ruled 1825–1855) was not to blame, and the fault lay with Alexander (ruled 1855–1881).

6. According to Ramann (*Franz Liszt als Künstler und Mensch*, I, 25–26), Liszt gave his first concert at the age of nine, in the home of Baron von Braun at Oedenburg.

7. Gustav Steinacker, Hungarian pastor who also composed several *Festspiele* under the pseudonym of "Treumund."

Letter 106

1. Member of one of the oldest Roman princely houses; not to be confused with Felice Orsini (1819–1858), attempted assassin of Napoleon III and agent of Mazzini.

2. August Klughardt (1847–1902), composer, conductor, and director of the Weimar Orchestra for a four-year term in the 1880's.

Letter 107

1. Jessy Laussot-Taylor (1827–1905), writer and music critic who sought to spread German music in Italian artistic circles.

2. Probably a kind of Tokay.

Letter 108

1. Liszt's unfinished oratorio, begun 1874.

2. Carolyne.

3. Ella Adaiewsky (1846–1926); Russian pianist and pupil of Henselt and Rubinstein.

4. Michael Ivanovitch Glinka (1803–1857), Russian composer and chief representative of the Russian nationalistic school in the nineteenth century. Glinka's *Life for the Tzar* (1836), his first opera, was an immediate and patriotic success; and in 1842 he produced *Russlan and Ludmilla*, based on a Pushkin story. He was a friend of such Western composers as Donizetti, Bellini, and Rossini (the latter musician had a particularly strong influence); and late in his career he started, but did not finish, a symphonic poem inspired by Gogol's *Taras Bulba*. Several compositions based on Spanish thematic material attest to his enjoyment of a trip to Spain. There is one letter to Liszt from Glinka in the La Mara collection (No. 161), dated June 19, 1852.

5. Verdi's *Requiem Mass* for the death of the Italian writer Manzoni was completed and performed in 1874. Verdi's operatic music had great appeal for Liszt: there are at least ten piano transcriptions of Verdi arias, and so forth, made by Liszt. Verdi's *Hernani*, based on Hugo's Romantic drama, was performed at Weimar during the 1860–61 season.

Letter 109

1. "With expectation I have awaited upon the Lord, and He was attentive to me" (Psalm XXXIX, Douay Version). This device was one of Liszt's favorites. He mentions the line several times in this correspondence; and in a letter to Carolyne on February 28, 1848 (*L.M. I*, No. 18), he said that he had the words engraved on a locket given to Mme. d'Artigaux in 1828.

2. Monte Pincio, northernmost hill in Rome; site of the villas of Lucullus and Sallust.

3. Schönbrunn, the Imperial Palace outside Vienna.

Letter 110

1. Part II of Longfellow's *Christus: A Mystery* (1851) is entitled *The Golden Legend;* and the third portion of the *Legend* takes place in Strassburg. The poem is written mainly in rhymed iambic tetrameter, although there are a large number of the dactylic lines that Longfellow loved so well:

"*Still is the night. The sound of feet*
Has died away from the empty street . . ."

Cf. *Christus* (Boston: Houghton Mifflin, 1886), p. 89.

2. Liszt's *Glocken des Strasburgen Münsters* (1874) for chorus and orchestra.

3. Frédéric-François-Xavier de Mérode (1820–1874), who started his career as an officer in the Belgian army and later took orders in the Church. Mérode became Vatican Privy-Councillor and confessor to Pius IX. The summit of his ecclesiastical career was reached when he was appointed Archbishop of Mélitène just before his death. Mérode also acted as military adviser to Pius IX during the 1860's and 1870's.

4. Eugène, Prince de Savoye-Carignan (1816–1888), leading member of the cadet branch of the House of Savoy, who was chosen Regent for Central Italy (1859) but who made *il gran refiuto*. He was at one time Admiral, and later Count, of Villafranca.

5. Mme. de Montalambert was wife of Charles de Montalambert (1810–1870), French writer and Catholic apologist, head of the Catholic Party in the Chamber of Deputies in 1844. His book *La Vie de Sainte Elizabeth de Hongrie* (Paris, 1936) was one of the sources of Liszt's inspiration for the oratorio, *St. Elizabeth.*

Letter 112

1. Town west of Rome on the Aniene. Cardinal Hohenlohe's estate was at Tivoli.

2. Carolyne's servants at the Babuino Street house in Rome.

Letter 113

1. Adelheid von Schorn (1841–1916), daughter of the art historian Ludwig von Schorn (1793–1842) and Henrietta von Schorn (1807–1869), Lady-in-Waiting to Grand Duchess Maria Pavlovna in 1832. One of Liszt's many female admirers, Adelheid von Schorn was authoress of two of the books used extensively as references in this correspondence: *Das nachklassische Weimar* (1911–12) and *Zwei Menschenalter* (1920). It is she whom Liszt describes as "The duenna — the housewife — sort of a white raven — who is so impatiently requested" in Letter 110. She acted as director of the Wittgenstein household in Rome. Moreover, letters to and from Carolyne indicate that Adelheid's function was to act as spy on Liszt's Weimar activities, since the Abbé, despite advancing age and clerical garb, was still not insensitive to the young women who idolized him. The correspondence of Adelheid von Schorn and Carolyne was published in 1904 (Paris: Dujarric).

2. Unidentified, but evidently the owner of a *pension* in Rome.

3. Piazza di Spagna on the east side of the Tiber, northeast of the Quirinal and east of the Vatican in Rome.

4. Felix-Otto Dessoff (1835–1892), piano pupil of Moscheles at the Leipzig Conservatory and conductor of the Viennese Court-Opera from 1860 to 1875.

5. Joseph Weil, Ritter von Weilen (1828–1889), minor Austrian poet and novelist. He taught history at Graz University and later became professor at the Vienna General Staff School, where his specialty was military history and theory.

Letter 114

1. Liszt's fourth *Étude d'Exécution Transcendante* (published 1854); also the Sixth Symphonic Poem which is virtually a transcription of the earlier piano piece, with a Tartar March added as coda.

The real Mazeppa was Ivan Stepanovitch Mazepa-Koledinsky (1644?–1709), Hetman of the Don Cossacks and educated at the Polish court of John Casimir. Mazeppa later fought for Peter the Great in the Azov campaigns, and subsequently allied himself treasonably with Charles XII of Sweden. When the Swedes were defeated at Poltava, Mazeppa went to Turkey. The Cossack adventurer had great appeal for Romantic artists. The legend of his being tied to a horse when a page by the irate husband of an unfaithful wife caught the attention of both Byron (*Mazeppa*: " 'Twas after dread Pultowa's day" — 1813) and Hugo (*Mazeppa*, in *Les Orientales*: "Ainsi, quand Mazeppa, qui rugit et qui pleure . . ." — 1828). If Byron is any index, the Romantics found their original source in Voltaire's *Histoire de Charles XII* (1731). Cf. also Vogüé, author of a curious book, *Mazeppa: Le Fils de Pierre le Grand*.

2. Giovanni Sgambati (1843–1914), Italian composer and conductor who made his debut in 1866 at Rome with Liszt's *Dante Symphony*. He was both disciple and friend of Liszt, and he also introduced the music of Brahms and Schumann into Italy. Mrs. Winthrop Chanler discusses Sgambati, with whom she studied, in *Roman Spring* (Boston, 1925) and *Memory Makes Music* (1948), where his fine ability as pianist and conductor, as well as his fear of fame and his inordinate shyness, is stressed.

3. Church in Rome, north of the Vatican and on the opposite side of the Tiber.

4. Bretschneider, a Roman piano-merchant.

5. Ollivier (1825–1913), French statesman and husband of Liszt's daughter Blandine. He was appointed Prime Minister in 1869 by Napoleon III. The events of 1870 forced Ollivier, a moderate Liberal, unwillingly into action against Prussia; and he lost his office after the initial French defeats at Wörth, Spicheren, and Reichshoffen. He became Minister of Justice under the Republic.

6. Robert von Keudell (1824–1903), German ambassador to Rome and an amateur pianist.

7. Probably Robert Jauner, director of the Vienna Court Opera in 1875.

Letter 115

1. Botho von Hülsen (1815–1886), Intendant of the Court Theater at Berlin.

2. It is difficult to ascertain who this "candidate" was. Liszt's remark is indicative, however, of the complex relations of the Dual Monarchy with the Vatican.

Letter 116

1. The concert took place at St. Gall (a small town in the Swiss Alps east of Zürich and south of the Bodensee) on November 23, 1856. Liszt and the young Wittgensteins were visiting the exiled Wagner at Zürich. The director of the St. Gall Orchestra, Henri Sczadrowsky, ventured to ask these two lions to participate in a concert with his small group, and to his surprise they accepted. The program was Beethoven's Symphony No. 3 and Liszt's Orpheus and Les Préludes. Sczadrowsky had wanted the pianist to play a concerto; but Liszt stuck to his determination not to be the virtuoso and declined to play. He conducted his own works as well as two short excerpts from Gluck's Armide and Iphigénie en Aulide.

During the stay at St. Gall, Wagner apparently found the idiosyncrasies of Carolyne trying — particularly after she woke him one night by shouting in the next room! Cf. Robert Bory, "Un Concert mémorable à St. Gall," Formes et Couleurs (Lausanne: No. 1, 1943).

2. Cardinal Hohenlohe's maître-domo.

3. Rauden, a city near Breslau in Lower Silesia.

4. Die heilige Cecilia, Liszt's oratorio published 1876 for mezzo-soprano, chorus, and orchestra.

5. Delphine de Girardin (1804–1855) née Gay, wife of Émile de Girardin (1806–1881), French newspaper-editor and founder of La Presse (1836). She was authoress of several plays and novels and also the Hymne à Sainte Généviève (1825). Her husband was descended from Rousseau's last patron.

6. Probably Via dei Greci, a street in Rome running from the Corso Umberto to the Via del Babuino, not far from Princess Carolyne's apartment.

7. Wife (née Beccadelli) of Marco Minghetti (1804–1855), Italian statesman twice Minister (1862–1864 and 1873–1876). A Conservative, he supported Cavour's notion of a "free Church in a free State"; and Minghetti's plan (1861) to divide Italy into six districts might have avoided the centralism believed by many political theorists to have been the essential fallacy of the Italian government in the nineteenth century.

Minghetti had been a student of Sismondi in his youth. He also was a great admirer of German culture and the Bismarckian state. Sitwell mentions "Minghetti" in another context. Carolyne was an inveterate cigar smoker; and as time went on, her tastes were less easily satisfied, and she sought for still stronger brands. "Eventually through political influence, she had special cigars manufactured for her by the Roman tobacco monopoly. They were of the Minghetti type — still familiar to Italian travellers — but of special length and double strength, dipped in iron filings, so it was said, to impart a special metallic tang to their flavour" (Sitwell, *Liszt*, pp. 265-266).

Letter 117

1. Wagner.

Letter 119

1. Marie's personal servant.

Letter 121

1. Royal residence of Wilhelm III (1817-1890) of Holland. In the La Mara collection (III, 191-192) there is a letter from the King to Liszt, May 23, 1875, thanking the musician in enthusiastic, affectionate terms for his visit to Loo, and promising to send "a cask of that Amsterdam beer which seemed to please you so much."

Letter 122

1. Mother of Albert Apponyi.

2. The Hohenlohes had just bought property in Styria, the Austrian district that includes Graz and is bordered by the Eastern Alps.

3. Part of the Compline Service, and originally the last prayer said by the Benedictine monks before retiring.

4. Adolph von Donndorf (1835-1910), Weimar sculptor and student of Rietschel at Dresden. Donndorf made a bust of Duke Carl Alexander (1860) and Carl August (1872).

Letter 123

1. Oskar II (1829-1905), who was also an amateur poet and published a volume of verse in 1857.

2. Wife of Carl I (reigned 1864-1891) and daughter of Czar Nicolas I of Russia.

3. This quotation has not been found in Napoleon's *Maximes*.

4. The closest statement to this alleged remark of Frederick the Great appears in E. Schröder, *Vom Alten Fritz* (Leipzig: Wigend, 1876) p. 58: "It is quite true that virtue possesses pleasures capable of making Beautiful Souls [Schöne Seelen] love her of herself; but let us not allow this to have us condemn that good which has us cast a backward glance at fame — for this good also is a compelling element for virtue."

5. Home of Mme. Lauchert, Princess Marie's sister-in-law.

Letter 124

1. Marie's four children.

2. A large rococo building in the Weimar Park, east of the Liszt Museum and north of the Liszt Monument.

3. Wife of Karl Maria, Graf von Coudenhoven, and daughter of Kalergis and his first wife, Mme. Moukhanoff.

Letter 125

1. Sankt Wolfgang, summer resort in Upper Austria.

2. There is no evidence that Adelheid von Schorn ever published this novel.

3. Wilhelm I (1797–1888) and Empress Augusta (1811–1890) of Germany.

4. Alfonso XII, who came to the Spanish throne in December 1874 (six months before this letter was written), after the short-lived republic of 1873. He died in 1885.

5. Otto Bach (1833–1893), pianist and composer, appointed director of the Salzburg *Mozarteum* (1869). He wrote six operas, among them *Lenore* (1874).

Letter 126

1. Liszt.

2. The wall of fire Wotan establishes around Brünnhilde. Cf. *Die Walküre*, Act III.

3. This remark has not been located in any of Pascal's writings.

4. Gräfin Schleinitz (1842–1912), who remarried in 1886 and became Gräfin von Wolkenstein.

5. Town in the Swiss Alps, south of Liechtenstein and east of Lucerne.

6. Edouard Schuré (1841–1921), Strassburg musicologist who attempted to spread the new German music among French musical circles. *Le Drame musical* appeared in 1871, and the second part of the book dealt with Wagner's contribution to contemporary music. Schuré also wrote *Précurseurs et Révoltés* (1904) and *Erinnerungen an Richard Wagner* (1900).

7. Wagner's opera, completed in 1840 and first performed at Dresden in 1842. It was based on Bulwer-Lytton's *Rienzi: The Last of the Roman Tribunes* (1835), and the German text was by Bärmann.

Letter 127

1. Mme. de Staël's preference is mentioned by Sainte-Beuve in *Portraits de Femmes*, "Mme. de Staël" (Paris: Garnier, 1876), p. 143. Before her exile, she had lived on the Rue de Grenelle-Saint-Germain near the Rue de Bac in Paris. " 'Oh, the gutter of the Rue de Bac!' she cried when she was shown the mirror-like Lake Leman."

2. Unidentified.

3. On the Gulf of Trieste, north of the city. The castle belonged to the Von Thurn und Taxis-Hohenlohe family. It was there that Marie von Thurn und Taxis invited the poet Rainer Maria Rilke, who was subsequently inspired to write his ten *Duiniser Elegien*, from 1912 to 1922.

Letter 130

1. Alexander von Hohenlohe-Waldenburg-Schillingsfürst (1794–1849), Bishop of Groswardein in 1844. He enjoyed the reputation of being a mystic and faith-healer.

2. Aquila and his wife Priscilla were Jews from Pontus, later converted with Paul to Christianity. Aquila later became Bishop of Heraclea.

Letter 131

1. This verse has not been located.

2. Alfred Grünfeld (1852–1924), Prague pianist, composer, and writer of several operettas.

Letter 132

1. The Wagners.
2. Allusion to Dingelstedt's recent acquisition of the particule before his name.
3. It is difficult to untangle this complicated avian reference. The Phoenix was the mythical red and gold, eagle-like bird, sacred to the Egyptian sun-god, which dwelled in Arabia and had a life span of five hundred years. It then burned to arise from its own ashes. To relate the Phoenix to the humble swan is a feat of Liszt's own literary imagination.

Letter 133

1. Karl Onken (b. 1846), minor Viennese landscape-painter and etcher.

Letter 134

1. The Seville Cathedral was begun in 1402 and is the largest Gothic church in the world: 460 feet long, 295 feet wide, and with a nave 132 feet high. "A cathedral rose above the tiled roofs of Seville on such a vast scale that the canons boasted succeeding generations would think them mad, and as is unusual in such boasts . . . the cathedral was actually completed." Cf. Bernard Bevan, *History of Spanish Architecture* (London: Batsford, 1938), p. 128.

Letter 135

1. *Née* Amalia Adelheid von Hohenlohe-Schillingsfürst, wife of a German painter (1825–1868).
2. In Saxe-Weimar, near the city of Weimar.
3. Prince Otto von Wittgenstein.
4. Elder cousin of Franz Josef and the Emperor's military adviser — along with Belcredi, Crenneville, and Franck — on the eve of the Austro-Prussian War in 1866.
5. The words uttered at the moment of the Elevation of the Host during the Mass. This is also the title of Liszt's seventh piece in the *Années de Pélérinage, 3e année*, published in 1890.

Letter 136

1. Szegszard is the Hungarian spelling for *Sexard*, a small town in southern Hungary.
2. Eduard Schönfeld (1839–1885), Düsseldorf painter; or Heinrich Schönfeld (1809–1845), portrait painter. There is no record of a painter named Schönfeld from Vienna.
3. Mme. Lindemann-Frommel, wife of the German painter Karl Lindemann-Frommel (1819–1893) living in Rome. Mrs. Chanler (*Roman Spring*) mentions that Liszt knew them when he visited Rome between 1847 and 1855.

Letter 137

1. Keudell.
2. Probably Beethoven's Concerto No. 5 in E Flat (the "Emperor").

1. Carolyne's street in Rome.
2. The Duchesse du Maine (1676–1753), a *grande-dame* of the early eighteenth century. Her salon was famous for its collection of wits and *précieux.* Cf. Sainte-Beuve, *Causeries du Lundi* and *Portraits Littéraires.*
3. Unidentified.
4. Literally, "to extend or project one's self into the future." The verb was a coinage by Dante. Cf. *Divina Commedia,* "Paradiso," Canto XVII, lines 97–99.
5. Gasparo Spontini (1774–1851), made Conti di Sant' Andrea in 1844, prolific and popular opera composer in the tradition of Auber, Méhul, and Grétry. Spontini's first success was *La Vestale* (1807). He was a musical favorite of the Empress Josephine and court composer for Louis XVIII. Cf. Wagner's essay about Spontini, in *Werke,* Vol. V.
6. Possibly Max Wirth (1822–1900), folklorist and historian, or Carl Friedrich Wirth, who was at one time Weimar Minister for Internal Affairs.

Letter 140

1. Cf. Letter 28, Note 14 and Letter 22, Note 21. George Sand met Liszt during the winter of 1835–36 at her home on the Quai Malaquais in Paris, where Liszt brought Lamennais so that the three might discuss plans for *Le Monde.* She went to Geneva in 1836 and stayed with Liszt and Marie d'Agoult.

The *Correspondance* (1812–1876) of George Sand contains fifteen letters to Marie d'Agoult and five to Liszt. These are fascinating documents. Her first letter to Liszt (May 5, 1836) mentions her new antipathy toward Sainte-Beuve and fondness for Lamartine, with whom she enjoyed smoking. (She shared an affection for strong cigars with another "emancipated" female, Carolyne Wittgenstein.) The remaining letters discuss Parisian gossip; and in one letter, George Sand points with curious pride to the popular belief in society circles that it was she and not Marie d'Agoult with whom the composer was living at Geneva. The final notes have a recriminatory tone: the lovers were brought together at her house, and now they do not even bother to write to her.

George Sand's letters to Countess d'Agoult are more revealing of her tempestuous nature. The opening letter (May 1835) states her desire to meet "my lovely countess with beautiful blonde hair"; the second (November 1, 1835) contains the following astounding pronouncement: "You must quickly reconcile yourself to the fact that I love you. This should be very simple. First, I am in love with Franz. He has told me to love you. He answers for you as well as for himself." Marie offered to give George Sand financial aid, and the latter accepted (in her letter of February 26, 1836) with these exalted sentiments: you are rich, you recognize your duty to the needy artist, and if your affection for me cannot possibly equal mine for you, I am at least gracious enough to accept this testimony of homage! "I love you tenderly, although you are capable of poisoning me. Fortunately I am not afraid of Monsieur Franz; and if he had such an idea, I would kill him with a snap of my fingers [*d'une chiquenade*]."

Their mutual endeavor as editors of *Le Monde* has already been described. Sand pictured them all as soldiers fighting for their commander-in-chief,

Lamennais, in the great battle for humanity. Her last letters to Liszt, like those to Marie d'Agoult, show her to be querulous and hurt since he had left her letters unanswered.

2. Georges-Louis Leclerc, seigneur de Buffon (1707–1788), French botanist and naturalist. Buffon's chief contribution was the large and comprehensive *Histoire naturelle* (published 1748–89).

3. Liszt refers to a letter found *in toto* in *L.M.* IV, No. 170; hence it is not reproduced here.

Letter 141

1. Friedrich Wilhelm, Fürst von Hohenzollern-Hechingen (d. 1869).

2. Younger son of an old Polish family who were among Liszt's early patrons.

3. Léonille zu Sayn-Wittgenstein (1825–1907), a distant cousin-by-marriage of Carolyne. Her *Souvenirs* (Paris, 1903) mention neither Liszt nor Carolyne, although she probably met the musician when she lived in Berlin, 1830–1848.

4. This may be Graf Zalewski-Kasimierz (1849–1919), newspaper editor, author of comedies, and Polish translator of Molière.

Letter 143

1. Gugliemo Audisio, minor Roman critic and author of pamphlets dealing with the relations of Church and State: *Della società politica e religiosa, etc.* (1876) and *Storia religiosa e civile dei papi* (1864–68).

2. Carolyne's massive work on the Church.

3. The Oecumenical Council (1869), which put forth the Doctrine of Papal Infallibility in 1870. (Cf. Letter 45, Note 9.)

4. Cf. Molière, *Les Fourberies de Scapin,* Act II, Scene 11. Scapin informs the miser Géronte that the latter's son has been abducted by Turkish pirates. Géronte repeats the line "Que diable allait-il faire dans cette galère?" six times, and declines to pay the necessary ransom.

Letter 144

1. Dr. Josef Standhartner, Viennese doctor, musical amateur, and friend of Wagner and Liszt.

2. One of the fifty-three Schubert songs transcribed for piano by Liszt, published in a set in 1838.

Letter 145

1. Ignaz Brüll (1846–1907), Austrian pianist and composer. Brüll wrote several light operas, among them *Das goldene Kreuz* (1875), *Der Landfriede* (1877), and *Bianca* (1879).

2. Leo Délibes' (1836–1891) most famous ballet, written and first performed in 1870.

3. Liszt means here the two parts of Goethe's work.

Letter 146

1. Bad Reichenhall, in the Austrian Tyrol west of Salzburg.

1. Probably another nickname for Carolyne.
2. Liszt's Montenegrin valet, who was with the musician from 1876 to 1886.
3. Carolyne.
4. The Bayreuth *Festspielhaus* was already a year old when this letter was written, and the circle of Wagnerites was growing. Wagner first conceived the notion of a huge theater designed specially for performances of his music dramas in 1850. The plan took gradual shape in his mind; and in 1867 he wrote a series of fifteen letters, printed in the Munich papers, to Ludwig II, informing that erratic monarch of his sacred duties to German music and drama. The fifteenth letter sketched the idea for the *Festspielhaus*. Wagner was customarily vague about the financial details; but the artistic aim was simple: to provide an adequate setting for the *Ring*. Ludwig agreed to undertake the subsidies in 1871, after Wagner had hinted he would take his plan to Prussia unless positive measures were forthcoming. In May 1873, the cornerstone was laid. Despite difficulties which included a temperamental cast, Ludwig's meddling, and the complexities in constructing the dragon *Fafnir*, the theater opened in August 1876. It was designed by the Leipzig architect Brüchwald, and both Wagner and Semper contributed many of the plans. Richter conducted in 1876; Wagner directed the productions until his death in 1883; Cosima took over the management from 1886 to 1906, when she was relieved by her son Siegfried.
5. Unidentified.

1. February 18.
2. Eduard von Liszt.

1. Probably Napoleon III's widow.
2. Leo XIII (Joachim Vincent Pecci, 1810–1903) succeeded Pius IX as Pope in 1878. His most successful political effort was to ameliorate the strained relations between the Vatican and Italy, France, and Germany. Leo XIII's most famous encyclical was that of 1878 concerning the Church's stand on Socialism.
3. Remark made by Voltaire (at a rehearsal of his tragedy *Mérope*) directed at the actress Mlle. Dumesnil:
[Mlle. Dumesnil:] " 'I'd have to have the devil in me [*le diable au corps*] to get at the tone you'd like me to produce.'
[Voltaire:] 'Ah, right you are, Mlle. Dumesnil . . . you have to have the devil within you to excel in all the arts.' "
4. *Née* Marie Bischof (1842–1920), singer at the Berlin Opera. She sang at Bayreuth in 1882.
5. Gheza Zichy (1849–1924), pianist, composer, poet, and pupil of Liszt. He lost his right arm when young, and attained remarkable virtuosity with his left hand. He was Intendant of the Budapest *National Theater* from 1891 to 1894. Among his operas was a *Rakoczy* trilogy based on patriotic Hungarian themes (1905–12). His autobiography, *Aus meinem Leben*, was published in 1911.

6. Gustav Walter (1834–1910), Austrian tenor.
7. Felix Mottl (1856–1911), Viennese singer and conductor. His opera, *Agnes Bernauer* (cf. note on Hebbel; Letter 57, Note 14) was given at Weimar in 1880. Mottl directed the Bayreuth *Festspielhaus* for one year (1886).

Letter 150

1. Prince Rudolph von Lichtenstein, amateur musician.
2. Victor Emmanuel (1820–1878).
3. Archduke Franz-Karl, father of Franz Josef, who renounced the succession to the Austrian throne in 1848.
4. Remmert (b. 1854), Berlin pianist and pupil of Liszt. She founded a Berlin *Liszt-Akademie* in 1905.
5. The Grand Duchess of Saxe-Weimar.
6. Cf. Letter 30, Note 16.

Letter 153

1. Wagner's music drama, completed 1882 and first performed July 1882, at Bayreuth.
2. The Grand Duchess.
3. Oskar II (cf. Letter 123, Note 1).
4. Unidentified.
5. Christina Nilsson (1843–1921), Swedish singer who made her debut in Paris in 1864.
6. Amelia Materna (1845–1918), *prima donna* of the Vienna Opera. She was the first Brünnhilde in Wagner's *Ring*, and she also sang the role of Kundry in *Parsifal*.
7. Ortrud is in *Lohengrin*, Elizabeth in *Tannhäuser*; Armide is in Gluck's *Armide*. Rossini also wrote an *Armida* (1817) with a libretto by G. Schmidt.
8. The three-act opera *Samson et Dalila* by Saint-Saëns (1835–1921) was given at Weimar in 1877, the same year it was published. The text was by F. Lemaire. It was not performed in France until 1890, at Rouen.
   Brilliant pianist and talented orchestrator, Saint-Saëns as composer is an example of the late nineteenth-century eclectic school of musicians in France. The influence of Liszt on his writings is unmistakable. He made revealing remarks about Liszt in *Portraits et Souvenirs* (Paris: Lévy, pp. 22 ff.). The impact of Liszt on nineteenth-century music he saw as similar to that of Hugo on verse: both were Titans in an age of pygmies, and they presented the age with an unequaled sense of the grandiose and magnificent. Saint-Saëns censured the Wagnerites for their lack of appreciation of Wagner's debt to Liszt. His final assertion of Liszt's superiority over Wagner was based on religious rather than aesthetic grounds, since Liszt was a Christian and a Catholic — and Wagner was not. This emphasis on Liszt's religiosity occurs also in *École Buissonière* (Paris, 1909). One other judgment of the French musician is worth mentioning. Liszt for him was the incarnation of the Magyar spirit, and hence free from the debilitating gentility that marked his contemporaries. "He never looked like a *gentleman who was playing at the piano.*" (*Portraits*, p. 42.)
9. *Étienne Henri Méhul* (1763–1817), French operatic composer. Gluck encouraged him to write operas, and Méhul's first success was *Cora et Alonso*

(1791). He wrote twenty-four operas in seventeen years, and among these was *Joseph* (1807). He also composed a Mass for Napoleon I's coronation, but it was never sung.

10. Rossini's *Mosè in Egitto* was written in 1818. An opera, it was also performed as an oratorio. The *trio* "Mi manca la voce," mentioned by Liszt a few lines further on in his letter, is listed by Clément-Larousse as a quartet.

11. Giovanni Rubini (1795–1854), Italian tenor who enjoyed a phenomenal success at the Paris *Opéra* in 1825–26. He went with Liszt to Berlin in 1843. He retired in Italy as a millionaire in 1845, after extensive and profitable concert tours on the Continent.

12. Antonio Tamburini (1800–1876), Italian baritone who, like Rubini, was managed by the brilliant *impresario* Barbaja.

13. August Tréfort (1817–1888), Hungarian writer and politician and author of agricultural studies concerning Central Europe. He was Minister of Agriculture in 1848, and Minister of Education under the Dual Monarchy in 1872.

14. Anton Jules Szapary (1802–1883), Hungarian Minister of Finance at this date. His family possessed the elegant title of "Szapary von Muraszombat, Szechysziget, und Szapar."

15. The Paris Exposition of 1878 lasted from May 1 to November 20. It took place on the *Champ de Mars*, and a huge palace was erected at the *Trocadero.* Thirty-six nations were represented; Prussia, understandably enough, was the sole exception among the major powers. The "Jury" of which Liszt speaks included eight hundred members. Half of these were French. The others, like Liszt, were prominent foreigners.

Letter 154

1. Either Heinrich von Reuss-Köstnitz (1855–1910), who wrote one symphony and a quartet, or possibly Heinrich VII von Reuss (1825–1906).

2. A reference to the meeting of Napoleon I and Alexander of Russia at Erfurt on September 27, 1808. Goethe was present, who occasioned Napoleon's remark, "Here is a man!" Talma also performed before this audience of kings [*"parterre des rois"*].

Letter 155

1. Philip von Hohenlohe-Schillingsfürst, attached to the German Embassy at Paris.

2. Schumann's cycle of songs for male voice, the *Dichterliebe* (Op. 48), based on seventeen poems from Heine's *Lyrisches Intermezzo.* Liszt transcribed four of Schumann's songs for piano: *Widmung* (1849), *An den Sonnenschein* (1860), *Frühlingsnacht* (1872), and *Provinzialisches Minnelied* (1881).

3. Princess de Caraman et Chimay, wife of the Belgian Minister Plenipotentiary to Paris and Rome. As one of Napoleon III's last loves, she enjoyed the privilege of that monarch's frequent visits via a subterranean passage between her house and the *Élysée Palace.*

4. The title of "Comte de Flandres" had disappeared in the eighteenth century, and was revived by the King of Belgium in 1840 for his second oldest son, Philippe.

345

5. Marshal MacMahon, president of the Third Republic, 1872–1879, succeeded by Grévy. As a Catholic, a Conservative, and a simple military man, he had little real affection for the new state; but he fulfilled his task with loyalty and honesty. (Cf. Letter 98, Note 4.) The remark, "We have no right to be here," is attributed to his wife when they took up residence in the *Tuileries.*

6. Northeast of the Quirinal in Rome and opposite the War Ministry buildings.

Letter 156

1. Marie von Sachsen-Weimar, daughter of Carl Alexander, who married Prince Heinrich von Reuss.

2. Von Reuss.

3. Nasir ud-Din (reigned 1848–1896), who visited Europe in 1873, 1878, and 1889. Evidently these meetings of East and West provided amusement in society circles. Maurice Baring (*Cat's Cradle,* p. 541) has a character relate an anecdote of the Shah killing a sheep in his bedroom at Windsor Castle.

4. Julius Gläser (1831–1885), Austrian jurist and statesman appointed Minister of Justice in 1871. Gläser was founder of modern jurisprudence in Austria, a system that reflected his admiration for English law.

Letter 157

1. Unidentified; apparently not the pianist Gottfried Heermann (1808–1878), since he died eight months before Liszt wrote this letter.

2. Unidentified.

3. Liszt repeated the same remark apropos of Martha Remmert in Letter 151.

4. Victorien Sardou (1831–1908), popular French playwright and Scribe's successor in composing "well-made" plays. His production was immense: his dramas ranged from comedies of intrigue (*Les Pattes de Mouche,* 1860) to society satire (*La Famille Benoîton,* 1865), political satire (*Rabagas,* 1872), and historical plays such as the often-performed *Madame Sans-Gêne* (1893).

With Sardou the nineteenth-century sentimental comedy reached its greatest heights — or depths. Typical of those plays presenting attitudinizing heroines were those written as vehicles for Sarah Bernhardt, and *Tosca* (1897) and *Fédora* (1882) are good examples.

Letter 158

1. Eduard von Liszt had just died.

2. Carolyne von Gomperz-Bettelheim.

3. Unidentified.

4. Viktor, Freiherr von Rokintansky (1836–1896), Viennese singer and *Lieder* composer.

Letter 160

1. The letter to Countess Andrassy is not reproduced here, although it does not appear in any other collection of Liszt's correspondence. In it Liszt merely reiterates his decision not to play the piano in public.

2. City in southern Hungary.

3. Gustave Doré (1832–1883), doubtlessly most famous of all nineteenth-century illustrators. He started his artistic career sketching for Philipon's *Journal pour Rire* in 1848. His first major effort was illustrations for an edition of *Rabelais* (1854); and in the same year he undertook what might be considered an ancestor of the modern comic strip — *Histoire* . . . *de la Sainte-Russie* — a work that had appropriate political connotations, since the Crimean War had just begun. His important illustrations included those for Balzac's *Contes Drolatiques* (1855), Dante's *Inferno* from the *Divina Commedia* (1861), Chateaubriand's *Atala* (1863), and Cervantes' *Don Quixote* (1863). A trip to England and an exhibition at London inspired Doré to attempt Coleridge's *Ancient Mariner* (1875).

Liszt played several times at Doré's house in Paris, Rue St. Dominique; and Liszt mentions "a Dantean session at Doré's" on May 11, 1866 (*L.M.* III, No. 110). There are at least three cases of similarities of interest between artist and musician: their treatments of *Faust*, the *Divina Commedia*, and the *Wandering Jew*. For a critic desirous of correlating style in music and the fine arts, certainly a comparison of the work of Liszt and Doré would be fruitful.

Letter 164

1. Catholic priest and Liszt's confessor at Weimar.

2. Elizabeth von Sachsen-Weimar, daughter of the Grand Duke and Duchess.

3. Wagner's house at Bayreuth, built in 1874.

4. Suburb of Naples and supposed site of Virgil's tomb. Donizetti's *Trois Nuits d'Été à Pausilippe* were transcribed for piano by Liszt and published in 1838 as part of the *Soirées Italiennes*.

5. Probably Princess Luise, daughter of Wilhelm I and Augusta of Prussia.

6. Unidentified.

7. Helmuth Karl von Moltke (1800–1891), German Chief-of-Staff for thirty years and the greatest military strategist of the last half of the century. Moltke served with the Turkish army 1835–1839; and the value of this experience in the field first appeared in 1854, when his skillful direction turned possible failure into victory over the Danes. The overwhelming defeat of the Austrians at Königgrätz (Sadowa) showed Moltke to be an apt disciple of Clausewitz; and for perhaps the first time, modern military principles of mobility, concentration, and judicious employment of railroad transportation were displayed. In 1870 Moltke beat one French army under Bazaine and then a second under MacMahon. From 1871 until his death, Moltke was a member of the newly-formed German *Reichstag*.

8. Johann Joseph Ignaz von Döllinger (1799–1890), one of the leaders of the Catholic theologians who advocated separation of the German Church from Rome. In 1832, Döllinger received Lamennais at Munich after the latter's return from Rome, and the influence of the French Catholic on Döllinger is important. He made a strong plea for separatism when the Bishops' Conference was held at Würzburg (October 1848). The plan might have succeeded had not Bishop Geissel, with a powerful opposition, suppressed Döllinger and his group.

347

Döllinger, with Bismarck's cognizance, refused to accept the Doctrine of Papal Infallibiltiy when it was issued in July 1870 — "as a Christian, as a theologian, as a historian, as a citizen." He was excommunicated and lost his University chair. The Doctrine became *casus belli* for Bismarck's *Kulturkampf* (1871–78) with Rome, and the so-called "May Laws," a series of articles formulated between 1873 and 1876, took up the fight with the Vatican. The struggle was resolved by the Concordat (1878), which Cardinal Gustav Hohenlohe helped to engineer. Among Döllinger's works were *Kirche und Kirchen* (Munich, 1869) and *Das Papstthum* (1892). Schorn (*Zwei Menschenalter*, p. 254) says that he was one of the few to receive a copy of Carolyne's theological masterpiece, *Les causes extérieures de la faiblesse intérieure de l'Église.*

9. Cf. Letter 139, Note 3.

10. Possibly Okraszewski.

11. This may be one of the priests attached to Cardinal Hohenlohe's household. "Don Marcello" was also the pseudonym used by Duchess Adele Colonna di Castiglione when she became a sculptress in her old age.

12. Small town southeast of Rome; a health resort in the mountains and the property of the Popes since 1687.

Letter 165

1. *Othon III von Deutschland*, opera by Carl Edler, who was tutor to the Hohenlohe children at the Augarten in Vienna. Marie tried unsuccessfully to interest Liszt in this work.

2. Cf. Virgil, *Aeneid*, Book II, lines 723–725: ". . . Little Iulus, his hand fast in mine, follows his father with unmatched steps. Behind us my wife comes after."

Letter 166

1. Ferdinand Jäger (1838–1902), Viennese tenor who sang the first "Siegfried" at Vienna and also played the role of Parsifal at Bayreuth in 1882 and 1888.

2. Giovanni Bottesini (1821–1889), double-bass player, composer, and Milanese conductor. His opera *Ero e Leandro* was written and performed in 1879, and he also wrote *Marion Delorme* (1862), based on Hugo's drama, and *Cristoforo Columbo* (1847). Bottesini at one time conducted the Havana Orchestra, and he directed the opening of Verdi's *Aïda* at Cairo.

3. Sardanapalo, book by C. d'Ormeville, music by G. Libani, produced in Rome, April 29, 1880.

4. Louis Étienne Reyer (originally "Rey" — 1823–1909), French operatic composer and music critic for the *Journal des Débats. Sigurd* was composed in 1884; another opera was the five-act *Salambô* with libretto by Camille du Locle based on Flaubert's novel. This was published in 1892 and performed in 1900. One of his operas was given at Weimar during the 1863–64 season.

Letter 167

1. Jäger.

2. This remark attributed to Balzac about Alexis de Tocqueville (1800–1858) has not been located.

Balzac and Liszt met at Paris in the late 1830's, and the writer dedicated *La Duchesse de Langeais* to "Frantz Liszt" in 1839. This melodramatic tale, the love affair of Duchesse Antoinette and General Armand de Montriveau, has two obvious points of reference with Liszt. First, Balzac devotes several pages to an analysis of the powers of music. "Are not religion, love, and music triple expressions of the same thing — the need for expansion by which every noble soul is moved?" This might be taken as a résumé of Liszt's career; in any case, one can speculate whether the two men had occasion to discuss music, since Balzac's ideas are so similar to Liszt's. The description of Montriveau is more important. An intensely Byronic, dynamic figure, his eyes flash with power and arrogance, his features are sharp and impelling, and a commanding forehead is crowned with a huge mane of long black hair. One need only look at contemporary pictures of Liszt to see the resemblance. True, Montriveau joins those Romantic heroes who apparently all shared the same physical traits, but this particular creation of Balzac seems too close to Liszt to be merely an artistic accident. André Billy, in his *Vie de Balzac* (Paris: 1944, pp. 151 ff.) mentions that Balzac's original admiration for Liszt turned to active dislike by 1844, when Balzac called Liszt "monkey, juggler, and bohemian." Billy also suggests that Liszt may have made advances to Countess Hanska, Balzac's mistress and later his wife. Liszt briefly discussed Balzac's *Une Fille d'Ève* in an article entitled "De l'art musical en Allemagne," written for the *Constitutionel*, January 7, 1855. Balzac's story contains the ludicrous figure, the German music-master Schmucke. The hero is the dandy, Raoul Nathan, also presented unfavorably, and in him one may perceive certain Lisztian qualities. It may be that the writer had the musician in mind, and was taking his literary revenge.

3. Napoleon Moriani (1806–1847), Florentine tenor.

4. Edgardo is the hero of Donizetti's *Lucia di Lammermoor;* Gennaro is from the same composer's *Lucrezia Borgia.*

5. This reference to a "vision" is difficult to interpret, unless it may concern the work of Moses Jacob Ezekiel (1844–1912), an American sculptor who studied under Wolff at the Berlin Academy. Ezekiel was a member of the artists' colony at Rome during the 1870's and 1880's and a friend of both Liszt and Cardinal Hohenlohe. Schorn (*Zwei Menschenalter*) says that he was working on a bust of the composer in 1880. This must be the one now in the *Deutsche Kunst-Museum* in Rome. Or perhaps Liszt refers to a projected composition based on the apocalyptic Book of Ezekiel.

6. Strassburg was ceded, along with almost all of Alsace and a third of Lorraine, to Germany in 1871. Consequently it was the scene of continual political unrest up to 1918.

Letter 168

1. Probably the *Mass for Men*, published in 1848 and revised in 1871.

2. Symphonic poem, written and published in 1859. It was inspired by Schiller's poem, *Die Ideale.*

> *"So willst du treulos von mir scheiden*
> *Von deinen holden Phantasien,*
> *Mit deinen Schmerzen, deinen Freuden,*
> *Mit allen unerbittlich fliehn? . . ."*

3. The protagonists in Grillparzer's tragedy.

4. Keats had the same difficulty in his sonnet, *On a Picture of Leander* (1816): "He's gone: up bubbles all his amorous breath!"

Letter 170

1. Unidentified.

Letter 171

1. Filippo Neri (1515–1595), founder of the Brotherhood of the Holy Trinity.

2. Meiningen.

3. Liebenstein, a spa in northern Meiningen about twelve miles south of Eisenach.

4. The Grand Duke of Saxe-Weimar.

5. Empress Augusta of Germany.

6. The two parts of Goethe's drama.

7. The line, misquoted by Liszt, is from Molière's *L'Avare*, spoken by La Flèche in Act I, Scene 3: "La peste soit de l'avarice et des avaricieux!"

8. Countess Gizycka-Zamoiska, Lady-in-Waiting to the Duchess Sophia and an amateur composer.

Letter 172

1. Georg von Meiningen.

2. Weilen never did write a biography of Grillparzer, although he edited an edition of Grillparzer's poetry: *Gedichte von Grillparzer* (Stuttgart: Cotta, 1872). A signed copy may be found in Widener Library, Harvard University.

3. Eugène Marie Melchior, Vicomte de Vogüé (1848–1910), cousin of the French ambassador to Austria and later to Turkey. Eugène Vogüé also pursued a diplomatic career after service with the French army in 1870. His contributions to Russian studies started in 1879. *Le fils de Pierre le Grand* appeared in 1889. *Le Roman Russe* (1886), his best known work, was a collection of essays on Pushkin, Gogol, Turgeniev, Tolstoi, and Dostoievski, and served to introduce Russian literature to France and the West. The influence exercised by *Le Roman Russe* was considerable, since it represented currents running counter to those of Naturalism: a new mysticism, religiosity, and concern with psychology.

Letter 173

1. A Benedictine cloister, *Notre Dame des Ermites*, built 1704–1720. It is in the Canton of Schwyz in Switzerland.

2. Town in the Canton of Uri, south of Zürich and east of Lucerne.

3. Wagner's opera *Die Meistersinger von Nürnberg*, a comic opera in seven acts. Wagner started the work in 1844 and completed it in 1867. The first performance, under Bülow, was given at Munich in 1868.

4. Carolyne.

5. Georg von Meiningen.

Letter 174

1. Georg von Meiningen.

Letter 175
1. Resort in the Reichensteiner Gebirge, south of Breslau and east of Prague.
2. A series of twelve articles written by Liszt for the *Gazette Musicale*. It is strange that he makes a mistake here about their date of publication: all twelve were written between February 1837 and March 1839 — and not in 1835. The articles and their dates follow:

    I. À un poète voyageur (February 12, 1837)
    II. [no title] (July 16, 1837)
    III. À M. Adolphe Pictet (February 11, 1838)
    IV. À M. Louis de Ronchaud (March 25, 1838)
    V. Le lac de Como (July 22, 1838)
    VI. La Scala (May 27, 1838)
    VII. À M. Heine (July 8, 1838)
    VIII. À M. Lambert Massart (September 2, 1838)
    IX. La pensée de Benvenuto Cellini (January 13, 1839)
    X. La Sainte Cécile de Raphäel (April 14, 1839)
    XI. À M. Hector Berlioz (October 24, 1839)
    XII. De l'état de la musique en Italie (March 28, 1839)

3. Lina Ramann (1833–1912), musician and musicologist. The biography mentioned by Liszt appeared two months after this letter. Ramann's other writings about Liszt were *Liszts Christus* (1880), *Liszt-Pädagogium* (in five series), *Franz Liszt als Psalmensänger* (1886), *Liszts Biographie* (1880–94), and *Liszts Schriften* (1880–83).

Letter 176
1. Daniel de Charnacé, grandson of Marie d'Agoult, son of Claire Christine d'Agoult who married Marquis Guy de Charnacé. He wrote *Portraits des femmes d'aujourd'hui* and it was Charnacé who coined the title of "La reine peste" for Pauline de Metternich.

Letter 177
1. Cf. Saar, *Werke*, vol. I, p. 22: *Schlummerlied.*

    "Des Tages laute Stimmen Schweigen,
    Und dunkeln wird es allgemach;
    Ein letztes Schimmern in den Zweigen —
    Dann zieht auch dies der Sonne nach."

2. Cf. Letter 164, Note 11.

Letter 178
1. Cardinal Antonelli (1806–1876), Secretary of State under Pius IX 1850–1876, and noted for his cleverness in diplomatic and political affairs. Antonelli was instrumental in formulating Vatican foreign policy during the troubled 1860's and 1870's. Léonille Wittgenstein (*Souvenirs*, p. 83) describes him as "polite, prepossessing; his black eyes sparkled with wit; his intelligent appearance displayed the great capabilities and resources of which he was master." Antonelli brought to Liszt and Carolyne the news of the Pope's refusal to annul Carolyne's previous marriage, on the night of October 21, 1861.

1. Probably Jäger.

2. Pierre Lanfrey (1828–1877), French politician and historian; author of the *Histoire politique des Papes* (Paris, 1860).

1. Earlier reference has been made (Preface to Letter 108) to the immense literary labors of Carolyne. "Her great historic, monumental, administrative work" was the gigantic *Causes extérieures de la faiblesse intérieure de l'Église,* of which twenty volumes were completed when she died in March 1887. It has been mentioned that Döllinger was given several parts of this work, which was always in progress, but I have been unable to ascertain whether other copies exist, or whether the original is still preserved. There is no statement by Liszt or Carolyne that publication of any portion took place; Sitwell (*Liszt,* p. 355) speaks of her quiet death a fortnight after she "accomplished her readerless task." Schorn says of this study that it was "the masterpiece of her life, which she finished a week before her death and which was published 25 years later — only a few copies were ever shared by her with friends and scholars" (*Zwei Menschenalter,* p. 110). Twenty-five years later would have been in 1912; but since in the light of all obtainable information, actual publication seems highly dubious, the problem remains a mystery — interesting, although certainly unimportant. A list of Carolyne's other writings follows:

> *Buddhisme et Christianisme*
> *De la prière pour une femme du monde*
> *Entretiens pratiques, etc.* (3 vols.)
> *La matière dans la dogmatique chrétienne* (3 vols.)
> *L'Église attaquée par la médisance*
> *Petits entretiens, etc.* (8 vols.)
> *Sagesse des colombes, prudence des serpents*
> *Souffrance et prudence*
> *Sur la perfection chrétienne et la vie intérieure*

2. Marcelline Czartoryska (1817–1894) *née* Radziwill, pupil of Chopin; wife of Prince Adam Czartorysky (1770–1861), Polish nobleman, Russian diplomat, Minister of Foreign Affairs in 1802. Czartorysky figures briefly in Tolstoi's *War and Peace,* when Andrei points "Tchartoriszhsky" out to Boris Bolkonski at the staff meeting just before Austerlitz. He also became head of the Polish revolutionary government during its short existence in 1830, and later emigrated to France. His portrait was painted by Scheffer in 1850.

1. Either Op. 11 in E Minor or Op. 21 in F Minor.

2. Czech: "elegy" or "lament."

3. Wife of Eduard Hanslick.

4. Beethoven's *Trio* for piano, violin, and 'cello, the so-called "Archduke" (Op. 97, in B Flat). Among other works dedicated by Beethoven to Rudolph von Hapsburg are the Fourth and Fifth Piano *Concerti; Fidelio;* the *Sonata* for piano, Op. 81a ("Les Adieux"); the *Hammerklavier Sonata;*

the last piano *Sonata*, Op. 111; the *Missa Solemnis;* and the *Grand Fugue*, Op. 133.

Letter 183

1. Unidentified; possibly Baron Konrad von Reisach (cf. Letter 62, Note 3) who married Amalia zu Sayn-Wittgenstein (d. 1876). Her memoirs, *Une famille princière d'Allemagne* (Paris: Ollendorff, 1886) are of interest to anyone caring to investigate the complicated history and genealogy of that family.

Letter 184

1. Liszt had a bad fall on the steps of the *Hofgärtnerei* in 1881.

Letter 186

1. Michael von Munkacsy (originally "Lieb"; 1844–1909), Hungarian painter. Munkacsy was a student of Courbet in Paris in 1867; and his best known work was *Milton*, exhibited in 1878. *Christ devant Pilate* was painted in 1881. Focillon (*La peinture au XIX* siècle, vol. II, p. 67) calls it "a somber and sonorous oratorio which has a certain theatrical grandeur."

Letter 188

1. Carl Pohlig (1864–1928), pupil of Liszt in Budapest and Rome, and later conductor of the Philadelphia Symphony.

Letter 189

1. The *Weihnachtsbaum* (1882), a collection of twelve piano pieces by Liszt.

2. Godefroi. This may be Félix Godefroid, minor French harpist and pianist.

Letter 191

1. Michael Zichy (1827–1906), Hungarian painter attached to the Russian court.

2. Liszt's symphonic poem, *Von der Wiege bis zum Grabe* (1883), written some twenty-five years after the earlier ones. The movement to which Liszt refers is the second of three.

3. Benjamin Bilse (1816–1902), who conducted his own orchestra in Berlin from 1868 to 1902.

4. Freiburg im Breisgau, archiepiscopal see in Baden, twelve miles east of the Rhine.

5. Probably Adolphe Goupil (1806–1893), art dealer in Paris.

6. Paul von Joukowski (b. 1845), attached to the Russian court.

7. Unidentified.

8. The Vendramin-Calergi Palazzo is on the Grand Canal in Venice, in the northern section of the city.

9. Duchesse de Berry (1798–1870), *née* Marie-Louise de Naples, daughter of Francis I of Austria. Her husband was assassinated February 13, 1820. Liszt knew her at Paris in the 1820's: she and Louis-Philippe fought to get "le petit Litz" [*sic*] to play in their rival salons in 1824–25. Her son was the Comte de Chambord, and her schemes to get the French throne for him ended when she remarried in 1837. The Duc della Grazia mentioned by Liszt in this letter was the product of the second match.

10. Alt Heinrichsau in Silesia, south of Breslau and north of the Riesengebirge.

11. Eugene d'Albert (1864–1932). He was born in Glasgow and studied with Sir John Stainer and Sir Arthur Sullivan; later, after 1881, he continued his training under Liszt. D'Albert wrote one opera, *Tiefland* (1903), and published critical editions of both Bach and Beethoven.

Letter 192

1. Summer resort and Benedictine monastery in the Klagenfurt district of Austria.

2. Alonso Cano (1601–1666), Spanish architect, noted for his altar carvings, and friend of Velasquez.

3. Ludwig Johann Passini (1832–1903), Viennese painter and watercolorist. Passini lived in Rome 1853–1870.

4. This little-known work of Wagner's was written in six weeks, in 1832, and first performed at Prague. It was then played, January 1833, at the *Gewandhaus* in Leipzig; and the performance was reviewed by Heinrich Laube, member of *Junges Deutschland*.

5. Count Contini.

6. Ernst Wilhelm Fritzsch (1840–1902), Leipzig musician and head of the Bromnitz publishing house after 1866, which published works by such artists as Wagner, Grieg, Cornelius, Rheinberger, and Nietzsche.

7. Mother of Prince Philip Hohenlohe and owner of Schloss Duino.

8. This is an error on Liszt's part: there were two and not three grenadiers. Cf. *Buch der Lieder* (1827): "Nach Frankreich zogen zwei Grenadier, Die waren in Russland gefangen . . ."

9. Op. 53.

10. Karl Reissiger (1798–1859), prolific and mediocre composer and conductor. Reissiger taught at Berlin, Leipzig, and the Hague and succeeded Marschner as director of the Dresden Opera in 1828.

Letter 193

1. Capital of Carinthia (Kärnten) in Austria.

2. Christian Ströbel (1855–1899), Hungarian sculptor and architect. Liszt's statue was placed at the entrance of the new theater on the *Radialstrasse* in Budapest, along with one of Franz Erkel (1810–1893), Hungarian composer of patriotic operas and songs.

3. Ströbel also did a bust of Marie's husband, Prince Constantin.

Letter 194

1. Richard Herberger (1850–1914), director of the Vienna *Singakademie* in 1878. He was music critic for the *Wiener Tageblatt*, *Münchner Allegemeine Zeitung*, and the *Neue Freie Presse*.

Letter 198

1. In Hesse-Nassau, north of Frankfurt and east of Cologne.

1. The gardener's cottage off the *Belvedere Allee* in the Weimar park, used by the painter Carl Emil Doepler as a studio before Liszt took it over. He lived in the *Hofgärtnerei* 1869–1886. After Liszt's death it became the Liszt Museum.

Letter 205
1. Countess Gizycka-Zamoiska.
2. A portion of the *St. Stanislas* Oratorio.
3. Baroness Olga von Meyendorff, *née* Gortchakoff (1838–1926), wife of the Russian diplomat Felix von Meyendorff.

Letter 207
1. Probably Marie's daughter, Dorothea — later Countess von Lamberg.
2. Carolyne's *magnum opus.*
3. Cardinal Hohenlohe.
4. Kurt von Schlözer (1822–1894), German representative at the Vatican 1882–1894.

Letter 214
1. Chairman of the *Concerts Colonnes* at Paris, to which Liszt had been invited.
2. Olga de Lagrené (b. 1836), daughter of the French diplomat Joseph de Lagrené (1800–1862).
3. Church in Paris where Liszt's *Graner Mass* was performed March 28, 1866. Pauline Metternich arranged the affair for her "abbé lion." Hurand conducted; and the organist improvised beforehand on themes from *Tannhäuser* in order to satisfy the crowd of Wagnerites who attended the service.

Letter 215
1. Cf. Letter 214, Note 1.
2. Francis Planté (1839–1920), French pianist. Planté had retired ten years earlier in order to perfect his technique, and this concert marked his triumphant return.

Bibliography

Albrecht, F., *Lesefrüchte aus dem Leben Friedrich des Grossen* (Ulm: Nöbling, 1860).

Allgemeine Deutsche Biographie (Leipzig: Duneker & Humblot, 1888).

Almanach de Gotha (Gotha: 1855–1861).

Apponyi, Graf Albert, *Erlebnisse und Ergebnisse* (Berlin: Keil, 1933).

Arnim, Bettina von, *Goethes Briefwechsel mit einem Kind*, ed. Dehlke (Berlin: Propyläen, 1920).

Baldensperger, Ferdinand, "L'Entrée pathétique des Tziganes dans les lettres occidentales," *Revue de littérature comparée* (October–December 1938).

——*Sensibilité musicale et Romantisme* (Paris: Les Presses françaises, 1925).

Balzac, Honoré de, "Une Fille d'Ève," *Histoire des Treize* (Paris: Lévy, 1925).

Baring, Maurice, *The Cat's Cradle* (London: Heinemann, 1925).

Barzun, Jacques, *Berlioz and the Romantic Century* (Boston: Little, Brown, 1950).

Bauer, Marion, "The Literary Liszt," *Musical Quarterly*, Vol. XII, No. 3 (July 1936).

Bayard, Jean-François, *Théâtre* (Paris: Hachette, 1855–1858).

Bedrow, Otto, *Rahel Varnhagen* (Stuttgart: Greiner & Pfeiffer, 1900).

Bekker, Paul, "Liszt and His Critics," *Musical Quarterly*, Vol. XII, No. 3 (July 1936).

Benoit-Lévy, E., *La Jeunesse de Victor Hugo* (Paris: Michel, 1928).

Berlioz, Hector, *Correspondance inédite*, ed. Berraud (Paris: Lévy, 1899).

——*Lettres intimes*, ed. Gounod (Paris: Lévy, 1882).

Bertha, A. de, *La Hongrie moderne, 1849–1901* (Paris: Plon, 1901).

Bevan, Bernard, *A History of Spanish Architecture* (London: Batsford, 1938).

Bielschowsky, *Life of Goethe*, trans. Cooper (New York: Putnam, 1908).

Billy, André, *La Vie de Balzac* (Paris: Flammarion, 1944).

Biré, E., *Victor Hugo avant 1830* (Paris: Gervais, 1883).

Bithell, Jethro, *Modern German Literature* (London: Methuen, 1946).

Blaze, de Bury, Henri, *Les écrivains modernes de l'Allemagne* (Paris: Lévy, 1868).

——*Musiciens contemporains* (Paris: Lévy, 1856).

——*Les salons de Vienne et de Berlin* (Paris: Lévy, 1861).

Blok, Petrus, *History of the People of the Netherlands*, trans. Bierstadt (New York: Putnam, 1912).

Bode, Wilhelm, *Das Leben in Alt-Weimar* (Leipzig: Haessel, 1922).

Boecklen, Adolf, *Sprichwörter in Sechs Sprachen*, ed. G. Schmidt (Stuttgart: Klett, 1938).

Boesch, B. (ed.), *Deutsche Literaturgeschichte in Grundzügen* (Berlin: Francke, 1946).

Bory, Robert, "Un concert mémorable à Saint-Gall," *Formes et Couleurs*, no. I (Lausanne: 1943).

—— *Une retraite romantique en Suisse* (Geneva: Sonor, 1923).

—— *La vie de Franz Liszt par l'image* (Geneva: 1936).

Brogan, Denis, *France under the Republic* (New York: Harpers, 1940).

Brown, Calvin S., *Music and Literature* (Athens: University of Georgia, 1948).

Bute, John, Marquess of (trans.), *The Roman Breviary* (London: Blackwood, 1878).

Chanler, Margaret, *Memory Makes Music* (New York: Stephen-Paul, 1948).

—— *Roman Spring* (Boston: Little, Brown, 1935).

Chateaubriand, François René de, *Mémoires d'Outre-Tombe*, ed. V. Giraud (Paris: Garnier, 1946).

Chopin, Frédéric, *Letters*, trans. Voynich (New York: Knopf, 1931).

Clark, C. W., *Franz Joseph and Bismarck before 1866* (Cambridge: Harvard University Press, 1941).

Clark and Freedley, *A History of Modern Drama* (New York: Appleton-Century, 1947).

Combarieu, Jules, *Les rapports de la musique et de la poésie* (Paris: Alcan, 1894).

Croce, Benedetto, *A History of Italy, 1871-1915* (Oxford: Clarendon, 1929).

Croner, The Earl of, *Modern Egypt* (New York: Macmillan, 1916).

Czartoryski, Adam, *Mémoires*, ed. Mazade (Paris: 1865).

Dawson, W. H., *The German Empire* (New York: Macmillan, 1919).

"Demophilos," *Friederichs des Grossen Gedanken über Staat, Kirche, u.s.w.* (Leipzig: Brüggemann, 1933).

Denziger, H., *Enchiridion etc.*, trans. Bettenson, 15th ed. (Freiburg: 1922).

Dézé Louis, G. *Doré: Bibliographie et Catalogue* (Paris: Séheur, 1930).

Dresch, J., *Gutzkow et le Jeune Allemagne* (Paris: Société nouvelle, 1904).

Dyson, C. C., *The Life of Marie-Amélie, 1782-1860* (New York: Appleton, 1910).

Eberlein, Karl, *Die Malerei der deutschen Romantiker und Nazarener* (Munich: Wolff, 1928).

Eckermann, Johann Peter, *Gespräche mit Goethe*, ed. Beutels (Leipzig: Diederichs, 1902).

Engel, Carl, "Six Letters from Franz Liszt to Marie zu Sayn-Wittgenstein," *Musical Quarterly*, Vol. XII, No. 3 (July, 1936).

Fallersleben, Hoffmann von, *An Meine Freunde*, ed. Gerstenberg (Berlin: Ehbock, n.d.).

Fétis, F. J., *Biographie universelle des musiciens* (Paris: Didot, 1870).

Focillon, Henri, *La peinture au XIXᵉ siècle* (Paris: Renouard, 1927).

Freytag, Gustav, *Briefe an Albrecht von Stosch* (Stuttgart: Deutsche Verlags-Anstalt, 1913).

Friedrich III, Kaiser, *Tagebücher 1848-1866*, ed. Meissner (Leipzig: Koehler, 1929).

Fuller, J. V., *Bismarck's Diplomacy at its Zenith* (Cambridge: Harvard University Press, 1922).

Geibel, Emanuel, *Gesammelte Werke*, 4th ed. (Berlin: 1906).

Geiringer, Karl, "The Friends of Music in Vienna," *Musical Quarterly*, Vol. XX, No. 6 (July, 1938).

Gesztes, Jules, *Pauline de Metternich* (Paris: Flammarion, 1947).

Gilbert & Kuhn, *A History of Aesthetics* (New York: Macmillan, 1939).

Goethe, Johann W. von, *Sämtliche Werke* (Stuttgart: Cotta, 1851).

Grand Dictionnaire Universel du XIX⁰ siècle (Paris: Larousse, 1874).

Grande Encyclopédie (Paris: 1894).

Grimschitz, Bruno, *Maler der Ostmark im 19. Jahrhundert* (Vienna: Schroll, 1940).

Grove, *Dictionary of Music and Musicians*, ed. Maitland (New York: Macmillan, 1911).

Grube, Max, *Geschichte der Meininger* (Stuttgart: Deutsche Verlags-Anstalt, 1926).

Hadow, Sir Henry, *The Place of Music among the Arts* (Oxford: Clarendon, 1937).

Hamann, Richard, *Die deutsche Malerei im 19. Jahrhundert* (Leipzig and Berlin: Teubner, 1914).

—— *Die deutsche Malerei vom Rokoko bis zum Expressionismus* (Leipzig and Berlin: Teubner, 1925).

Hanslick, Eduard, *Von Musikalisch-Schönen* (Leipzig: Barth, 1881).

Hebbel, Friedrich, *Briefe* (Berlin: Behr, 1900).

Heine, Heinrich, *Sämtliche Werke*, ed. Elster (Leipzig: Biographisches Institut, 1924).

Helmholtz, Hermann F. L., *Die Lehre von den Tonempfindungen*, 4th ed. (Brunswick: 1877).

Heyse, Paul, *Jugenderinnerungen und Bekenntnisse* (Berlin: Hertz, 1900).

Hoffmann von Fallersleben, Baron H. A., *Au meine Freunde*, ed. Gerstenberg (Berlin: Ehbock, 1895).

—— *Mein Leben* (Berlin: Fontane, 1893).

Hugo, Victor, *Lettres à la fiancée* (Paris: Charpentier, 1901).

—— *Oeuvres*, ed. Maurice (Paris: Garnier, 1926).

—— *Oeuvres poétiques complètes*, ed. Goffin (Montreal: Valiquette, 1944).

Joachim, J., *Letters*, trans. Bickley (London: Macmillan, 1902).

King, Bolton, *A History of Italian Unity* (London: Nisbet, 1904).

Kingsley, Charles, *Alton Locke, Tailor and Poet* (New York: Harpers, 1850).

Kloss, E. (ed.), *Briefwechsel zwischen Wagner und Liszt* (Leipzig: Breitkopf & Härtel, 1910).

Kolb, Marthe, *Ary Scheffer et son temps* (Paris: Boivin, 1937).

La Mara, *Liszt und die Frauen* (Leipzig: Breitkopf & Härtel, 1911).

La Mara (ed.), *Briefe Hervorragender Zeitgenossen an Franz Liszt* (Leipzig: Breitkopf & Härtel, 1895).

—— *Briefwechsel zwischen Liszt und Bülow* (Leipzig: 1898).

—— *Briefwechsel zwischen Franz Liszt und Carl Alexander* (Leipzig: 1909).

—— *Franz Liszts Briefe an eine Freundin* (Leipzig: 1899).

—— *Liszts Briefe an die Fürstin Carolyne Sayn-Wittgenstein* (Leipzig: 1899–1902).

Lamennais, Hughes Félicité Robert de, *Paroles d'un Croyant* (Paris: Reudeul, 1834).

—— *Portefeuille*, ed. Goyau (Paris: Renaissance du Livre, 1930).

Láng, Paul Henry, "Liebestraum," *Saturday Review of Literature*, Vol. XXV, No. 14 (January 25, 1947).

—— "Liszt and the Romantic Movement," *Musical Quarterly*, Vol. XII, No. 3 (July 1936).

Larousse du XXe siècle (Paris: 1921).

Lavisse, *Histoire de France contemporaine* (Paris: Hachette, 1921).

Lefebvre, G., *Napoléon* (Paris: Alcan, 1935).

Lelkes, Stephan, *L'Age d'or de l'amitié franco-hongroise* (Budapest, 1933).

Levi, Primo, *Gustave Adolfo, cardinal principe di Hohenlohe-Schillingsfürst* (Rome: 1896).

Lewald, Fanny, *Zwölf Bilder nach dem Leben* (Berlin: 1888).

Liszt, Franz, F. *Chopin* (Leipzig: Breitkopf & Härtel, 1852).

—— *Gesammelte Schriften*, ed. Ramann (Leipzig: Breitkopf & Härtel, 1880–1883).

—— *Pages Romantiques*, ed. J. Chantavoine (Paris: Alcan, 1912).

Loewenberg, A., *Annals of Opera* (Cambridge: Heffner, 1943).

Longfellow, Henry W., *Christus: A Mystery* (Boston: Houghton Mifflin, 1886).

Ludwig, Otto, *Gesammelte Werke*, ed. Stern (Leipzig: Grunau, 1891).

—— *Die Makkabäer*, ed. M. S. Briel (Saarlouis: Haufen, 1930).

Mollberg, Dr. Albert (ed.), *Weimars klassische Kulturstätten* (Weimar: Pause, 1925).

Morin, F., *St. Francis d'Assise et les Franciscains* (Paris: Hachette, 1853).

Necker, Bernhard, *Franz Grillparzer: Sein Leben und seine Werke* (Berlin: 1910).

Newman, Ernest, *Richard Wagner* (New York: Knopf, 1933).

Niecks, Frederick, *Programme Music in the last four Centuries* (London: Novello, 1907).

Niemann, W., *Brahms*, trans. C. A. Phillips (New York: Knopf, 1929).

Nietzsche, Friedrich, *Werke* (Leipzig: Naumann, 1899).

Ollivier, D. (ed.), *Correspondance de Liszt et de Mme. d'Agoult* (Paris: Grasset, 1933).

Pailleron, Marie-Louise, *Les derniers Romantiques* (Paris: Perrin, 1923).

—— *George Sand* (Paris: Grasset, 1938).

Pascal, Blaise, *Oeuvres*, ed. Brunnschwigg (Paris: Hachette, 1921).

Piépape, Général de, *La Duchesse du Maine* (Paris: Plon, 1910).

Ploetz, *Manual of Universal History*, trans. W. H. Tillinghast (Boston: Houghton Mifflin, 1925).

Purdie, Edna, *Friedrich Hebbel* (London: Humphrey Milford, 1932).

Ramann, Lina, *Franz Liszt als Künstler und Mensch* (Leipzig: Breitkopf & Härtel, 1880).

Raphaël, Gaston, *Otto Ludwig* (Paris: Rieder, 1920).

La Revue des Deux Mondes; Cent Ans de Vie française (Paris: Hachette, 1929).

Riemann, Hugo, *Musik-Lexikon* (Berlin: Hesse, 1919), 9th ed. completed by Einstein.

Robertson, C. Grant, *Bismarck* (London: Constable, 1929).

Roenneke, Rudolf, *Franz Dingelstedts Wirksamkeit am Weimarer Hoftheater* (Griefswald: Adler, 1912).

Roosevelt, Blanche, *The Life of Gustave Doré* (New York: Cassell, 1885).

Rovigny, The Marquis of, *The Titled Nobility of Europe* (London: Harrison, 1914).
Royce, W. H., *A Balzac Bibliography* (Chicago: Chicago University Press, 1929).
Saar, Ferdinand von, *Gesammelte Werke*, ed. Minor (Leipzig: Hesse, 1908).
Sainte-Beuve, Charles-Augustin, *Causeries du Lundi* (Paris: Lévy, 1869).
—— *Correspondance générale*, ed. Bonnerot (Paris: Stock, 1935).
—— *Mes Poisons*, ed. Giraud (Paris: Plon, 1926).
—— *Nouveaux Lundis* (Paris: Lévy, 1869).
—— *Portraits de femmes* (Paris: Garnier, 1876).
Saint-Saëns, Camille, *École buissonière* (Paris: Lafitte, 1904).
—— *Portraits et Souvenirs* (Paris: Calmann-Lévy).
Salvatorelli, L., *Concise History of Italy*, trans. B. Miall (New York: Oxford, 1940).
Sand, George, *Correspondence, 1812–1876* (Paris: Lévy, 1882).
Sayn-Wittgenstein, Léonille, *Souvenirs, 1875–1907* (Paris: Léthielleux, 1907).
Sayn-Wittgenstein-Berlebourg, Emile de, *Souvenirs et Correspondances* (Paris: Lévy, 1888).
Sayn-Wittgenstein-Sayn, Amélie, *Souvenirs d'une famille princière d'Allemagne* (Paris: Ollendorff, 1886).
Scheffel, Josef Viktor von, *Der Trompeter von Säkkingen* (Stuttgart: Metzler, 1874).
Schmidt, Paul Friedrich, *Biedermeier-Malerei* (Munich: Delphin, 1922).
Schopenhauer, Artur, *Schriften über Musik*, ed. Stabenow (Ravensburg: 1922).
Schorn, Adelheid von, *La Correspondance d'Adelheid von Schorn et la Princesse Carolyne zu Sayn-Wittgenstein* (Paris: Dujarric, 1904).
—— *Das nachklassische Weimar* (Weimar: Kieponheuer, 1911).
—— *Zwei Menschenalter* (Stuttgart: Greiner & Pfeiffer, 1912).
Schrickel, Leonhard, *Geschichte des Weimaren Theaters* (Weimar: Pause, 1928).
Schröder, E., *Von alten Fritz* (Leipzig: Wigend, 1876).
Servières, Georges, *Tannhäuser à l'Opéra en 1861* (Paris: 1895).
Sitwell, Sacheverel, *Liszt* (London: Faber & Faber, 1934).
Staiger, Emil, "Deutsche Romantik in Dichtung und Musik," *Trivium*, Vol. III (Zürich: 1947).
Stern, Daniel, *Nélida* (Paris: Moussin, 1846).
Strobl von Ravensburg, Ferdinand, *Metternich und seine Zeit, 1773–1859* (Vienna: Stern, 1906).
Terry, W., *A Wagner Dictionary* (New York: Wilson, 1939).
Thayer, W. R., "Cardinal Hohenlohe — Liberal," *Italica* (Cambridge: Riverside, 1908).
Thieme & Becker, *Allgemeine Lexikon der bildenden Künstler* (Leipzig: Seemann, 1938).
Tiersot, Julian, "Liszt in France," *Musical Quarterly*, Vol. XII, No. 3 (July 1936).
Treisch, L. (ed.), *L'Esprit de Voltaire* (Paris: Gallimard, 1927).
Turner, W. J., *Berlioz: the Man and his Music* (London: Dent, 1935).

Valentin, Veit, 1848: *Chapters of German History*, trans. E. T. Scheffauer (London: Allen & Unwin, 1940).

Vehle, Dr. Eduard, *Der Hof zu Weimar* (Leipzig: Dietz, 1854).

Wagner, Richard, *Mein Leben* (Munich: Bruckmann, 1914).

——— "Über Franz Liszt's Symphonische Dichtungen." *Gesammelte Schriften und Dichtungen* vol. V (Leipzig: Fritsch, 1872).

Wallace, William, *Liszt, Wagner, and the Princess* (London: Kegan Paul, Trench and Trubner, 1927).

Wogue, Jules, "Un aumônier israélite de l'Impératrice Eugénie" *Mercure de France* (July 1936).

Zak, Alfons, *Österreichisches Klosterbuch* (Vienna: Kirsch, 1911).

INDEX TO LETTERS AND NOTES

Note

Items included in the Index are the names of persons, places, musical compositions, titles of books and paintings, et cetera, mentioned in the letters. There are no references to material from the Introduction, the various Prefaces to the letters, or Liszt's own footnotes. Arabic numerals refer to letters and not to pages.

In general the note to any specific item follows (in Roman numerals) the first text reference to it. In a few cases (indicated by parentheses) it seemed advisable to change the order, since a musical work, for example, may have been treated in the footnote concerning the composer before the composition itself appeared in the correspondence. When no Roman numerals are used, it is an indication either that the item was too well-known to require explanation or that the surrounding text of the letter provided adequate identification.

A dash between Arabic numerals indicates inclusiveness. Titles of books, paintings, musical works, and journals are italicized.

Index to Letters and Notes

Hannover, 81, 154, 173.
Hanslick, 30–iii; 33, 34, 42, 181, 182.
Harpagon, 10–xii; 32.
Härtel, 9–viii.
Härtel, Kistner, & Senff, 15–ii; 41, 60.
Haslinger, 42–xx.
Haus Pudel, 44, 66.
Hausner, 1–iii.
Haydn, 22–iii; 76.
Haynald, 97–i; 98, 104, 135, 136, 186.
Hebbel, 57–xiv; 59.
Hébert, 63–ii; 64.
Hebrews, 23.
Hegel, 23.
Heine, 19–xvii; 192.
Heinrichsau, 191–x.
Helgoland, 135.
Hellmesberger, 75–v; 95, 155, 158, 167, 181.
Hellwig, 81–iii.
Hemsen, 33–iii; 57.
Henri, 20–xxiii.
Henry of Holland, 22–ii; 156.
Henry V, 98–iv.
Henry VII, 156–ii.
Hens, 190.
Herbeck, 48–ix; 49, 51, 65, 66, 69, 76, 77, 91, 97, 109, 113, 114, 115, 168.
Herberger, 194–i.
Herder, 123.
Hero and Leander, 168–iii.
Herrmann, 157–i.
Herwegh, 18–v; 191.
Heyse, 45–xxviii; 46–114.
Hietzing, 62–iv.
Hildebrand, 47–iv; 114.
Hiller, 22–xv; 34, 35, 52.
Hippogriffe, 9–iii.
Hobbema, 45–xvii.
Höfer, 8–xvi.
Hoffmann von Fallersleben, 23–xxvii; 25, 38, 48, 51, 56, 57, 59, 97, 104, 114.
Hofgärtnerei, 204–i, (171).
Höfliche Mann, Der, 14–vi.
Hofmann, 90–ii; 91, 95.
Hohenlohe, Alexander, 130–i.
Hohenlohe, Chlodwig, 60–v; 155, 201.
Hohenlohe, Constantine, 48, 55, 64, 75, 83, 85, 91, 107, 108, 112, 135, 138, 142, 144, 152, 166, 167, 184, 207.
Hohenlohe, Dorothea, 207–i.
Hohenlohe, Gustav (Cardinal), 64–v; 65, 75, 97, 107, 122, 125, 133, 135, 138, 146, 155, 156, 164, 166.
Hohenlohe, Philippe, 155–i; 192.
Hohenlohe, Theresa, 192–vii.

Hohenlohe family, 51–x; 135, 137, 138.
Hohenzollern-Hechingen, F., 42–i; 44, 45, 55, 57, 141.
Hohlstein, 45–i.
Hohmann, 164–i.
Holle, 41–xiii.
Hopfgarten, 20–v.
Horpacs, 75–i; 94–97.
Hübner, 48–vi.
Hugo, 27–ix; 104, 105.
Huguenots, 33–vi.
Hülsen, 115–i.
Humboldt, 23–i; 29, 57, 104.
Hungaria, 32–ii; 114, 168.
Hungaria Hotel, 159, 162.
Hunnenschlacht, 60–ii.

Ideale, 168–ii.
Impératrice Elizabeth, Hotel de l', 42.
Infanta, 26, 27.
Institut (e), 10–v; 11–13, 15, 20, 114.
Iron Crown, 45–xxxii; 194, 209.

Jaëll, 29–viii.
Jäger, 166–i.
Jan, 12–xx.
Janko, 41–iv; 42.
Jauner, 114–vii; 124, 126, 144, 167, 179.
Jena, 11, 32.
Joachim, 10–xiv; 29, 41, 59, 168.
Johannot, 54–ii.
Joseph, 153–ix.
Josika, 13–i; 15.
Joukowski, 191–vi; 192.
Journal des Débats, 166–iv.
Judas Maccabeus, 46–viii.
Juive, La, 39–viii.

Kacha, 12–ii.
Kaiser Heinrich IV, 78–i; 79, 81.
Kalckreuth, 57–vi; 84.
Kalergis, 59–ii; 60.
Kalocsa, 97–ii; 98, 104, 135, 136, 186, 194.
Kamiensky, 28–ii.
Karatsonyi, 41–vii; 72, 150.
Karoly, 30–vi; 141.
Kassel (Cassel), 33–ii; 33, 34.
Kaulbach, 23–iv; 46, 81, 104.
Kauser, 158–iii.
Keck, 17–xv.
Kehren, 37–v.
Keudell, 114–vi; 137, 138, 191, 207.
Khedive, 83–iii.
Khevenhüller, 30–xi.
Kieter, 170–i.

Nottebohm, 22–xvii.
Nuellens, 39–vii.

"O," 164–x.
Oberammergau, 60–xvi.
Oberon, 91–iv.
O'Brien, 9–iv; 17, 24.
Oedenburg, 97–iii; 182, 183.
Oehringen, 51–x.
Ofen, 41–xii.
Offenbach, 95–v.
Okraszewski, 50–vi; 56, 164.
Olfers, 23–viii.
Ollivier, 114–v.
Olmütz, 53–iv.
Onken, 133–i.
Orczy, 68–iv.
Orléans, Duchess of, 13–viii; 46.
Ormuzd, 5–iv.
Orpheus, 42–xiii; 63, 215.
Orsini, 106–i.
Ortrud, 153–vii.
Ossiach, 192–i.
Othello, 21a–vi.
Othon III von Deutschland, 165–i.
Outremont, 34–xiv.

Paderborn, 34–ii.
Palatin, Joseph, 42–xxiii.
Palermo, 142.
Palleske, 62–vii.
Pan Lapin (e), 8–iv; 9, 12, 14, 17.
Panin, 14–xii.
Panthée, 1–vi.
Paradise Lost, 27–xi.
Paris, 19, 20, 23, 26–28, 46, 48, 52, 55,
   56, 114, 153–155, 157, 165, 166, 191,
   215; Congress of, 50–ix; Exposition
   of (1857), 34–vii; Exposition of
   (1878), 153–xv.
Parma, Duke of, 21b–i.
Parsifal, 153–i; 164, 176.
Pas Floup, 18, (3–v)
Pasabée, 18–iii; 19.
Pascal, 60–iv.
Passini, 191–iii.
Pastoral Symphony (Beethoven), 55–i.
Patersi, 22–xviii; 26, 28.
Pedro II, Don, 22–xi; 145.
Pericles, 8–ii.
Persia, Shah of, 156–iii.
Pest (Pesth), 30–32, 34, 41, 42, 49, 66,
   68–73, 75–83, 86, 89, 90, 94, 97–100,
   102–107, 110, 113–118, 127, 130, 139,
   140, 150, 153, 157, 158, 164, 167. *See
   also* Budapest.

Petersburg. *See* Saint Petersburg.
Pétrarque, 23–xiv.
Pflughaupt, 40–ii.
Philotechnus, 42–v.
Phoenix, 132–iii.
Piloty, 57–ix.
Pincio, 109–ii.
Pischek, 22–vii.
Pisa, 207.
Pius IX, 45–ix; 149, 150, 156.
Planté, 215–ii.
Platen, 44–vi.
Ploërmel, Pardon de, 45–xxx.
Podolia, 12–iv; 14.
Poet and Tailor, 13–xiv.
Pogwisch, 27–iii.
Pohl, 23–xx; 46, 95.
Pohlig, 188–i.
Polimenes, 42–x.
Pordenone, 42–vii.
Posen, 8–v.
Posillipo, 164–iv.
Prague, 30, 32, 40, 41, 42, 53.
Prechtler, 44–viii.
Preller, 24–i.
Préludes, Les, 29–ii; 32, 215.
Pressbourg, 95–vi; 98, 104, 105, 182, 194.
Prokosch, 40–iv.
Prometheus, 19–xviii; 49, 60.
Prophète Fantasia, 27–xiv.
Propstin, 127–ii; 130.
Prussia, Charles of, 11–x; 45.
Prütz, 57–xvi; 59.
Psalm XIII, 29–iv; 60, 178.
Psalm CXVI, 70–i; 163.
Pütlitz, 44–v.
Pütsch, 10–xv.
Pyrrhus, 12–xiv.
Pythagorus, 23–ii.

Quatre Saisons, 22–iii.
Quatre-vingt-treize, 104–ii; 105.

Raab, 157–ii.
Racine, 2–iii.
Raff, 8–xv; 9–14, 41.
Ragaz, 126–v; 127.
Raiding, 75–iii; 183.
Ramann, 175–iii.
Ramberg, 57–vii.
Raphael, 50–v.
Ratibor, 48–xi; 150, 151.
Rauden, 116–iii; 135.
Raupach, 14–vii.
RD (Talleyrand), 25–i.
Ream, 66–iii.